Early and Middle Woodland Landscapes of the Southeast

Florida Museum of Natural History: Ripley P. Bullen Series

UNIVERSITY PRESS OF FLORIDA

Florida A&M University, Tallahassee
Florida Atlantic University, Boca Raton
Florida Gulf Coast University, Ft. Myers
Florida International University, Miami
Florida State University, Tallahassee
New College of Florida, Sarasota
University of Central Florida, Orlando
University of Florida, Gainesville
University of North Florida, Jacksonville
University of South Florida, Tampa
University of West Florida, Pensacola

Early and Middle Woodland Landscapes of the Southeast

Edited by Alice P. Wright and Edward R. Henry

UNIVERSITY PRESS OF FLORIDA
Gainesville/Tallahassee/Tampa/Boca Raton
Pensacola/Orlando/Miami/Jacksonville/Ft. Myers/Sarasota

Copyright 2013 by Alice P. Wright and Edward R. Henry
All rights reserved
Published in the United States of America

This book may be available in an electronic edition.

First cloth printing, 2013
First paperback printing, 2019

24 23 22 21 20 19   6 5 4 3 2 1

Library of Congress Cataloging-in-Publication Data
Early and middle woodland landscapes of the Southeast /
edited by Alice P. Wright and Edward R. Henry.
pages cm — (Florida Museum of Natural History: Ripley P. Bullen series)
Includes bibliographical references and index.
ISBN 978-0-8130-4460-6 (cloth : alk. paper)
ISBN 978-0-8130-6446-8 (pbk.)
1. Woodland culture—Southern States. 2. Adena culture—Southern States.
3. Mound-builders—Southern States. 4. Excavations (Archaeology)—Southern States.
5. Southern States—Antiquities. I. Wright, Alice P. II. Henry, Edward R.
III. Series: Ripley P. Bullen series.
E99.W84E37 2013
976.01—dc23   2013015098

The University Press of Florida is the scholarly publishing agency for the State University System of Florida, comprising Florida A&M University, Florida Atlantic University, Florida Gulf Coast University, Florida International University, Florida State University, New College of Florida, University of Central Florida, University of Florida, University of North Florida, University of South Florida, and University of West Florida.

University Press of Florida
2046 NE Waldo Road
Suite 2100
Gainesville, FL 32609
http://upress.ufl.edu

Dedicated to William S. Webb (1882–1964)
and James B. Griffin (1905–1997),
who set the standard for
Woodland research in the Southeast

Contents

List of Figures ix
List of Tables xi
Acknowledgments xiii

1. Introduction: Emerging Approaches to the Landscapes of the Early and Middle Woodland Southeast 1
   Alice P. Wright and Edward R. Henry

Part 1. Extensive Landscapes: Between and Beyond Monuments

2. The Early–Middle Woodland Domestic Landscape in Kentucky 19
   Darlene Applegate

3. The Adena Mortuary Landscape: Off-Mound Rituals and Burial Mounds 45
   David Pollack and Eric J. Schlarb

4. Like a Dead Dog: Strategic Ritual Choice in the Mortuary Enterprise 56
   R. Berle Clay

5. The Early and Middle Woodland of the Upper Cumberland Plateau, Tennessee 71
   Jay D. Franklin, Meagan Dennison, Maureen A. Hays, Jeffrey Navel, and Andrew D. Dye

Part 2. Monumental Landscapes: Mound and Earthwork Sites

6. Winchester Farm: A Small Adena Enclosure in Central Kentucky 91
   Richard W. Jefferies, George R. Milner, and Edward R. Henry

7. Persistent Place, Shifting Practice: The Premound Landscape at the Garden Creek Site, North Carolina 108
   Alice P. Wright

8. Biltmore Mound and the Appalachian Summit Hopewell 122
   Larry R. Kimball, Thomas R. Whyte, and Gary D. Crites

9. The Woodland Period Cultural Landscape of the Leake Site Complex   138
   Scot Keith

10. The Creation of Ritual Space at the Jackson Landing Site in Coastal Mississippi   153
    Edmond A. Boudreaux III

Part 3. Landscapes of Interaction

11. Late Middle Woodland Settlement and Ritual at the Armory Site   167
    Paul N. Eubanks

12. Constituting Similarity and Difference in the Deep South: The Ritual and Domestic Landscapes of Kolomoki, Crystal River, and Fort Center   181
    Thomas J. Pluckhahn and Victor D. Thompson

13. Ritual Life and Landscape at Tunacunnhee   196
    Victoria G. Dekle

14. Swift Creek and Weeden Island Mortuary Landscapes of Interaction   204
    Neill J. Wallis

15. Working Out Adena Political Organization and Variation from the Ritual Landscape in the Kentucky Bluegrass   219
    Edward R. Henry

Part 4. Woodland Landscapes in Historical and Regional Perspective

16. On Ceremonial Landscapes   237
    James A. Brown

17. Social Landscapes of Early and Middle Woodland Peoples in the Southeast   247
    David G. Anderson

References   263
List of Contributors   311
Index   315

Figures

1.1. Location of sites and subregions discussed in the text 2
1.2. Timeline of data discussed in chapters 2–15 10
2.1. Early–Middle Woodland sites and survey areas in Kentucky 21
3.1. Location of Evans and surrounding sites, Kentucky 46
3.2. Map of the Evans site, Kentucky 48
4.1. Woodland mounds in present-day cemeteries 58
4.2. Auvergne Mound, Kentucky 60
4.3. Auvergne Mound central burial 60
4.4. Artifact distribution in mound fill and off-mound area at Auvergne Mound 61
5.1. Western Escarpment, Upper Cumberland Plateau, Tennessee 73
5.2. Rim sherd from Eagle Drink Bluff Shelter, Tennessee 79
5.3. Biface use wear from Horn Dog Pictograph Site, Tennessee 84
6.1. Elkhorn Creek earthwork complex, Kentucky 92
6.2. Rafinesque's 1820 map, "Monuments on North Elkhorn Creek" 94
6.3. The Mt. Horeb earthwork 95
6.4. Part of a 1952 aerial photo of the Winchester Farm earthwork 97
6.5. Various images of the Winchester Farm earthwork 98
6.6. Remote sensing images of the Winchester Farm earthwork 101
6.7. Areas of 171 small circular enclosures 103
6.8. Small square enclosures at Junction Group, Camargo, and Seal Township sites in Kentucky and Ohio 105
7.1. Aerial map of Garden Creek site, North Carolina 111
7.2. Structure 1 below Garden Creek Mound No. 2 113
7.3. Posthole patterns below Garden Creek Mound No. 2 117
8.1. Location of Biltmore Mound, North Carolina 123
8.2. Construction stages of Biltmore Mound 125
8.3. Biltmore Mound excavation plan 126
8.4. Profiles and features at Biltmore Mound 127
8.5. Map of Biltmore Mound, Mt. Mitchell, and Mt. Pisgah 130
8.6. Summer solstice sunrise over Mt. Mitchell 130

9.1. Map of the Leake site complex and environs, Georgia   139
9.2. Map of the Leake site   139
9.3. Features south of Mound B at the Leake site   145
9.4. Post alignments in the Swift Creek midden   147
9.5. Structures at the Leake site   150
10.1. Location of Jackson Landing site, Mississippi   155
10.2. Map of Jackson Landing site   156
10.3. Mound profile drawing from Jackson Landing   161
11.1. Location of the Armory site, Alabama   168
11.2. Map of mounds and occupation at the Armory site   169
11.3. Ceramic density across the Armory site   170
11.4. Location of Walthall's (1985) Southern Appalachian aggregation centers   171
11.5. Ceramic seriation from Armory site vicinity   172
11.6. Distribution of check- and rocker-stamped pottery at the Armory site   173
11.7. Copper ear spool from the Armory site   176
12.1. Location of Kolomoki, Crystal River, and Fort Center   182
12.2. Map of the Fort Center site   185
12.3. Map of the Kolomoki site   186
12.4. Map of the Crystal River site   187
12.5. Calibrated radiocarbon dates from the Crystal River site   190
12.6. Calibrated radiocarbon dates from the Fort Center site   191
12.7. Calibrated radiocarbon dates from the Kolomoki site   192
13.1. Map of Tunacunnhee site and nearby regions   198
13.2. Ear spool from the Tunacunnhee site, Georgia   203
14.1. Swift Creek and Weeden Island sites   206
14.2. Paddle match connections with the Dent and Mayport mounds   213
14.3. Late Swift Creek Complicated Stamped vessel   216
15.1. The Inner and Outer Bluegrass regions of Kentucky   222
15.2. Adena subregions and sites in the Kentucky Bluegrass   223
15.3. Distribution of submound cremations   228
15.4. Distribution of submound architecture   228
15.5. Distribution of log tombs   229
15.6. Distribution of puddled-clay basins   229

Tables

2.1. Early–Middle Woodland sites in Kentucky 22
2.2. Domestic structures at Early–Middle Woodland sites in Kentucky 28
3.1. Evans site calibrated radiocarbon dates 47
5.1. Early and Middle Woodland AMS dates from the Upper Cumberland Plateau 75
5.2. Early and Middle Woodland luminescence (OSL) dates from the Upper Cumberland Plateau 76
5.3. Flaking debris data for Woodland sites on the WEUCP study area 81
5.4. Faunal information for the WEUCP study area 85
8.1. Archaeobotanical remains from Biltmore Mound and village 133
8.2. Seeds from Biltmore Mound and village 134
8.3. Identified wood charcoal from Biltmore Mound and village 135
11.1. Significance of difference between the north–south distribution of check and rocker stamping 174
11.2. Significance of difference between the east–west distribution of check and rocker stamping 174
11.3. Significance of difference between the thicknesses of check- and rocker-stamped ceramics 175
15.1. Attributes observed from mounds across the Kentucky Bluegrass 225
15.2. Radiocarbon dates from examined mound sites in the Kentucky Bluegrass 230

Acknowledgments

This volume is the happy result of a series of conferences, conversations, and collaborations among the Southeastern archaeological community. First, we must thank David Anderson and Ken Sassaman, who motivated us to pursue the topic of Early and Middle Woodland landscapes at the 2009 meeting of the Southeastern Archaeological Conference in Mobile, Alabama. However, that motivation might not have resulted in much if not for the assistance and support of George Crothers, organizer of the 2010 meeting of the Southeastern Archaeological Conference in Lexington, Kentucky; among all his other responsibilities, George was able to schedule the exhaustive lineup of the symposium that led to this volume, and for that, we are extremely grateful. We must also acknowledge George and several other contributors to that original symposium, although they were not included in this book: Joe Saunders, John Blitz, Lauren Downs, Logan Kistler, Karen Smith, Keith Stephenson, N'omi Greber, and William Dancey. We look forward to reading the data and insights offered by these scholars in other publications.

Over the years, we have received support, critique, and insight from numerous mentors, some of whom are contributors here. Others include Rob Beck, Joyce Marcus, Paul Thacker, Bryan Tucker, Sarah Sherwood, John Speth, Lisa Young, Henry Wright, Scott Ashcraft, Bennie Keel, Jay Johnson, Robbie Ethridge, Matthew Murray, Gabe Wrobel, David Pollack, Gwynn Henderson, and George Crothers. We are also grateful to know a new generation of scholars who inspire us to work hard and think creatively, including Casey Barrier, Stephen Carmody, David Cranford, Jeremy Davis, Lydia Dorsey, Meg Kassabaum, Logan Kistler, D. Shane Miller, Matt Sanger, Anna Semon, and Erin Stevens. We must particularly acknowledge the over-the-top intellectual and emotional support of the occupants of the University of Michigan North American Archaeology Range: Ashley Schubert, Christina Perry-Sampson, Travis Williams, Shaun Lynch, honorary member Tim Horsley, and most especially Casey Barrier, perpetual SEAC roommate and the reason the editors met in the first place.

Despite many (*many*) warnings about the hassle of compiling an edited volume, at the time of writing these acknowledgments, we feel as though we got off easy. This is entirely attributable to the enthusiasm and dedication of our many contributors and to the editorial staff at the University Press of Florida, whose professionalism and encouragement left us prepared and willing to complete this venture. Thank you.

Finally, on a more personal note, we must offer the most heartfelt thanks to those who have put up with us, in person and over the phone, in the two years we've been on this journey—our families. So thank you to our parents, John, Rita, Mike, Debbie, Dina, Nan, and to our partners, Andrea and Cameron. It might be a stretch to say you kept us entirely sane throughout this process, but we don't want to think about what it would have been like without your support.

1

Introduction

Emerging Approaches to the Landscapes
of the Early and Middle Woodland Southeast

ALICE P. WRIGHT AND EDWARD R. HENRY

On a pleasantly balmy morning in November 2009, several dozen archaeologists crowded into a small conference room in Mobile, Alabama, to hear David Anderson and Kenneth Sassaman comment on the current state of archaeological research in the American Southeast. Their paper, now expanded into a book (Anderson and Sassaman 2012), covered considerable topical, chronological, and theoretical ground. In a mere 20 minutes, they discussed how new techniques for archaeological prospection, dating, data management, and environmental reconstruction were changing our views of the southeastern past, from the Paleo-Indian period through European contact, and they outlined several directions for future study of these issues.

Notably absent from their presentation, however, were the Early and Middle Woodland periods, dating, respectively, to circa 1000–200 BC and 200 BC–AD 600–800.[1] For researchers interested in the Woodland period, this omission by two giants of southeastern archaeology was, to say the least, disconcerting. Surely, future research in the region could not ignore nearly two millennia of cultural development, which encompass critical social, political, and economic changes associated with the adoption of horticulture and semipermanent settlement and with a florescence of ceremonial activity and subcontinental interaction networks? Surely, the methodological developments and theoretical perspectives discussed in the context of Archaic and Mississippian research could be applied with equal success to the intervening periods? Surely, we could not be the only people interested in this stuff?

In an effort to answer these questions, we mustered a sizable contingent of Woodland period specialists at 2010's Southeastern Archaeological Conference in a symposium entitled "Ritual and Domestic Landscapes of Early and Middle Woodland Peoples in the Southeast." This more manageably titled volume is the outcome of our session. The chapters herein demonstrate the

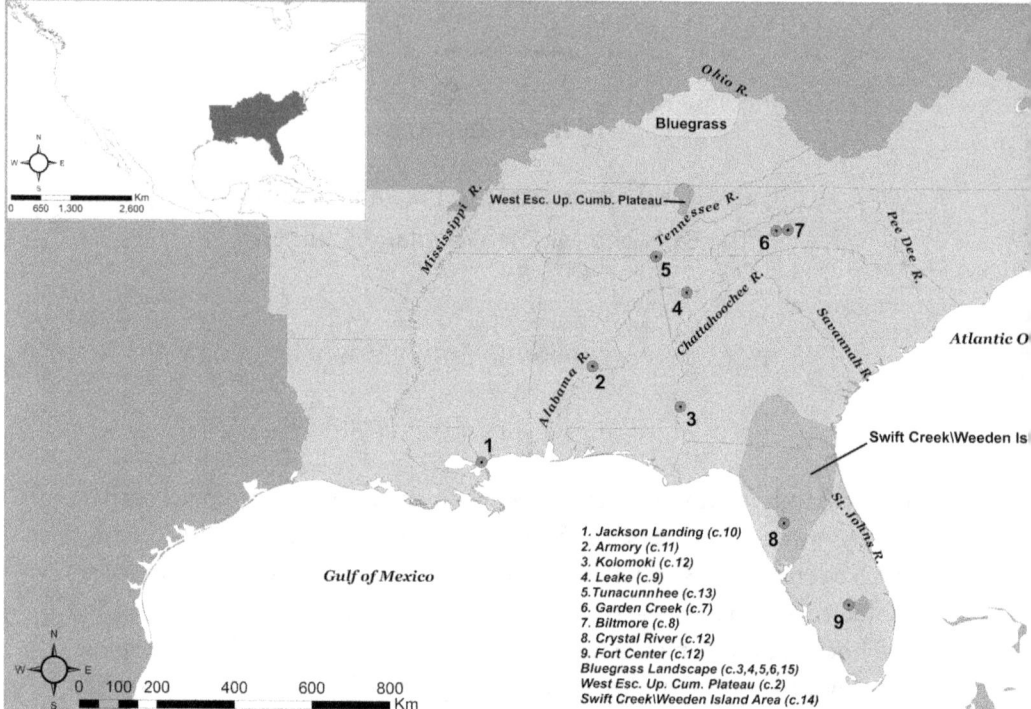

Figure 1.1. Location of Early and Middle Woodland sites and subregions examined in this volume. Map prepared by Edward Henry.

vibrancy of research across the Early and Middle Woodland Southeast (figure 1.1) and argue strongly for their continued investigation and inclusion in discussions of recent developments in southeastern archaeology (Anderson and Sassaman 2009).

As the titles of both the symposium and the volume indicate, this assembly of Early and Middle Woodland research finds collective footing in the concept of *landscape archaeology*. Although this approach to prehistory is not lacking in southeastern archaeological research, this umbrella term has never been explored, unabridged, in one publication. In the remainder of this introduction, we explore the theoretical foundations of landscapes in archaeological research, examine the methodological challenges and opportunities inherent in investigating past landscapes, and propose how landscape-based perspectives can shed light on the Early and Middle Woodland periods in particular. Our goal—and that of our contributors—is twofold. We aim not only to present cutting-edge interpretations of diverse Early and Middle Woodland data sets, which were last synthesized more than a decade ago (Anderson and Mainfort 2002a), but also to develop a flexible theoretical framework with the potential to illuminate the dynamic and multiscalar historical processes exhibited in the archaeological record of the Greater Southeast.

Theoretical Background: A Diversity of Landscapes

Encompassing high mountains and rolling hills, wide floodplains and meandering river valleys, dense forests and sandy coastlines, the American Southeast has provided a stage and a means of human habitation, sociopolitical and economic interaction, and ceremonial performance for more than 10,000 years. During this time, native peoples engaged with and modified the physical landscape in a variety of ways. They built houses, villages, and towns; erected earthworks and burial facilities; established overland trails and traveled along rivers and streams; and visited and marked special natural places. Archaeological studies in the Southeast have tended, at least for the past several decades, to examine the records of these and other activities in relative isolation—in other words, with a topical emphasis on subsistence strategies, exchange patterns, mortuary ritual, and so forth. At least partially attributable to increasing demands for technical expertise and contextual specialization in particular times and places, this body of research provides the building blocks for new interpretations of the southeastern past that simultaneously consider the many different ways in which native communities experienced their natural and cultural surroundings. To that end, this volume presents new research on the social landscapes of the Early and Middle Woodland Southeast, drawing on diverse concepts of landscape archaeology developed over the past three decades.

As others have noted (Anschuetz et al. 2001; Knapp and Ashmore 1999), there are, in fact, many different archaeologies of landscape. The field is unified by a common purpose: to detangle the relationships between people, their natural environment, and their cultural domain. Different sorts of landscape archaeology, however, entail different field methodologies, theoretical foundations, and interpretive biases. Distinctions between American and British schools of landscape research comprise the most commonly cited intellectual and methodological divides in landscape archaeology.

Briefly, and with admitted oversimplicity, the American school emerged in the context of processual archaeology (Johnson 2007; Kantner 2008) and has traditionally been associated with rigorously empirical investigations of human-environment interaction. Influenced by Julian Steward's (1955) ecological approach in anthropology, large-scale regional surveys in the Western Hemisphere (e.g., Sanders et al. 1979; Willey 1953) generated data poised to address several issues central to the American school and, more generally, the processual endeavor. For example, the identification of sites and settlement patterns had the potential to reveal relationships between human populations and environmental resources, as well as various forms of political and economic organization (Knapp and Ashmore 1999). Marching to the beat of a processual drum, seminal studies of the American school collected and interpreted these data to produce cross-cultural generalizations regarding fundamental human-environmental processes, such as risk management strategies and the establishment of regional settlement hierarchies.

Meanwhile, the British school of landscape research in archaeology, arguably shaped by long-standing Romantic views of the English landscape (Johnson 2007), emerged in the context of the postprocessual critique.[2] In sharp contrast to the empirical approach of the American school, hardline postprocessual landscape archaeologists claimed the fact that the past can be known only from the perspective of the present invalidated objective or universalizing truth claims about past landscapes (Bender 1998). The ways in which this position has been implemented in actual landscape research have varied widely.

Phenomenologists, for example, have undertaken multiscalar and multisensory investigations of past landscapes, tackling the movements of individual bodies, the evocation of collective memories, and the tangible and intangible experiences rendered by the built environment (e.g., Pearson and Shanks 2001; Thomas 1996; Tilley 1994, 1999; but see Barrett and Ko 2009; Lekson 1996). More generally, postprocessual or British approaches are credited with promoting "a more 'peopled' form of landscape history, especially for periods which are not text-aided" (Fleming 2006: 271). Rather than subsuming all past landscape interactions within an environmentally determined or systemic framework, the British school considers the myriad ways that past peoples shaped, cognized, and dwelled in the world around them (Ingold 1995).

These days, the epistemological fault lines that served to differentiate American and British landscape approaches in the 1990s and early 2000s are less pronounced, particularly with the fairly regular incorporation of processual-plus (Hegmon 2003) and historical processualist (Pauketat 2001) frameworks, at least by archaeologists in North America. Nevertheless, similarly distinctive research agendas continue to characterize the study of landscapes of certain "types" of societies. In his review of place, landscape, and environmental research in anthropological archaeology, Christopher Rodning (2010: 183) noted that "[m]any archaeological studies of mobile hunter-gatherer societies emphasize themes of risk management and resource procurement . . . and many studies of sedentary societies emphasize the social dimensions of architecture and monuments." Put another way, research on mobile foragers has followed in the footsteps of the American school by examining cultural responses to the environment. In contrast, researchers concentrating on sedentary societies have adopted social and ideational perspectives to understand how so-called complex societies influenced, experienced, and understood the world around them.

Certainly, this trend results in part from the differences in the archaeological records of mobile and sedentary societies. The latter have a considerably higher impact on the landscape through the establishment of a permanent built environment amenable to long-term preservation and, in turn, archaeological analysis. Yet the result of this research trend is a false dichotomy between environmentally determined and culturally mediated landscapes, as if sedentary societies did not require the natural environment to survive or as if mobile foragers did not imbue their surroundings with cultural significance.

In our minds, the inadvertent perpetuation of this patent fiction demands a more holistic approach to past landscapes. Fortunately, the blurring of transAtlantic differences in landscape research suggests that such an approach is both possible and in practice among anthropological archaeologists. Historical ecologists (Crumley and Marquardt 1990: 74), for instance, have maintained their processual roots by conducting scientifically informed research on "physical structures" (such as climate and topography) as well as "sociohistorical structures" (such as social and political institutions). At the same time, they have also sought to identify the "aesthetic, symbolic, religious, and ideological" dimensions of such structures and their interrelationships. In so doing, historical ecology eschews the stereotypical American school view of landscapes as "passive backdrops[s] or forcible determinant[s] of culture" (Knapp and Ashmore 1999: 2) and encourages an examination of the recursive relationships between humans and their surroundings: "how human impact has created a particular landscape and how that resulting landscape has in turn shaped human behavior" (Kantner 2008: 56).

In many ways, the chapters in this volume follow historical ecology's lead, in that the authors espouse theoretical perspectives derived from both the American and the British school of landscape archaeology. This effort is especially relevant for Early and Middle Woodland research. As we discuss below, these time periods witnessed the gradual reduction of mobility among indigenous communities in the Southeast as they began to cultivate native plants and establish sedentary or semisedentary lifestyles. A comprehensive approach to Early and Middle Woodland landscapes thus has the potential to bridge the divide Rodning (2010) identified in modern landscape research, and to clarify the roles of the natural, built, and ideational environments in the important shift from mobile to sedentary social landscapes.

To that end, we have adopted Christopher Fennell's (2010: 1) thoroughly inclusive definition of the field: "Landscape archaeology addresses the complex issues of the ways that people have consciously and unconsciously shaped the land around them ... for a variety of purposes, including subsistence, economic, social, political, and religious undertakings." Like the editors of other volumes on archaeological landscapes (e.g., Ashmore and Knapp 1999; David and Thomas 2008), we embrace this diversity and the resulting complexity of our interpretations of the interactions among Early and Middle Woodland peoples, their environment, and each other. Collectively, this volume's contributors have begun to answer Kurt Anschuetz and colleagues' (2001: 163–64) call for an "objective demonstration of the usefulness of a landscape approach as a processual, interactive, contextual, and interdisciplinary framework ... [that] helps contribute to the building of fuller understandings of relationships among the various spatial, temporal, ecological, and cognitive contexts in which people creatively interact with their environments."

Scalar Challenges and Methodological Opportunities in Landscape Research

The convergence (or, minimally, the complementarity) of such diverse forms of landscape archaeology likely stem from the challenges faced by *all* researchers when it comes to the actual implementation of landscape research. Questions of scale and units of analysis have provided considerable fodder for debate for as long as there have been spatial interpretations of the archaeological record. For some, landscape analysis is to be undertaken at a regional scale, juxtaposing site-based studies that have historically received the most archaeological attention. In this regard, distributional archaeology, off-site archaeology, and siteless archaeology (e.g., Dunnell 1992; Dunnell and Dancey 1983; Ebert 1992; Foley 1981; Wandsnider 1992) have been adopted by investigators striving to overcome the subjectivity of site identification (Cherry 1983) and to "facilitate the study of diffuse human remains—such as field systems, farms, industrial sites, roads, and the generally more ephemeral traces of non-sedentary people—that never fit comfortably within traditional operational definitions of 'sites'" (Knapp and Ashmore 1999: 2). Additionally, these approaches enable a more explicit investigation of natural caves, springs, mountaintops, and other locations as places with special, often sacred, significance to the people who experienced them (e.g., Bradley 2000).

While these non-site-centric approaches to the landscape have undeniably allowed for more thorough accounts of people's relationships with their surroundings, we hesitate to throw the baby out with the bathwater. Limiting our focus to those culturally significant spaces "in-between sites" means that our interpretations of past landscapes are incomplete. Those places with sufficient anthropogenic activity to merit the designation of "site" are arguably among the most important features on the landscape and should not be left out of the interpretive equation because they require analytic flexibility for thorough study (such as excavation as opposed to survey). As geographer Yi-Fu Tuan (1977: 12) cogently noted, "[S]pace can be variously experienced as the relative location of objects or places, as the distances and expanses that separate or link places, and—more abstractly—as the area defined by a network of places."

A complete investigation of the landscape therefore requires contextualized explication of many places and multiple scales—from major sites to ephemeral scatters, from meaningful natural landmarks to the trails and waterways that link them all. Of course, a multiscalar approach takes quite a bit of work—perhaps more than can be productively managed in a single project. The diverse assembly of chapters in this volume is a first response to this challenge. By bringing together scholars working at different analytical scales, we can generate a more holistic picture of southeastern landscapes during the Early and Middle Woodland periods.

The difficulties and opportunities of scale, however, are not the only factors that crosscut and link various theoretical approaches to archaeological landscapes. Whether ecological or ideational in orientation, many modern landscape studies are productively engaging a variety of new methodologies in the field and for interpretation. Geographic information systems (GIS) and geophysical techniques represent two increasingly utilized toolkits for landscape research, as several chapters in this volume illustrate (e.g., Henry, chapter 15; Jefferies et al., chapter 6; Pluckhahn and Thompson, chapter 12; and Wright, chapter 7).

Since the 1980s, GIS has provided archaeologists with a means of simultaneously projecting, visualizing, and analyzing many types of spatial data at various scales (e.g., Allen et al. 1990; Connolly and Lake 2006; Kvamme 1999; Wheatley and Gillings 2002). The many applications of GIS to the archaeological record are beyond the scope of this chapter, but a few examples from pre-Columbian Southeast highlight its capabilities. These range from analyses of ancient land and water travel routes (e.g., Livingood 2009; Whitley and Hicks 2003), to an exploration of Paleo-Indian artifact distributions as indicators of regional population changes (Anderson et al. 2010), to more rigorous investigations of intrasite spatial data using decades-old excavation records (e.g., Boudreaux 2007; Hally 2008).

Geophysical prospection is another important method that southeastern archaeologists are increasingly adopting to explore diverse aspects of past landscapes. Kenneth Kvamme's (2003) seminal article on this topic explicitly described the many ways in which geophysical methods can benefit archaeologists who are interested in landscape analysis. Specifically, he identified the successes of geophysical surveys in the wide-area mapping of settlement spaces, site organization, intersettlement forms of domestic architecture, and individual house size, shape, and orientation (Kvamme 2003: 436).

The ability to detect archaeological features at scales that exceed those possible through excavation has encouraged archaeologists to use geophysical data in the development and testing of long-standing and new archaeological and anthropological hypotheses (Aspinall et al. 2008; Conyers 2010; Conyers and Leckebusch 2010). Victor Thompson and colleagues (2011) outlined four lines of inquiry to which geophysical data sets are especially well suited. Specifically focused on the anthropological analysis of space at persistent places, these issues include (1) variation between constructed features within built environments; (2) continuity and discontinuity of space as arranged within sites; (3) separation of natural from cultural phenomena in architectural site remains and depositional processes; and (4) the identification of regional-level patterning (Thompson et al. 2011: 198–99, 203, 204, 206). To date, many (though not all) of the anthropological applications of archaeogeophysics have targeted late prehistoric sites in the Southeast (e.g., volume 29, no. 2 and volume 30, no. 1 of the journal *Southeastern Archaeology*), but Early and Middle Woodland specialists are increasingly using geophysical techniques to explore diverse research questions (see Henry 2011; Jefferies et al., chapter 6, this volume; Thompson and Pluckhahn 2010; Pluckhahn et al. 2010; Mainfort et al. 2011).

A Laboratory for Landscape Approaches: The Early and Middle Woodland Southeast

Overview of the Early Woodland Southeast

The Early Woodland period (circa 1000–200 BC) in the Southeast is commonly, although (sometimes) jokingly, referred to as "Archaic with pottery" (Anderson and Mainfort 2002b: 5). It is true that many of the defining characteristics of the Early Woodland (the adoption of pottery, the creation of interregional trade networks, mound construction, and the advent of plant cultivation) have roots dating as far back as the Middle Archaic and were certainly prevalent in some Late Archaic societies (Gremillion 1996; Jefferies 2004; Sassaman 2002; Saunders 2010; Saunders et al. 2005). However, during the Early Woodland, these technologies and aspects of human behavior became widespread across the Eastern Woodlands, linking far-flung communities even as they mapped onto distinctive subregional traditions (Anderson and Mainfort 2002b: 6; Anderson and Sassaman 2012: 114; Kidder et al. 2010: 141).

Relative to the preceding Late Archaic period, Early Woodland settlement and land use across much of the Southeast "begins at a point of diminished archaeological resolution" (Anderson and Sassaman 2012: 115). For the most part, Early Woodland settlement patterns reflect residential mobility and dispersed community organization. Nevertheless, typically small-scale occupations are rendered archaeologically visible thanks to the increasingly dominant presence of pottery in site assemblages. Researchers have identified regional traditions of pottery manufacture in the Gulf Coastal Plain, the interior Midsouth, the Southern Appalachians, the mid-Atlantic seaboard, and peninsular Florida (Bense 1994; Caldwell 1958; Milanich 2004). The widespread adoption of ceramic technology speaks to some form of interaction among geographically dispersed groups, which is also indicated by shared repertoires of mortuary ceremonialism and monumentality after around 700 BC.

The Tchefuncte tradition of the lower Mississippi Valley and the Adena tradition of the lower Midwest represent the best-known records of such activities, including conical burial mounds and accretional burial contexts that often include nonlocal materials, themselves indicative of regional interaction or exchange (Clay 1998; Hays and Weinstein 2010). Add to these processes the intensification of plant-food collection and, in some areas, the increased cultivation of starchy and oily seed crops, and the dynamism of Early Woodland historical trajectories becomes even more apparent. We suggest that all of these issues are amenable to investigation through the lens of social landscapes. With few exceptions, the cultural changes observed during the Early Woodland entailed novel relationships among people, the natural world, and the built environment at multiple scales, from the small farmstead cultivating seed-bearing plants to interregional networks that involved marking significant places and practices with mounds.

Unfortunately, very little Early Woodland research is being published these days, and this volume, with its majority of chapters focusing on the Middle Woodland period, is no exception (see figure 1.2). Standing in contrast to this dearth of publication, however, are the many Early Woodland sites encountered and recorded by cultural resources management (CRM) archaeologists across the region. The mere identification of artifact scatters and feature clusters—the bread and butter of Phase I surveys—has generated rich Early Woodland data sets compatible with various sorts of landscape analysis. As Anderson and Mainfort (2002c: 542) recognized nearly a decade ago, southeastern archaeologists—and Early Woodland specialists in particular—would be well served by examining, synthesizing, and publishing CRM records, rather than leaving them on the shelves of state historic preservation offices and the firms conducting the research (but for examples of archaeologists placing CRM work in the published record see Espenshade 2008 and Keith, chapter 9, this volume). Applegate (chapter 2,

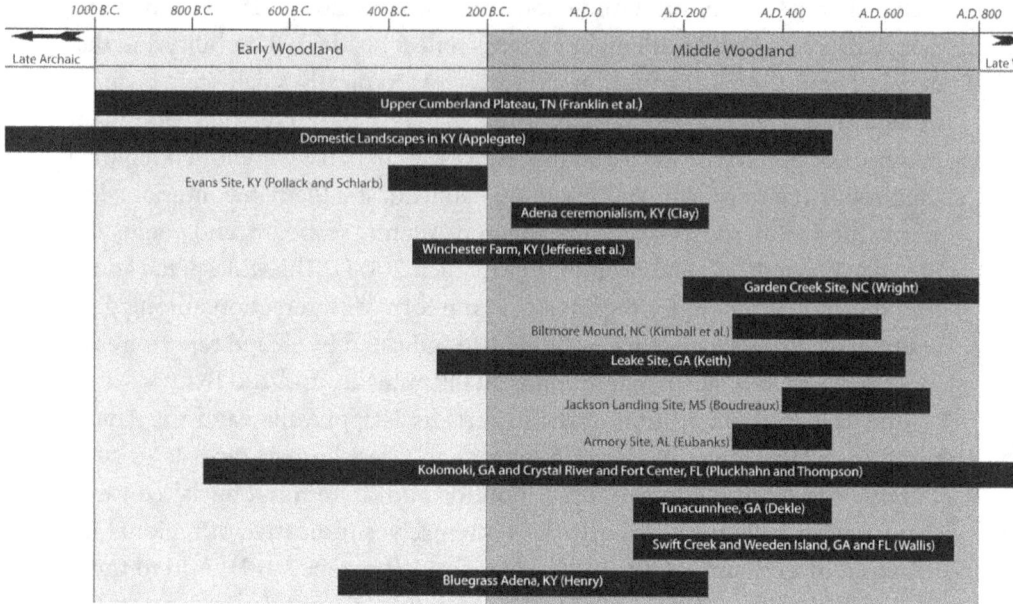

Figure 1.2. Timeline of the Early and Middle Woodland Southeast, including approximate dates relevant to subsequent chapters. Figure prepared by Alice Wright.

this volume) demonstrates the potential of this approach; her integration of CRM and academic literature illustrates that domestic sites are in fact well represented for the Early and Middle Woodland periods in Kentucky, contrary to the oft-cited trope that archaeologists have identified few or no such occupations.

Despite the challenges of disseminating CRM research, several advances in Early Woodland research have been made since the previous compilation of Woodland literature from the Southeast (Anderson and Mainfort 2002a), with important implications for research on social landscapes. For example, the "Adena" concept (mentioned above) has undergone considerable revision. The concept's long-presumed homogeneity has now been discounted (Clay 2005, 2009, chapter 4, this volume), and the relationships and differences among Adena domestic and ritual architecture indicate the need for new frameworks by which to understand social and ceremonial organization and interaction at the northern fringes of the Southeast (Clay 2009).

Paleo-environmental research also stands to make important contributions to Early Woodland landscape archaeology. In particular, the emergence of the Early Woodland period is now being linked to trends of global climate change that disrupted Late Archaic cultural stability and, in some cases, led to subregional abandonments (in the lower Mississippi River basin, Kidder

2006: 220–21; on the Georgia coast, Thompson and Turck 2009: 269–72). Furthermore, T. R. Kidder and colleagues (2010: 141) have attributed later Early Woodland forms of "material culture, settlement organization, social structure, and exchange relations" to reoccupation of the region following its environmental restabilization.

As these few (but by no means exhaustive) examples demonstrate, archaeologists *are* conducting interesting anthropological research on the Early Woodland Southeast. As Clay's (2005, 2009) and Kidder and colleagues' (2010) projects have highlighted, it is important that researchers examine *what* exactly happened on the Early Woodland landscape, before tackling broader, more anthropologically significant *how* and *why* questions. With a more detailed picture of the material patterns encountered across Early Woodland sites and broader landscapes, we can better assess the changes and transitions that have been commonly associated with this period. In this way, we can exhume the Early Woodland from "the dustbin of history," where it has traditionally represented "an interval of 'good gray' culture thus meriting no further interest" (Kidder et al. 2010: 141).

Overview of the Middle Woodland Southeast

Although many aspects of the Middle Woodland archaeological record represent the intensification or elaboration of existing Early Woodland cultural trends, the dramatic appearance of panregional religious movements at this time set the Middle Woodland apart from preceding and subsequent periods. Exact dates for the Middle Woodland vary slightly from subregion to subregion, but traditional culture history frameworks usually place it between 300/200 BC and AD 500 (Anderson and Mainfort 2002b: 9). As highlighted by several of the chapters in this volume, however, a precise terminus for the Middle Woodland is far from certain, particularly where ceremonial practices persist until AD 600–800 (e.g., Boudreaux, chapter 10, this volume; Kimball et al., chapter 8, this volume), and in areas in which Late Woodland adaptations are poorly understood (such as the Cumberland Plateau [Franklin et al., chapter 5, this volume] and the Southern Appalachians [Ward and Davis 1999]).

Following trajectories established during the Early Woodland period, pottery manufacture, intensive plant-food collection and modest plant cultivation, and small-scale, semipermanent settlement strategies persisted through the Middle Woodland in much of the Southeast. Interaction in the form of shared ceremonial monumentality and nonlocal materials also bridged these periods, but evidence for such phenomena is especially pronounced during the Middle Woodland. Most famously, the midwestern Hopewell tradition involved elaborate mound and geometric earthwork construction and the assembly of massive quantities of exotic and presumably ritually charged artifacts, including mica and quartz crystals from the Southern Appalachians, marine shell and shark teeth from the Gulf Coast, copper from the Upper Great Lakes, galena from Missouri, and even obsidian and grizzly bear teeth from the Rocky Mountains.

For at least 20 years, archaeological research in the Hopewell core (essentially the Scioto River drainage in southern Ohio) has focused on the relationships between ritual and domestic landscapes, as represented by apparently "vacant" ceremonial centers and dispersed homesteads, respectively (e.g., chapters in Byers 2011; Byers and Wymer 2010; Carr and Case 2005a; Case and Carr 2008; Charles and Buikstra 2006; Dancey and Pacheco 1997). On the one hand, this research has underscored the regional distinctiveness of Ohio Hopewell, but on the other, it has suggested that the social catchments involved in Hopewell monument construction and exchange may have extended across a much greater geographic area than has previously been recognized (e.g., Bernardini 2004; Seeman 1995).

With that in mind, we can see that the appearance of Hopewell material culture across the Southeast during the Middle Woodland period has been a focus of southeastern archaeological research for the past few decades (e.g., Brose and Greber 1979). Importantly, the nature of southeastern Hopewell varies considerably across space; as succinctly put by Anderson and Sassaman (2012: 132), "Hopewell religion was motivated by local needs and rationalized by local logics ... 'being' Hopewell meant different things to different people." It is also important to note that monumental ceremonial practices and extralocal interactions in the Middle Woodland Southeast were *not* just a matter of Hopewell influence. Middle Woodland specialists have identified distinctly southeastern interaction spheres and ceremonial complexes, as evidenced in the widespread distributions of ceramic styles, exotic artifacts, and particular forms of monumental architecture.

In fact, the Middle Woodland archaeological record bears witness to the existence of at least two intraregional interaction networks that, to varying degrees, overlapped with each other and with evidence of Hopewellian ceremonialism across the southeastern landscape. The first is defined by the distribution of a particular kind of complicated-stamped pottery called Swift Creek, centered in southeastern Georgia and northeastern Florida. Studying paddle matches and conducting petrographic, geochemical, and iconographic analyses (Snow and Stephenson 1998; Stoltman and Snow 1998; Wallis 2008, 2011, and chapter 14, this volume), archaeologists have posited that long-distance interaction in and beyond the Swift Creek core area involved utilitarian and nonutilitarian activities and that Swift Creek pottery served as tangible manifestations of "spatial relationships among mounds, objects of ritual importance, places of dwelling, and mobile human bodies" (Anderson and Sassaman 2012: 140).

Middle Woodland interaction across the Southeast is also indicated by the emergence of platform mound architecture, particularly in interior Florida, in the Southern Appalachians, and along the Gulf coast. These monuments, conforming to what Vernon J. Knight (1990, 2001) has labeled the "Kolomoki pattern," includes iconic sites such as Pinson (Mainfort 1988), Marksville (Toth 1974), Crystal River (Pluckhahn et al. 2010; Weisman 1995), and (of course) Kolomoki (Sears 1956; Pluckhahn 2003). These and other sites were plausibly the locations of integrative public performances, perhaps involving the aggregation of otherwise dispersed groups (Lindauer and Blitz 1997). Many of these mounds, as well as other types of earthen monuments dating to the Middle Woodland period (e.g., Jefferies 1976; Mainfort and Sullivan 1998; Wright 2012), also include exotic material culture indicative of long-distance communication and exchange. Ongoing investigations at several of these sites—including Biltmore (Kimball et al. 2010 and chapter 8, this volume) and Garden Creek (Wright 2012 and chapter 7, this volume) in North Carolina, Tunacunnhee in Georgia (Dekle, chapter 13, this volume), and Crystal River and Fort Center in Florida (Pluckhahn et al. 2010; Thompson and Pluckhahn 2010, 2012)—promise to shed light on the mechanisms by which extralocal interaction and innovations in the monumental built environment came to shape the social landscapes of the Middle Woodland period.

Not surprisingly, the nonmonumental components of the Middle Woodland landscape have received comparatively less archaeological attention, at least in the published literature. In general, Middle Woodland groups in the Southeast appear to have lived in permanent and semipermanent base camps and hamlets (Anderson and Mainfort 2002a; Smith 1992). Some groups practiced horticulture, cultivating crops in the Eastern Agricultural Complex, although wild plant and animal resources appear to have provided a subsistence base in many localities (Fritz 1993; Gremillion 2002). Some of the chapters in this volume strive to better articulate the monumental (and, we assume, ceremonial) and nonmonumental aspects of the Middle Woodland landscape (e.g., chapters 2, 5, and 7), but a more comprehensive synthesis, with the potential to elucidate the interrelated cultural structures at work in Middle Woodland societies, requires additional comparative research across the Southeast.

Emerging Issues in Early and Middle Woodland Landscape Research

Contributions to this volume highlight how diverse landscape-based approaches to the archaeological record can clarify the cultural dynamics of the

Early and Middle Woodland Southeast and, in turn, provide valuable case studies with the potential to further our anthropological understanding of human interactions with their landscapes more generally. The perspectives adopted by the authors target different spatial and social scales, and we have tried to parse this variability into three interrelated categories of archaeological inquiry: examinations of extensive landscapes, including domestic and nonmonumental ritual landscape features; the evaluation of intensive landscape use, particularly at monumental sites; and analyses of human interaction across landscapes. The last section of our volume includes reflections on and future directions for these various landscape approaches in the Southeast.

Part 1 explores the ways by which southeastern archaeologists investigate social landscapes at relatively extensive scales during the Early and Middle Woodland periods. With a geographic focus on Kentucky, chapters 2–4 bring to light complementary data sets that contextualize Early and early Middle Woodland Adena landscapes. Using both site descriptions and technical CRM reports, Applegate explores the evidence for seemingly elusive Early and Middle Woodland domestic components and reveals that archaeologists know much more than they realize when it comes to the domestic landscapes associated with more archaeologically visible monumental complexes. Pollack and Schlarb's chapter examines another aspect of the nonmonumental archaeological record—specifically, evidence of mortuary ritual that occurred in off-mound contexts yet certainly related to mound interment at other sites. Clay takes some of their arguments a step further and makes the case that Adena burial mounds, often viewed as specific loci of memorialization, can be more fruitfully interpreted as part of dispersed mortuary processes taking place across larger spatial and temporal scales. In the final chapter in this section, Franklin and colleagues take up these themes of extensive landscape use in their examination of upland rockshelter sites on the relatively understudied Cumberland Plateau of Tennessee. They engage lithic and ceramic artifacts, subsistence data, and a variety of chronometric dating techniques to refine previous interpretations of how people were using and interacting (or not interacting) within this remote and rugged portion of the Southeast.

Zeroing in to particular sites, part 2 features research on the monumental landscapes constructed by Early and Middle Woodland peoples in the Southeast. Jefferies and colleagues approach this topic by using geophysical methods to locate and assess the structural organization of an Adena ditch-and-embankment earthwork in central Kentucky. Natural and modern human effects on this constructed feature have left it barely visible on the landscape. However, geophysical methods allow it to be compared with other known geometric earthworks in the Eastern Woodlands.

Moving southward, Wright uses geographic information system (GIS) software to contextualize a massive collection of seemingly random submound postholes at the Garden Creek Mound No. 2, a Middle Woodland platform mound in western North Carolina. The possible structural patterns she teases out from these scatters suggest diachronic changes in the nature of occupation at this particular, eventually monumental, site on the landscape, perhaps related to the emergence of new forms of social and ceremonial organization. Also in North Carolina, Kimball and colleagues present new research from the Biltmore Mound, including detailed subsistence and stratigraphic information. These data are assembled to argue for feasting and ritual activities at the site and for a connection to a seasonal archaeoastronomical event associated with nearby Mt. Mitchell.

Keith's chapter on the excavations at the Leake site complex in northern Georgia demonstrates how the horizontal exposure of a monumental site, rather than the more common vertical exposure/trenching of a mound proper, can clarify activities through the lens of a landscape approach. Keith describes how inhabitants and visitors to the site were connected, possibly via ritual events, to nearby natural features on the landscape. Further, he suggests that the presence of various nonlocal artifacts at Leake and its location on a significant waterway indicate that it may have been a gateway between Hopewell sites in the Midwest and the Deep South.

Lastly, Boudreaux draws attention to the monumental earthen constructions that took place during the early Late Woodland[3] at the Jackson Landing site of the Mississippi Gulf Coast. Monumental on both vertical and horizontal scales, the area of ritual space at Jackson Landing is uncommon at Woodland ceremonial centers in the Southeast, meriting the testing of hypotheses related to the site's function as a locale for community integration.

The third set of contributions to this volume address how the southeastern landscape served as a medium for human interactions. Both Dekle and Eubanks achieve this by focusing on single sites as nexuses for interaction. Eubanks assesses the Armory site in central Alabama as a center for ritual activity and population aggregation over short periods of time, and he explores various situations that may have encouraged this aggregation. Meanwhile, Dekle examines the distribution of sacred objects recovered from the Tunacunnhee site in northwestern Georgia to understand how interactions among various peoples who visited Tunacunnhee reverberated in individual experiences.

The other three chapters in part 3 examine interaction through the analysis and comparison of site and artifact distributions *across* the landscape. Pluckhahn and Thompson provide a comparative analysis of Kolomoki, Crystal River, and Fort Center, three monumental Woodland sites in the Deep South.

They provide evidence for low-level interactions between these sites and propose the sorts of experiences travelers could have had going from one site/landscape to another. In the same area, Wallis investigates types of community interactions and forms of kin group organization among Weeden Island and Swift Creek cultures by mapping the distribution of ceramic vessels found within burial mound contexts. Finally, back in Kentucky, Henry examines the form and organization of burial mounds and evidence for premound ritual across three subregions of the Kentucky Bluegrass. The variation he identifies is used to generate a hypothesis of temporary leadership and to explain how specific mortuary traditions were adopted between subregions.

Together, these chapters highlight how archaeologists are addressing a variety of landscape issues in southeastern archaeology. At the risk of fostering a "catch-all" mentality, we have encouraged each researcher to approach his or her investigations with whatever aspect of a broad landscape perspective is best suited to answer the question(s) at hand. Embracing such theoretical diversity allows for unique and innovative research strategies and has the greatest potential to flesh out a comprehensive understanding of past human societies and the worlds that surrounded them. By conducting archaeological research on prehistoric landscapes in different ways and on multiple scales, we can elucidate how interaction with the natural and built environments impacted the lives of Early and Middle Woodland peoples. Such research will not only enrich our interpretations of the long-term trajectories of southeastern history but also, on a global scale, open our eyes to general anthropological issues relevant to similarly organized societies and their relationships with landscape.

Notes

1. As the chapters in this volume make clear, these dates vary some from subregion to subregion. We also acknowledge that our ending date for the Middle Woodland is fairly late compared to most cultural historical frameworks. Anderson addresses this issue specifically in chapter 17.

2. As Fleming (2006: 267) has pointed out, the term *landscape archaeology* actually appeared first in Britain before the postprocessual critique gripped archaeology. At least initially, the concept was a means to link the rigorous methods of site identification through field archaeology with the production of histories of complex cultural landscapes (Aston and Rowley 1974)—a framework quite reminiscent of that adopted in this volume.

3. Although Boudreaux's dates for Jackson Landing place it in the early Late Woodland period on the Gulf Coast, they overlap with late Middle Woodland dates for other portions of the Southeast and other sites discussed in this volume (see figure 1.2).

PART ONE

Extensive Landscapes

Between and Beyond Monuments

2

The Early–Middle Woodland Domestic Landscape in Kentucky

DARLENE APPLEGATE

Archaeological studies of the Early–Middle Woodland subperiods in Kentucky have long been associated with research on Adena, an archaeological culture best known for earthwork construction and elaborate mortuary ritual. Since the 1930s, archaeologists have made great progress in understanding the Adena ritual landscape, including recent studies of developmental trajectories (Clay 1991), regional variation in mortuary practices (Henry, chapter 15, this volume; Rafferty 2005), earthwork formal variation (Jefferies et al., chapter 6, this volume), protracted ritual performance at mounds (Clay, chapter 4, this volume), and off-mound ritual activity (Pollack and Schlarb, chapter 3, this volume). Less attention has been paid to the Adena domestic landscape, as well as the domestic-ritual landscapes of peoples who preceded and were contemporaneous with Adena in Kentucky. Because of recent work by academic and contract archaeologists, however, more is now known about Early–Middle Woodland settlement strategies in Kentucky. In this chapter I synthesize research on Early–Middle Woodland domestic landscapes in Kentucky using a multiscalar perspective.

Past human settlement strategies may be investigated at several levels. Microsettlement studies consider structure construction and the manner in which space was used within individual structures. Intrasite patterning examines the distribution of contemporaneous activities within one site. Intersite patterning considers the spatial relationships (settlement pattern) and functional relationships (settlement system) among contemporaneous sites (Evans and Gould 1982; Winters 1969). Though mortuary and ritual sites certainly are components of human settlement strategies and must be considered in relation to domestic space, this chapter focuses on multiscalar domestic components of Early–Middle Woodland settlement in Kentucky.

Here defined, the Early–Middle Woodland subperiods in Kentucky span about 1,750 years, circa 1250 BC to AD 500. The earliest evidence of pottery, known from dated contexts in northwestern and southeastern Kentucky, marks the lower boundary. Pottery technology spread unevenly across Kentucky, meaning that many early Early Woodland sites are aceramic, but pottery was in most places by 500 BC. The upper boundary of AD 500 is delineated by the development of subconoidal and subglobular cord-marked pottery jars (Applegate 2008).[1]

Early–Middle Woodland Microsettlement

Thirty domestic sites in Kentucky provide evidence of Early–Middle Woodland microsettlement (figure 2.1, table 2.1). Data about the structures at each of these sites are summarized in table 2.2 (see Applegate 2011 for details), and considered together, they provide a small but adequate sample for identifying patterns of Woodland microsettlement.

A majority of the 70 Early–Middle Woodland structures in this database are lightly built domestic structures intended for short-term (one or two seasons) rather than year-round use. These structures include circular and rectangular enclosed houses, open ramadas or sunscreens, and open cabanas, windbreaks, or lean-tos. Such structures are documented at numerous Early–Middle Woodland sites elsewhere in the Southeast and Midwest (e.g., Faulkner and McCollough 1974; Kline et al. 1982; Mocas 2007, n.d.; Smith 1992). In contrast, fewer than one-fifth ($n = 11–12$) of the Kentucky structures are heavily built domestic structures intended for long-term or cold-season occupation. These include roofed rectangular domiciles at Sim's Creek, large rebuilt cabanas at Sim's Creek and Grayson, a windbreak secured in a rock-lined trench at Big Turtle Shelter, and daub-covered structures at three sites (see below). External associated domestic furniture (e.g., drying racks and storage racks) likely was present at about one-third of the sites: Lawrence, Plum Springs, Main, Shippingport, Stone, Cloudsplitter, Cold Oak, Pine Crest, and Sim's Creek.

Most Early–Middle Woodland structures had a single use-life, the average length of which has not been estimated. Rotted, broken, and pulled posts at Newt Kash, Cloudsplitter, and Shippingport indicate that structures were abandoned or dismantled at the end of that use-life. Evidence of structure burning consists of charcoal-bearing or charcoal-lined postmolds at one-third of the sites, as well as burned daub/clay at Lawrence and Site 15Ml134.

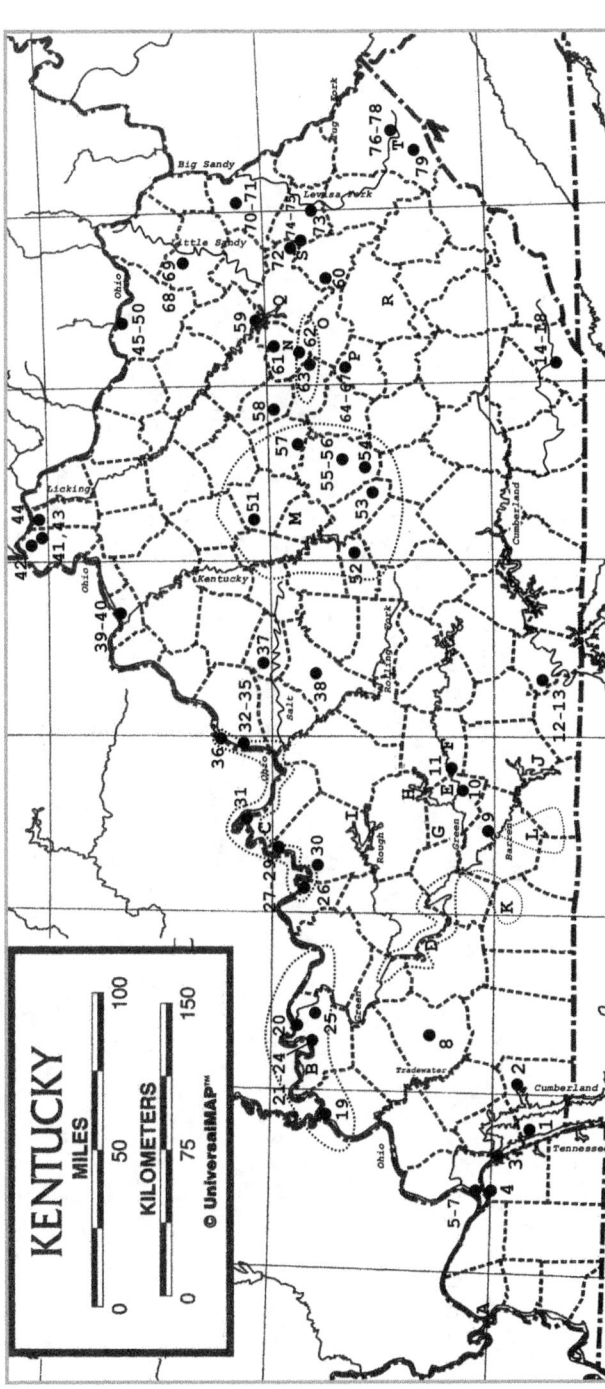

Figure 2.1. Locations of Early–Middle Woodland sites and settlement surveys discussed in chapter: (1) Roach, (2) Lawrence, (3) Owen, (4) 15Ml134, (5) 15Lv204, (6) 15Lv208, (7) Chestnut Lake, (8) Morris, (9) Plum Springs, (10) Mammoth Cave, (11) Salts Cave, (12) 15Cu27, (13) 15Cu110, (14) Main, (15) Cumberland Ford II, (16) Cumberland Ford I, (17) Mills, (18) Bailey, (19) Slack Farm, (20) Smith, (21) 15He33, (22) 15He34, (23) 15He315B, (24) 15He323B, (25) 15He847, (26) 15Ha151, (27) Rockmaker, (28) Yellowbank, (29) Chenaultt Crematory Pit, (30) Beech Fork, (31) Carver's Lake, (32) Spadie, (33) Rosenberger, (34) Villier, (35) Longworth-Gick, (36) Shippingport, (37) 15Sp26, (38) Withrow Creek, (39) Panther Rock, (40) Hayes, (41) West Runway, (42) Wackenstein, (43) 15Be509, (44) Gibson Greeting Card, (45) 15Lw301C, (46) 15Lw314C, (47) 15Lw316A, (48) 15Lw302A, (49) 15Lw325E, (50) 15Lw353, (51) Peter Village, (52) Danville Tank, (53) Miller, (54) Indian Fort Mountain, (55) Harvey Tudor, (56) Gate Eleven, (57) Stone, (58) 15Mm140, (59) Zilpo, (60) Short Fork, (61) Newt Kash Hollow Rockshelter, (62) Cloudsplitter Rockshelter, (63) Seldon Skidmore, (64) Zachariah Shelter, (65) Cold Oak Shelter, (66) Big Turtle Shelter, (67) Pine Crest Shelter, (68) 15Cr61, (69) Grayson, (70) Graham, (71) Calloway, (72) Patoker, (73) C&O Mounds, (74) Dameron Rockshelter, (75) McKenzie Farmstead, (76) Martin Justice, (77) Sim's Creek, (78) Blackburn, (79) 15Pi303; (A) Big Bottoms, (B) Crab Orchard area, (C) constricted Ohio River floodplain, (D) middle Green River Shell Mound area, (E) Mammoth Cave National Park, (F) WKU Upper Green River Biological Preserve, (G) Edmonson County, (H) Nolin Reservoir, (I) Rough River Reservoir, (J) Barren River Reservoir, (K) Gasper River Drainage, (L) Drakes Creek Drainage, (M) Adena core area, (N) Clifty Wilderness, (O) North Fork Red River, (P) Middle Fork Red River, (Q) Cave Run Reservoir, (R) Robinson Forest, (S) Paintsville Reservoir, (T) Fishtrap Reservoir. Map prepared by Darlene Applegate.

Table 2.1. Early–Middle Woodland sites in Kentucky

Site name	Site no.	County	Drainage	Chronometric date[a] or relative period	Reference
Roach	15Tr10	Trigg	Tennessee	Early Woodland	Rolingson and Schwartz 1966
Lawrence	15Tr33	Trigg	Cumberland (lower)	758–173 BC[b]; 370 BC–AD 60[b]	Mocas 1977, 1991b
Owen	15Ml69	Marshall	Tennessee	352–295, 229–220, 211–128 BC; 167 BC–AD 251; 357–284, 256–248, 234 BC–AD 546	Allen 1976; Nance 1974
None	15Ml134	Marshall	Tennessee	384–53 BC	Schenian and Mocas 1993
None	15Lv204	Livingston	Tennessee	Middle Woodland	Anderson et al. 1992
None	15Lv208	Livingston	Tennessee	Early Woodland	Schock 1994
Chestnut Lake	15Lv222	Livingston	Tennessee	Early–Middle Woodland	Herndon 2003
Morris	15Hk49	Hopkins	Tradewater	Early–Middle Woodland	Rolingson and Schwartz 1966
Plum Springs	15Wa981	Warren	Green	389 BC–AD 72; 186 BC–AD 93, 97–125; 88–77 BC, 55 BC–AD 239; AD 252–874; AD 540[c]	Dowell 1981, n.d.; Schock 1979; Applegate and McCray 2006
Mammoth Cave	15Ed1	Edmonson	Green	756–684, 699–360, 274–260 BC; 387–203 BC; 1112–1101, 1086–1063, 1058–753, 685–668, 611–597 BC; 926–781 BC; 914–748, 688–665, 643–589, 580–558 BC; 914–517 BC; 891–879, 844–505, 492–490, 462–450, 441–417 BC; 791–485, 464–416 BC; 781–413 BC (two different assays); 759–683, 670–355, 290–232 BC; 537–528, 525–355, 288–233 BC	Crothers et al. 2002; Gremillion and Sobolik 1996; Kennedy 1992, 1996; Nelson 1917a, 1917b; Watson 1997; Watson et al. 1969
Salts Cave vestibule	15Ht4	Hart	Green	2131–2085, 2051–1527 BC; 1958–1493, 1476–1460 BC; 2282–2249, 2232–2218, 2214–1112, 1100–1087, 1063–1059 BC; 1427–893, 876–847 BC; 1054–507, 460–452, 440–418 BC; 800–482, 467–415 BC; 796–485, 464–416 BC; 767–411 BC; 755–684, 669–607, 601–401 BC; 756–684, 669–394 BC; 756–684, 669–373 BC; 748–687, 666–644, 590–578, 562–348, 317–207 BC; 393–107 BC	Crothers et al. 2002; Gardner 1987; Kennedy 1992; Watson et al. 1969; Watson 1997
None	15Cu27	Cumberland	Cumberland (upper)	401–163, 130–119 BC; 351–300, 227–224, 210 BC–AD 138, 197–207; AD 421–655	Kerr et al. 2004

Site	Number	County	Period	Dates	Reference
None	15Cu110	Cumberland	Early–Middle Woodland		French 2004
Main	15Bl35	Cumberland (upper)		889–881, 843–401 BC; 799–407 BC; 761–682, 671–403 BC; 773–175 BC; 748–687, 665–644, 590–579, 559–197 BC	Creasman 1994
Cumberland Ford II	15Bl52	Cumberland (upper)		810–483, 466–415 BC; 817–399 BC; 793–413 BC	Maslowski et al. 1995; Autry and DuVall 1985
Cumberland Ford I	15Bl59	Cumberland (upper)	Early–Middle Woodland		Kimball 1988
Mills	15Bl80	Cumberland (upper)		1007–799 BC; 1024–774 BC; 997–795 BC; 745–689, 664–647, 551–341, 326–204 BC; 390–94 BC; 359–275, 260 BC–AD 0	Creasman 1994, 1995
Bailey	15Bl100	Cumberland (upper)		1263–916 BC; 345–322, 205 BC–AD 69[b]	Stokes and Shields 1999
Slack Farm	15Un28	Union		107 BC–AD 181, 187–214; AD 53–259, 295–322; AD 434–493, 506–520, 527–666	DeNeeve 2004; Pollack 1993
Smith	15He16	Henderson	Middle Woodland		DeNeeve 2004
None	15He33	Henderson	Middle Woodland		Schock and Stone 1985; Dowell 1979
None	15He34	Henderson	Middle Woodland		Schock and Stone 1985; Dowell 1979
None	15He315B	Henderson	Early–Middle Woodland		Schock and Stone 1985; Dowell 1979
None	15He323B	Henderson	Middle Woodland		Schock and Stone 1985; Dowell 1979
None	15He847	Henderson		356–285, 255–249, 234 BC–AD 87, 104–121	Versluis 2004
None	15Ha151	Hancock	Early–Middle Woodland		Turnbow et al. 1980
Rockmaker	15Bc138	Breckenridge		1258–1232, 1218–829 BC; 789–482, 467–415 BC; 763–680, 673–405 BC	Bader 1996a, 1996b

(*continued*)

(Table 2.1. continued)

Site name	Site no.	County	Drainage	Chronometric date[a] or relative period	Reference
Yellowbank	15Bc164	Breckenridge	Ohio	750–687, 666–641, 593–172 BC	Bader 1996a, 1996b
Chenault Crematory Pit	None	Breckenridge	Ohio	789–482, 467–415 BC	Bader 1996a
Beech Fork	15Bc168	Breckenridge	Ohio	Early Woodland	Bader 1991
Carver's Lake	15Md318	Meade	Ohio	Early Woodland	Bader 1996a
Spadie	15Jf14	Jefferson	Ohio	Early–Middle Woodland	Boisvert 1979
Rosenberger	15Jf18	Jefferson	Ohio	Early Woodland	Driskell 1979
Villier	15Jf110	Jefferson	Ohio	766–369 BC; 255 BC–AD 45	Robinson and Smith 1979
Longworth-Gick	15Jf243	Jefferson	Ohio	Early Woodland	Collins 1979
Shippingport	15Jf702	Jefferson	Ohio	1460–1310 BC; 767–411 BC; 754–685, 668–610, 598–406 BC; 757–684, 669–397 BC	Mocas et al. 2010; French et al. 2007
None	15Sp26	Spencer	Salt	10±140 BC[d], AD 10±250[d], AD 73–603; AD 360±100[d], AD 400±110[d]; AD 630±100[d]	Driskell et al. 1984
Withrow Creek	15Ne55	Nelson	Salt	AD 410–637	Davis et al. 1997
Panther Rock	15Cl58	Carroll	Ohio	Early–Middle Woodland	Stallings 2007
Hayes	15Cl67	Carroll	Ohio	AD 74–380	Hall 2005
West Runway	15Be391	Boone	Ohio	1188–1181, 1155–1146, 1130–752, 686–667, 632–625, 612–596 BC; 1111–1102, 1084–1064, 1057–355, 288–233 BC; 895–868, 856, 850–536, 533–521 BC; 761–682, 671–403 BC; 756–684, 669–606, 604–389 BC; AD 79–397	Duerksen et al. 1994, 1995
Wackenstein	15Be467	Boone	Ohio	164–128, 121 BC–AD 179, 188–213[b]; AD 63–416[b]	Walley et al. 1997
None	15Be509	Boone	Ohio	347–318, 207 BC–AD 180, 187–214; 44 BC–AD 436, 490–509, 517–529; AD 91–99, 124–538	Breetzke 2001
Gibson Greeting Card	15Kt4	Kenton	Ohio	AD 79–397	Schock 1984; Duerksen et al. 1994

Site	Number	County	State (region)	Period	Dates	References
None	15Lw301C	Lewis	Ohio	Middle Woodland		Schock and Langford 1978, 1980, 1981
None	15Lw314C	Lewis	Ohio	Early–Middle Woodland		Schock and Langford 1978, 1980, 1981
None	15Lw316A	Lewis	Ohio		348–316, 207 BC–AD 240[b]; 349–314, 208 BC–AD 995, 1008–1011[b]	Schock and Langford 1978, 1980, 1981
None	15Lw302A	Lewis	Ohio	Early–Middle Woodland		Schock and Langford 1978, 1980, 1981
None	15Lw325E	Lewis	Ohio		AD 85–110, 116–604	Schock and Langford 1978, 1980, 1981
None	15Lw353	Lewis	Ohio	Early–Middle Woodland		Schock and Langford 1978, 1980, 1981
Peter Village	15Fa166	Fayette	Kentucky (middle)		891–879, 844–409 BC; 409–171 BC; 516 BC–AD 1; 399 BC–AD 68	Clay 1985
Danville Tank	15Bo16	Boyle	Kentucky (middle)	Early Woodland		Boedy and Niquette 1987
Miller	15Gd44	Garrard	Kentucky (middle)		86–79, 54 BC–AD 229; 162–132, 117 BC–AD 139, 154–169, 195–209	Elmore and Ross-Stallings 2006; Ross-Stallings and Stallings 2007
Indian Fort Mountain	15Ma25	Madison	Kentucky (middle)		917–960, 935–375 BC; 39–7, 5 BC–AD 236	Moore 1982
Harvey Tudor	15Ma70	Madison	Kentucky (middle)	Early–Middle Woodland		Brenyo 1983
Gate Eleven	15Ma218	Madison	Kentucky (middle)		AD 132–468, 479–534	French and Bader 2001; Ensor et al. 1996
Stone	15Ck89	Clark	Kentucky (middle)		751–686, 667–637, 622–614, 595–387 BC	Turnbow et al. 1983
None	15Mm140	Montgomery	Licking		352–295, 229–220, 211–42 BC; 48 BC–AD 93, 97–125	Anderson 2003

(continued)

(Table 2.1. continued)

Site name	Site no.	County	Drainage	Chronometric date[a] or relative period	Reference
Zilpo	15Bh37	Bath	Licking	Early Woodland	Rolingson and Rodeffer 1968; Marquardt 1970
Short Fork	15Mg38	Magoffin	Licking	775–347, 319–206 BC; 38–9, 4 BC–AD 242	Richmond et al. 2002
Newt Kash Hollow Rockshelter	15Mf1	Menifee	Licking	1419–1118 BC; 1500–53 BC; 1449–19, 13–1 BC	Gremillion 1995; O'Steen et al. 1991; Webb and Funkhouser 1936b; Crane 1956
Cloudsplitter Rockshelter	15Mt36	Menifee	Kentucky (upper)	1114–1097, 1091–818 BC (two assays)[b]; 1040–840 BC[b,c]; 995–988, 980–785 BC[b]; 910–710 BC[c]; 799–477, 474–413 BC; 762–681, 672–403 BC; 125 BC–AD 135[c]; AD 320–480[c]	Cowan 1985; Cowan et al. 1981
Seldon Skidmore	15Po17	Powell	Kentucky (upper)	Early Woodland	Cowan 1985
Zachariah Shelter	15Le44	Lee	Kentucky (upper)	Early Woodland	O'Steen et al. 1991
Cold Oak Shelter	15Le50	Lee	Kentucky (upper)	1373–1341, 1318–969, 962–932 BC; 1381–1334, 1323–891, 879–845 BC; 1192–1174, 1164–1143, 1132–836 BC; 1048–805 BC; 997–795 BC; 907–481, 468–415 BC; 787–477, 473–414 BC; 791–402 BC; 767–411 BC; 757–684, 669–397 BC; 401–163, 130–119 BC; 396–149, 140–112 BC; 395–51 BC; 384–53 BC; 352–295, 229–220, 211 BC–AD 80; 345–322, 205 BC–AD 69; 20–12, 1 BC–AD 232	Gremillion 1997, 1998; Gremillion et al. 2000; Ison 1988; O'Steen et al. 1991
Big Turtle Shelter	15Le55	Lee	Kentucky (upper)	753–685, 668–611, 597–39, 8 BC–AD 4[b]	O'Steen et al. 1991
Pine Crest Shelter	15Le70	Lee	Kentucky (upper)	1739–1706, 1698–1487, 1484–1454 BC; 1192–1176, 1163–1143, 1132–814 BC; 766–369 BC; 383–17, 15 BC–AD 0	O'Steen et al. 1991
None	15Cr61	Carter	Big Sandy	775–400 BC; 756–684, 669–394 BC	Stallings et al. 1995

Site	Number	County	Point type	Dates	Reference
Grayson	15Cr73	Carter	Big Sandy	1606–1572, 1559–1549, 1539–1304 BC[b,e]; 1679–1674, 1669–903 BC; 1430–1190, 1178–1159, 1144–1131 BC[b]; 1428–1123 BC; 2032–92, 68–61 BC; 1114–1097, 1094–810 BC; 1494–348, 318–207 BC; 805–345, 322–205 BC[b]	Ledbetter et al. 1991; Ledbetter and O'Steen 1992
Graham	15La222	Lawrence	Big Sandy	913–732, 691–661, 650–545 BC; 395–51 BC; 338–330, 203 BC–AD 30, 37–51	Niquette 1989; Niquette et al. 1987
Calloway	15Mt8	Martin	Big Sandy	755–685, 668–608, 600–50 BC; 310±120 BC[d]; 130±210 BC[d]; 198 BC–AD 240; 39–8, 4 BC–AD 259, 284–323	Niquette and Boedy 1986
Patoker	15Mo13	Morgan	Big Sandy	Early Woodland	Adovasio 1982
C&O Mounds	15Jo2, 15Jo9	Johnson	Big Sandy	Early–Middle Woodland	Webb et al. 1942
Dameron Rockshelter	15Jo23A	Johnson	Big Sandy	1488–1483, 1454–1006 BC	Adovasio 1982; Vento et al. 1980
McKenzie Farmstead	15Jo67	Johnson	Big Sandy	766–677, 675–359, 275–259 BC; 166 BC–AD 93, 97–125; AD 85–109, 117–413[b], AD 87–104, 121–428	McBride 1994
Martin Justice	15Pi92	Pike	Big Sandy	907–961,932–405 BC[b], 405–171 BC[b]; 37–30, 22–11, 2 BC–AD 263, 277–331[b]	Kerr and Creasman 1998; Kerr et al. 1995
Sim's Creek	15Pi7	Pike	Big Sandy	AD 183–185, 214–776	Dunnell 1966a, 1972
Blackburn	15Pi12	Pike	Big Sandy	Middle Woodland	Dunnell 1966a, 1972
None	15Pi303	Pike	Big Sandy	Middle Woodland	Schock et al. 1976; Dowell 1979

[a] Except where otherwise noted, all chronometric dates are calibrated two-sigma radiocarbon dates; standard radiometric ages were converted to calendar dates using the radiocarbon calibration program Calib v. 5.0.1 (Stuiver and Reimer 2005), and ages were calibrated using the IntCal04 data set (Reimer et al. 2004).
[b] Date for postmold or feature associated with domestic structure.
[c] Uncalibrated.
[d] Thermoluminescence date.
[e] Date rejected by authors as inconsistent with other archaeological evidence.

Table 2.2. Domestic structures at Early–Middle Woodland sites in Kentucky

Site Name	No.	Structure				Postmolds			
		Shape	Dimension(m)	Area (sq m)	No.	Dimension (cm)	Depth (cm)	Orientation	Type
Lawrence	1	Oval	5.4 × 4.0	17	42	N/A	N/A	N/A	Single and paired
	2	Rectangular	3.0 × 1.2	3.6	5–6	N/A	N/A	N/A	Single
	3	Rectangular	2.6 × 1.8	4.7	7	N/A	N/A	N/A	Single
	4	Linear	2.4 × 1.2	~2.9	9–10	N/A	N/A	N/A	Single
Plum Springs	1	Circular	1.6	2	5	7.5–10	Unknown	Unknown	Single
	2	Linear	0.9	—	4	7.5–10	Unknown	Unknown	Single
	3	Circular	2.1	3.4	13	7.5–10	Unknown	Unknown	Single
	4	Linear	1.6	—	4	7.5–10	Unknown	Unknown	Single
	5	Linear	3.6	—	12	7.5–10	Unknown	Unknown	Single
	6	Curvilinear	3.0 × 1.2	~2.3	5	7.5–10	Unknown	Unknown	Single
	7	Circular	3.7	10.7	N/A	7.5–10	Unknown	Unknown	Single
	8	Circular	3.7	10.7	N/A	7.5–10	Unknown	Unknown	Single
Main	1	Rectangular or oval	3.85 × 2.6	9.0–10.0	14+	8–20	3–23	Vertical	Single
	2	Linear	3.85	—	4	8–20	3–23	Vertical	Single
Bailey	1	Unknown	Unknown	Unknown	5	10–19	6–16	Vertical	Single

Site	#	Shape	Dimensions					Orientation	Type
Cumberland Ford II	1	Circular	7.8	47.5	N/A	N/A	N/A	N/A	N/A
Cumberland Ford I	1	Rectangular	>4.4 × 1.7	>7.5	3	N/A	N/A	N/A	Single
	2	Curvilinear	2.8	—	5–6	N/A	N/A	N/A	Single
	3	Curvilinear	3.3 × 1.3	~2.5	7–9	N/A	N/A	N/A	Single
	4	Curvilinear	3.1 × 1.3	~3.2	9	N/A	N/A	N/A	Single
	5A	Curvilinear	1.7	—	3	N/A	N/A	N/A	Single
15Ha151	1	Circular	~2.0	3.1	3	18–20	Unknown	Unknown	Single
Shippingport	1	Curvilinear	4.0 × 2.5	~8.0	9	8–26	4–24	Vertical	Single
	2	Curvilinear	5.0 × 2.5	~10.0	9	8–20	2–20	Vertical	Single
Wackenstein	1	Circular	1.3	1.3	1	45	23	N/A	N/A
15Lw301C	1	Rectangular	>2.5 × 2.0	>5.0	5	20–30	N/A	N/A	Single
15Lw314C	1	Curvilinear	3.75 × 0.9	~2.6	10	9.5–19	29.5–68	Vertical	Single
	2	Linear	1.6	—	9	6–15.5	38–39	Vertical and slanting	Single
15Lw316A	1	Curvilinear	7.5 × 2.5	~15.2	17–19	15–35	46–57	Slanting	Single
15Lw302A	1	Curvilinear	5.1 × 1.5	~5.9	5	15.5–23	25–70	Vertical	Single
15Lw325E	1	Rectangular	>4.0 × 1.0	>4.0	4	24–47	31–44	Vertical	Single
15Lw353	1	Rectangular	1.5 × >1.0	>1.5	8	5–10	N/A	Vertical	Single

(continued)

(*Table 2.2. continued*)

		Structure			Postmolds				
Site Name	No.	Shape	Dimension(m)	Area (sq m)	No.	Dimension (cm)	Depth (cm)	Orientation	Type
Grayson	3	Curvilinear	10.0 × 8.0	~62.0	22	15–30	3–30	Vertical	Single and paired
	4	Curvilinear	6.0 × 3.0	~13.0	6	N/A	N/A	N/A	Single
Stone	1	Curvilinear	6.8 × 2.1	~11.2	6	11–40	5–42	Vertical	Paired
	2	Linear	3	—	2	23–53	35–38	Vertical	Single
	3	Curvilinear	5.0 × 2.5	~9.8	3	25–50	11–26	Vertical	Single
	4	Linear	2	—	2	17–26	14–15	Vertical	Single
Cloudsplitter	1	Curvilinear	1.6 × 1.5	~2.5	5	11–14	24	Slanting	Single
	2	Linear	1.7 × 1.6	~3.0	6	11–13	N/A	Slanting	Single
Newt Kash Shelter	1	N/A	N/A	—	11	5	10–15	N/A	Single
	2	N/A	N/A	—	3	5	10–15	N/A	Single
Cold Oak Shelter	1	N/A	N/A	—	5	10–27	5–32	Vertical	Single and paired
	2	N/A	N/A	—	6	10–25	>4–25	Vertical	Single
Pine Crest Shelter	1	N/A	N/A	—	5	15–40	15–35	Vertical	Single and paired
	2	N/A	N/A	—	8	16–25	37–39	Vertical	Single
Zachariah Shelter	1	Circular	1.3	1.3	8	10	5–10	Vertical	Single and paired

Site	No.	Shape	Dimensions					Orientation	Arrangement
Big Turtle Shelter	2	Circular or curvilinear	1	~0.3–0.8	7	10	Unknown	Unknown	Single and paired
Patoker	1	Linear	>1.0	—	2	15	30	Vertical	Single
McKenzie Farmstead	1	Circular	2.15	3.6	7	10–17	14–20	Vertical	Single
	1	Curvilinear	3	—	5	7.5–15	14–40.5	Vertical	Single
Martin Justice	1	Rectangular	5.5 × 3.5	19.3	11	17–24	6–28	Vertical	Single and paired
Sim's Creek	1	Rectangular	7.6 × 4.8	36.5	50	N/A	N/A	N/A	Single?
	2	Rectangular	3.6 × 2.8	10.1	25	N/A	N/A	N/A	Single and paired?
	3	Curvilinear	9.0 × 5.0	~32.5	9–11	N/A	N/A	N/A	Single
	4	Curvilinear	9.0 × 8.0	~53.9	15–17	N/A	N/A	N/A	Single
	5	Curvilinear	7.0 × 1.5	~7.3	11	N/A	N/A	N/A	Single and paired?
Blackburn	1	Curvilinear	N/A	N/A	N/A	N/A	N/A	N/A	N/A

Note: Excludes structures evidenced by daub/burned clay concentrations at Site 15Ml134 (Feature 3), Lawrence (Structures 5–6), and Site 15Sp26, as well as structures evidenced by nonpostmold features at Main (Structures 3–11).

About one-fifth of the structures ($n = 12–14$) have indications of reconstruction and reuse. There were two to three total construction episodes per rebuilt structure. Structures at Lawrence, Main, Sites 15Lw314C and 15Lw353, Cold Oak, Grayson, and Sim's Creek are marked by superimposed or overlapping postmold patterns. The latter two sites, and probably Bailey, Cumberland Ford I, and Martin Justice, have artifact cache features, suggestive of intended reuse, associated with domestic structures.

Early–Middle Woodland domestic structures varied in size, largely in relation to season of occupation, site function, group size, and social residence patterns. The estimated floor areas of 60 structures range from 1 m² to 62 m², but two size clusters are apparent. Over 90 percent ($n = 55$) are smaller than 20 m², and the other five range from 32 m² to 62 m². If we assume that each occupant (up to six occupants) would have required about 2.25 m² of space and each additional occupant (after six) would have required 9 m² (per Cook 1972), then the smaller structures could have accommodated up to six or seven individuals and the larger structures, eight to eleven or twelve individuals. A substantially larger proportion (80 percent) of the large structures exhibited evidence of reconstruction or reuse, in contrast with less than one-fifth ($n = 8–10$) of the smaller structures. A bimodal size distribution is evident within the cluster of smaller structures, with two-thirds ($n = 35$) smaller than and one-third ($n = 20$) larger than 4 m².

Structure shape is unknown in 12 instances, but 35 percent of 58 structures are curvilinear, 31 percent are circular/oval, and 17 percent each are linear and rectangular. Rounded structure forms thus outnumber nonrounded forms by 2:1, a general pattern that mimics Early–Middle Woodland submound ritual architecture in Kentucky. Whether this apparent shape preference in domestic architecture is symbolic, aesthetic, functional, and/or structural is unclear. Rectangular domestic structures are not well represented at Early–Middle Woodland sites outside Kentucky, though a notable example is the Middle Woodland Patton site in southern Ohio (Weaver 2009). In the Kentucky sample, 70 percent of the rectangular structures have corners oriented in the cardinal directions.

When covariation in structure size and shape is considered, the size distribution of the 20 curvilinear structures is bimodal and skewed, as 85 percent are small (≤ 15 m²) and 15 percent are large (32–62 m²). In addition, there is a bimodal distribution within the sample of small curvilinear structures, as nearly equal proportions are very small (≤ 3.2 m²) and moderately small (6–15 m²). Similarly, 94 percent of the 18 circular/oval structures are small (≤ 17 m²) and 6 percent are large (47.5 m²). Of the former, about one-third are very small (≤3.6 m^2) and two-thirds are moderately small (10.7–17 m^2). The ten rectangular structures also exhibit a bimodal and skewed size distribution, as 90 percent are small (<20 m^2) and 10 percent are large (36.5 m^2). However, all are moderately small (at least 3.6–19.3 m^2). Floor area was not calculated for most linear structures, although the area behind each windbreak would likely fall into the very small group (<4 m^2).

Early–Middle Woodland structure walls were constructed with wooden posts that tend to be small to medium in size. Maximum postmold diameters for 41 structures range from 5 cm to 53 cm with a mode of 10 cm. Postmold diameters for 75 percent of these structures cluster between 10 cm and 27 cm. Because most of the posts were inserted into pre-dug postholes, occasionally using erection trenches (such as at Cold Oak and Pine Crest), the postmold diameters are indirect indicators of the wooden post sizes. At Cloudsplitter, however, archaeologists uncovered pointed structural posts driven into the shelter sediments; one such fragment measured about 5 cm across and 26 cm long. Driven posts were also documented at Sim's Creek, where the average postmold diameter is 6 cm. In terms of depths, postmolds from 28 structures tend to be shallow, with maximum depths ranging from 10 cm to 70 cm and modes of 15 cm and 23 cm. Most postmold depths cluster between 15 cm and 44 cm.

Postmold form, when reported, varies at Early–Middle Woodland domestic sites. Postmolds with in-sloping walls were uncovered at 4 sites, vertical walls at 2 sites, and both forms at 5 sites. Six sites yielded postmolds with rounded bases, 2 had flat-based postmolds, and 4 had both types. In contrast with many submound ritual structures in Kentucky, domestic structures with unpaired posts account for 82 percent of the 55 structures for which data are available. About 16 percent of the structures have both single and paired posts, while only 2 percent have paired posts. Of 27 structures for which data are available, 85 percent have vertical postmolds, 11 percent have slanting postmolds, and 4 percent have both.

Slanted postmolds often indicate tensioned structures, and this likely was the case with linear and curvilinear cabanas at Sites 15Lw314C and 15Lw316A. The slanted postmolds at Cloudsplitter likely demark two cabanas angled toward the back wall, at least one of which is associated with tension posts along the back wall. Based on the presence of single interior posts, tensioned linear and curvilinear cabana structures were erected at Lawrence, Cumberland Ford I, and Shippingport.

Chinked postmolds are another indicator of tensioned structures. Postmolds with dolostone chinking, fire-altered rock, nonaltered rock, and gravel fill were documented at Stone, Grayson, Cold Oak, Big Turtle, Pine Crest, and Martin Justice, but only in the case of Site 15Lw316A are these features associated with a tensioned structure.

Indirect evidence of tensioned structures is the apparent absence of interior support posts in the enclosed houses. These structures likely were constructed by bending and securing saplings in a dome-like shape. Such structures are known from Middle Woodland sites outside Kentucky (e.g., Mocas 2007, n.d.; Wiant and McGimsey 1986).

In terms of wall coverings, few Early–Middle Woodland structures were plastered with mud, as daub and burned clay are associated with only five or six structures at Lawrence and Sites 15Ml134 and 15Sp26. The absence of large quantities of daub at most sites indicates that structures lacked vertical walls, to which daub is more easily applied, and/or were used during warm seasons when insulation was not needed. Instead, most walls likely were constructed of perishable material only, such as poles, bark, cane, thatch, mats of woven or sewn plants, and, in the case of Newt Kash, woven textiles.

Internal features are associated with 41–46 percent of the structures at half of the sites in this database, though for individual structures the number and diversity of internal features are limited. Thermal features include surface and pit hearths and, less commonly, earth ovens. Other internal features are refuse pits, ephemeral basins, debitage concentrations, and lithic cache pits, while food storage pits are notably absent. When documented, such features tend to be clustered, sometimes near doorways (as at Martin Justice) or along walls (as at Grayson). Internal postmolds are uncommon, suggesting that Early–Middle Woodland structures were not partitioned and/or lacked benches, platforms, and roofs. Internal floor maintenance was documented in six or seven structures at Main, Cumberland Ford I, Grayson, and Martin Justice. Gaps in postmold patterns of several enclosed structures suggest that some had entryways. At Martin Justice, two pairs of double posts in the southeast suggest a more formal opening or doorway into the rectangular structure.

In conclusion, though the database of Early–Middle Woodland domestic structures in Kentucky is growing, further research on Woodland microsettlement is needed. Postmolds should be excavated routinely. Data recovery in the field should include recording postmold dimensions, spacing, and orientations, as well as the methods of post insertion and nature of backfilling or chinking. Careful attention must be paid to apparent gaps in postmold patterns, in order to distinguish structural openings from the effects of site formation processes. Researchers should carefully examine the interior spaces of structures for additional postmolds, other associated features, functionally diagnostic artifacts, and evidence of floor maintenance. These detailed field data must be reported in the literature.

Armed with additional data, future researchers investigating Woodland microsettlement should focus on identifying specific structure types and describing the functional use of space within structures. With additional chronometric dating and the discovery and documentation of additional sites, it may be possible to discern seasonal, diachronic, and geographic variation in Early–Middle Woodland domestic structures in Kentucky.

Early–Middle Woodland Intrasite Patterning

Archaeological projects involving extensive lateral excavation and mechanical stripping provide information about intrasite patterning in Kentucky. Early–Middle Woodland open habitations, rockshelters, and caves often contain midden deposits, artifact and feature clusters, evidence of mortuary activities, and, in some cases, remains of domestic structures (described in the previous section). Unlike the Late Woodland subperiod, with its distinctive circular villages (Pollack and Henderson 2000), Early–Middle Woodland domestic sites lack a distinguishing and recurring pattern of spatial organization and instead are characterized by considerable variation in site form and use of space.

Starting with open habitation sites, evidence suggests that there is a dichotomy in general intrasite patterning, which likely is explained by variation in occupational intensity.[2] First, domestic loci at more substantial sites have clusters of artifacts and features from a variety of food preparation, food consumption, food storage, tool manufacture, and resource-processing activities. In some cases, structural remains are found at these sites. While *multipurpose* activity areas are evident at these sites, generally speaking, there is limited evidence of *activity-specific* space differentiation, exceptions being Rockmaker and Shippingport. Sites illustrating this pattern include Lawrence, Plum Springs, Main, Cumberland Ford I, Bailey, 15He847, Withrow Creek, Panther Rock, West Runway, Gibson Greeting Card, Miller, Stone, Grayson, McKenzie Farmstead, Martin Justice, and Sim's Creek (figure 2.1, table 2.1).

In contrast, low-intensity habitations are marked by artifact scatters or clustered artifacts, fewer or no features, and no activity areas. At these sites a variety of activities may be evidenced, but those activities were distributed broadly without spatial patterning. This is the more common Early–Middle Woodland site pattern, and examples include Roach, Owen, 15Ml134, 15Lv204, 15Lv208, Chestnut Lake, Morris, 15Cu110, Mills, 15He33, 15He34, 15He315B, 15He323B, Yellowbank, Beech Fork, Spadie, Rosenberger, Villier, Longworth-Gick, Hayes, Wackenstein, 15Be509, Danville Tank, Gate Eleven, 15Mm140, Zilpo, Short Fork, 15Cr61, Graham, Calloway, Patoker, and 15Pi303 (figure 2.1, table 2.1). Four sites exemplify this dichotomy in Early–Middle Woodland open habitation intrasite patterning: Grayson, Martin Justice, Yellowbank, and Graham.

Investigations at Grayson, an intensely occupied winter habitation, revealed at least 23 early Early Woodland features and midden concentrated along a terrace crest. Postmolds marking at least two structures (table 2.2), chert-filled cache pits, and various thermal features were clustered spatially, suggesting several domestic activity areas. Multiple activities occurred in each of these loci, including stone tool manufacture and maintenance, food processing, and food storage. One set of features immediately adjacent to and partially outlining Structure 3 suggests a tightly clustered houselot measuring 20 × 17 m; associated features include a nut-roasting pit and an earth oven later used as a storage or refuse pit. About 35 m north, the cluster of features around Structure 4 may represent a smaller and less dense houselot (Ledbetter and O'Steen 1992; Ledbetter et al. 1991).

Archaeologists documented two intensive Middle Woodland fall–winter occupations at Martin Justice. The earlier occupation encompassed two contemporaneous activity areas that together resemble a houselot. The residential portion included a rectangular structure (table 2.2), two hearths, a shallow basin, and an unspecified pit. Located 3–8 m south was an associated kitchen area with an earth oven, two hearths, and possibly a shallow basin and a cache of dart points. The later occupation was located 8–17.5 m south and downslope of the earlier kitchen area. It encompassed thin midden deposits and eight features in a broad arc spanning 5 m: two hearths, an earth oven, a shallow basin, and four unpatterned postmolds that may represent a drying rack. The area immediately around this feature cluster had a lower artifact density and may have been the primary work area or drop zone, while the area north of the feature cluster yielded a high density of artifacts and may represent a discard or toss zone (Kerr and Creasman 1998; Kerr et al. 1995).

In contrast, Yellowbank is a low-intensity, spatially undifferentiated Early Woodland residential site occupied in the fall–spring. Artifact assemblages from the site, which lacked cultural features, indicate a narrow range of activities: chert acquisition, stone tool manufacture, and acquisition, processing, and consumption of riverine resources. Lithic production activities at Yellowbank were similar to those at nearby, and more intensive, Rockmaker but were not spatially segregated (Bader 1996a, 1996b; Evans et al. 1994).

An example of a Middle Woodland unpatterned open domestic site is Graham. Multiple groups frequently used Graham as a transient or short-term encampment, resulting in the accumulation of midden deposits. Domestic activities included stone tool manufacture, nut gathering and processing, and gardening. Despite the high frequency of occupation, feature numbers and diversity are comparatively limited, and Middle Woodland storage pits and thermal features are unpatterned across the site (Niquette 1989; Niquette et al. 1987).

In addition to open habitation sites, Woodland domestic sites are found in Kentucky's numerous rockshelters and caves, as in eastern Tennessee (Franklin et al., chapter 5, this volume). In many cases, the Early Woodland components at these typically multicomponent sites represent the most intensive occupations. Given the circumscribed nature of rockshelters and caves, the spatial distribution of human activities is partly related to avoiding physical constraints such as breakdown accumulations and water drainages. At the same time, it is common for activity areas to cluster along the natural walls of these sites.

Early Woodland domestic occupations are well documented in eastern Kentucky's rockshelters, with Middle Woodland occupations considerably less intense and less numerous (Applegate 1997; Mickelson 2002). The more substantial rockshelter sites have clusters of domestic features and thick midden and ash deposits that were stabilized with vegetal mats, sand, grass, or leaves when they became too deep. The main activity areas were within the drip line; peripheral activities sometimes occurred outside the drip line, and refuse often was discarded on talus slopes outside the drip line (Cowan et al. 1981; Funkhouser and Webb 1929; Knudsen 1985; Vento et al. 1980). Structural remains tend to be light structures oriented near the back wall or along the drip line to serve as windbreaks (see previous section).

Excavations at Cloudsplitter, for example, revealed a substantial Early Woodland component with at least 44 features in several clusters along the back wall. The cluster of six large-capacity storage pits and four hearths at the southern end of the rockshelter represents a 20 m^2 work area. In the central portion of the site, two clusters of postmolds (table 2.2) and associated features spaced 3 m apart indicate a residential area. Ash lenses, hearths, charcoal-filled basins, and other features indicate a 4 m^2 work area between the two windbreaks (Cowan 1985; Cowan et al. 1981). (See Franklin et al., chapter 5, this volume for an analysis of rockshelter occupational intensity focused on artifactual evidence, as opposed to feature evidence, at Early–Middle Woodland sites in eastern Tennessee.)

An example of a less intensely occupied rockshelter is Site 15Cu27. Excavation of 80 percent of the usable space inside the small rockshelter revealed only two late Early Woodland–early Middle Woodland features—a burial pit with a vertically flexed or seated adult male and a large storage pit or cache—about one meter apart in the center of the rockshelter. The late Middle Woodland component is associated with reuse of the large storage pit and construction of a smaller storage pit that intruded the burial feature. The storage and mortuary features represent special-use functions unrelated to other domestic activities (hunting, nut consumption, initial core reduction, tool production) that took place at different times and focused in the back-central portion of the rockshelter. There is no indication that the rockshelter floor was maintained or cleaned (Kerr et al. 2004).

Like Kentucky's rockshelters, few Kentucky caves have been subject to extensive lateral excavations. Domestic occupations, however, occurred in many cave vestibules, and these sites are important components of the Woodland domestic landscape. In western Kentucky, many caves were utilized most intensely during the Early Woodland subperiod, when cave exploration and mineral mining peaked (Crothers et al. 2002; Watson 1997). At caves such as Mammoth and Salts, where archaeologists conducted extensive investigations, there is some indication of differentiation in the use of space but little evidence of structures.

Detailed study of the Salts Cave vestibule, for example, revealed a complex sequence of midden and ash deposits separated by natural strata marking periods between short-term human occupations. Across the vestibule, Early Woodland assemblages indicate intermittent accumulation of domestic debris from small groups engaged in hunting, animal butchering and other food processing, food preparation and consumption, stone tool manufacture and maintenance, clothing manufacture, hide preparation, and mortuary processing/interment. Substantial midden deposits and features were found along the north wall. Two small postmolds oriented perpendicular to the wall, which may represent domestic furniture, separate two clusters of features. Within two meters to the west were four pockets of midden within the breakdown, suggesting that this was a dedicated area of primary refuse disposal. Within three meters to the east was a work area with eight unspecified pits, two bone/stone clusters, and several charcoal and charcoal/burned clay concentrations (Watson 1997; Watson et al. 1969).

Future research on Early–Middle Woodland intrasite patterning will require lateral excavations and clearing at sites in a variety of topographic settings. Whenever possible, contemporaneity of and associations among features should be demonstrated through artifact analyses (e.g., refitting, stylistic comparison, and microwear analysis), feature analyses (e.g., superimposition, origination depths, and functional analysis), and chronometric dating, rather than simply assuming such relationships. Intrasite research at featureless sites can fruitfully utilize lithic, faunal, and pottery artifacts and analytical techniques such as microwear analysis (Franklin et al., chapter 5, this volume). Interpretive models (e.g., Bartram et al. 1991; Binford 1980, 1983; Gilman 1987; Kozarek 1997; Logan and Hill 2000; O'Connell 1987; O'Connell et al. 1991) should continue to inform research on intrasite patterning. As the database of sites expands, it may be possible to investigate seasonal, diachronic, and geographic variations in Early–Middle Woodland intrasite patterning.

Early–Middle Woodland Intersite Patterning

In Kentucky, reconstructions of Early–Middle Woodland settlement patterns far outnumber settlement system studies, which require more data. Regarding the former, archaeologists have studied the relevance of landform, aspect, soils, and other variables in site selection, and some archaeologists have proposed intersite patterning predictive models. Regarding the latter, archaeologists have investigated functional relationships among sites, settlement hierarchies, and links between settlement and subsistence strategies. The spatial coverage of research has been uneven, with many studies focused in the Ohio, Green, Kentucky, Licking, and Big Sandy river drainages (figure 2.1).

Ohio River Drainage

There are several notable studies from the lower Ohio River valley (e.g., Bader 1996a; Ottesen 1985; Turnbow et al. 1980). In the Big Bottoms at the Mississippi-Ohio confluence, Kreisa and Stout (Kreisa 1987, 1988; Kreisa and Stout 1991) documented a mostly stable settlement pattern but a significantly different settlement system over the Woodland period. Generally small in size (less than two hectares), Early Woodland villages, base camps, and extractive locations (see Binford 1980) are dispersed across floodplain, loess bluff, tributary stream valley, and dissected upland contexts, though fewer sites are documented in the latter. Middle Woodland occupations continued in all ecological zones, though most sites larger than one hectare are found on floodplains and near backwater lakes, and settlements became more aggregated. The settlement system encompassed two site types: large ceremonial centers (with or without domestic deposits) and small domestic sites.

Upstream, DeNeeve (2004) studied 31 Crab Orchard floodplain, terrace, and upland sites, which were preferentially located within one to three kilometers of major streams, on nonterrace floodplain landforms, and at low elevations providing access to upland zones and edge environments. The 12 sites with Early Woodland components are small in size and dispersed within two site clusters, and floodplain sites vastly outnumber terrace and upland sites. The 27 sites with Middle Woodland components are more densely packed but roughly equally spaced within seven clusters, especially on floodplain and terrace landforms. All sizes of habitation sites are documented, though small sites predominate. The two large-sized Middle Woodland sites, Slack Farm (Ohio-Wabash) and Smith (Ohio-Green), are located near major confluences.

Green River Drainage

There have been a number of settlement studies in the middle to upper Green River drainage, focusing on both the trunk stream and tributary valleys and including several reservoir projects (e.g., Applegate 2001, 2007; Applegate and Furlong 2001; Foster 1972; Hensley 1991; Schock and Langford 1979; Schwartz 1960; Schwartz et al. 1958a, 1958b).

For example, Prentice's (1993, 1996) diachronic study of site selection factors in Mammoth Cave National Park included rockshelter, cave, and open sites with 43 Early Woodland and 31 Middle Woodland components. Rockshelter selection was based primarily on size; for large shelters, habitability and accessibility were additional relevant variables but aspect and rocky substrate were not. Smaller rockshelters tend to be single-component sites with low artifact densities representing few activities, while large shelters are multicomponent sites with more artifacts and activities.

Open-air sites in bottomland zones outnumber those in the uplands. Large bottomland sites representing repeated occupations are located near tributary confluences with the Green River, where the floodplain is wider and occupants had easy access to uplands. Small bottomland sites were used infrequently and are found on levees and ridges away from stream confluences. Large upland sites, which are within one kilometer of the Green River or near springs, are artifact scatters lacking features but representing moderate-intensity occupations, especially as locales for fall hunting and nut harvesting. Small upland sites, which are located away from the Green River but within one kilometer of water sources such as ponds or intermittent stream confluences, are characterized as lithic scatters representing single-component, short-term occupations. Chert extraction activities occurred predominantly in upland valleys south of the Green River at about 213 meters (700 feet) in elevation (Prentice 1993, 1996).

Kentucky-Licking River Drainage

Settlement studies in the middle Kentucky River drainage, the Adena core area, have focused on relationships among ritual and domestic sites (e.g., Clay 1991; Railey 1991). In the upper Kentucky-Licking River drainage, archaeologists have conducted many settlement studies in conjunction with reservoir projects and resource inventories of government properties (e.g., Gremillion et al. 2000; Marquardt 1970; Rolingson and Rodeffer 1968; Sussenbach 1990). Two related studies are described here.

Along the North Fork Red River, Cowan (1985) found that the adoption of cultigens was associated with an increased number of rockshelter sites, more intense rockshelter occupations with a wider range of activities, and less intense floodplain occupations. The 29 Early Woodland site components outnumbered Late Archaic components by three times, especially rockshelter sites. Early Woodland rockshelter occupations varied in intensity, with small shelters housing one to two nuclear families and large shelters like Cloudsplitter housing larger groups for multiple seasons. Early Woodland components at six floodplain sites, which represent seasonal camps for small groups, are smaller in size and have fewer features and lower artifact densities compared to their Late Archaic components.

Building on Cowan's work, Mickelson (2002) documented concomitant shifts in settlement and subsistence with little temporal lag. The Early Woodland transition to food production was accompanied by more widely distributed occupations across the landscape and utilization of more landform types (as Wyss and Wyss [1977] documented previously), increased residential intensity at rockshelter sites, and continued intensive use of lowland locales (the latter in contrast with Cowan's [1985] findings). This strategy of very generalized landscape use and broad-spectrum subsistence indicates logistical mobility. Site types include primary and secondary residential bases, extractive locations, and processing locations.

Later, during the Middle Woodland, settlement strategies shifted in some respects as reliance on cultigens increased. There were fewer sites, site size decreased, utilization of midslope landforms including rockshelters declined, and upland usage increased, though utilization of all landform types continued. There was a preference for lowland and lower slope environs, as Wyss and Wyss (1977) documented previously. Logistical mobility continued, and although the same site functional types were situated in similar zones, those sites were relatively smaller in size (Mickelson 2002).

Big Sandy Drainage

Like the upper Kentucky-Licking drainages, many intersite settlement studies in the Big Sandy drainage are associated with reservoir projects, including Paintsville Lake (Adovasio 1982; Sanders and Duffield 1976; Vento et al. 1980) and Fishtrap Reservoir (Dunnell 1966a, 1966b, 1972). Other studies provide regional syntheses of Woodland settlement strategies.

Niquette's (1992) regional study of the upper Big Sandy drainage is based on 71 Early Woodland and 59 Middle Woodland components. He documented greater continuity in settlement patterns along tributary streams compared to the three trunk streams (Big Sandy, Levisa Fork, and Tug Fork) over time. During both periods, about three-fourths of sites are situated along upland tributary streams, where there are about 1.5 times as many floodplain sites as rockshelter and hillside bench sites, as well as equally small proportions of sites on saddles and ridgetops. Along the trunk streams, the proportion of sites on floodplain landforms decreased slightly over time, from about 21 percent in the Early Woodland to 15 percent in the Middle Woodland. Rockshelter and hillside sites are more common during the Early Woodland, and ridgetop and saddle sites are more common during the Middle Woodland along the trunk streams.

Kerr and Creasman's (1998) study of Middle Woodland settlement systems in the upper Big Sandy drainage complements Niquette's work on settlement patterns. Four site functional types comprised a logistically organized collector strategy (see Binford 1980): long-term residential camps such as Martin Justice, Sim's Creek, and McKenzie Farmstead; short- to medium-term residential camps such as Graham, Calloway, and Dameron Rockshelter; short-term field camps or locations; and mortuary sites such as C&O Mounds.

Intersite Summary

In sum, despite regional variation in settlement strategies, there are several common themes in Early–Middle Woodland intersite patterning across Kentucky. In all studies, domestic sites with Early Woodland components outnumber those with Middle Woodland components. While the Early Woodland is a longer time period, some of this variation relates to changes in settlement strategies.

Regarding settlement patterns, the widespread distribution of Early–Middle Woodland domestic sites in multiple ecological zones and on various landform types suggests generalized utilization of the landscape. In most studies, Early–Middle Woodland bottomland habitations slightly or considerably outnumber upland sites, and colluvial slopes were infrequently occupied. Within the bottomland zone, floodplain terraces, ridges, and levees were strongly preferred, and rockshelters were preferred within midslope and upland zones.

At the same time, there is temporal variation in preferred use of certain zones and landforms. Within individual drainages, Early Woodland sites are located along a larger number of streams, while Middle Woodland sites are found along fewer streams. Further, Early Woodland habitations along tributaries typically outnumber those along trunk streams, while Middle Woodland habitations are exclusively or predominantly along trunk streams in many drainages. In both western and eastern Kentucky, utilization of rockshelters and caves was more intense during the Early Woodland subperiod.

Factors that influenced the placement of open habitation sites during the Early–Middle Woodland are landform, elevation, and soil drainage, as well as proximity to chert resources, stream confluences, major stream or other water source, and edge environments or upland zones. Ground slope was an important selective factor in some studies but not others. Aspect and soil fertility were not significant factors. Rockshelter selection was related to absolute size or usable area, habitability, and accessibility but not aspect or substrate. Larger rockshelters were used more intensely than smaller ones.

Regarding settlement systems, domestic and ritual spaces are physically separate in most parts of Kentucky. Notable exceptions are large open sites in the lower Ohio Valley with both residential and mortuary-ceremonial functions, as well as a number of caves and rockshelters in western and eastern Kentucky. Early–Middle Woodland site types common across Kentucky are large and small residential camps, special-purpose resource extraction or production locales, and ritual-mortuary sites, though not all areas have all types. Residential sites are situated in both open and rockshelter-cave contexts.

In contrast with small residential camps and special-purpose sites, large residential camps have more extensive midden deposits, larger numbers and more diverse types of artifacts and cultural features, activity areas or loci, and, in some cases, structural remains. The large Early–Middle Woodland residential sites, however, do not represent population nucleation. Such sites date to both subperiods in most areas, though they are predominantly Early Woodland in the upper Kentucky River drainage and mostly Middle Woodland in the upper Big Sandy.

In most cases, Early–Middle Woodland settlement strategies involved residential mobility, with relatively short-term occupations spanning several weeks to several months. There is little indication of year-round habitation of individual domestic sites. Further, Early–Middle Woodland domestic sites are dispersed across the landscape in most areas, indicating limited concentrations of human groups on the landscape. In the lower Ohio Valley, however, research demonstrated increased settlement aggregation in the Middle Woodland period. Large residential sites were clustered on floodplains and around backwater lakes at the Ohio-Mississippi confluence, and large Crab Orchard sites in northwestern Kentucky are clustered at stream confluences and in river bends with extensive floodplains. Logistical mobility associated with a collector subsistence strategy best characterizes the nature of Early–Middle Woodland settlement across Kentucky.

Future research on Early–Middle Woodland intersite patterning should include investigations of more drainages in the Commonwealth, especially the lower Tennessee-Cumberland, upper Cumberland, and lower Kentucky-Licking drainages. As archaeologists gather more data about site functions across Kentucky, the preliminary findings about settlement systems reported here can be evaluated and updated. In the course of such research, archaeologists must be careful about the site typologies employed, which should be tied to clearly delineated interpretive models. For example, archaeologists continue to ambiguously characterize certain residential sites as base camps, a site type that means different things in different models (e.g., Winters 1969 vs. Binford 1980).

Conclusion

This synthesis of Early–Middle Woodland domestic landscapes demonstrates that archaeologists know much more about the nature of human settlement in Kentucky than is commonly thought. Compilations such as this are possible only because of the numerous compliance projects and academic investigations completed over the last several decades and the detailed reports and papers generated by those archaeologists. A significant finding relates to Woodland microsettlement: Who knew there are 70 Early–Middle Woodland domestic structures reported in the literature? Another important development concerns identification of two general forms of intrasite patterning at Early–Middle Woodland open habitation sites. Settlement patterns and settlement systems delineated for several drainages can inform similar research needed in other drainages. I hope this chapter will be a helpful basis for contextualizing future research, especially studies that address "how" and "why" questions (Wright and Henry, chapter 1, this volume) about Early–Middle Woodland landscapes in Kentucky.

Notes

1. Because of the Early Woodland subperiod beginning date of 1250 BC used here, some sites or site components originally assigned by archaeologists to the late Terminal Archaic period, as traditionally defined, are included in this chapter. For example, Cogswell phase sites, which date to ca. 1200–800 BC, are considered early Early Woodland in this analysis. Newtown sites, which span the late Middle–Late Woodland subperiods, are not considered in this analysis.

2. Occupational intensity describes how intensely a site was used in the past. It varies along several dimensions, including duration, frequency, group size, range of activities, and season. Data on these variables in relation to intrasite patterning are provided whenever known.

3

The Adena Mortuary Landscape

Off-Mound Rituals and Burial Mounds

DAVID POLLACK AND ERIC J. SCHLARB

The central Kentucky Adena mortuary landscape comprised burial mounds (Applegate 2008; Clay, chapter 4, this volume; Henry, chapter 15, this volume) and off-mound ritual localities. Mounds ranged in height from less than 50 cm to more than 30 m. Small, low-lying mounds would have been used once for a single interment, while large, taller mounds would have been used for more extended periods of time, as people returned year after year to bury the dead, reconnect with their ancestors, and reaffirm social relationships. Because of their low visibility on the landscape, the location of small mounds eventually would have faded from the collective memory of those living nearby (Clay, chapter 4, this volume; Pollack et al. 2005). In comparison, because of their greater heights, large mounds would have remained highly visible landscape features long after they ceased to be used as burial mounds (Clay, chapter 4, this volume; Hays 2010; Henry, chapter 15, this volume; Rafferty 2005; see also Littleton and Allen 2007; Schlanger 1992).

Because many of the larger Adena mounds have been excavated, archaeologists know a great deal about how they were constructed and the different ways the dead were interred within these mounds (such as primary inhumation in a log tomb, cremation in submound pits, or secondary interment of cremated skeletal remains) (Funkhouser and Webb 1935; Henderson and Schlarb 2007; Henry, chapter 15, this volume; Webb 1940, 1941a; Webb and Funkhouser 1940). Much less is known, however, about sites where Adena rituals were undertaken away from, but within sight of, a mound. As with low-lying burial mounds, these localities did not leave a lasting visual impression on the landscape. That most were used for very short periods of time, with the activities conducted at them rarely resulting in a large material culture signature, also hampers efforts to document these sites.

The Evans site in Montgomery County provided us with an opportunity to examine an off-mound ritual activity locality. Situated on an upland ridge spur overlooking a small stream that flows into nearby Hinkston Creek, a tributary of the Licking River, the Evans site is located 350 m east and within sight of a large burial mound (15Mm11) (figure 3.1). Examination of the spatial distribution of features and posts within a 29 × 17 m area at this site, coupled with analysis of the associated material culture and cremated human remains, led to the identification of a locality where Adena people gathered to process the dead before their remains were interred in 15Mm11. An unusual aspect of this site is that the two largest pits appear to have been used to store yellow clay for use at a later date. The same yellow clay was found in direct association with cremated human remains and plant remains that are interpreted as representing the by-product of ritual feasting.

For the living, mortuary rituals conducted at off-mound localities, such as Evans, would have served to affirm their connection to the dead and help maintain the fabric of Adena life. As Rafferty (2005: 153–54; see also Clay, chapter 4, this volume and Hays 2010) has noted, "Adena rituals can

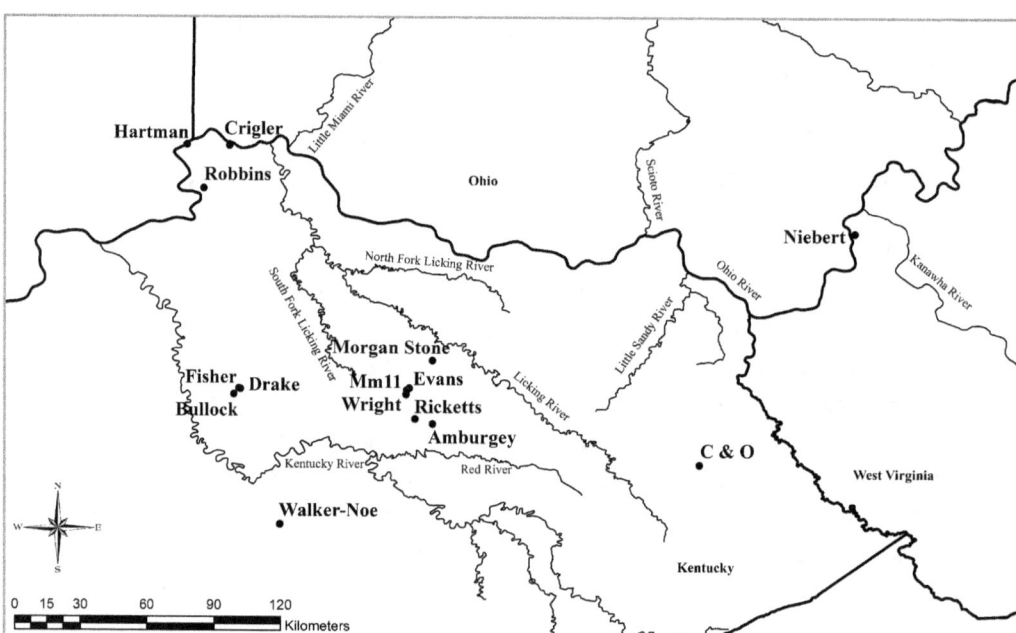

Figure 3.1. Location of the Evans site, 15Mm11, and surrounding sites in central Kentucky. Map prepared by Kary Stackelbeck, Chris Pappas, and Hayward Wilkirson.

be viewed as programmatic, goal-oriented, repetitive social practices that communicate ideological messages and represent one way in which society reproduces itself." Mortuary rituals thus would have been important components of the social memories of Adena groups (Dillehay 2007; Mills and Walker 2008; Van Dyke 2009; Van Dyke and Alcock 2003). By repeatedly undertaking the same rituals at mounds and off-mound localities, Adena groups would have reaffirmed their identity while also maintaining their social and political structure (see Dillehay 2007).

In this chapter, we begin by situating the Evans site in time and describing its internal structure. This is followed by a review of the use of clay in Adena mounds as a means to contextualize its use and presence at the Evans site. We conclude by considering the Evans site's spatial relationship to 15Mm11, as well as the role that off-mound localities played in the central Kentucky Adena mortuary landscape.

Dating

The Evans site's material culture, in particular the ceramics and projectile points, and radiocarbon determinations obtained from charcoal recovered from three features suggest that the site was used by Adena groups toward the end of the Early Woodland subperiod (1000–200 BC). All of the ceramics are consistent with the Adena Plain type (Haag 1940: 75–79). Most of the projectile points are Robbins points (Justice 1987) that were primarily manufactured from locally available, thermally altered Boyle chert.

The four radiocarbon determinations have a pooled calibrated mean that ranges from 400 to 200 BC (table 3.1). They are consistent with the material culture recovered from the site.

Table 3.1. Evans site calibrated radiocarbon dates

Lab no.	BP	Calibrated two standard deviations
ISGS-6034	2150±70	385–5 BC
ISGS-6035	2350±70	753–209 BC
ISGS-6036	2300±140	771–50 BC
ISGS-6037	2090±80	360 BC–AD 52
Calibrated pooled mean	2214±40	387–191 BC

Site Structure

The Adena component at the Evans site consists of 11 pits/basins and 14 posts within a 17 × 29 m area. Examination of the spatial distribution of these features led to the identification of several activity areas (figure 3.2). Of the pits, 2 were extremely large and deep, having a length in excess of 2 m and a depth of more than 1 m below the base of the plow zone. Both were located on the eastern side of the distribution of Adena features. The sides of both pits had been lined with a dark brown silty clay loam before being filled with a very dense yellowish-brown, plastic clay (figure 3.2). The clay was devoid of concretions and was extremely workable. The fact that this clay lacked hematite and manganese concretions, both typical Kentucky ridgetop soil inclusions, suggests that it had been processed and stored in these pits for use at a later date. Among the artifacts recovered from the dark brown soil were small fragments of mica and worked barite fragments. Mica could have been procured from the Blue Ridge Mountain range, located several hundred kilometers to the southeast of the site. However, the barite could have been obtained from deposits in nearby Fayette County, Kentucky. The presence of both is suggestive of ritual artifact preparation at the Evans site. Not surprisingly, no artifacts were recovered from the yellowish-brown clay.

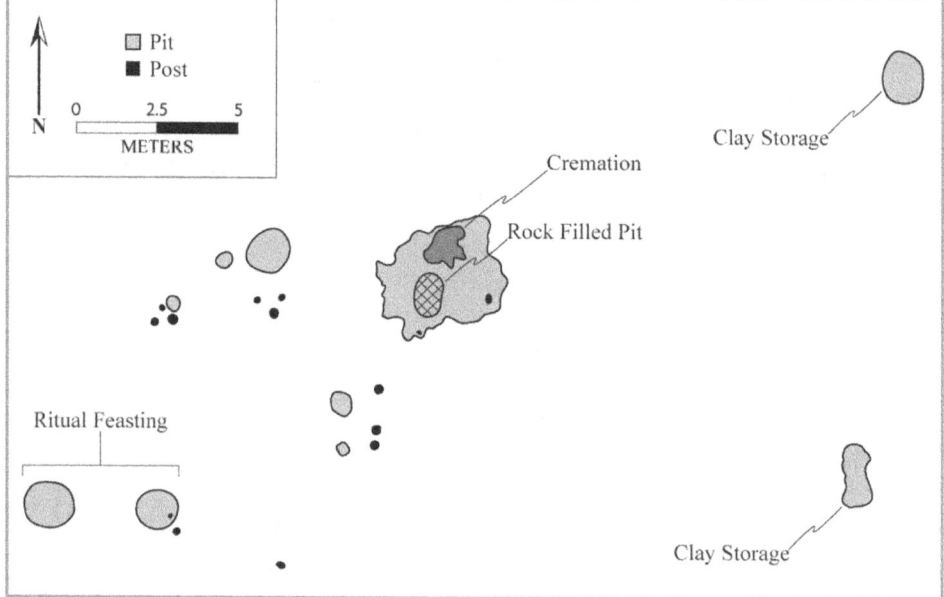

Figure 3.2. Map of the Evans site, including clay storage pits, postholes, and features indicative of ritual feasting. Figure prepared by Kary Stackelbeck, Chris Pappas, and Hayward Wilkirson.

A large shallow basin that measured approximately 3.5 × 4 m was located about 6 m to the west of the clay storage pits (figure 3.2). The basin extended to a depth of 15 cm below the base of the plow zone. Two large posts and two small pits had been dug into this basin. The larger post was located in the southeast portion of the basin, and the smaller post was located in the southwest portion. One of the small pits contained a compact concentration of light-gray to nearly white ash surrounded by the same yellowish-brown clay found in the large storage pits. Below the ash and clay were pockets of alternating layers of yellow clay, a mixture of ash and burned and calcined human bone, and pockets of a dark brown silty clay loam mottled with yellow clay. The other pit contained 32 kg of fire-cracked limestone, along with ash, charcoal, and burned and calcined human bone.

At the Evans site, burned and calcined human bone was recovered only from these two small pits, and in neither case did the recovered remains occur in sufficient quantities to represent the final resting place of a single or multiple individuals. Rather, the human bone appears to be what remained from rituals that involved the processing/cremating of individuals, whose remains were subsequently transported to another location for final interment. The association of the yellow clay with the cremated remains suggests that the clay was used in some way during these rituals. The burned rocks may have been used in the cremation process and then stored for reuse at a later date, as was noted at Walker-Noe in Garrard County (Pollack et al. 2005: 71).

Located about 7 m to the west of the shallow basin were two other large pits (figure 3.2). These features were nearly 2 m in diameter and extended 30–40 cm below the base of the plow zone. Both were characterized by a dark brown silty clay loam bordered on one side by the same yellow clay found in the eastern pits and in the central basin. Among the artifacts recovered from these two pits were one or perhaps two Adena Plain vessels, a ground stone celt, and large (nickel- to quarter-sized) pieces of mica. The celt was manufactured from geological formations associated with Mt. Rogers in the Appalachian Mountain range, located 258 km southeast of the Evans site in southwestern Virginia. The large number of mica fragments recovered from these pits is unusual and, as with the mica recovered from the clay storage pits, is suggestive of the manufacture of mica objects for use in rituals conducted at the Evans site and at nearby burial mounds.

Both pits yielded native cultigens (maygrass, chenopod, and sunflower), acorn, strawberries, persimmon, and squash (Rossen 2007). The presence of a large and varied native cultigen assemblage suggests that feasting similar to that documented at Walker-Noe and the nearby Amburgey site took place as part of mortuary rituals conducted at the Evans site (Pollack et al. 2005; Richmond and Kerr 2005; see also Kimball et al., chapter 8, this volume). The association of yellow clay with the pits within which these food remains were deposited again reflects its association with these rituals.

American chestnut is often present in Kentucky sites but usually accounts for less than 10 percent of the identifiable wood. At Evans, it constituted 61.1 percent of the wood (Rossen 2007), and it was the only wood type associated with one of the pits that yielded a large amount of native cultigens. American chestnut also accounted for most of the wood associated with the shallow basin where the cremations took place. The large amount of American chestnut in the Evans site archaeobotanical assemblage and its association with features that were used to process the dead and in ritual feasting suggests that it may have been purposely selected for use at this site, and its presence could have had some ritual significance.

The majority of the remaining posts ($n = 9$) at the Evans site occurred as clusters of two to three posts located near small or large pits (figure 3.2). The posts were rather large, averaging between 20 and 25 cm in diameter, with an average depth of around 25 to 30 cm below the base of the plow zone. As at the Amburgey site (Richmond and Kerr 2005: 80), these posts may represent the remains of a temporary circular structure or screens that served to separate the performers of certain rituals from the rest of the mourners.

The distribution of features and posts at the Evans site reflects a clear demarcation of space. Cremations took place in the center of this activity area. Ritual feasting occurred to the west of it. Yellow clay for use in mortuary rituals was stored to the east of the central cremation area. The large number of mica fragments found at the site points to the manufacture of objects for use in rituals conducted in the central or western portion of this activity area and elsewhere. Likewise, the barite fragments found at the site point to the manufacture of barite objects at the Evans site.

Adena Use of Clay in Mortuary Rituals

The presence of storage pits containing yellow clay, coupled with its use in cremations and association with pits that contained evidence of feasting, led us to question to what extent clay was used in Adena burial mounds, both in submound mortuary contexts and in the construction of mound stages. A review of Kentucky Adena reports revealed extensive use of clays similar to that found at the Evans site (Applegate 2008; Funkhouser and Webb 1935: 80; Schlarb 2005; Webb 1940, 1943a; Webb and Elliot 1942; Webb and Funkhouser 1940: 213; see also Kimball et al., chapter 8, this volume). Sometimes clays of contrasting colors were used in the construction of mound stages. Processed, or puddled, clay was utilized to build platforms on which the dead were placed (Henry, chapter 15, this volume), to permanently seal individual graves, to construct log tombs, to create crematory basins, and, as at Evans, in the cremation process itself.

In Montgomery County, the nearby Wright and Ricketts mounds are good illustrations of how clay was used in mound and grave/tomb construction (figure 3.1). At Wright, mounds were built of tough clays of contrasting colors (Webb 1940: 11–12; see also Kimball et al., chapter 8, this volume). Webb's description of these clays sounds very much like the clay encountered in the large eastern storage pits at the Evans site. Webb (1940: 11–12) stated that

> the secondary, tertiary, and quaternary mounds were built of exceedingly tough yellow and red clays, apparently gathered from the hilltop nearby.... The particular clay used for most of this mound construction was pure and tough. It was largely sterile of artifacts or midden....
> [T]he obliteration of individual loads did not prevent the formation of varicolored clays distinguished from each by color, texture, and density. This clay was very tough and hard and nearly impervious to water.

Webb's description makes it clear that the builders of the Wright Mound purposely selected clays for their color and texture and constructed the mound in such a way as to highlight these differences. Clay also was used in the construction of graves within this mound: the graves of five individuals had a puddled-clay bottom and top, one had just a puddled-clay bottom, and two had only a puddled-clay top (Webb 1940: 112). During the construction of log tombs within this mound, the logs were often pressed into wet clay or set together with clay (Webb 1940: 17–19).

At the Ricketts site, 12 of the 18 burials had been laid in a puddled-clay basin and then covered with puddled clay (Funkhouser and Webb 1935: 80; Webb and Funkhouser 1940: 213). Use of clay to cover graves also was noted at Morgan Stone Mound in nearby Bath County (Webb 1941a) (figure 3.1). At this site, one grave was covered with 15 cm of clay, and during the initial phase of mound construction, a clay platform was laid over the original ground surface (Webb 1941a: 226, 228, 230).

Use of clay for special purposes also was noted at several mounds in northern Kentucky (figure 3.1). For instance, a dark blue clay was used in the construction of the Crigler Mound in Boone County (Webb 1943a: 508–9). Webb (1943a: 508–9) suggests that this clay may have been obtained from a pond located 30 m southeast of the mound. At the Robbins Mound, also in Boone County, seven burials or tombs were covered with puddled clay. Though the color of the clay is not described for most of these tombs, mention is made of a layer of gray-yellow clay measuring 24 cm thick that covered one burial (Webb and Elliot 1942: 398–99). Also of note is the use of blue clay to line the floor of a tomb (Webb and Elliot 1942: 401).

At the Hartman Mound, also in Boone County, the fill of a fired basin consisted of a mixture of yellow clay and "humus," with charcoal and some burned human bone. While the sides of this pit had been burned, the yellow clay fill had not been fired, and the charcoal and clay had not been burned in situ. The contents of this pit are very similar to the contents of one of the small pits associated with the large centrally located shallow basin at the Evans site, which, as previously noted, consisted of alternating layers of yellow clay and ash with a small amount of burned and calcined human bone. The fill within the pits at Hartman and Evans represents the end products of a cremation that involved the use of yellow clay and resulted in most of the cremated remains being interred in another location(s).

At the central Kentucky Drake Mound in Fayette County, a lens of red clay measuring 3–9 cm (0.1 to 0.3 ft) thick was found encircling a large pit. Within this pit, "a layer of mixed, divided, yellow and red clay was laid over a thin layer of red ochre. In the center of this clay layer which spread to the walls of the pit an elliptical lens of white puddled-clay, about 6.5 × 5.5 feet and .3 of a foot thick at the center was laid down" (Webb 1941b: 171–75). The remains of eight individuals were placed on this clay before the pit was covered. Use of puddled clay with two burials was noted at Fisher Mound, also in Fayette County (Webb and Haag 1947), and puddled-clay use was noted in association with a hearth and a cremation at the Bullock Mound in Woodford County (Schlarb 2005).

Use of special clays also was noted at the eastern Kentucky C&O mounds in Johnson County (Webb et al. 1942) (figure 3.1). For instance, a layer of gray clay was spread over one body, being thickest at the head and shoulder (Webb et al. 1942: 323), and several cremations were capped with clay.

It is clear from these examples that Adena groups used colored clays for a variety of purposes as part of their mortuary program. Likewise, it is evident that by their use in the cremation process, to encase burials, and to construct graves/tombs and mound stages that these clays had some symbolic importance for Adena groups. The Evans site provides the first documentation of clay storage and use in off-mound rituals.

Summary and Discussion

It is clear from the kinds of features documented at the Evans site and the types of materials recovered from them that the Evans site has little in common with Adena habitations (Kerr and Creasman 1998; McBride 1994; Niquette and Boedy 1986). Domestic site assemblages tend to be dominated by Adena Plain pottery and chipped stone artifacts, and nonlocal materials are rare or nonexistent. Features tend to be small storage or trash pits, and hearths and posts tend to be small and shallow. Few features comparable in either size or complexity to those found at the Evans site have been documented at these habitation locales. In addition, the posts at Evans tend to be larger and to have been set deeper into the ground than posts at domestic sites.

In comparison to burial mounds, in addition to the obvious mound stages, the Evans site lacks the cremations, in-flesh burials, or tombs that are the hallmarks of these sites. The dead may have been processed at Evans as part of an Adena multistage mortuary program, but they were laid to rest elsewhere. The small amount of burned and calcined bone recovered from the Evans site clearly distinguishes it from sites, such as Walker-Noe, where the remains of more than 20 individuals were found (Pollack et al. 2005).

It has been suggested that mounds were often constructed over ritual spaces, such as circular paired-post structures. As Clay (1986, 1998) has noted, the initial rituals undertaken at these places need not have been conducted in anticipation of mound construction. They may have involved a period of use of a particular locality before a mound was ever anticipated. Construction of a mound represented a stage in the evolving use of a locality, but use of a particular place on the landscape for mortuary rituals did not always result in the construction of a mound.

It is tempting to speculate that the Evans site is similar to the Niebert site in West Virginia (Clay and Niquette 1992), where a mound was never constructed over circular paired-post enclosures. But unlike Niebert, where the types of structures and features present are consistent with those that have been found beneath many Adena mounds, the same cannot be said of the features found at, and artifacts recovered from, the Evans site. In particular, the large clay storage pits and debris from the manufacture of ritual items clearly distinguish Evans from Niebert. It is certainly within the realm of possibility that as use of the Evans site evolved, a mound could have been constructed at this locale; however, this does not appear to have ever happened.

Within the area at the Evans site where Adena rituals were conducted, space appears to have been clearly demarcated. The large shallow basin where the dead were processed was centrally located. Structures/screens and nearby smaller pits, as well as the two large pits associated with feasting, were located to the west. The clay used in the cremating of the dead and in ritual feasting would have been obtained from the two large pits to the east of the central basin.

The uniqueness of this suite of features, along with the presence of mica and barite and the storage and use of yellow clay, distinguishes the Evans site from other Adena sites. All of the mica fragments represent the by-products of the production of mica objects, and the barite was discarded during manufacture. The presence of these materials reflects the production of ritual objects for use at the Evans site and elsewhere. Perhaps mica and barite objects manufactured at the Evans site were placed with the dead interred in the nearby burial mound. Alternatively, they could have been retained by the living and used in other rituals before entering the archaeological record.

Conclusion

The Evans site appears to have served as a locality where Adena people processed their dead as part of a multistage mortuary program. They came to this spot to prepare the dead for placement in a nearby large burial mound, 15Mm11. While at the Evans site, they procured and purified clay for use in mortuary rituals and manufactured mica and barite objects from these materials. Some of the clay was used on-site in conjunction with rituals that involved the cremation of dead, the burning of American chestnut, and the consumption of a variety of plant foods.

The specific rituals performed at the Evans site would in part have been dependent on an individual's age, sex, and how they died. Their achieved status and the status of those responsible for leading and organizing the mortuary activities would have influenced the nature of the rituals performed. In addition to status, a leader's/organizer's age, knowledge, and past experiences also would have influenced the types of mortuary rituals selected.

The Evans site's ridgetop location would have provided a clear line of sight of a burial mound located on an adjacent ridgetop. Thus, any procession going to and from these two localities could have been observed from either site. The symbolic importance of this ritual landscape may have been further enhanced during activities conducted at night when fires were set on or adjacent to the mound. If this was the case, then any examination of the Adena mortuary landscape must take into consideration not only the burial mound and the off-mound activity locality but also the intermediate area between them. All need to be treated as an interrelated site complex.

At the Evans site, we have documented one step in the Adena mortuary program: a place where a group initiated their loved one's safe passage to the afterlife. They would have cremated the remains of family members or relatives at Evans in preparation for interment in a nearby burial mound. For short periods of time, the Evans site would have been an important place on the Adena mortuary landscape. But whereas 15Mm11 would have remained an important component of the Adena mortuary landscape for many generations, the Evans site would have quickly faded from their corporate memory.

Acknowledgments

The authors would like to thank the Kentucky Transportation Cabinet for giving us the opportunity to excavate the Evans site and Dan Davis in particular for his constant support of this project. We would also like to thank property owners Reid Evans and Vernon Tipton for supporting the archaeological investigations that took place on their land. The botanical remains were analyzed by Jack Rossen of Ithaca College, and the human skeletal remains were examined by Peter Killoran of the University of Wisconsin–Whitewater. A huge thanks goes to A. Gwynn Henderson for providing helpful editorial comments. Kary Stackelbeck, Chris Pappas, and Hayward Wilkirson prepared figures 3.1 and 3.2. Finally, we would like to thank Gary Sorrell for patiently operating the backhoe, as well as the many individuals who assisted in the field and laboratory.

4

Like a Dead Dog

Strategic Ritual Choice in the Mortuary Enterprise

R. BERLE CLAY

My deliberately provocative title is an attempt to move archaeological discourse away from more predictable, Western-oriented channels toward those that might be novel yet informative. It is taken from the words of a coastal New Guinea informant commenting on the "correctness" of a mortuary ritual sequence he had witnessed. In Tok Pidgin, his words were "Ol e troim wey nating long bik bus, olsem dok e dai pinis" (They buried him carelessly in the jungle, just the way you would throw away a dead dog). The deceased in question had been buried, as was custom, in an unmarked grave within the walls of a traditional men's house enclosure (B. J. Clay 1977: 85; R. B. Clay 1972). However, he was buried in the wrong enclosure, belonging either to a clan other than his or, worse yet, to his wife's clan. My informant indicated that this made it impossible for his kinsmen to conduct the final feast and exchange (B. J. Clay 1977: 121) some ten years after his death. Following such a feast, his bones might be recycled in a rain magician's rain magic; whereas his bones were not important in the final analysis, the mortuary ritual following his death was. This forward-looking complication in ritual performance was the most critical problem associated with the individual's burial in the wrong place.

Importantly for this village, the staged mortuary enterprise looked *forward* to prescribed rituals establishing and reinforcing chained exchange relationships through time and across generations between kin groups, not *backward* to memorializing the dead. Practices are changing somewhat today, primarily under Western influence: concrete grave markers are now being built by some to mark graves, though they seem to mark the performance of past ritual feasts as much as they memorialize the dead.

I suggest that this New Guinea example of mortuary practice, although a world apart, is relevant to interpreting the Ohio Valley Middle Woodland mortuary landscape. Specifically, it emphasizes how ritualized mortuary performances incorporate planning ahead, not simply looking back. Still, this ethnographic example is not a heuristic analogy for the Ohio Valley Middle Woodland. Instead, it is an invitation for Woodland archaeologists to move beyond "Western," perhaps peculiarly American, ways of thinking about death and burial.

A Recent History of the Memorialization of the Dead

In a recent book for the general public, George Milner made the following comment regarding Middle Woodland burial mounds (2004: 95):

> Once built, the mounds served as major landmarks that marked longstanding connections to particular areas. For example, many Adena mounds in the rolling country of Central Kentucky sit on locally high spots. They would have been a clear reminder that many generations had preceded the people that currently lived nearby. Thus, the Adena mounds and associated wooden structures were quite likely highly visible symbols of rights to particular territories; after all, survival rested squarely on undisputed access to the land.

This expresses a widely held view that burial mounds were built to mark territory: more elegantly, that the mounded countryside became a landscape of memory and ownership created by collective acts of ritualized mortuary behavior. Contra Seeman and Branch (2006: 109), who suggest that this may be traced most directly to recent archaeological thinking in Britain and its application in the U.S. Midwest (notably in Charles 1992), I see its deep roots in a very Euro-American tradition of memorializing the dead. Early on, this tradition was reflected in the republic's memorializing of its own past, most notably in the garden or memorial cemetery movement, which replaced the more haphazard burial of the dead in congested urban cemeteries and countless rural burial plots.

Current historiography recognizes that the American cemetery beautiful/memorial movement stemmed from the French example established with the Pere Lachaise cemetery outside Paris in 1804 (Linden 2007: 53). There it is interpreted as a conscious attempt through burial "memorialization" to transcend the social disruption caused by the recent French Revolution and reestablish a sense of order expressed in an elaborate, man-made mortuary landscape. Likewise, in the new American republic, the development of the cemetery beautiful was an attempt to bridge the social dislocations created by the American Revolution and, coinciding with the deaths of its younger revolutionary heroes, reestablish a sense of order and permanency in the fractured American social experiment (Jasanoff 2011). Beginning with the Mt. Auburn cemetery in 1831 at Cambridge, Massachusetts, the movement pro-

A

Drawn by Henry Howe in 1846.
THE MOUND AT MARIETTA.

B

Figure 4.1. Early and Middle Woodland mounds in present-day American cemeteries: (*upper*) Mound Cemetery, Marietta, Ohio (drawing by Henry Howe, from *Historical Collections of Ohio*, vol. 11 [1896]); (*lower*) Mt. Hill Cemetery, Sharpsburg, Kentucky (photo by Berle Clay [2010]).

duced many other memorializing cemeteries across the expanding frontier over the mid-nineteenth century.

Coincidentally, on the early American frontier, Middle Woodland burial mounds were noted by explorers and incorporated into this same cemetery beautiful movement, most notably, Mound Cemetery in Marietta, Ohio. They continue to be included in expanding Ohio Valley cemeteries. Once it was established that the mounds contained burials, the mounds were integrated into a more general approach to Native American earthworks taken by early writers, who effectively saw them as memorials to a past order identified with a vanished race of mound builders and a higher order of civilization (figure 4.1). Nineteenth-century Americans' interest in memorializing their own dead, I suggest, was in this case transferred to the earlier Native American landscape. In the latter case, the "disorder" that was being transcended was the tragic backcountry warfare with its roots in the dehumanizing of contemporary Native American adversaries, which had ended circa 1813 with the death of Tecumseh. By the time Cyrus Thomas (1894) straightened out all that mound builder nonsense, these earthen landscape features were thoroughly regarded as having a memorializing purpose, even for him.

Middle Woodland Burial Mounds in Context

With this outline of the memorializing view, it becomes clear that, influenced by our own national past, we potentially transfer the process of mound burial to a conceptual level that may not have been explicit in its actual performance. So, I propose that burial mounds may not have been *primarily* created to memorialize dead members of the society and landscape "ownership," but rather to strategically locate the dead for extended ritual events. I explore this possibility through several examples, beginning with a straightforward one.

The tiny Auvergne Mound (15Bb16) (figure 4.2) in central Kentucky was excavated in 1975–76 (Clay 1983), and its immediate vicinity was explored in 1985. It was less than one meter high and just happened to survive in a field that had never been plowed. I expect that there were many like it that did not survive early land clearing and subsequent agricultural practices, a corrective that must be kept in mind as we attempt to evaluate the complexity of the Middle Woodland mounded landscape. There was a single central and largely decomposed extended inhumation in a shallow grave (figure 4.3) oriented east to west with the head to the east (suggested by surviving tooth enamel). A deposit of eighteen local Boyle chert flakes was placed on the individual's chest, but no other artifacts were present in the grave. The shallow burial shaft had been refilled and covered with a low primary mound devoid of artifacts in its fill. A post was set beside this primary mound.

This small mound was later covered by a second stage raising it to its full height. The fill of this stage contained potsherds with formal variation possibly indicating manufacture by different stylistic groups, chert debitage, and scat-

Figure 4.2. Auvergne Mound (15Bb16), Kentucky, in 1963. Photo by Berle Clay (1963).

Figure 4.3. Central burial at Auvergne Mound (15Bb16), Kentucky. Photo by Berle Clay (1977).

tered chert and ground stone artifacts from an off-mound activity area. Scattered charcoal in this second mound stage was dated to 1680 ± 115 BP (UGA 3617, AD 270), which correlates with other regional ceramic dates and makes Auvergne a late mound for the region. An intriguing distribution of very fine calcined bone fragments was scattered on this second mound stage, suggesting that they were tossed on one side of the second mound stage as it was being thrown up. However, these could not be conclusively identified as human.

Exploration of the off-mound area indicated that certain activities were performed nearby (figure 4.4), but the lack of significant features suggests that they were brief and low impact. Faunal remains were scarce because of the acidic soil. I believe that this off-mound activity area is a clear example of one of those contexts in which the categorization domestic versus ritual, widely used in archaeological interpretation, can lead the interpreter astray (Chapman 2006: 514). Rather than seeing this total complex of mound and off-mound "domestic" activities as a microcosm of the larger society (that is, a small settlement with its dependent mound for its deceased), I believe that off-mound artifacts reflect activities deployed in support of specifically ritual behavior, here a mortuary event (Clay 1983; see also Abrams 1992b).

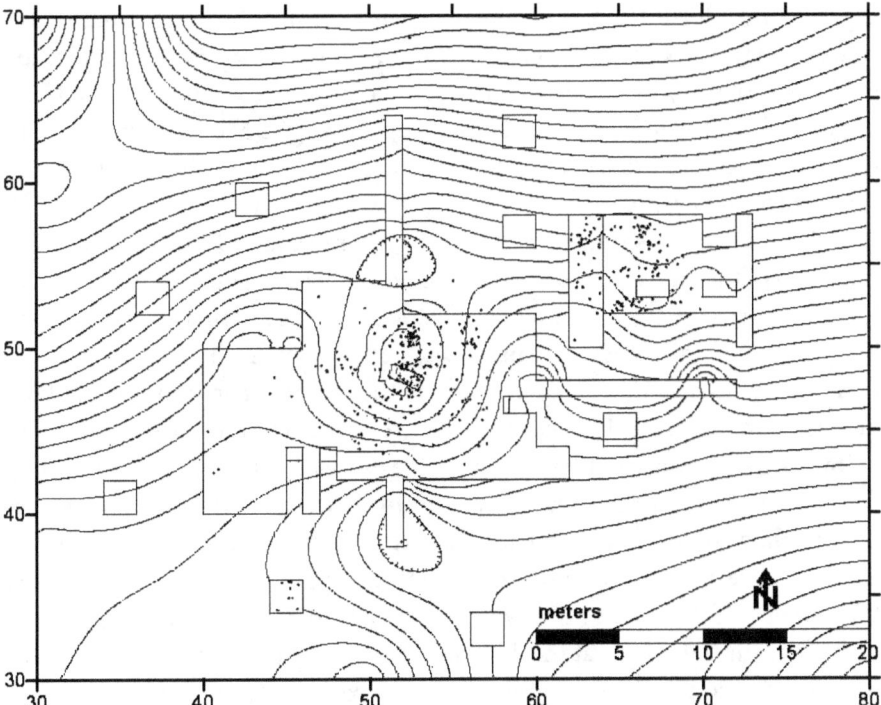

Figure 4.4. Distribution of artifacts in mound fill and across off-mound area at Auvergne Mound (15Bb16). Drawing prepared by Berle Clay.

I suggest that following the burial of the deceased by an intimate burial party, at a later date a more socially heterogeneous group—at least representing possibly differing potting styles—convened at this location marked with a minimal mound and post to conduct a graveside feast. I would emphasize that the *initial* act of mound burial was a way to strategically *locate* the grave specifically for this later graveside ritual feasting, which probably included exchange between social groups. However, this exchange is not reflected in the recovered artifacts and certainly not in the flakes placed with the dead, although it could have been reflected in an exchange of foodstuffs that have left no archaeological record. There is a possibility that cremated human remains were added to the fill of the final mound stage by these ritual participants, reflecting some aspect of a linked mortuary ritual for another individual.

Was the mound memorializing? In a sense it was. To categorically maintain that it was not is to ignore one meaning of the term *memorializing*. It did mark the grave of this individual so that it could be remembered—perhaps, more specifically, re-located—and the grave offering of Boyle chert no doubt "remembers" the persona of the deceased. Yet involved with this construction was the possibly more important strategic thinking simply to locate the grave for further mortuary-related ritual. Concluding that ritual, the mound was capped with a terminal mound stage. In this final stage, artifacts from graveside events were swept in by chance. With no other known cultural landscape evidence (for example, nearby earthworks or known archaeological sites dating to this time), I have no sense that the Auvergne Mound continued to serve as a memorial to the dead or as a space marker after the conclusion of these graveside events.

Using other terms I have tried out elsewhere (Clay 1976), I suggest that the death of this individual posed his/her immediate group—perhaps a small foraging party—with an immediate tactical question: what to do with the body? Because of some circumstances, perhaps where or when death occurred, or who may have been involved in the foraging party, they buried the deceased on the spot. However, the selected form of burial—flesh interment below a small mound with a post set beside it—was influenced by scheduling factors: they made a decision to strategically mark the burial location specifically so they could return at a later date. This interpretation may be more realistic than seeing this mound as comparable to a grave marker both recalling the persona of the dead and serving as a means of claiming landscape "ownership" by his/her death at this location. At Auvergne the burial party chose to bring the concluding prescribed mortuary ritual to this graveside: they rejected the alternative, to take the deceased as flesh and bones or cremated remains to another location for those extended rituals.

Because tactical decisions such as these tend to be variable, reflecting immediate field conditions, I assume that the Auvergne burial event may have been one possibility among many. In addition, this level of decision making is not simply reflected in the large burial mounds. The large mounds may in fact represent only a fraction of the ritual decisions that did occur, considerably complicated by multiple ritual episodes taking place in these accretional structures. This view finds some justification in the variability of disposal in mounds themselves (Prufer 1964: 50–52; Carskadden 2008: 262), such as the variable, yet consistent, roles that both cremation and inhumation played in mortuary ritual in the Ohio Valley Middle Woodland (Adena and Hopewell). For example, Webb and Snow (1945: 59) note that Greenman recorded 30 occurrences of cremation in 14 of the 70 mounds he listed as Adena. This is in marked contrast to the preceding Green River Late Archaic in Kentucky (Claassen 2010) and the following Late Woodland and Fort Ancient cultures, which almost exclusively practiced inhumation.

Mortuary evidence from the central Tennessee Columbia Reservoir echoes this interpretation. At the Middle Archaic Ervin site, for example, Hofman (1985: 14) reported three possible human cremations. He suggested that these were a logistical way to move the deceased from the point of death to their ultimate deposition at a ritual aggregation locus, rather than a way of treating individuals of a certain status in the society (contra Webb et al. 1942). Hofman further noted that cremation was used in the Middle Woodland McFarland phase (1985: 14), at which time it possibly represented a similar movement of "bodies in space" to aggregation sites, not simply a derivative Ohio Hopewell trait. In this example, Hofman (1985) expressed exactly the view that I suggest explains ritual performance in the Ohio Valley Middle Woodland: the variation in burial treatment exists principally to facilitate the execution of a future prescribed mortuary ritual. This position sharply contrasts with recently stated positions that factor such variation at a regional scale into very distinct regional mortuary traditions (Hays 2010: 118; see also Rafferty 2005: 165–67).

Some More Complex Examples

Two other well-known Kentucky "Adena" mound examples, Robbins (15Be3) (Milner and Jefferies 1987; Webb and Elliott 1942) and the larger Wright Mound (15Mm6) (Webb 1940), further illustrate my point. Robbins, in northern Kentucky, was a complex accretional burial mound built in part over a paired-post circle, which had at its center at least 11 redeposited cremations (Webb and Elliott 1942: 447). A radiocarbon determination of 2051 ± 140

BP (M-2242, 150 BC) (Crane and Griffin 1972) from materials associated with the submound post circle suggests that the mound was somewhat earlier than Auvergne. Unlike Webb, I consider the post circle here and elsewhere as a defined ritual space that was converted to a stage for mortuary ritual through the deposition of the human remains strategically cremated elsewhere then redeposited here for the conclusion of additional mortuary rituals (Clay 2009). The remaining 89 or more individuals at Robbins were buried in various types of simple log graves in an expanding burial mound built over this circular space. Milner and Jefferies have reanalyzed this structure (1987) and, using computer-generated graphics, present a valuable visualization of its construction. They trace the irregular expansion of the mound through eight stages as log-crib graves were added. I see this progression as attempts of funeral parties to deposit deceased persons for the conclusion of additional mortuary ritual involving feasting and probably exchange (as reflected in potsherds and other loose artifacts in the mound fill). At least 12 of 52 log tombs contained multiple burials (Webb and Elliott 1942: 414–15), many of these fragmentary. This suggests to me that the tombs had been used for multiple, sequential mortuary ceremonies before they were finally covered (see Brown 1979).

My conclusions are further supported by the inability of Milner and Jefferies (1987) to pinpoint a terminal conversion of the Robbins Mound into a memorializing monument. They (1987: 40) do identify a "terminal construction episode involving the deposition of a layer of soil that covered the entire mound.... [It] probably reduced some of the surface irregularities[;] ... many would have remained until the mound was smoothed further through years of erosion." In short, though looking like a conically symmetrical memorializing structure before excavation, the final aspect may still have reflected its piecemeal strategic use by multiple, sequential burial parties. In short, the structure reflected the many acts of mortuary ritual that produced it and was not a conscious monument to the mortuary activities it contained as a whole.

The large Wright Mound, 15Mm6 (Webb 1940), contained a variety of inhumations ranging from simple pits to large and deep log-cribbed grave chambers. A date of AD 216 from Feature 17 and associated with the third mound stage indicates that the site is quite late, possibly coeval with the Auvergne Mound less than ten miles away. As with Auvergne, the late date is supported by larger, regional ceramic evidence. According to Webb (1940: 11), there were four mound stages representing the construction of four large burial crypts, more or less centered over each other. Unfortunately, we lack a detailed reconstruction of mound building of the sort produced by Milner and Jefferies (1987) for the Robbins Mound.

The impressive scale of the Wright Mound log crypts has challenged archaeologists, and the assumption has often been that they were built for high-status individuals (Shryock 1987). James Brown (1979) distinguishes between what he called Hopewell "charnel houses" and "mortuary crypts" (essentially log tombs). This provides an alternative way to interpret the Wright Mound: a log burial crypt was essentially a storage container for the deceased with a removable cover. In Illinois Valley Hopewell, there is abundant evidence that the occupants of the crypt were frequently changed, suggesting that the container housed a deceased individual for only a period of time, probably while further mortuary ritual was conducted in the vicinity. For the Wright burial mound, the complex log tomb was the strategic successor to the simpler Robbins example: both involved reusable containers for the deceased, which held the bones of the dead for the duration of extended mortuary rituals. This form of burial treatment appears to have been contemporaneous with the much simpler inhumation at Auvergne.

The Wright Mound has not been reanalyzed to demonstrate that the log crypts were in fact reused. However at Crigler Mound (Webb 1943a) (another late, though undated, mound) in northern Kentucky, the one major log tomb was reused and parts of five individuals were buried in it. Thus, I would maintain that at all three sites, mound burial in an accretional mound structure and the use of log crypts were ways to position the deceased so that further mortuary rituals could be conducted graveside, perhaps even elsewhere. At Robbins and Wright, it is possible that bodies were removed from these log tombs at the conclusion of this ritual, their ultimate destination unknown. At Crigler, it is probable that burials were brought to the aggregated ritual locus (the burial mound) as cremations. What happened to the remains after these rituals may have been immaterial. Some survived piecemeal in reused tombs, but it is possible that others were incorporated in other future mortuary ritual (such as the fragmented cremation toss recorded at Auvergne). While inhumations might remain "in place" in the now-augmented Auvergne burial mound, Robbins, Wright, and Crigler allowed the funeral parties to remove the remains and replace them with others and add to them burials prepared elsewhere by cremation.

In these variable ways, funeral parties ensured that their deceased were not "cast away in the jungle" and separated from the full mortuary enterprise, although their final destination following graveside feasting may have been of lesser concern. Burial mounds in the Ohio Middle Woodland offer us important ways to examine the process of extended mortuary ritual in action and caution us to expect considerable variation in burial trajectory. The view, so important in the interpretation of burial variation for the past 45 years, that the burial directly reflects the status of the deceased must in the Ohio Valley

Middle Woodland case be filtered through the reality of lengthy burial manipulation that may not be directly related to status.

In short, when discussing most Adena mounds that, for better or worse, have been deemed Adena, I find it is instructive to consider them largely as the products of extended mortuary ritual rather than any planned attempt to memorialize the dead and thereby define the landscape according to some conceptual scheme. This does not mean, however, that when completed by mortuary parties, they continued thereafter to have symbolic importance. It is altogether too tempting to consider them ways to mark territories in exactly the same way that numerous Anglo pioneer family cemeteries marked family lands and in some cases still do. But to extend this interpretation to the Middle Woodland examples remains speculation.

Informing the Ongoing Dialogue

Two areas of investigation in Ohio, the Scioto drainage (importantly, the Scioto-Paint Creek confluence) and the Hocking drainage (importantly, the Plains), have been the focus of recent work asking some of the same sorts of questions of the Middle Woodland landscape of burial mounds and mortuary behavior as have been addressed here. I would like to suggest ways that my views might inform this work and the interesting conclusions that have developed from it—conclusions that support the points I have made. I owe a debt to the researchers who have made many of the following observations; they have informed me about archaeology in areas where I have no direct experience.

The first of these is a GIS-based study of the Scioto drainage mounded landscape (Seeman and Branch 2006). The authors see mound/earthwork construction as pertaining to two general purposes: the marking of territory and the covering of sacred places (Seeman and Branch 2006: 109). Concluding their interesting analysis of change from what they term Adena to Hopewell (which I would consider earlier and later Middle Woodland), Seeman and Branch (2006: 121) suggest that in Hopewell the sacred place aspects of mound building became more actively managed and any territorial aspects, which they saw as more characteristic of earlier Adena, somewhat less so. Their conclusion finds support in the apparent concentration of Hopewell "mounding activity" in sharply limited areas (that is, the Scioto-Paint Creek confluence) in contrast to the wide distribution of earlier Adena burial mounds. Because of this, Hopewell mounds could not mark territory, because they were so concentrated in space. Instead, they must reflect the aggregation of ritual behavior in a constrained area of the larger drainage. Still, Seeman and Branch also see evidence of continuity between Adena and Hopewell, expressed perhaps most importantly in the apparent concentration of late, large Adena mounds in the same general area of the Scioto and Paint Creek drainages (for example, at the Adena and Carriage Factory/Miller mounds) (Greber 1991: 3–9). This might reflect that later Adena was going through ritual "consolidation," which was later expressed in the complex Hopewell sites with mounds and ancillary earthworks (but see also Lloyd 1998: 24).

While a GIS approach is powerful in a study such as this, I think all can acknowledge that it is constrained by its data set. In the drainage under consideration, the authors consider countless small but otherwise unknown mounds as early and Adena. We must be mindful of just how complex the mounded landscape may have been and how little we may know of it, given the multitude of effects from European expansion. Recall that Auvergne was a very small mound that survived into the 1970s simply because the field in which it was located had never been turned. It was also apparently quite late, Hopewell in date though clearly not "Hopewell" in cultural expression. Therefore, I would add a caveat: Seeman and Branch's perception that a widespread distribution of small mounds with "territorial" implications was replaced by a concentration of mounds reflecting more intensely managed mortuary ritual could be modified if the unrecorded and unknown mounds reflect a contemporaneous continuation of dispersed and less complex ritual activities. Thus, likewise, Auvergne, by all accounts an expression of relatively simple mortuary ritual, seems to have been contemporaneous with the large Wright Mound, where ritual behavior may have been much more complex or, in Seeman and Branch's terms, aggregated.

Still, I am not willing to concede that Adena accretional burial mounds *marked* territory in any particular sense. I see these mounds as the existential products of mounding over concluded mortuary rituals, rather than an intent by the mound builders to produce a monument. However, what the restrained locations of late Adena mounds and major Hopewell earthwork sites in the Scioto Valley make clear is that in certain valley locations of southern Ohio the nature of strategic choices occasioned by death was restructured: different choices were made for different reasons. But these too, as in the earlier and "simpler" periods of burial mound construction, may still have been mainly choices to ensure that the bones of the dead were not "thrown away." The areal restriction of mounded landscapes of the later Ohio Middle Woodland and their incorporation into complex earthwork-defined landscape constructions remain for me the result of extended mortuary events. They were not principally built to memorialize the dead, and their existence does not negate the existence of contemporaneous, more ad hoc mortuary events elsewhere, which perhaps fed into subsequent rituals at the aggregated centers. Nevertheless, the concentration of mounds and earthworks at the Scioto-Paint Creek confluence and in the Plains on the Hocking does indicate that the ritual proscriptions of later Middle Woodland cultures, at least in certain places and after certain times, were shifting. In these areas, far more variable tactical decisions were needed to ensure the strategic performance of concluding ritual performance. Just why this was so remains problematic.

The approach taken by Seeman and Branch is nicely complemented by the ongoing and well-reported archaeological research of Abrams and his fellow workers and others in the Hocking drainage to the east (Abrams 1992a, 1992b; Abrams and Le Rouge 2008; Black 1979; Blazier et al. 2005; Joel Brown, pers. comm. 2011; Crowell et al. 2005; Murphy 1989; Skinner and Norris 1984; Stump et al. 2005; Waldron and Abrams 1999). Like the work of Seeman and Branch, their analysis has in part been informed by a GIS data set (see particularly Stump et al. 2005; Waldron and Abrams 1999), and I see in this the same potential problems that I feel are inherent for the Scioto drainage. The dispersion of burial mounds on the Hocking reflects the dispersion of "decisions" made in view of extended mortuary ritual over a long period of time. To assume that ridgetop mounds—which, by these researchers' GIS-informed reckoning, exist in each others' viewsheds—mark community territories and reflect communication between them (Crowell et al. 2005: 93; Waldron and Abrams 1999) is an interpretive stretch that ignores the reality that we know practically nothing about the dating and contents of the mounds. Demonstrating this point, recent re-excavation of the Daines I mound vicinity, long felt to represent a relatively simple mortuary location (Murphy 1989), has revealed the existence of a rather typical off-mound post circle and a potential temporal spread of over 300 years for Daines II (Joel Brown, pers. comm. 2011). Such a site suggests that small hilltop mound locations on the Hocking may be more complex than otherwise assumed, and I would judge that Carskadden's (2008) detailed distributional data on mounds and habitations in the upper Muskingum drainage would also serve as a caution in the interpretation of the Hocking hinterlands.

From the excavation of the Boudinot 4 and County Home sites (Crowell et al. 2005), the Hocking archaeologists have developed a conceptualization of the minimal Middle Woodland community in which the small burial mound is a component of a local habitation "unit" (Crowell et al. 2005: 92–93), whereas I would imagine that the mound may reflect the ritual needs of a much wider "community." Boudinot 4, a palimpsest covering perhaps some 1,000 years of prehistory (Crowell et al. 2005), is more than 2,000 feet from a small mound that is unexcavated (Crowell et al. 2005: fig. 6.8). Without knowledge of the structure of mortuary ritual in the mound, it may be far too restrictive, and in a larger sense conceptually misleading, to view it as the social landscape marker of the Boudinot 4 site inhabitants during the Middle Woodland. Carskadden (2008: 267) makes a similar caution from his analysis of habitation and mound site distribution on the Muskingum. I say this also in light of the excavation of the Armitage Mound (Abrams 1992b) and 33At441 (Blazier et al. 2005: 104–9), both of which revealed quite variable evidence that is somewhat difficult to decipher but would seem to reflect far more complex behavior than I would expect of a provincial, self-defining, mound benchmarked hamlet.

However, it is fascinating that on the Hocking (in the Plains archaeological district), as at the Scioto-Paint Creek confluence, there are concentrations of mounds and earthworks that are unknown elsewhere in these drainages. Furthermore, the Plains is the locus of the Coon Mound (Greenman 1932), which, given its size and its single internment, may in fact memorialize an individual. While the earthwork complexity of Hopewell is lacking in the Plains, there are numerous "ceremonial circles," some of which are no doubt contemporaneous with Hopewell circles on the Scioto, and the sites of the Plains suggest intense, aggregated activity in the later Middle Woodland. Blazier and colleagues (2005: 102) further suggest that contemporaneous habitation sites (as opposed to mortuary loci) may be absent among the earthworks. The sites of the Plains, like the complex sites of the Scioto-Paint Creek Confluence (which differ in landscape details, to be sure), suggest a distinctive system that was affecting mortuary choices (and perhaps other types of choices as well). The variability in mortuary treatment (which I assume is reflected in the mounds, even if we do not understand them at all well) suggests to me that more variable strategic choices—or sequences of strategic choices—were used in the conclusion of extended mortuary ritual, all in the context of a restricted geographic area. Initiating the dead into the ritual sequence (so that they were not thrown away in the jungle like a dead dog) may have involved more complex tactical decisions, such as, possibly, the complexity of burials that Abrams has recorded for Armitage Mound (1992b: 86–87), which included 14 cremations added at various times to a mound that covered at least one inhumation. It remains to be seen whether this was a drainage-wide temporal shift in the nature of decision making. For me, the late dating of the Auvergne Mound in Kentucky, where the simple decision was made to bury the dead and have done, then bring the terminal mortuary ritual to mound side at a later date, suggests that it coexisted with more complex examples nearby (the Wright Mound). Similar variability in strategic decisions may have occurred on the Hocking as well.

Some Concluding Comments

Such possible variability in how funeral parties concluded Middle Woodland mortuary events, which I see mainly as a product of planning ahead for prescribed, extended mortuary ritual, must ultimately be factored into attempts to produce broad culture reconstructions. Lloyd perhaps states it most succinctly (Lloyd 1998: 24) when he says that "the variability that exists within Adena and Hopewell sites, and between regions, almost certainly precludes the definition of a single Adena or Hopewell pattern." I would even go beyond Lloyd and add that a search for mortuary "patterns," if seen as normative ways of conducting mortuary ritual implied in the work of some (most recently in Hays 2010), misses the point in failing to grapple with the system of choices that were clearly made (that variability noted by Lloyd) by those Ohio Middle Woodland funeral parties.

It is perhaps more useful to view this variability as the result of decisions made with a view to the ultimate completion of ritual sequences appropriate to variable social contexts. At this level, similar decisions may have been made in what we might otherwise think of as quite different normative cultural contexts, namely, Adena *or* Hopewell. Just why these extended rituals took place is an additional question. They may have had little to do with the "remembrance" of the dead.

First, however, we must be prepared to sidestep the intellectual straightjacket that I see in the mound "interpreted" as a memorial to the dead and all that implies about landscape ownership. This constrained view of a prehistoric Native American landscape may be a part of the baggage we carry as colonial American archaeologists. Rather, the Middle Woodland burial mound was a product of ritual choices in the mortuary endeavor, not an end product by itself. This interpretive shift hardly detracts from the importance of the mounds to past Native American behavior. Possibly paradoxically, for me it expands their importance in understanding past lifeways.

Acknowledgments

I would like to thank Joel Brown for information on his recent excavations at Daines Mounds I and II, Mark Seeman and N'omi Greber for their encouragement, and the editors for both their invitation to participate in their Southeastern Archaeological Conference symposium in 2010 and their excellent editorial suggestions.

5

The Early and Middle Woodland of the Upper Cumberland Plateau, Tennessee

JAY D. FRANKLIN, MEAGAN DENNISON, MAUREEN A. HAYS,
JEFFREY NAVEL, AND ANDREW D. DYE

In this chapter, we address Early and Middle Woodland landscape use on the Upper Cumberland Plateau (UCP) of Tennessee. In keeping with this volume's perspectives on social landscapes, we consider how the residues of various technological processes—raw material procurement, stone tool production, ceramic manufacture, and obtaining and processing subsistence resources—shed light on certain social dimensions of Early and Middle Woodland occupation in this unique region. This approach yields a more comprehensive view of the interactions between UCP inhabitants and their natural environs than is possible with the taxonomic approaches that have historically characterized southeastern archaeology (Franklin et al. 2012).

As we discuss below, the UCP region is both geologically and culturally distinctive. For example, the region is littered with rockshelters and caves. As Franklin (2008a) has argued elsewhere, the geologic features were as much a part of the cultural landscape as they were the natural one. During the Early and Middle Woodland, they were as important to regional hunter-gatherer populations as mounds and earthworks were to Woodland peoples in other regions. Although mound construction, artistic expression, and regional interaction were all, in fact, part of the lives of Woodland peoples on the UCP, the sheer number and density of rockshelters and caves in this region provide a unique window onto the ways in which the daily lives and activities of Woodland peoples became imprinted on the physical landscape. Because such features are far less numerous and clustered in lowland floodplains, the UCP merits archaeological investigation as a distinct culture area and landscape. We believe that this recognition is critical and of broader anthropological concern because highland regions such as the UCP typically receive comparatively less systematic anthropological and archaeological inquiry than lowland regions. As such, stereotypes that highland regions are marginal areas and isolated cultural backwaters, which pervaded early twentieth-century ethnological research, unfortunately persist today.

The data discussed in this chapter are the result of several years of extensive and systematic archaeological surveys and excavations in the UCP region of Tennessee. There have been previous attempts to examine settlement and subsistence patterns on the UCP, primarily between the Archaic and Woodland time periods (Ferguson 1988; Pace and Hays 1991). However, these studies (out of necessity) focused only on lithic data to make these distinctions, albeit recognizing the shortcomings of such an approach (Pace and Hays 1991: 145). We build on this previous work by addressing Woodland settlement on the UCP with not only lithic data but also ceramic and faunal (subsistence) data. Included in our lithic analyses is use-wear analysis, something missing from previous studies.

Since 1996, we have recorded more than 500 prehistoric archaeological sites on the UCP, mostly along the western escarpment (Franklin 2002, 2006a, 2006b; Franklin and Bow 2008; Bow and Franklin 2009; Langston and Franklin 2010). Sites with an Early and/or Middle Woodland component account for about 25–35 percent of all prehistoric sites identified in our surveys (Franklin 2002, 2006a; Langston and Franklin 2010). The results presented here focus on data generated from excavations at four rockshelter sites: Eagle Drink Bluff Shelter (Franklin 2008a), York Palace (Langston et al. 2010), Hemlock Falls Rock House (Dye et al. 2010), and Indian Rock House (figure 5.1). Where applicable, we also use data from other sites, including Workshop Rockshelter (Franklin and Bow 2009, 2010) and Horn Dog Pictograph Site.

Environmental Setting

Our research area lies almost entirely within the Cumberland Plateau division of the Appalachian Plateaus physiographic province, as defined by Fenneman (1938). Des Jean and Benthall (1994: 115) further distinguish the Upper Cumberland Plateau as "bounded by the escarpment of Waldens Ridge and the Cumberland Mountains on the east, by a continuous escarpment of caprock along the western edge, on the north by the Cumberland River, and on the south by everything north of the Sequatchie Valley." We believe that the area of the Cumberland Plateau bisected by Interstate 40 is actually a more accurate southern boundary, as it seems to reflect differences between the northern and southern plateau in Tennessee, namely, the density and distribution of prehistoric rock art sites, most notably pictographs (Simek et al. 2008).

Under the bluff lines and in the gorges of the region are thousands of rockshelters and hundreds of caves. Their ubiquity made them ideal locations for shelter and habitation. Patty Jo Watson (2001: 320) stated, "Throughout Appalachia, almost by definition, rockshelters are extremely important repositories of archaeological materials." While rockshelters are self-contained places

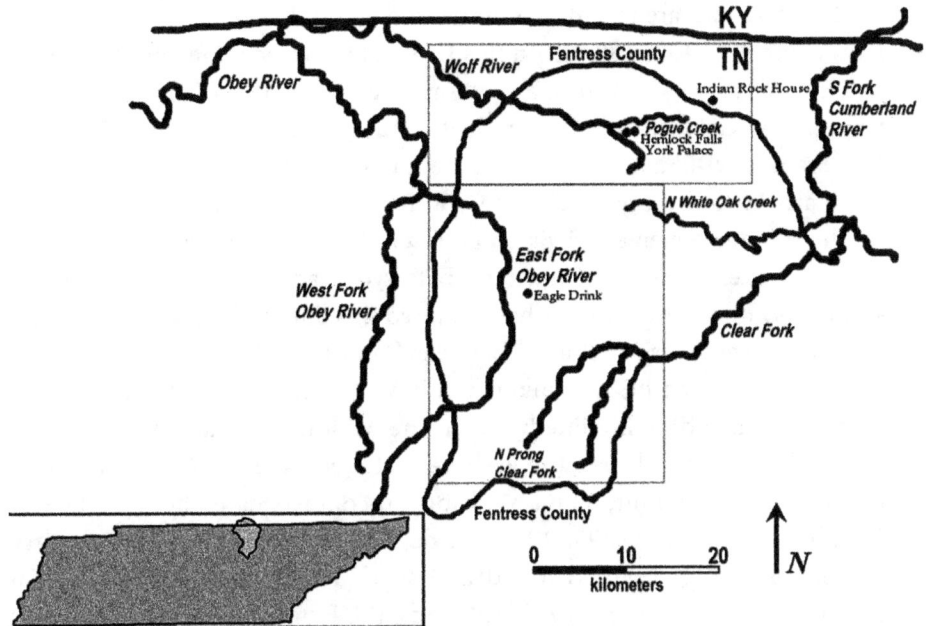

Figure 5.1. Location of western escarpment of the Upper Cumberland Plateau, Tennessee, with sites mentioned in the text. Map prepared by Jay Franklin.

on the landscape, their numbers and density on the UCP allow us to consider them collectively as an integral aspect of local social landscapes.

Much of our work has been conducted along the western escarpment of the Upper Cumberland Plateau (hereafter, the WEUCP; see figure 5.1). The escarpment is a well-defined, nearly uninterrupted boundary, although it bears many incisions where westward-draining streams have cut into it, sometimes deeply (Sasowsky 1992: 5). Here, the normally resistant sandstone caprock has been eroded into the underlying chert-bearing Mississippian-aged limestones, thus exposing numerous chert outcrops, particularly the Monteagle. In short, lithic raw material availability was not an issue for Woodland peoples on the WEUCP, though it may have been for those occupying more interior and upland portions of the UCP (e.g., Pace and Hays 1991).

Chronology

In many regions of the Southeast, there is little to differentiate the Early Woodland from the preceding Late Archaic except the wholesale addition of pottery. In this regard, the WEUCP is not unique. At many sites, Late and Terminal Archaic artifacts are found in the same archaeological levels as Early Woodland artifacts. At Eagle Drink Bluff Shelter, Terminal Archaic Wade bifaces, steatite vessel fragments, Adena bifaces, and fabric-marked and cord-marked ceramics are found together and dated to between 2800 and 3200 BP. Faulkner (2002: 188–89) notes these same associations in the central Duck River basin. Soot from a cross-mended Early Woodland Swannanoa vessel recovered from a shelter in Scott County was AMS dated to 2962 cal BP (Franklin 2008a). Thus, it is apparent that by 3,000 years ago, recognizable Early Woodland types of pottery were made on the WEUCP.

There is no convenient division between Early and Middle Woodland or, for that matter, between Middle and Late Woodland. This is not a novel assertion. Southeastern scholars have pointed this out for decades, particularly when using ceramics to delineate between Woodland phases (Faulkner 1968; Schroedl and Boyd 1991; Franklin and Bow 2010). We use AD 700–800 as an approximate dividing line between the Middle and Late Woodland on the WEUCP, primarily because we have yet to recover Late Woodland arrow points (such as Hamilton and Madison) in contexts dated before AD 800 (Cobb and Nassaney 1995: 208). We do recognize that this is an arbitrary distinction and agree with Schroedl and Boyd (1991: 77–78, 85) for material culture continuity between AD 400 and 900. However, because the focus of this volume is on the Early and Middle Woodland, we discuss sites and components dated to between 1000 BC and AD 800.

Diagnostic Early Woodland artifacts recovered on the WEUCP include ceramics and stone tools. We discuss the ceramics in the section on ceramic systematics. Diagnostic stone tools recovered on the WEUCP are largely stemless triangular bifaces such as the Greeneville and McFarland Series. For example, more than thirty McFarland bifaces were recovered from Workshop Rockshelter alone (Franklin 2002: 30, 230; Franklin and Bow 2010). These types also grade into the Middle Woodland. Other Middle Woodland types recovered in the study belong to the Lowe Cluster (Justice 1987) of expanding stemmed bifaces and, occasionally, Copena types.

To complement these artifact chronologies, AMS radiocarbon determinations from Early and Middle Woodland contexts on the WEUCP are presented in table 5.1. The radiocarbon dates indicate occupation of the WEUCP from about 1000 BC to AD 650.

Because of problems with southeastern Woodland ceramic typologies and chronologies highlighted by other scholars working in the Tennessee region (Kneberg 1961; Faulkner 1968; Schroedl and Boyd 1991), we began the Upper Cumberland Plateau Archaeological Luminescence Dating Project in 2007 to directly date ceramics in rockshelter contexts where they were not associated with archaeological carbon (Franklin 2008a; Franklin and Bow 2008, 2009, 2010; Bow and Franklin 2009). To ensure that the sample is spatially representative, the luminescence dating project includes survey-

Table 5.1. Early and Middle Woodland AMS radiocarbon determinations from the Upper Cumberland Plateau of Tennessee

Laboratory ID	Material	Provenance	Measure (rcBP)	1 sigma (calibrated)	2 sigma (calibrated)	2 sigma weighted
Beta-126040	River cane charcoal	3rd Unnamed Cave, gypsum mining passage, M35	2010 ± 60	90–71 BC, 59 BC– AD 65	173 BC–AD 90, AD 100–123	41 BC
Beta-134990	River cane charcoal	3rd Unnamed Cave, gypsum mining passage, M58	1920 ± 40	AD 30–37, 51–128	18–14 BC, AD 0–181, 187–214	AD 91
Beta-134991	River cane charcoal	3rd Unnamed Cave, gypsum mining passage, M59	1860 ± 40	AD 88–102, 122–215	AD 67–242	AD 154
AA45683	Wood charcoal	Pemberton Rock Shelter, prepared clay surface	2417 ± 50	728–693, 658–654, 542–404 BC	753–685, 668–610, 597–397 BC	497 BC
AA45684	Cervid metatarsal	Calf Rock Cave, TU1	2371 ± 33	506–459, 453–439, 419–394 BC	706–695, 539–387 BC	463 BC
AA60590	Charcoal soot	Griffin Rock Shelter, Swannanoa vessel	2837 ± 40	1046–968, 964–929 BC	1124–902 BC	1013 BC
AA71096	Wood charcoal	Eagle Drink Bluff Shelter, Feature 2	2308 ± 35	404–363, 267–266 BC	413–351, 299–227, 223–210 BC	382 BC
AA77118	Wood charcoal	Eagle Drink Bluff Shelter, Feature 3	1900 ± 42	AD 31–36, 52–138, 197–207	AD 21–227	AD 124
Beta-250176	Wood charcoal	Far View Gap Bluff Shelter, TU7, 20 cm bs	1540 ± 40	AD 435–91, 509–18, 528–69	AD 426–600	AD 513
Beta-250177	Wood charcoal	Far View Gap Bluff Shelter, TU7, 25 cm bs	1540 ± 40	AD 435–91, 509–18, 528–69	AD 426–600	AD 513
Beta-265066	Wood charcoal	Hemlock Falls Rock House, Feature 1	1380 ± 40	AD 622–71	AD 582–694, 704–5, 748–65	AD 638
Beta-265067	Wood charcoal	Hemlock Falls Rock House, Feature 2	2380 ± 50	536–530, 523–393 BC	751–686, 667–638, 620–615, 594–380 BC	487 BC
Beta-306622	Charred hickory nut	Indian Rock House (40Pt3), TU3, L4	2400 ± 30	510–400 BC	720–700, 540–400 BC	410 BC
Beta-306623	Charred acorn	Indian Rock House (40Pt3), TU3, L6	2430 ± 30	720–700, 540–410 BC	750–690, 660–640, 590–400 BC	510 BC

Table 5.2. Early and Middle Woodland luminescence (OSL) dates from the Upper Cumberland Plateau of Tennessee

Laboratory ID	Material	Provenance	Sherd thickness (mm)	Fine-grained measure
N/A	Limestone-tempered crisscross cord-marked body sherd	Eagle Drink Bluff Shelter, XU7, L4	5.4	AD 676 ± 45
N/A	Limestone-tempered cord-marked body sherd	Eagle Drink Bluff Shelter, XU7, L5	6.15	AD 3 ± 66
N/A	Limestone-tempered fabric-marked body sherd	Eagle Drink Bluff Shelter, XU7, L6	7.24	1218 ± 115 BC
LB289	Limestone-tempered cord-marked body sherd	Big Sandy Conor Rock Shelter (40Fn248), surface	13.00	177 ± 98 BC
LB288	Limestone-tempered cord-marked body sherd	Hemlock Falls Rock House (40Fn239), surface	7.60	AD 678 ± 36
LB350	Limestone-tempered cord-marked body sherd	York Palace (40Fn220), TU1, L4	9.54	AD 562 ± 84
LB351	Limestone-tempered cord-marked body sherd	York Palace (40Fn220), TU4, L6	9.06	AD 498 ± 50
LB352	Limestone-tempered zone check-stamped body sherd	York Palace (40Fn220), surface	4.5	AD 720 ± 35
LB353	Limestone-tempered cord-marked body sherd	Upper Falls Rock House (40Fn240), surface	14.18	362 ± 63 BC
LB355	Limestone-tempered plain body sherd	Pogue Creek Cave NR1 (40Fn303), surface	7.49	AD 625 ± 81
LB514	Quartz-tempered fabric/cord-marked body sherd	Hemlock Falls Rock House (40Fn239), TU1, Feature 2	11.9	AD 552 ± 132
LB515	Limestone-tempered plain body sherd	Hemlock Falls Rock House (40Fn239), TU1, L4	8.3	AD 850 ± 106
LB540	Quartz-tempered cord-marked body sherd	Green Squall Rock House, surface	7.0	AD 391 ± 146
LB544	Limestone-tempered fabric-marked body sherd	No Quarter Rock Shelter, surface	8.4	AD 544 ± 145
LB548	Limestone-tempered fabric-marked body sherd	Gwinn Cove Rock Shelter, surface	10.73	AD 79 ± 203
LB549	Quartz- (grit-) tempered cord-marked body sherd	Eagle Drink Bluff Shelter, XU27, L11	6.8	AD 77 ± 147
LB553	Quartz- (grit-) tempered cord-marked body sherd	Indian Rock House (40Pt3), surface	7.14	AD 680 ± 136
N/A	Limestone-tempered check-stamped body sherd	Indian Rock House (40Pt3), TU5, L2	6.8	AD 584 ± 86
N/A	Limestone-tempered fabric-marked body sherd	Honey Comb Rock Shelter, surface	10.9	AD 176 ± 190
N/A	Limestone-tempered fabric-marked body sherd	Twenty Rock Shelter	13.1	BC 9 ± 185
N/A	Limestone-tempered cord-marked body sherd	Bald Knob Rock Shelter (40Mo163), TU2, L3	7.1	AD 722 ± 61

level investigations (e.g., Dunnell and Feathers 1994). We use luminescence dates from controlled excavations to frame the ones recovered in our surveys (Franklin 2008a; Franklin and Bow 2009, 2010). The results thus far have been remarkably consistent, though we sometimes obtain larger error margins with surface dates. Table 5.2 lists luminescence dates obtained for the Early and Middle Woodland ($n = 21$). In cases where both radiocarbon and luminescence dates occurred in good stratigraphic contexts, they have been consistent, so we are confident of their mutual accuracy.

Ceramic Systematics

Franklin (2002, 2006a) initially hypothesized that conservative ceramic traditions persisted on the UCP throughout the Woodland period. During the Early Woodland, pottery was largely grit and/or quartz-tempered and cord-marked or plain. In these respects, it is generally typical of Early Woodland pottery. In addition, sites farther east on the UCP contain larger amounts of limestone-tempered fabric-marked ceramics (Ahler 1967; Franklin 2002: 223–26). While fabric marking is very typical of the Early Woodland in Middle and East Tennessee (Lewis and Kneberg 1957; McCollough and Faulkner 1973; Lafferty 1978; Faulkner 2002), to date, the recovery of fabric-marked pottery on the WEUCP has been less common, though we continue to recover it as our surveys of the UCP continue. During the Early Woodland period on the WEUCP specifically, cord marking was by far the preferred surface treatment, with lesser amounts of fabric marking and plain pottery (Franklin 2002: 223, 230; 2006a: 7).

Our OSL (optically stimulated luminescence) dates thus far indicate a wide temporal range for Early Woodland ceramics, from circa 1200 BC to AD 600 (table 5.2). In addition, we have obtained another very early OSL date of 1234 ± 339 BC for (Long Branch) fabric-marked pottery from the Red Velvet Spider Rockshelter (40Re243) on the Tennessee River, almost identical to that obtained from Eagle Drink Bluff Shelter (Franklin 2007). Long Branch pottery also persists into the early Middle Woodland McFarland phase of Middle Tennessee, perhaps as late as AD 200 (Faulkner 2002).

Early Woodland interregional interactions are indicated by the presence of the previously mentioned Swannanoa vessel and the recovery of six Early Woodland deeply cord-marked and incised limestone-tempered body sherds from Tevepaugh Rockshelter (Franklin 2002: 42, 230). These are reminiscent of Black Sand Incised (Munson 1986: 281) and Liverpool Cordmarked/Chevron Incised ceramics from central and southern Illinois (Munson 1986: 284; Farnsworth and Asch 1986).

In the Middle Woodland, limestone-tempered cord-marked wares continue to dominate and account for nearly two-thirds of all Middle Woodland ceramic assemblages. Limestone-tempered plain wares account for nearly 25 percent of Middle Woodland ceramics (Franklin 2006a). Our sample of OSL dates is consistent with these percentages (table 5.2).

At Eagle Drink Bluff Shelter, where we conducted our most extensive excavations from 2005 through 2009 (e.g., Franklin 2008a; Franklin et al. 2012), cord-marked ceramics outnumber other surface treatments by more than 2:1. Crisscross cord-marked and smoothed-over cord-marked sherds are common. Mixed tempering (such as limestone and grit) is typical. Several fabric-marked sherds were recovered, both limestone and limestone/grit tempered. One limestone-tempered simple-stamped sherd was recovered that yielded an OSL date of AD 984 ± 90. Finally, a grit-tempered cord-marked rim sherd was recovered in 2009 that has a chevron design incised over the cord marking (figure 5.2). We have yet to see this treatment anywhere else in East and Middle Tennessee.

Most ceramics recovered at York Palace are limestone tempered (Langston et al. 2010). Limestone-tempered cord-marked sherds constitute 31 percent of the ceramic assemblage. Two luminescence dates place this type in the Middle Woodland (table 5.2). Nearly 40 percent of the assemblage is limestone-tempered residual (i.e., too eroded to permit a determination of surface treatment). Ten percent are limestone-tempered check stamped, but we note that these sherds are from one vessel only. We also recovered one limestone-tempered simple-stamped sherd. Quartz and chalcedony are also common temper types.

The majority of the ceramic assemblage at Hemlock Falls Rock House is limestone-tempered cord-marked pottery, constituting 63 percent of the total assemblage (see OSL dates in table 5.2). The assemblage also includes plain limestone-tempered pottery, which accounts for 8.4 percent. Limestone-tempered residual ceramics constitute a smaller portion of the assemblage (4.2 percent). Siliceous stone–tempered pottery is present as well and accounts for approximately 5 percent of the total (Dye et al. 2010).

The ceramics from Indian Rock House are consistent with other Middle Woodland assemblages. The majority of sherds recovered (75 percent) are limestone-tempered cord marked. Limestone-tempered plain sherds, quartz-tempered plain, limestone-tempered check stamped, limestone-tempered brushed, and grit-tempered cord-marked make up minority amounts of the assemblage. One grit-tempered cord-marked sherd was OSL dated to AD 680, and one limestone-tempered check-stamped sherd was dated to AD 584 (table 5.2).

In previous archaeological investigations on the UCP of Tennessee, Ferguson and colleagues (1986: 132) found that plain surfaces were most common in Middle Woodland limestone-tempered pottery, followed by cord marking.

Figure 5.2. Grit-tempered cord-marked rim sherd with chevron incising, Eagle Drink Bluff Shelter, Tennessee. Photo by Jay Franklin.

Examination by Franklin and Faulkner (Franklin 2002) of a Middle Woodland ceramic collection from Big South Fork yielded results that differ somewhat from that pattern. In this sample, check stamping appears to be prevalent ($n = 19$), followed by cord marking ($n = 18$). There were 16 simple-stamped sherds, 5 of which were sand-tempered Connestee sherds. Only 1 plain-surfaced sherd was identified in the sample. This sample size is small, but there may be differences between the WEUCP area and more interior and eastern areas of the UCP. Conversely, the differences may reflect finer temporal resolution in our surveys due to the inclusion of luminescence-dated ceramics.

In sum, Middle Woodland ceramic assemblages on the UCP are dominated by limestone tempering and cord marking. In this regard they are similar to contemporaneous assemblages from adjacent river valley regions of Middle and East Tennessee. However, check stamping is much more common in the East Tennessee Valley (Faulkner 1968: 26; Franklin et al. 2008: 186). On the WEUCP, stamping in the Middle Woodland appears to have been comparatively rare. Simple stamping is most common but does not account for more than 10 percent of ceramic assemblages (Franklin and Bow 2009, 2010). In fact, OSL dates on stamped pottery (simple and check) from the UCP all postdate AD 700 (some significantly). Unfortunately, although discussion of these dates is beyond the scope of this chapter, they may represent an interaction lag in temporal terms. We would also note that in the course of our surveys on the UCP, we continue to record stamped wares.

Technology and Resource Procurement

Ferguson (1988: 21–32, 166–72) proposed that different strategies for resource procurement existed during the Archaic and Woodland periods on the UCP. Because lithic resources are relatively scarce in the region, most strategies focused on the need to curate chert. Generally speaking, Archaic hunter-gatherers seemed to have practiced curated lithic technologies, while Woodland groups appear to have been somewhat more expedient. This is reflected in relatively low ratios of tools to flaking debris and the general lack of bifaces recovered at Woodland sites.

Pace and Hays (1991) also address Woodland lithic strategies on the UCP in their work at Station Camp in the Big South Fork. They suggest that the differences between Archaic and Woodland patterns are due to underrepresentation of bifaces at Woodland sites. If, however, flake tools are included, tool to flaking debris ratios for the Woodland are comparable to the Archaic (Pace and Hays 1991: 130). We caution here that these studies do not appear to have included use-wear analyses of stone tools. We believe that their interpretations are incomplete and thus problematic.

Another difference that Pace and Hays (1991) suggested between Archaic and Woodland lithic assemblages on the UCP deals with raw material variability. Monteagle chert (Upper Mississippian) is the most ubiquitous tool stone in the region. At the Station Camp sites, Pace and Hays identified that Archaic groups used a wider array of raw materials (with other Mississippian-aged cherts such as Fort Payne and St. Louis sometimes accounting for more than 30 percent of assemblages). Woodland groups, conversely, used local Monteagle chert almost exclusively (Pace and Hays 1991: 132, 142).

We use these previous studies to frame our work and discussion of lithic technology and mobility within the Woodland of the UCP. We note two important points: first, we include lithic wear analyses in our study, and second, the sites where we have done the most work are all located on the WEUCP. Therefore, access to raw materials was not an issue for prehistoric hunter-gatherers in this area.

The results of lithic analyses from our sites contrast with those presented by Ferguson (1988) and Pace and Hays (1991). At all sites, it is clear that local Monteagle chert was the most widely used raw material (table 5.3). However, it is also clear that Woodland peoples used other raw materials routinely, including Fort Payne chert and chalcedony. These other raw materials make up as much as 30 percent of some Woodland assemblages. We must draw the conclusion that the exploitation of different raw materials was no more variable in the Woodland than in the Archaic on the WEUCP (contra Pace and Hays 1991:

Table 5.3. Lithic flaking debris data by raw material category for Woodland sites on the WEUCP

A. Eagle Drink Bluff Shelter

Size grade	Monteagle (weight, count)	Chalcedony (weight, count)	Fort Payne (weight, count)	Unidentified local (weight, count)
1"	0 g, 0	0 g, 0	0 g, 0	17.4 g, 1
3/4"	35 g, 4	0 g, 0	12.9 g, 2	8.7 g, 1
1/2"	60.7 g, 18	3.9 g, 1	18.8 g, 7	12.7 g, 3
1/4"	66.3 g, 113	5.1 g, 9	17.7 g, 28	8.9 g, 20

Flake portion	Monteagle (count)	Chalcedony (count)	Fort Payne (count)	Unidentified local (count)
Complete	30	3	7	2
PRB	52	4	14	3
Broken	40	2	12	5
Blocky shatter	7	1	0	3
Thermal shatter	2	0	0	10
Split flake	4	2	0	0

Debitage stages	Monteagle (count)	Chalcedony (count)	Fort Payne (count)	Unidentified local (count)
Early	56	3	14	5
Middle	18	6	5	1
Late	52	2	16	4
Blocky shatter	7	1	0	3

B. York Palace

Size grade	Monteagle (weight, count)	Chalcedony (weight, count)	Fort Payne (weight, count)	Unidentified local (weight, count)
1"	0 g, 0	0 g, 0	0 g, 0	0 g, 0
3/4"	0 g, 0	0 g, 0	0 g, 0	0 g, 0
1/2"	24.1 g, 11	14.1 g, 4	14.4 g, 8	7.1 g, 4
1/4"	34.4 g, 78	6.9 g, 13	14.5 g, 41	10.8 g, 16

Flake portion	Monteagle (count)	Chalcedony (count)	Fort Payne (count)	Unidentified local (count)
Complete	10	1	10	2
PRB	31	5	15	6
Broken	31	7	18	5
Blocky shatter	6	4	2	4
Thermal shatter	11	0	4	3

(continued)

(*Table 5.3. continued*)

Debitage stages	Monteagle (count)	Chalcedony (count)	Fort Payne (count)	Unidentified local (count)
Early	16	1	6	3
Middle	13	5	3	2
Late	13	7	6	0
Blocky shatter	5	4	1	4

C. Hemlock Falls Rock House

Size grade	Monteagle (weight, count)	Chalcedony (weight, count)	Fort Payne (weight, count)	Unidentified local (weight, count)
1"	0 g, 0	0 g, 0	0 g, 0	0 g, 0
3/4"	0 g, 0	0 g, 0	0 g, 0	0 g, 0
1/2"	66.3 g, 24	11.6 g, 5	4.3 g, 2	0 g, 0
1/4"	68.4 g, 64	12.3 g, 13	12 g, 19	33.8 g, 46

Flake portion	Monteagle (count)	Chalcedony (count)	Fort Payne (count)	Unidentified local (count)
Complete	0	0	0	0
PRB	0	0	0	0
Broken	40	7	8	5
Blocky shatter	3	2	1	12
Thermal shatter	5	1	0	11

Debitage stages	Monteagle (count)	Chalcedony (count)	Fort Payne (count)	Unidentified local (count)
Early	66	5	9	14
Middle	5	5	7	7
Late	9	5	4	2
Blocky shatter	14	2	1	12

143). This likely also means that Archaic and Woodland peoples practiced similar mobility strategies and were as likely to engage in the curation of lithic tools. The recovery of numerous Woodland bifaces at Workshop Rockshelter and Eagle Drink Bluff Shelter supports this contention (Franklin and Bow 2010).

While we recovered comparatively fewer Woodland bifaces at York Palace, Hemlock Falls, and Indian Rock House, this could be related to greater degrees of vandalism in the shallower Woodland components than the more deeply buried Archaic components (Eagle Drink was undisturbed). Unfortunately, vandalism and looting is a decades-long tradition in the shelters of the UCP (Des Jean 1987; Des Jean and Benthall 1994; Pace and Hays 1991; Franklin 2002). It is incumbent upon archaeological scholars to accurately discern how this has impacted the nature of the archaeological record in the region. For example, in our survey of Pogue Creek State Natural Area, we found that only 1 of 17 Archaic component sites had been looted. At sites that also had later Woodland components, conversely, more than 80 percent had been looted (Langston and Franklin 2010).

This clearly has implications for the appearance of the archaeological record. With that in mind, we suggest that Woodland groups engaged in bifacial tool production even if we fail to recover these tools. Our flake debris analyses support that contention—significant numbers of biface thinning flakes and flakes with lipped platforms were recorded at all sites. In sum, Woodland peoples on the WEUCP used variable raw material sources in the region as did their Archaic predecessors (Franklin et al. 2012), conducted all stages of lithic reduction in rockshelters, and engaged in curated behavior.

Lithic use-wear analyses were conducted on stone tool assemblages from Eagle Drink ($n = 20$), Indian Rock House ($n = 18$), and the Horn Dog Pictograph Site ($n = 2$). Tools were analyzed microscopically using the high-power approach (Keeley 1980). At Eagle Drink, activities represented at the site were varied, ranging from butchering/processing meat to hide processing to woodworking. The overall functional composition of the assemblage indicates that 25 percent of the pieces had some evidence of use (15 percent butchering/processing meat, 5 percent hide working, and 5 percent woodworking); for 75 percent of the pieces, no wear could be detected. At Indian Rock House, the activities were not particularly varied. Fifty percent of the tools had traces of use indicating some form of early-stage animal processing. Interestingly, one piece had wear that may be the result of contact with shell.

Two Middle Woodland bifaces from Horn Dog Pictograph Site bear use-wear polish: the Bakers Creek biface has hafting mastic on one shoulder and bone and hide polish along the blade edges; the Copena biface has bone polish along one blade edge (figure 5.3). As a whole, use-wear analyses from three Woodland sites indicate that a variety of activities occurred at each site, comprising a full range of behavior expected for a foraging community. It thus appears that these lithic assemblages reflect occupation by residentially mobile families, rather than more specialized, logistically organized hunting groups.

In addition to securing raw materials for chipped-stone tools from chert outcrops, Woodland peoples on the UCP also exploited dark-zone cave envi-

Figure 5.3. Lithic use wear of bifacial stone tools from Horn Dog Pictograph Site, Tennessee. Photos by Maureen Hays.

ronments for mineral resources. This has been well documented in the karstic regions of the Southeast (Watson 1969, 1974, 1986; Crothers et al. 2002). On the UCP, Early Woodland groups at least explored Jaguar Cave (Franklin 2002: 94, 2008b: 152). More specifically, 3rd Unnamed Cave was used by Late Archaic groups mining for chert (Simek et al. 1998; Franklin 1999, 2001) and by Early Woodland peoples mining gypsum. This latter use is supported by three radiocarbon assays (table 5.1) from river cane charcoal samples collected from sediment surfaces directly underneath areas of the Meander Passage walls where gypsum crusts were evident. These crusts were battered with hammer stones by Woodland peoples to remove gypsum (Franklin 2002, 2008b). This is consistent with similar evidence from other Tennessee caves such as Big Bone and Hubbards (Crothers 1987; Pritchard 2008).

Subsistence

Descriptive analyses were conducted on faunal remains from York Palace, Hemlock Falls, and Indian Rock House (no faunal remains were present at Eagle Drink). A few general statements can be made regarding the assemblage compositions from all three sites (table 5.4). First, more than 95 percent of the faunal remains from each site is highly fragmentary. This may be a result of

Table 5.4. Summary faunal information for the WEUCP study area

A. Species representation

	York Palace NISP	York Palace MNI	Hemlock Falls NISP	Hemlock Falls MNI	Indian Rock House NISP	Indian Rock House MNI
White-tailed deer	3	1	27	2	37	3
Wild turkey	1	1	6	1	2	1
Black bear	1	1	0	0	0	0
Eastern box turtle	0	0	1	1	1	1
Gray fox	0	0	1	1	0	0
Woodchuck	0	0	1	1	0	0
Beaver	0	0	0	0	1	1

B. Comparison of taxonomic classes (including unidentifiable)

	York Palace	Hemlock Falls	Indian Rock House
Mammal	58	380	208
Bird	1	22	10
Reptile	1	27	13
Amphibian	0	1	0
Fish	0	4	0
Invertebrate	0	13	15
Unidentifiable	13	181	743
Total	73	628	989

C. Modifications across taxonomic classes

	York Palace	Hemlock Falls	Indian Rock House
Mammal—cut	1	10	0
Mammal—burned	19	130	39
Mammal—gnawed	0	35	1
Bird—cut	0	0	0
Bird—burned	0	4	1
Bird—gnawed	0	4	0
Reptile—cut	0	0	0
Reptile—burned	1	3	2
Reptile—gnawed	0	1	0
Amphibian—cut	0	0	0
Amphibian—burned	0	1	0
Amphibian—gnawed	0	0	0
Unidentifiable—cut	0	0	0
Unidentifiable—burned	9	44	341
Unidentifiable—gnawed	0	1	0

looting, but in undisturbed levels, it may also indicate that bones were being broken to obtain marrow. Large quantities of burned bones are also common at each site, and many of these are calcined, indicating that they were heated to a high degree. Mammals are the most common class of animals identified at each site by far; however, the presence of aquatic and avian resources indicates that these were also part of the Woodland diet on the WEUCP. White-tailed deer and wild turkey were the only species consistently distributed among all three sites; however, turtle and small- to medium-sized mammals (e.g., squirrel, beaver, and fox) were also regularly encountered.

Eagle Drink and Indian Rock House are the only sites that yielded archaeobotanical remains. Feature 2 at Eagle Drink yielded carbonized remains of acorns, and several charred acorns and hickory nuts were recovered in Early Woodland levels at Indian Rock House. The implications of these assemblages for seasonal occupation of rockshelters are discussed below.

Settlement and Site Formation Processes

Woodland adaptations on the UCP were fairly uniform but broad in terms of subsistence and technology. Because it has not been vandalized, Eagle Drink is the only site where we can document assemblage formation processes based on the lithic assemblage, though given certain intersite consistencies, we can hypothesize for Workshop Rockshelter and perhaps the others. Eagle Drink appears to represent an intermittently occupied situational camp during the Woodland where a variety of activities took place, as evidenced by use-wear analysis. In fact, it is clear that the entire range of lithic reduction was conducted at all of the Woodland sites we have investigated. This suggests that they were not simply special-purpose camps, as posited by Pace and Hays (1991: 142–43). With the possible exception of Eagle Drink, all sites may have served as residential base camps during the Woodland. Eagle Drink may in fact have also served as a residential camp, just not as intensively as it was during the Late Archaic (Franklin et al. 2012).

Fauna at all sites indicates a broad subsistence range with a focus on larger mammals such as white-tailed deer but also wild turkey. The recovery of fish, shellfish, and reptilian species suggests warm-weather occupations in addition to fall occupations (contra Pace and Hays 1991: 142–43). This is consistent with our lithic analyses in that the variable reduction strategies indicated by technological analyses and use-wear analyses that indicate a variety of activities suggest seasonal movement *within* the uplands of the UCP by family groups, as opposed to fall and winter forays *into* the uplands by logistical hunting groups.

This is an important point because rockshelters in the northern hemisphere have typically been viewed as late fall and winter sites, if only implicitly. This is largely based on the idea that prehistoric peoples mostly sought out south-facing shelters for increased solar insulation and protection against winter winds and storms (see Hall and Klippel 1988: 161). While Eagle Drink Bluff Shelter and Indian Rock House face southeast, York Palace opens mostly to the north and south (it is a four-footed natural arch shelter). Hemlock Falls Rock House opens to the northwest. In our survey of Pogue Creek State Natural Area, we recorded nearly as many north- and west-facing rockshelters ($n = 51$) as south- and east-facing shelters ($n = 57$). Further, of shelters with only Woodland components, more than 58 percent faced north or west (Langston and Franklin 2010). In short, in unique regions such as the UCP that are dominated by rockshelters, selection was not dependent upon facing direction. Rather, it was likely influenced by seasonality (north-facing shelters are quite hospitable during the hot southern summers).

Interactions, Expressions, and Future Directions

Thus far we have recovered no artifacts that suggest direct Hopewell influence on the UCP. This is interesting because Late and Terminal Archaic peoples on the UCP clearly had significant regional interactions. This is evidenced by the recovery of steatite vessel sherds from dozens of sites, as well as bifaces typical of the Midwest (e.g., Adena, Matanzas, and Merom). Most of the bifaces are made from locally available raw materials, however (Franklin et al. 2010).

Copena bifaces are not uncommon on the UCP, and we have recovered them from four rockshelter sites. While these do not indicate Hopewell interaction per se, they do suggest interaction with the Copena Complex. One of these sites, Horn Dog Pictograph Site, has two pictographs in spatial association with Copena and Bakers Creek bifaces, and a sand-tempered Connestee potsherd. However, we cannot be certain that the spatial association reflects cultural association. We stress that our work at this site is preliminary, and we continue our investigations there with Jan Simek and the Cave Archaeology Research Team at the University of Tennessee.

There do appear to be a few Middle Woodland mounds in the region. Myer (n.d.) was the first to mention the Pile Mound on the Wolf River 500 m north of Jaguar Cave. We re-located the mound in 2001. It measures 1.5 m high and 30 m in diameter (Franklin 2002). These measurements are consistent with Myer's account. The mound remains undisturbed and has never been plowed. We have begun GPR survey of the Pile Mound but unfortunately do not yet have results to present. We have also recently been informed of two similar mounds several kilometers downstream from the Pile Mound, which we also plan to investigate.

Although our investigations of cultural expressions in rock art and mounds are in their preliminary stages, we are fortunate on the UCP to now have a comprehensive database of landscape use during the Early and Middle Woodland, against which we can contextualize new findings. Multiple lines of evidence, in particular lithic raw material types and use-wear patterns, reflect a wide range of activities occurring across a complex and distinctive physical landscape. We believe that these reflect a wide range of people (families). Taken together, the Early and Middle Woodland archaeological record of the WEUCP appears to reflect occupation by small but numerous groups of residentially mobile hunter-gatherers. These peoples used the shelters and caves of the UCP for many purposes: hunting and gathering, shelter, residential occupations, mineral extraction, the production of artwork, and burial. Woodland peoples were intimately familiar with these myriad geological features and thus imprinted their experiences onto this landscape in ways not possible in the adjacent lowland river valleys.

Acknowledgments

We would like to thank the Estate of Bruno Gernt, Inc. for permission to conduct archaeological investigations on their landholdings. We are particularly indebted to Jerry Gernt for his interest, enthusiasm, hospitality, and support. Jay Franklin wishes to thank the Research Development Committee, Office of the Vice Provost for Research and Sponsored Programs, the College of Arts and Sciences, and the Department of Sociology and Anthropology, East Tennessee State University for funding and material support. Funding was also provided in the form of several competitive survey and planning grants awarded to Jay Franklin for the work in York Palace, Hemlock Falls, and Indian Rock House by the Tennessee Historical Commission. Archaeological survey and testing permits were granted by the Tennessee Division of Archaeology. The AMS determinations were done by the NSF-Arizona AMS Facility and Beta Analytic, Inc. (all radiocarbon measures were calibrated using Calib 6.0 with IntCal 09 atmospheric data). We would also like to extend our sincere thanks to Tennessee State Parks and Forests, in particular, Alan Wasik, John Froeschauer, Travis Bow, and Brandon Taylor. We would like to thank the folks at the Hangin' Hog BBQ for providing food for our crews while in the field. We appreciate the suggestions and cogent comments provided by Alice Wright and Eddie Henry.

PART TWO

Monumental Landscapes

Mound and Earthwork Sites

6

Winchester Farm

A Small Adena Enclosure in Central Kentucky

RICHARD W. JEFFERIES, GEORGE R. MILNER,
AND EDWARD R. HENRY

Earthen constructions of various sizes and shapes have attracted the attention of people interested in the prehistoric remains of the middle Ohio River valley for over 200 years. In fact, in 1803, Meriwether Lewis described the celebrated Grave Creek mound on the Ohio River in West Virginia as a "remarkable artificial mound of earth" encompassed by a wide ditch. The mound was a memorable stop during the initial stage of the Corps of Discovery's long journey, which in due course would take them entirely across the continent (Moulton 1986: 77).[1]

One particular kind of earthwork, a small ring that has long been considered "sacred," was by far the most common form of enclosure to survive into the nineteenth century (Squier and Davis 1848: 8).[2] Yet despite once being a prominent part of the archaeological landscape, these small rings have not received the attention one might expect given their former abundance, with notably few exceptions (Burks 2010; Burks and Cook 2011; Fenton and Jefferies 1991; Griffin 1947; Henry 2009, 2011; Webb 1941b). Perhaps that is attributable to their disappearance in many places through erosion, plowing, and construction, although recent excavation and remote-sensing projects demonstrate that much can still be learned about them (Burks 2006, 2010; Burks and Cook 2011; Cowan 2005; Henry 2011).

Here we present the results of a mapping and geophysical survey project focused on the Winchester Farm earthwork in the Kentucky Bluegrass (figure 6.1). The geophysical survey was an inexpensive and efficient means of data collection that added new information to what was already available from topographic maps and aerial photographs. However, no single source of information—surface elevation characterized by contour maps, soil stains visible in aerial photographs, or subsurface distinctions identified by remote sensing procedures—provided a complete picture. Furthermore, our re-

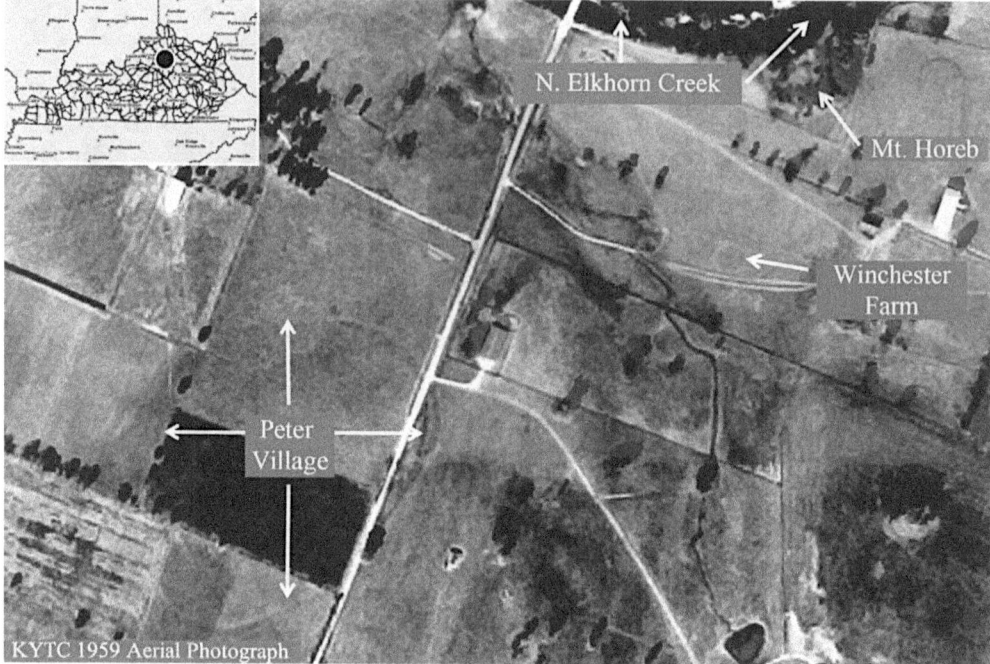

Figure 6.1. Major components of the Elkhorn Creek earthwork complex on North Elkhorn Creek, Fayette County, Kentucky. Photo courtesy of the Kentucky Transportation Cabinet, Frankfort.

search, like the recent work of Burks (2006, 2010; Burks and Cook 2011) in Ohio, demonstrates that the internal structure of small circular earthworks cannot be judged solely by their external appearance.

The fieldwork is placed in a broader context by assembling information on the distribution and characteristics of small Adena (Early to Middle Woodland) earthworks in the middle Ohio Valley, specifically, sites in Kentucky, Ohio, West Virginia, and Indiana. For the most part, data were gleaned from published sources, although some unpublished information from state site files is also included. Additional information can certainly be collected from various other sources, especially by regional specialists who comb through obscure nineteenth-century accounts. It is doubtful, however, that such information would greatly alter the general picture provided here, because the existing sample is already large and the number of reasonably well-documented earthworks that have been missed is likely to be small.

Small Earthworks

Many earthworks that varied greatly in size and shape were built in the middle Ohio River valley during the Early and, especially, Middle Woodland periods.

In the early nineteenth century, small circles were recognized as the most common form of earthen enclosure, although many have since succumbed to erosion, agricultural practices, and urban sprawl (Squier and Davis 1848). A distinction between small and large earthworks is maintained here as well, both for convenience and because the two likely served different functions, although all were "sacred" in nature.

There is, of course, no single correct way to classify the diverse group of middle Ohio River valley earthworks, because whatever is done depends on a researcher's specific objectives and the nature of the data at hand. For the purposes of this chapter, it was sufficient to identify a group of small earthworks and then characterize their general features. In our survey of the literature, small enclosures of various shapes encompassed from 0.01 to 1.35 ha ($n = 226$, median = 0.16 ha). These earthworks are for the most part separate structures, although some are joined to long embankments that form part of much larger enclosures. The distinction between these enclosures and others found in the middle Ohio River valley, which is based on the areas encompassed and their appearance, is admittedly somewhat arbitrary. The size distributions, for example, overlap, as the earthworks excluded from further consideration ranged from 0.78 to 56.66 ha ($n = 85$; median = 7.53 ha). If size was used as the sole criterion for separating the two kinds of earthworks and, say, 1.5 ha was chosen as the sectioning point, then only four earthworks would be shifted to the group of primary interest.[3] Such minor changes in the composition of the sample of small earthworks would have little effect on the summary of their general characteristics.

There is a further and potentially more serious problem with attempting to say anything at all about a particular type of earthwork, no matter how it is defined. Much must be made of early descriptions, as many sites have been utterly destroyed. That is particularly true of the small earthworks that do not withstand much plowing. Over a century ago, the embankments were often "scarcely traceable," and today the situation is much worse (Fowke 1902: 220). Earlier sources, however, are not always accurate, a problem Thomas (1894) noted over a century ago with regard to one of Squier and Davis's (1848) small circular embankments.

For earthworks like Winchester Farm, Squier and Davis's (1848) designation "sacred" is appropriate insofar as such earthworks have long been recognized as having had something other than a defensive purpose. That was apparent early on because of their small size, the arrangement of ditches and embankments relative to one another, the insignificant height of many earthen ridges, and their positioning in terms of local topographical features. If we are to confine ourselves to circles, by far the most common shape, the enclosures are usually characterized by an exterior earthen embankment that surrounds a ditch and, in turn, an interior space. The interiors are often accessed by an entryway, and sometimes more than one of them, that passes through the embankment and across the ditch. By its very nature, an entrance that allowed passage across the earthen barrier, which separated the interior from the world outside, channeled movement into a space that presumably possessed great ritual significance. At the Mt. Horeb earthwork just uphill from Winchester Farm, the interior was further demarcated and effectively hidden from view by a screen of closely spaced upright posts (Webb 1941b).

Several archaeologists have remarked upon the rather obvious distinction drawn between external and internal space (Clay 1987; Squier and Davis 1848; Webb 1941b). What took place within these enclosures is largely unknown, primarily because so few have been excavated. Some circles, however, were probably associated with Adena mortuary rituals since large and small mounds were constructed in the areas encompassed by embankments and ditches. One well-known example is the large conical mound at Marietta, Ohio, known as the Conus, which has been preserved in an old city cemetery (see figure 4.1).

Small enclosures are frequently located near one another, often in the vi-

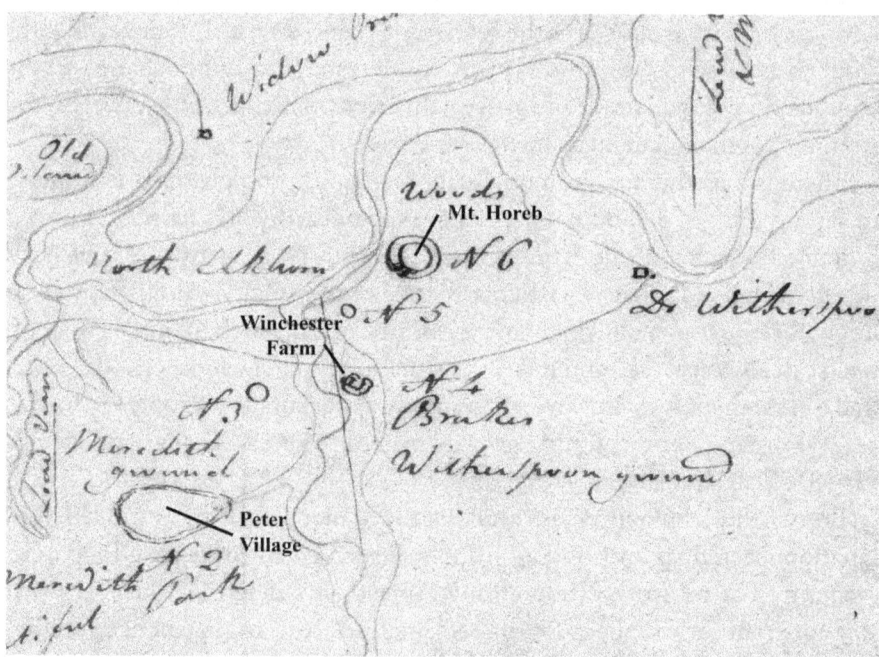

Figure 6.2. Location of "Monument 4," now known as the Winchester Farm earthwork, as shown on Rafinesque's 1820 map titled "Monuments on North Elkhorn Creek." Entire map not shown. Image courtesy of Special Collections Division, University of Kentucky Libraries.

cinity of mounds and larger earthworks, as Squier and Davis (1848), among others, noted long ago. That was the case with Winchester Farm, as recognized in the earliest map of the earthwork and nearby archaeological features (Rafinesque 1820) (figures 6.1 and 6.2).

Winchester Farm

Old Descriptions

Excavations of several mounds and earthworks near North Elkhorn Creek indicate that they are associated with the Early to Middle Woodland Adena culture (Clay 1985, 1988; Webb 1941b, 1943c; Webb and Haag 1947). Other groups of Adena mounds and earthworks are scattered across the Bluegrass and beyond, throughout eastern Kentucky (Applegate 2008; Railey 1996; Webb 1941b; Webb and Snow 1945).

Winchester Farm is situated within a cluster of sites that was first described by Rafinesque (1821: 53) as the "principal ancient monuments of Fayette county." Winchester Farm—monument 4 on his 1820 sketch map (figure 6.2)—is located between the large enclosure now known as Peter Village and Mt. Horeb (figure 6.3), which Rafinesque (1821: 54) considered, with reason, as "one of the best preserved monument[s] of [its] kind in Kentucky." The

Figure 6.3. The Mt. Horeb earthwork showing (*left to right*) the wall, interior ditch, and interior space. Photo by Richard Jefferies.

Winchester Farm enclosure is situated on the flank of the rise upon which Mt. Horeb sits. It was said to have a circumference of 400 ft, a ditch 2 ft deep, an outer embankment 1 ft high, and an opening to the northeast oriented toward Mt. Horeb. Rafinesque (1821: 54) believed that the less notable Winchester Farm enclosure was a "small temple." Warming to his subject, he wrote that it was perhaps a "temple of the Moon" that complemented Mt. Horeb's dedication to "the Sun." Of such idle speculation are great stories made, then and now.

Additional archaeological explorations took place along North Elkhorn Creek later in the nineteenth century, but the small and inconspicuous Winchester Farm enclosure received little further attention (Peter 1873a, 1873b). It was, however, still visible as a "small ditch, quite shallow, inclosing a circle of about 82 feet in diameter" (Peter 1873a: 423). While Rafinesque's and Peter's dimensions do not match—both are rough estimates of an indistinct ditch and embankment—it is clear from the location that they refer to the same enclosure.

Mt. Horeb, in particular, continued to attract attention early in the twentieth century (Funkhouser and Webb 1928; Young 1910). Webb and Funkhouser (1932: 115), for example, called it "one of the archaeological treasures of Kentucky" in their statewide site survey. With Webb at the helm of Kentucky's archaeological work funded by various New Deal agencies during the Great Depression, it was only natural that an excavation was conducted at Mt. Horeb. It occurred in the latter half of 1939 with a Works Progress Administration (WPA) crew directed by Claude Johnston (Milner and Smith 1986: 45–46; Webb 1941b). Designated Unit A, it had a ring of closely spaced postmolds located just inside the interior space. The upright posts, along with the high outer embankment, would have effectively screened the enclosure's interior from view. A recently collected charcoal sample found on top of a buried A soil horizon beneath the embankment yielded a two-sigma calibrated date of 358 BC to AD 80 (Henry and Crothers 2010).

The WPA archaeologists also visited the Winchester Farm earthwork, which they identified as Unit D (Webb 1941b). It was reported to be roughly 125 ft in diameter, and the difference in elevation between the top of the embankment and bottom of the interior ditch was at most 2 ft. A "gateway," oriented toward the southwest, was "formed in the usual way by failure to excavate the ditch as a complete circle" (Webb 1941b: 142). The earthwork's overall dimension corresponded closely to Rafinesque's estimate; in fact, they are extraordinarily close considering that both were rough assessments of an indistinct earthen feature. There is, however, a discrepancy in the direction of the opening.

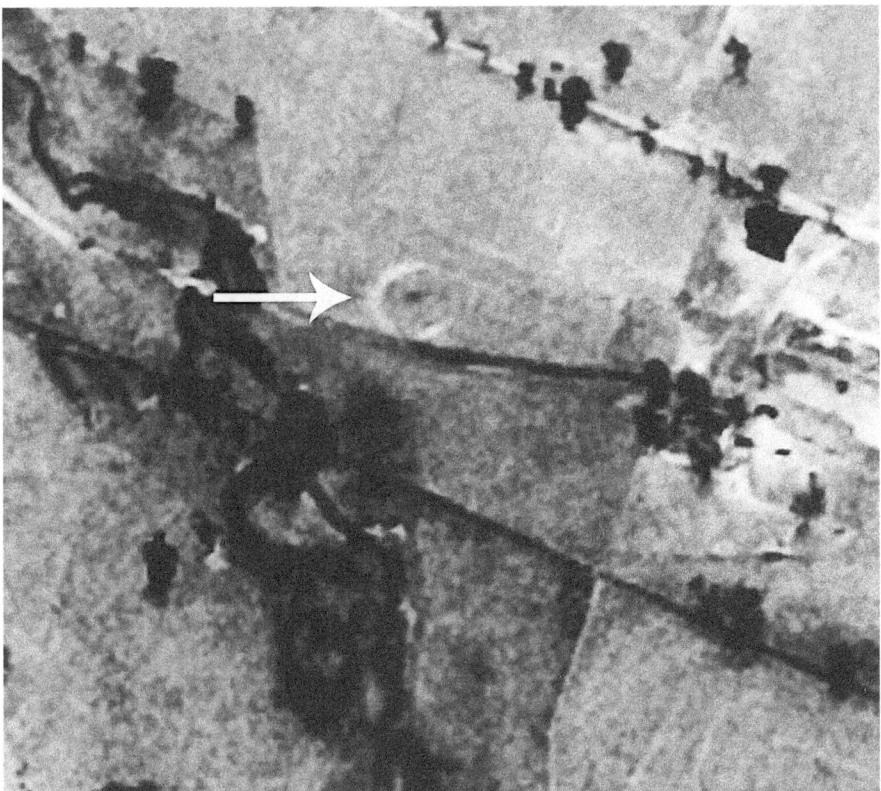

Figure 6.4. Part of a 1952 aerial photo showing the Winchester Farm earthwork. Photo courtesy of the Kentucky Transportation Cabinet, Frankfort.

In short, descriptions from the nineteenth century onward are consistent in describing a small circular earthwork similar to those reported by many archaeologists, amateurs and professionals alike, throughout the middle Ohio River valley region. The early accounts of a circular enclosure conform to what is visible in aerial photographs (figure 6.4) from the mid-twentieth century to the present (KYTC 1952).

Topographic Map

Nothing else of archaeological interest happened at Winchester Farm until December 1985, when two of us (GRM and RWJ) used a transit to map the enclosure, which was then in a horse pasture. The intent was to document what remained of the site, as it seemed likely to disappear from view in due course. In the mid-1980s, the earthwork was quite difficult to discern from ground level. In fact, it was best seen from some distance, being clearest when the observer was standing near the crest of the rise on which the site was located, somewhat downslope from Mt. Horeb (figure 6.5A). A topographic

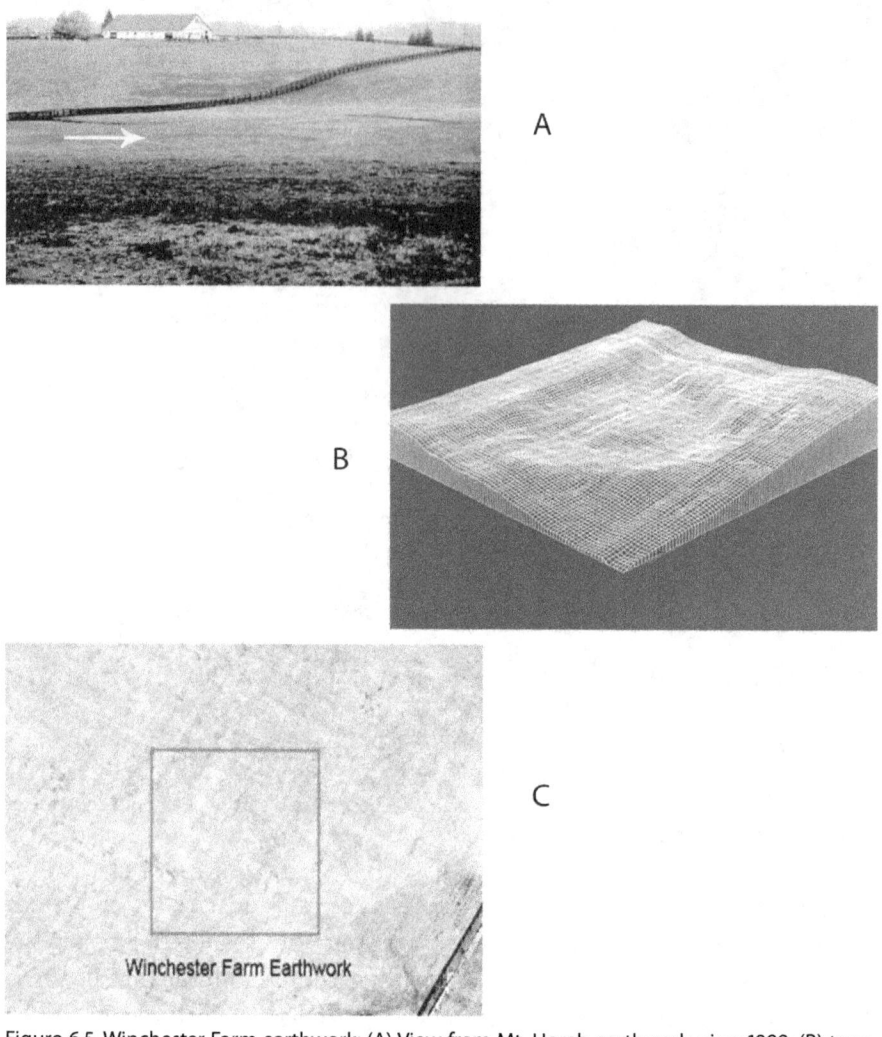

Figure 6.5. Winchester Farm earthwork: (A) View from Mt. Horeb earthwork, circa 1999; (B) topographic map of the Winchester Farm earthwork based on elevation data collected by Milner and Jefferies in 1985; (C) recent aerial photo of Winchester Farm earthwork (from Bing 2010).

map was made by taking elevation readings at one-meter intervals; it remains the only detailed map of the earthwork.

In figure 6.5B, produced immediately after mapping the site, the vertical scale is exaggerated to emphasize subtle elevation differences. The image shows what is interpreted as a roughly circular embankment, ditch, and internal area. Although indications of a slight elevation are visible in the interior, little was made of it at the time. The topographic map indicates that two openings perhaps existed; if so, that might resolve the discrepancy between Rafinesque's and Webb's descriptions.

The topographic map indicates that the earthwork measured 35.2 × 38.3 m, as estimated from the top of the embankment. The outer edges are vague and blend into the uneven ground of the sloping hillside. The embankment dimensions, estimated without knowledge of earlier figures, are essentially identical to the diameters reported by Rafinesque (1820, 1821) in 1820, 38.8 m, and Webb (1941b) in 1939, 38.1 m.[4] Their measurements are remarkably similar given the problems everyone would have experienced in seeing subtle differences in elevation on a vegetation-covered hillside.

Geophysical Survey

Based on the early descriptions of Winchester Farm, aerial photographs taken over the past 50 years (figures 6.1, 6.4, 6.5C), and our topographic map, we were confident that our more recent field investigations would simply confirm its circular shape. That, however, was not the case.

In August and September 2010, two of us (ERH and RWJ) conducted a multi-instrument geophysical survey to clarify the earthwork's size and shape, and to identify internal anomalies. Multiple geophysical survey techniques were used to increase the chance that subsurface features with various soil properties would be detected (Clay 2001; Kvamme et al. 2006).

A Bartington Instruments Grad-601-2 dual fluxgate gradiometer and a Geonics EM38B electromagnetic induction meter were used. Gradiometers and electromagnetic meters have been widely employed in geophysical surveys elsewhere in North America (Clay 2006; Dalan 2006; Johnson et al. 2000; McKinnon 2009; Perttula et al. 2008). Moreover, they have been used successfully on Middle Woodland earthwork sites in Ohio and Kentucky that exhibit little, if any, topographic relief (Burks 2006, 2010; Burks and Cook 2011; Henry 2009, 2011).

Gradiometers measure thermoremnant and induced magnetism (Clark 1996). Enhanced remnant magnetism occurs when ferrous minerals in the soil are heated above their Curie point at approximately 1,000–1,200°F (Aspinall et al. 2008). Examples of thermoremnant magnetic features include brick kilns, hearths, and heavily burned structures. Induced magnetism refers to a material's magnetic susceptibility. Detectable induced magnetic signatures can be produced by discarded magnetic materials such as broken pottery, as well as bacteria-rich organic waste that, in turn, creates reducing or oxidizing conditions for magnetic minerals (Aspinall et al. 2008).

Electromagnetic instruments can measure soil conductivity—that is, the ability of a material to conduct an electromagnetic signal (Bevan 1998). Archaeological features detectable by variations in soil conductivity typically consist of redistributed soils that retain or resist water saturation more so than surrounding soils (Clay 2006). This equipment can also measure induced magnetism or magnetic susceptibility, the ability of a material to be magnetized. Examples of induced magnetic features that are identifiable include mound and earthwork remnants, buried ground surfaces, and filled pits and ditches.

Data were collected with the gradiometer across a 60 × 60 m area, with readings taken every 25 cm along transects spaced 50 cm apart. The electromagnetic data were collected on a 50 × 45 m grid, with readings taken every 50 cm on transects 1 m apart.

The earthwork's ditch is represented as a magnetic high in a map of the gradiometer data. This high magnetic anomaly is likely the result of the ditch being filled with magnetically enhanced topsoil (figure 6.6A). The embankment is indicated by a magnetic low surrounded by a faint outer magnetic high. The outer magnetic high represents topsoil that eroded to the outer edge of the embankment, while the magnetic low over the embankment may represent displaced magnetic minerals from the construction of the earthwork. Two magnetic highs inside the earthwork could represent cultural features. Other anomalies are attributable to historic farm use, including a long-abandoned field road and metal debris.

The ditch can also be identified in the electromagnetic data as magnetic susceptibility highs, suggesting elevated levels of induced magnetism from topsoil that accumulated in the depression (figure 6.6B). Additionally, a circular area of high induced magnetism occurs inside the earthwork, presumably representing some sort of feature. This area corresponds to the area where the gradiometer detected two magnetic highs. Maps of the conductivity component of the electromagnetic data revealed low conductivity in the ditch and high conductivity in the embankment, in addition to an old road south of the earthwork (figure 6.6C).

The geophysical maps indicate that the earthwork's interior differs substantially from what might be assumed from earlier descriptions, the topographic map, and aerial photographs. Winchester Farm has long been referred to as one of the "sacred circles" scattered across the middle Ohio River valley (Webb 1941b: 141). The geophysical data, however, show that the ditch was not circular but instead defined an interior space that was square with rounded corners. The internal area measures approximately 293 m^2, to judge from the geophysical survey data.

The geophysical results indicate that the earthwork's dimensions, measured from the midpoint of the embankment, are 25 × 29 m. These dimensions are smaller than those estimated from topographic data. The difference between the surface and subsurface dimensions is partially attributable to erosion and plowing that spread the embankment soil. But it is also a result

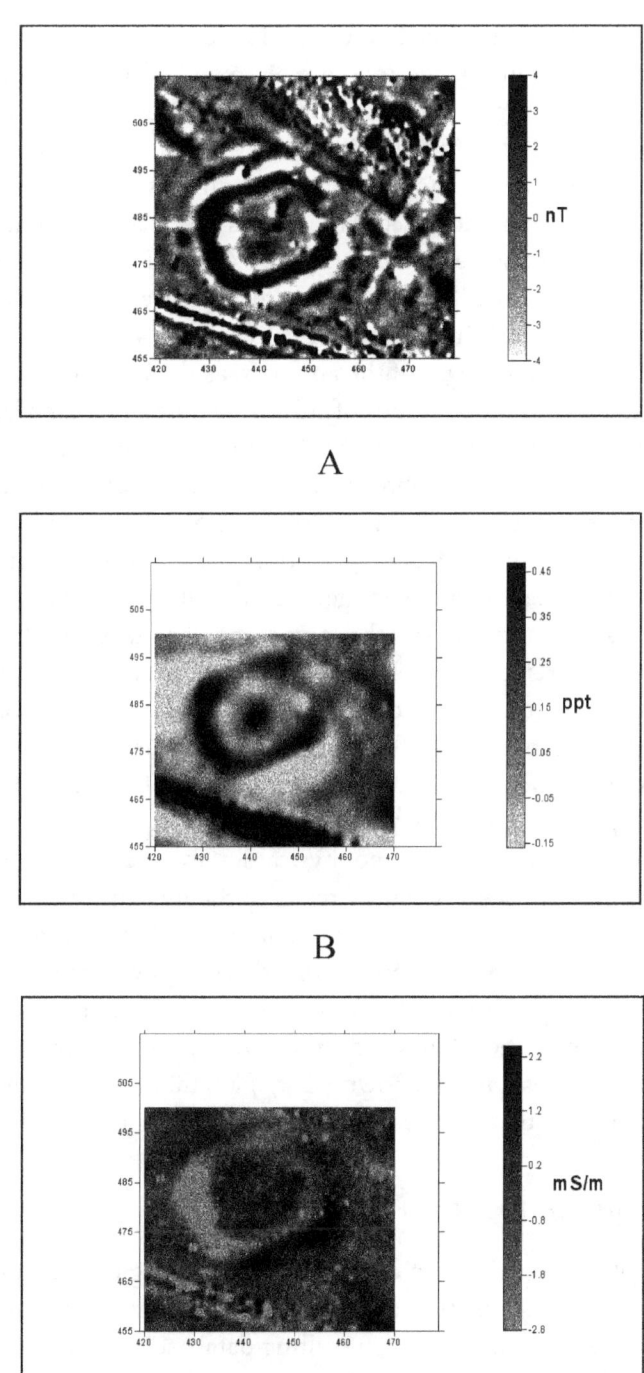

Figure 6.6. Remote sensing images of the Winchester Farm earthwork: (A) gradiometer; (B) magnetic susceptibility; and (C) conductivity.

of the difficulty experienced in identifying both the crest and the midpoint of the embankment on the topographic map and in the geophysical data, respectively. That said, the correspondence between old and new estimates based on the visible, although difficult to discern, embankment make us inclined to believe that the topographic map dimension is closer to the mark.

The gradiometer and susceptibility data reveal a circular anomaly in the middle of the enclosure's interior (figure 6.6A,B). It corresponds to a slightly elevated area on our 1985 topographic map (figure 6.5B) and a dark area on an aerial photograph from March 1952 (figure 6.4). For now, we can only speculate about the origin of the anomaly, as the interiors of enclosures are known to contain various kinds of cultural features including large and small mounds, posts, and burned areas (Clay 1987; Griffin 1947; Squier and Davis 1848; Webb 1941b; Webb and Funkhouser 1932). Because of the topographic map, however, we lean toward the anomaly being a low mound only discernible through vertical exaggeration of elevation data. That is, it is not visible today, even though the vegetation is quite low in the pasture.

Our research underscores the long-recognized fact that the small Adena enclosures consist of four elements. The outermost is an embankment, which can be mapped using traditional methods. In general, the embankments are the most apparent feature of these earthworks, unless there is also a large internal mound, such as the Conus in Marietta (Squier and Davis 1848). Next, there is a partly or completely filled ditch. After years of erosion, determining its shape generally requires a geophysical survey. The ditch's inner margin defines an interior space, generally circular or square. Finally, there is everything else, including mounds, located on what is, in effect, an internal platform. Not all sites, of course, conform to the general pattern. Some of them are reported as having only an embankment or a ditch. These enclosures should be checked again, as the ditches and embankments can be devilishly hard to see. In most instances it is not known what, if anything, was located on the interior platforms—that requires conducting geophysical surveys or excavations.

Small Earthworks in General

To put Winchester Farm in context, the archaeological literature was examined to extract information about what was known about the nature of the small "sacred" enclosures. The resulting database represents an elaboration of Webb's (1941b: 161–66) earlier effort to do the same. Information was mostly gleaned from published sources, although unpublished materials including state site files were also consulted. The total of 259 enclosures is certainly far less than the number originally present in the middle Ohio River region and falls short of the sites mentioned in numerous and often obscure sources.[5] Nevertheless, the sample is large enough to provide an overall impression of the general characteristics of the small enclosures.

The small earthworks have several shapes, although most are circular. The shape was reported for 257 of the enclosures, and 198 (77.0 percent) are circles. Other common forms are arcs, ovals, and rectangles.

The areas of circular enclosures, the great majority of the earthworks, are shown in figure 6.7. Size information is available for 171 circular earthworks, which range from 0.01 ha to 1.35 ha (median = 0.16 ha).[6] Clearly, most of the earthworks were small, although the smallest of them are likely to be underrepresented in the literature. The anomalously high bar in the middle of the histogram is of little consequence, as it is a result of estimate bias. Squier and Davis (1848) reported many enclosures as having 250 ft diameters (hence enclosing 0.46 ha). This tendency no doubt resulted from rounding to a convenient distance. At approximately 0.11 ha, Winchester Farm falls in the small end of the distribution, being somewhat less than the median of 0.16 ha.

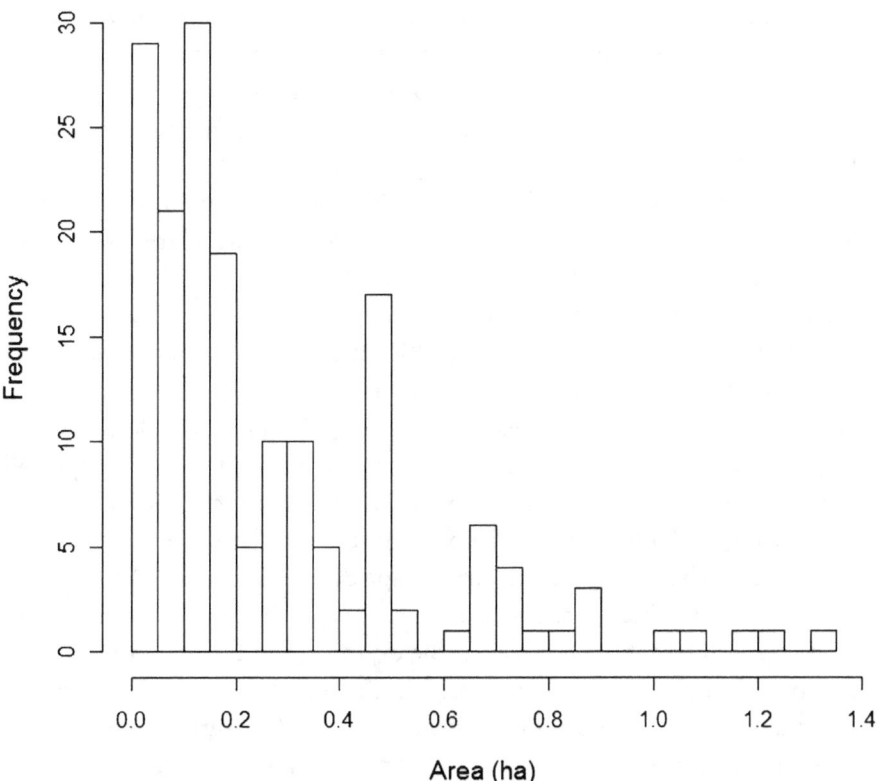

Figure 6.7. The areas of 171 small circular enclosures. The spike in the middle of the distribution results from estimation error by the original investigators.

Of 152 circular enclosures with enough information to determine whether openings were present, 113 (74.3 percent) had noticeable gaps in the embankments. Generally, the enclosures had only a single passageway allowing access to their interiors, but a few had more. Gaps in enclosure walls could be oriented toward any point on the compass, although eastern openings predominated. Of 98 circular earthworks with single openings for which discerning the direction of the gaps was also possible, 31 (31.6 percent) had passageways with orientations between east-northeast and east-southeast, as usually estimated from site maps. That is consistent with what Squier and Davis (1848: 48) stated in the mid-nineteenth century: the "opening [is] oftenest to the east, though by no means observing a fixed rule in that respect." It is also similar to what Webb (1941b) found in an earlier tally of circular earthworks, although his sample was smaller than what was used here.

The enclosures often encircle mounds. Of the 198 circular earthworks, 43 (21.7 percent) had one. Winchester Farm is included among the sites that lack internal mounds, as whether the slight rise visible on the topographic map is indeed a mound has not yet been determined. Should equivalent piles of soil occur elsewhere, they would be invisible without similarly detailed mapping. It should be noted that most mounds are rather small piles of earth, such as Biggs in Kentucky (Hardesty 1965; Squier and Davis 1848). There are, however, some large ones that mostly or completely fill their enclosure's interior, such as Marietta's Conus (Squier and Davis 1848).

Winchester Farm is unusual, but not unique, since a roughly circular embankment surrounds a square platform. Internal square platforms are, of course, often associated with square enclosures (figure 6.8A). There are, however, a number of circular embankments around square internal platforms known in Kentucky and Ohio (Burks 2006, 2010; Fenton and Jefferies 1991; Squier and Davis 1848; Thomas 1894) (figure 6.8B).

Of particular interest in this regard is Burks's (2006, 2010; Burks and Cook 2011) recent geophysical surveys at several of Ohio's Adena and Hopewell earthwork sites. As is true of many other parts of the Eastern Woodlands, erosion, plowing, and other forms of land use have nearly flattened many of these earthworks and have obscured the true shape of others. Burks's (2006, 2010) work has revealed ditches and embankments whose subsurface characteristics are quite different from those visible on the ground. He discovered that a number of small earthworks recorded in the nineteenth century as circles are actually squares with rounded corners. In our literature review—based mostly on earlier accounts, many dating to the nineteenth century—only 25 of 257 (9.7 percent) enclosures are square to rectangular, counting the Winchester Farm embankment as a circle (as opposed to the internal space).

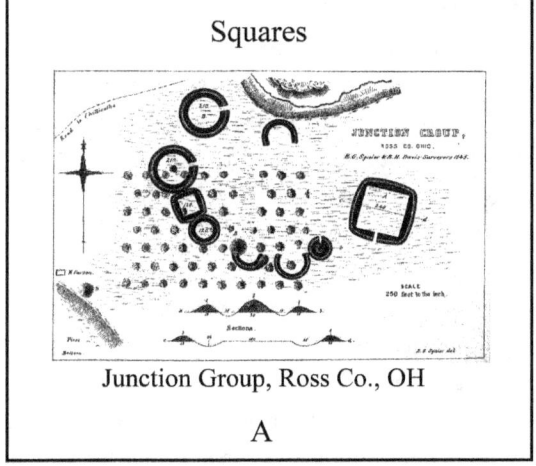

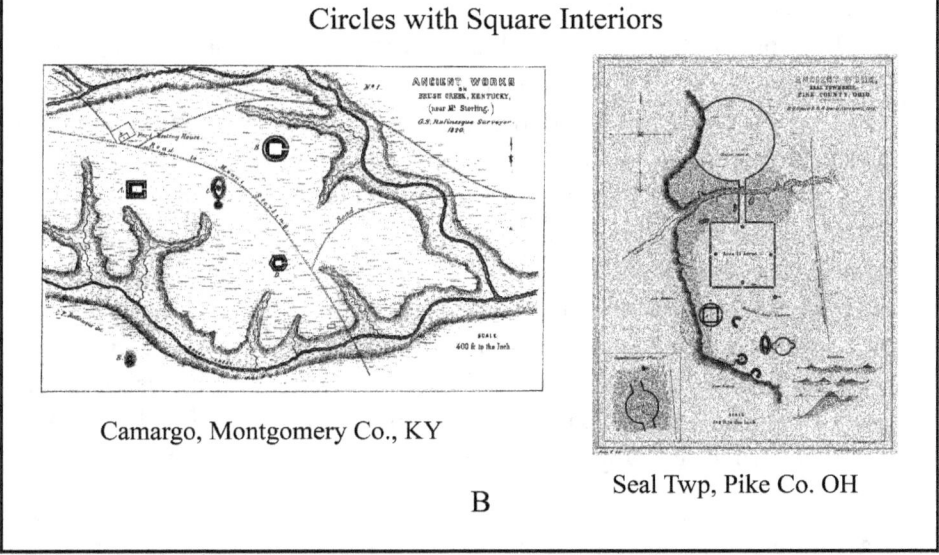

Figure 6.8. Small enclosures that are partly or entirely squares at the Junction Group, Camargo, and Seal Township sites in Kentucky and Ohio. Images from Squier and Davis 1848: plates 22, 24, and 33.

If more were known about these sites, and if the recent geophysical work is any guide to the real state of affairs, then the proportion of square enclosures would increase at the expense of those long thought to be circles.

Summary

The recent fieldwork at Winchester Farm clearly indicates that the earthwork's dimensions match what was recorded much earlier by Rafinesque (1820, 1821) and Webb (1941b). That is encouraging because although Rafinesque's work is often considered to be erroneous, clearly in some instances he was right on target. While the embankment was a circle, the interior platform was a square with rounded corners. The square interior—hitherto thought to be unusual—is consistent with Burks's (2006, 2010; Burks and Cook 2011) recent work in Ohio that has called into question the assumed circular shape of many small earthen enclosures. There might even be a previously unrecognized mound on the interior platform; if so, it was a quite small heap of earth.

Most of the recorded small Adena earthworks are described as circles, and that is likely to remain the case even when some are reclassified as squares with further geophysical work. Gaps in the embankments were usually oriented toward the east, just like what was noted in the mid-nineteenth century (Squier and Davis 1848). Many have mounds within them, and occasionally other features have been identified through excavation, so the interiors were more than open areas.

Perhaps the most important lesson from the Winchester Farm project is that it serves as an example of the benefits of combining traditional mapping, aerial photography, and geophysical survey techniques when characterizing past cultural features. No procedure was sufficient in and of itself. Individually, the various sources of information yielded incomplete, hence wrong (and equally wrong), conclusions. The topographic map and aerial photos lead one to emphasize the circular shape of the embankment, and that is precisely what earlier observers recorded when they visited the site as much as two centuries ago. The geophysical survey, however, focuses attention on the ditch and square internal platform. What one chooses to emphasize depends on whether one is discussing the embankment, ditch, or internal space. Winchester Farm is not simply a circle or a square, but a combination of both.

Acknowledgments

This project would not have been possible without the cooperation and assistance of the current owners of Winchester Farm, Dr. and Mrs. Naoya Yoshida, and Ms. Kara McDermott, client and public relations representative for Winchester Farms. The farm's former owner, the late Mr. Lee Eaton, gave us access to the site in 1985 for the initial topographic mapping. The authors greatly appreciate their interest and long-standing concern for the farm's archaeological resources. Jarrod Burks kindly provided unpublished data and images of the Ohio earthworks he has investigated for over a decade. His work, combined with that of other geophysical specialists working in the Ohio Valley, is establishing an excellent database that in due course will clarify the internal structure of these poorly understood earthen constructions. Terry Tune,

Nick Laracuente, Jeremy Love, Allison Esterle, Cara Mosier, and Brandon Ritchison provided valuable assistance in the field.

Notes

1. The expedition's journey had just begun when the Grave Creek mound was visited on September 10, 1803. Meriwether Lewis was then leading only a small group, and William Clark would later join them farther downstream on the Ohio River, along with other men (Moulton 1986: 77).

2. Squier and Davis (1848: 50–103) referred to "sacred enclosures"—works that made up much of their seminal volume on midwestern earthworks, especially those of Ohio—as one of their two major earthwork categories, the other being defensive in nature. Regardless of the accuracy of the supposed function of these earthworks, which is often questionable with regard to those originally considered defensive works, there is much to recommend the "sacred" appellation with regard to the small circles covered in this chapter.

3. Only two additional earthworks would be added to those of interest if the largest of the "sacred" enclosures, at 1.35 ha, is used as the upper bound of the size range. Once again, no matter how the two groups are separated, the change in sample composition—hence the general characteristics of the small enclosures—is of little consequence.

4. Our size figures were estimated independently of other information about the earthwork, including both earlier reports and the work we did at various times. That was purposeful because we wanted to ensure that any correspondence in estimates was real rather than a result of numbers conforming to expectation.

5. In fact, Squier and Davis (1848: plate 2) show some small circles on their map of the Chillicothe, Ohio, area that are not otherwise described. One such group, however, was recently the subject of a geophysical survey by Burks and Cook (2011), and their work resulted in the discovery of additional enclosures near the ones depicted a century and a half earlier.

6. The average for these 171 circular enclosures is 0.27 ha, but it is a poor measure of central tendency because of the nature of the distribution. Note that Webb (1941b) reported an average diameter of 212 ft, which corresponds to an area of 0.33 ha, for his compilation of 76 circular enclosures. The two area estimates are similar, despite our sample being much larger, indicating that more earthworks are unlikely to result in markedly different results.

7

Persistent Place, Shifting Practice

The Premound Landscape at the Garden Creek Site, North Carolina

ALICE P. WRIGHT

The social landscapes of the Middle Woodland Southeast comprised a variety of culturally meaningful places, from camp sites and settlements to burial grounds and ceremonial centers. Historically, these latter constituents of the landscape, often consisting of monumental mounds and earthworks, have undergone the most intensive archaeological investigation. Thanks to excavations at many of these sites, particularly in the midwestern Hopewell core (e.g., Baby and Langlois 1979; Brown 1979; Greber 1979), extensive information exists regarding the activities that took place at and around Middle Woodland monuments and the social relationships and institutions that those activities reflect (as further demonstrated in the Southeast by several other chapters in this volume).

To complement this body of knowledge, I adopt a diachronic approach to those places on the landscape that eventually supported mounds and earthworks. In the Southeast, although most Middle Woodland platform mounds are a locally unprecedented form of architecture, the sites of their ultimate construction often experienced some sort of occupation before the advent of mound building. I therefore argue that such sites qualify as *persistent places*—loci of repeated anthropogenic activities that "represent the conjunction of particular human behaviors on a particular landscape" (Schlanger 1992: 97; see also Thompson 2010). While the persistence of some places is attributable to their natural suitability for certain (essentially functional) requirements (such as proximity to fertile soils, raw materials, and so forth), persistent places can also emerge where the remains of earlier human activities play a major role in "attracting reuse and reoccupation and structuring the activities associated with ... various occupations" (Schlanger 1992: 97).

With this in mind, it is important to emphasize that the ways in which the remnants of previous occupations shape subsequent occupation at a persistent place may vary. At one end of the continuum, people may repeatedly conduct specific activities at a particular spot for many generations, suggesting the endurance of certain social practices and institutions over time (e.g., Mann 2005; Thompson and Turck 2009). At the other end, a place may undergo a drastic shift in the sorts of activities carried out there, indicating changes in, resistance to, or rejection of existing social structures (e.g., Cobb and King 2005; Thompson 2009, 2010). At southeastern Middle Woodland platform mound sites, the appearance of the mounds themselves represents a substantial change in the long-term use of these places by their occupants. With a more thorough consideration of the history of other on-site activities that predate and/or are contemporaneous with the mounds, the nature of the social changes associated with unprecedented monument construction during the Middle Woodland may become clearer, and Southeastern archaeologists will be able to contribute to worldwide discussions of how and why monuments emerged in different, historically contingent landscapes (e.g., Bradley 1998; Childe 1950; Kolb et al. 1994; Renfrew 1973; Trigger 1990).

In this chapter, I explore the potential of this approach using the Garden Creek Mound No. 2 site, a well-known Middle Woodland platform mound in western North Carolina, as a case study. After describing the various corporate-ceremonial activities that took place on the summits of Mound No. 2 and similar mounds in the region, I use extant data from earlier excavations to evaluate the precedent (or lack thereof) for such activities in submound deposits. Methodologically, this undertaking involved the development of a new technique for identifying structural outlines from the scattered posthole clouds that typify many Middle Woodland sites in the region (Smith 1992). I describe this method in detail with the hope that it may be applied to similar data sets from other sites. My preliminary results reveal both differences and similarities in the ways that the Garden Creek site was persistently used before and immediately after mound construction. When complemented by future analyses, these interpretations may shed light on social processes related to the emergence of monumental architecture in the Appalachian Summit and across the wider landscape of the Southeast during the Middle Woodland period.

On and Under Middle Woodland Platform Mounds

An assessment of the premonumental precedent for certain activities at a persistent place such as a Middle Woodland platform mound requires an understanding of those activities directly associated with the mounds themselves. More than 30 such mounds have been identified and subjected to varying degrees of archaeological study across the Southeast (Keith 2010; Knight

1990). Some of these, including Garden Creek Mound No. 2 and other platform mounds in Georgia, Florida, and Alabama, appear to have been involved with intervillage alliance building and integrative feasting activities (Knight 2001; Lindauer and Blitz 1997). Knight (1990) has referred to this form of mound architecture as the "Kolomoki pattern."

The Kolomoki pattern is defined by a suite of traits related to mound construction and use (Knight 1990, 2001). Such mounds consist of multiple stages of construction, sometimes with contrasting colors of fill. Mound summits lack evidence of roofed structures and are instead marked by irregular scatters of postholes. These have been interpreted as the remains of scaffolds for drying or displaying meat during a feast (Knight 2001). Other features associated with mound summits include large, funnel-shaped postholes, burned areas, hearths, pits, and thin midden lenses. Faunal and paleobotanical data from these contexts at McKeithen (Milanich et al. 1997), Walling (Knight 1990), Kolomoki (Pluckhahn 2003; Pluckhahn et al. 2006), and Biltmore (Kimball et al. 2010) provide additional lines of evidence in support of feasting, such as the remains of diverse plant species and (in most cases) faunal assemblages dominated by high-yield cuts of white-tailed deer. Finally, Kolomoki-pattern summit contexts include exotic artifacts and special-use ceramics, the presence of which may be explained as the result of gift-giving activities associated with feasts (Hayden 2001).

Is there any evidence that feasting or related social-ceremonial activities took place at Kolomoki-pattern mound sites before the mounds were constructed? Unfortunately, at most Middle Woodland platform mounds, there have not been sufficient excavations of submound/premound deposits to allow for an exploration of this issue. While the horizontal extent of premound surface exposure varies from site to site, premound levels tend to get short shrift in site reports and interpretation. For example, in the brief descriptions of the Kolomoki-pattern sites Block-Sterns and Waddells Mill Pond (Brose 1979), submound surfaces are not mentioned at all. At McKeithen (Milanich et al. 1997) and Cold Springs (Jefferies 1994), the platform mounds are acknowledged to have been built over a midden (and in the case of Cold Springs, at least partially over one structure), but no further interpretation is offered.

Knight (1990) provides the most thorough extant description of a premound midden in his report of the Walling site. Though only a small surface area was exposed, Knight (1990: 158) makes the case that "the pre-mound knoll surface was already the locus of special, nondomestic activity," because the ceramic type diversity of the premound midden was higher than that in the mound fill (which was interpreted as redeposited

The Premound Landscape at the Garden Creek Site, North Carolina 111

domestic refuse), the premound midden included rare and/or exotic artifacts, and premound faunal remains included a high proportion of meat-bearing portions of deer. These lines of evidence suggest continuity in some of the activities conducted before and after mound construction at certain persistent places across the Middle Woodland landscape. This scenario may be clarified through an investigation of materials from more horizontally extensive excavations of premound contexts, such as those from Garden Creek.

Garden Creek Mound No. 2 (31Hw2) occupies the western edge of a small floodplain along the Pigeon River in Haywood County, North Carolina (Dickens 1976; Heye 1919; Keel 1976) (figure 7.1). Mound No. 2 was fully excavated by Bennie Keel as part of the University of North Carolina's Chero-

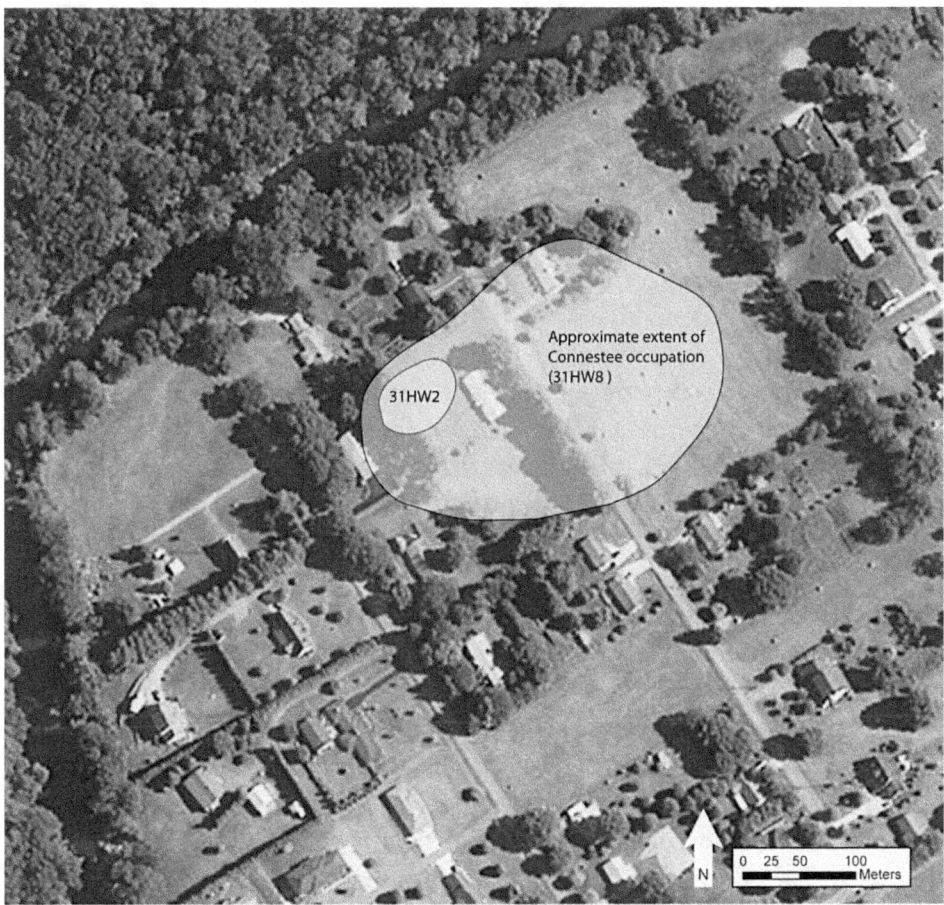

Figure 7.1. Location of Garden Creek Mound No. 2 (31Hw2) and the surrounding Connestee phase occupation (31Hw8), based on Keel's 1965–66 fieldwork. Overlaying aerial image of present-day landscape at the site. Figure prepared by Alice Wright.

kee Project in 1966 (Keel 1976). His efforts revealed many of the characteristics that Knight would later include in the Kolomoki pattern: multiple stages of mound construction (two); irregular patterns of postholes and features on consecutive mound summits; and a small but notable assemblage of exotic artifacts indicative of regional interactions with groups to the north and south. Although the upper portions of the mound were partially destroyed before excavations began, a premound midden was exposed and excavated to subsoil across a 13.7 × 25.9 m excavation block, where it ranged from 6 cm thick (adjacent to the mound and truncated by the plow zone) to 20 cm thick (under and protected by the mound). The quantity of ceramics in the midden suggests that the premound occupation was "intense and relatively continuous" (Keel 1976: 95). The midden dates to no later than the Middle Woodland Connestee phase (AD 200–800), to which the construction stages of the mound are also assigned.

The broad horizontal exposure of submound deposits allowed Keel to identify among a seemingly random scatter of more than a thousand postholes the complete outline of a single rectangular structure (figure 7.2). Measuring roughly 5.9 × 6.1 m, the areal extent of this building (36.2 m^2) falls within the predicted range of Middle Woodland/Hopewellian residential structures, 13.5–85.5 m^2 (Smith 1992). The posts that constituted Structure 1 were recognized at the base of the midden by their distinctive fill, which consisted of dark midden soil in the upper third of the hole and white, coarse sand in the lower two-thirds. According to Keel (1976: 95), "It appeared that this structure was removed and the holes filled with sand in one continuous operation, perhaps to clear the area for the construction of the primary mound." This pattern might reflect the closure of a ritually significant or otherwise special structure in advance of subsequent, ritually significant constructions (i.e., the mound) (e.g., Heitman 2007), although analogous posthole evidence from other sites (such as the ditch at Biltmore Mound; Kimball et al., chapter 8, this volume) must be thoroughly considered before drawing any firm conclusions. At the very least, the sand-filled postholes do set this structure apart from the few known Middle Woodland residential structures in the Southern Appalachians. Last, in addition to Structure 1, Keel also recorded and individually excavated 21 discrete intact features in the premound midden.

Given this sort of premound archaeological record, the Garden Creek site provides an excellent opportunity to examine the early life history (sensu Ashmore 2002) of a platform mound site. Instead of the premound midden being treated as a single unit of analysis, a common strategy employed during assessment of Middle Woodland platform mounds, the Garden Creek

Figure 7.2. Structure 1 below Garden Creek Mound No. 2, with paper plates marking constituent postholes. Photo courtesy of the University of North Carolina Research Laboratories of Archaeology (1966).

archaeological record makes possible the analysis of particular features/feature classes and architectural structure(s). These categories represent an archaeologically recoverable record of specific events, activities, or sequences of activities at the scale at which they were experienced in the past. As a result, a diachronic consideration of these more discrete units of analysis can reveal the histories or genealogies of certain social practices at persistent places (Joyce and Lopiparo 2005; McAnany and Hodder 2009; Mills 2009; Pauketat and Alt 2005). Moreover, this approach renders premound and mound summit deposits more directly comparable, since the latter are already conceptualized as the remains of a series of particular activities (such as feasts, post emplacement, and so forth). This sort of comparison allows for a more nuanced evaluation of continuity and change in various activities concomitant with mound construction at Garden Creek. In the remainder of this chapter, I explore the premound histories of practice at this persistent place—a process that involves not only the examination of existing feature data sets but also a methodology for assessing the potential "architectural significance" of scattered posthole clouds below the mound.

Pits and Hearths: A Material Record of Premound Activities

As mentioned above, Keel identified 21 intact features below Mound No. 2 proper. On the basis of published descriptions and field notes, I have divided these features into two categories: hearths (both surface and pit hearths) and pits. Although the sample size is certainly small, the 14 submound hearths occur in three size classes based on approximate areal extent: small (approximately 0.20–0.49 m^2), medium (0.5–0.99 m^2), and large (greater than 1.0 m^2). Unfortunately, insufficient analysis has been conducted on these features' faunal and paleobotanical assemblages to determine whether they differ by size class, and sherd counts from hearths predictably increase with hearth size.

However, in contrast to small hearths, six of the nine hearths with areas greater than 0.5 m^2 included artifacts that might be indicative of gift giving and other activities commonly associated with feasting: bar gorgets, gorget blanks, prismatic bladelets made from exotic raw materials, and figurine fragments. Similar sorts of artifacts are known from some mound summit hearths at Mound No. 2 and from Kolomoki-pattern mound summits. In general, though, summit hearths ($n = 8$) at Garden Creek are larger than those below the mound, particularly when the outlier 3.1 m^2 submound hearth is excluded from comparison. This pattern is perhaps a preliminary indication that there might be differences in degree, rather than differences in kind, between some activities in premound and mound summit contexts. For instance, the feasting/gift-giving ceremonies inferred for the mound summits may have involved more people than similar events that predated the mound, which may have required more food and larger hearths. Further analysis of subsistence remains from the premound hearths and comparison between cooking/serving ceramic assemblages in premound and mound summit contexts could be used to evaluate this hypothesis.

Pit features at Garden Creek suffer from smaller samples (seven that predate the mound, and five from the mound summits), negating meaningful statistical comparison across contexts. There is, however, one submound pit that stands out: a small basin dug into the subsoil that was lined with cut mica, which Keel assigned to the early Middle Woodland Pigeon phase (300 BC–AD 200). Based on analogy to mica-lined burial pits from Hopewell sites such as Mound City, Ohio (Mills 1922; Squier and Davis 1848), it is probable that this feature had some specialized, ceremonial purpose. Whatever the purpose, its expression as a mica-lined pit is exclusive to the premound contexts at Garden Creek. Meanwhile, other ostensibly ceremonial features are unique to the summits of Mound No. 2, including exceptionally large postholes and a cache of green steatite. It therefore seems likely that ceremonial activities were taking place both before and after mound construction, but the exact types of activities and their significance may have changed over time, in concert with the emergence of the platform mound.

Postholes and Premound Architecture

At first glance, plan maps of the top of the premound midden and the top of the subsoil at Garden Creek resemble the summit maps: they are all dominated by dense scatters of postholes. In fact, the map of the subsoil includes nearly as many postholes as observed on the primary and secondary summits and top of the premound midden combined. However, there is no reason to assume on the basis of this resemblance that the scaffolding activities proposed to explain mound summit postholes also occurred during premound occupation. It is possible that meat-drying/displaying scaffolds emerged only in ceremonial contexts afforded by monumental architecture, whereas postholes in premound deposits represent a palimpsest of architectural features—a hypothesis preliminarily supported by the identification of Structure 1. What remains to be seen is whether Structure 1 was, in fact, the sole structure below Mound No. 2. Although there are challenges in detangling structural patterns from site maps rather than field observations (Knight 2007; Prezzano 1988), I have attempted to go beyond merely connecting the dots by using digitized plan maps, field notes, and metric posthole data to clarify architectural remains.

Methodology

Evaluating the presence of premound architecture at Garden Creek required a set of expectations for the sorts of structures that were most likely to be encountered. To that end, I considered the recently excavated Middle Woodland record from the Macon County Airport site in southwestern North Carolina, which included at least 49 structures from this period (Tasha Benyshek, pers. comm. 2010). Based on these data, Connestee structures can be either rectangular or circular and range considerably in size. Posts in the center of walls tend to be deeper than corner posts (if corner posts preserve at all), and some structures have a single central support post. Posts can be up to a meter apart, though this may be as much a product of preservation as aboriginal building techniques. In the case of both Garden Creek's Structure 1 and the Macon County Airport site, no hearths have been identified inside the structures.

More specific to Garden Creek, Keel's Structure 1 suggests a range of posthole variability that might be expected within the remains of a single building. Structure 1 consisted of 29 postholes, approximately 13.5–33.3 cm in diameter and 12.7–71.1 cm deep. Combined, the Macon County Airport site and Structure 1 data provided the basic parameters I used to identify additional structural remains from the premound archaeological record at Garden Creek.

Keel's subsoil plan map includes 1,297 total postholes. Recorded depth measurements exist for 663 of these, concentrated in the northwestern portion of the excavation unit; diameter measurements could be calculated for all 1,297 posts. Using ArcGIS 9.3 software, I first isolated all posts that matched the diameter and depth of postholes in Structure 1. Selecting only posts between 13.5 cm and 33.3 cm in diameter eliminated considerable noise, increasing the possibility that architectural patterns may be identified. However, nearly all posts for which depths were measured fell between 12.7 cm and 71.1 cm deep; to create tighter parameters, I began selecting posthole depths within a range of 20.3 cm, roughly double the standard deviation of posthole depths observed in Structure 1. Though this method might have missed especially deep or shallow posts in a given structure, it should have captured the majority of posts in any given structure's outline.

Within my subset of posts 13.5–33.3 cm in diameter, I selected several iterations of posthole depths encompassing 20.3 cm ranges: in other words, I selected all posts 2.5–22.8 cm deep, 5.1–25.4 cm deep, and so forth, up to 48.3–68.6 cm deep. I chose to display some of these selections simultaneously to assess whether variable depth patterns, such as deeper posts in the middle of walls, were apparent. As linear arrangements of posts and potential structures became visible in these selections, I removed their constituent posts from my sample, reducing noise that would impede the identification of additional structures.

Because circular Connestee structures have been difficult to identify even in the midst of excavation, I limited my identifications to rectangular structures. Furthermore, I identified only those structures for which the majority of posts were assigned depth measurements; there may indeed be additional structures in the half of the excavation block for which posthole depth was not recorded, but they could not be identified using the present methods.

Results

These efforts led to the tentative identification of at least five additional structures underneath Garden Creek Mound No. 2 (figure 7.3). All of these structures were identified from the plan map of the subsoil. Applying the same technique to postholes mapped on the top of the premound midden identi-

The Premound Landscape at the Garden Creek Site, North Carolina 117

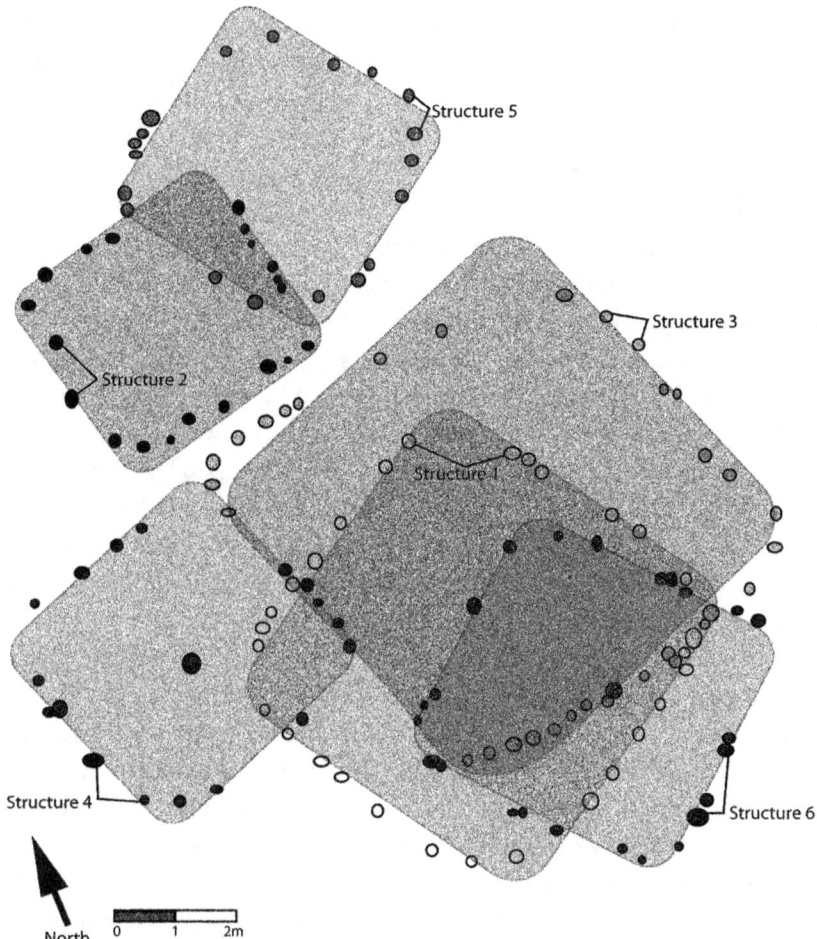

Figure 7.3. Posthole outlines of six structures below Garden Creek Mound No. 2, including Structure 1. Figure prepared by Alice Wright.

fied no structures, suggesting that architecture analogous to Structure 1 was present only early in the life history of this persistent place.

Structure 2 consists of 20 postholes that demarcate a nearly complete rectangle measuring 3.4 × 4 m, with a noticeable gap only in the northeast corner. Interestingly, posts in the center of the east and west walls are deeper than posts near the corners, as suggested by the Macon County Airport site data. The only feature found inside the structure was a refuse pit that included Early Woodland Swannanoa pottery, but whether the structure postdates or is contemporaneous with this pit is unclear.

Structure 2 overlaps Structure 5, a roughly rectangular arrangement of posts at the northern end of the excavation block measuring 3.7 × 4.3 m. Major gaps in the pattern occur in the west wall and northeast corner, so acceptance of this structure must be cautious. A pit appears at the northern edges of the structure but is probably intrusive from later levels, while another, larger pit that contained very few artifacts is near the center of the structure. Based on existing data, it is impossible to say whether this latter pit and the surrounding structure are contemporaneous. Similarly, it is presently unclear whether Structure 2 or Structure 5 appeared first.

Chronological ambiguity also characterizes the other four structures (including Structure 1), which overlap each other to varying degrees. Structure 3 represents the largest building yet identified on the site, at approximately 6.1 × 6.4 m. There are obvious linear arrangements of posts for the north, south, and east walls and a clearly defined northwest corner, but the northeast and southeast corners are not well defined. Interestingly, no west well is apparent. On the one hand, these posts may have been obliterated by subsequent activities. On the other hand, the existing posthole pattern might represent a series of screens or walls rather than an enclosed structure, comparable, perhaps, to open-ended C-shaped posthole alignments at Middle Woodland sites in other parts of the Eastern Woodlands (Smith 1992). A small hearth was identified at the subsoil inside Structure 3's northeast corner, but again, its temporal relationship with the building cannot be specified at this time.

Immediately west of Structure 3, Structure 4 exhibits a roughly square shape, notably lacking northeast or southeast corners. It measures 4.6 m per side. Like Structure 2 and structures from the Macon County Airport site, Structure 4 has especially deep posts in the middle of at least two walls. Additionally, Structure 4 is one of two structures at Garden Creek with a probable central support post. Two rock-filled hearths—one associated with Early Middle Woodland Pigeon sherds and the other with Late Middle Woodland Connestee sherds—were identified within the margins of Structure 4.

Finally, Structure 6 measures approximately 4.3 × 4.9 m, with noticeable gaps in the eastern corner and northwestern wall. No features appear within the margins of the pattern, but like Structure 3, there is a central support post.

These structures can be classified into two groups based on their orientations. Structures 2, 3, and 4 are aligned so that the center of each wall nearly faces a cardinal direction (i.e., the middle of the north walls face 13–15° west of north). Structures 1, 5, and 6 are rotated slightly, so that the corners of the structures point nearly to the cardinal directions (i.e., the northernmost corners face 3–12° east of north). In my mind, the apparently nonrandom positioning of the posthole patterns increases the likelihood that they represent real structural remains, not simply chance connections between dots. Although the emic significance of different orientations is unknown, these groupings may correspond to successive occupations, in which structures sharing the same orientation were in use at the same time. Of course, this hypothesis and other temporal aspects of the premound occupation would benefit from additional radiocarbon dates from different structural and feature contexts.

Discussion

To summarize, the postholes identified in the subsoil beneath Garden Creek Mound No. 2 align to form at least six structures, not all of which could have been in use simultaneously during the early life history of the site. This discovery has several implications not only for the comparison of social practices in premonumental and monumental contexts but also for our understandings of continuities and changes that entirely predate mound construction. Unlike Structure 1, none of the newly identified structures show signs of being specially dismantled, and none of their constituent postholes were specially marked with unique fill. Whereas these traits suggest some possible ceremonial significance for Structure 1, there is no architectural evidence that Structures 2–6 played this sort of specialized role. Additionally, features in four of the five new structures included no ritually suggestive artifacts; the exception is a hearth with a gorget blank in Structure 4, but as mentioned above, whether the hearth and the structure were contemporaneous is unknown.

Given these results, it seems possible that all of the newly identified structures represent the remains of residential (as opposed to corporate-ceremonial) structures from a series of occupations. The surface areas of the structures bolster this hypothesis, because (admittedly, like Structure 1) they fall within the expected range for Middle Woodland residential buildings (Smith 1992). Furthermore, based on existing assemblage inventories, many of the premound pits and hearths could just as easily represent domestic activities as those associated with ceremonial feasting, though, of course, additional faunal/paleobotanical analyses are necessary to demonstrate this point. This sort of palimpsest of post alignments and features representing a sequence of domestic occupations would be expected if seasonally dispersed groups were aggregating at this ecologically rich location for part of the year, as some models of Middle Woodland settlement in the Southeast have proposed (Fortier et al. 1989).

However, the presence of the still incompletely understood Structure 1 indicates that social practices at this location underwent some change even before the construction of Mound No. 2. Though extant evidence is limited, it suggests that Structure 1 played some specialized role that required its purposeful deconstruction, complete with unique posthole treatment, perhaps as part of a closure and/or renewal ritual. There is also evidence from some submound features that more than residential activities took place before mound construction: that is, the gorgets, bladelets, and figurine fragments in certain hearths, as well as the mica-lined pit. But importantly, these data suggest that premound ceremonial practice differed in some ways from subsequent mound-summit feasting activities as proposed for the Kolomoki pattern. Certain ostensibly nonresidential features exist only in the premound midden (i.e., the mica-lined pit) or only on the mound summit (i.e., the steatite cache and massive postholes). Perhaps more strikingly, there is no known, structural posthole pattern comparable to Structure 1 on either mound summit at Garden Creek or at other Kolomoki pattern mound summits.

Together, extant feature and architectural data from submound deposits at the Garden Creek site reveal a history of shifting social practices that predated mound construction. Some aspects of this history, such as Structure 1 and the mica-lined pit, suggest that there was a precedent, at least in a general sense, for ceremonial activities at this spot on the landscape before mound construction, as Knight observed at the Walling site. When the available remains of these "special, non-domestic" activities are compared between premound and mound summit deposits at Garden Creek, however, it becomes clear that not all activities subsumed under the Kolomoki-pattern umbrella, such as larger-scale communal feasting and possibly gift giving, were practiced at the site before Mound No. 2 provided a platform for their performance. Similarly, certain premound practices—perhaps, most importantly, residential occupation—ceased at this particular location once the mound was erected.

In any attempt to discover broader social implications of this diachronic trajectory of site use, several additional lines of evidence merit consideration. In particular, further interpretation would benefit immensely from more precise stratigraphic and radiometric dating of submound deposits to determine the chronological relationships among different structures and features. Additionally, as emphasized by Littleton and Allen (2007), one aspect of persistent places that should be explored for Garden Creek is the way in which this locality structured the organization activities across the wider landscape. Ongoing surveys and excavations in the Appalachian Summit have the potential to clarify such interplace relationships and reveal other patterns of continuity and change in landscape use that may be related to shifts in ceremonial practice and the emergence of platform mound architecture at Garden Creek.

Lacking these data sets, I am hesitant to offer a definitive statement of the broader, structural social implications of the observed shifts in the activities that occurred before and alongside mound building at Garden Creek.

However, as indicated above, the changes in a general sense seem to represent differences in degree rather than differences in kind. Before and after mound construction, this persistent place was the site of ceremonial activities, though their particulars differed over time. Moreover, although there is no evidence of mound-contemporaneous residences on or immediately adjacent to Mound No. 2, the tradition of domestic occupation at Garden Creek—first observed in the newly identified structures below Mound No. 2—may have persisted across the surrounding floodplain or at other nearby locations.

In sum, the Garden Creek site appears to have witnessed the elaboration and adjustment of social practices that were *not* locally unprecedented immediately before and coincident with the construction of Mound No. 2. The monument itself, conversely, was a novel architectural development in the Appalachian Summit Middle Woodland landscape. Together, these details suggest that this persistent place was the site of neither a wholesale perpetuation of traditional activities nor their total, radical transformation/abandonment but rather something in between. I tentatively suggest that this pattern may be clarified by considering how Middle Woodland interaction networks encouraged various forms of culture contact (sensu Silliman 2005) across the Eastern Woodlands landscape (for the Appalachian Summit, see Chapman and Keel 1979). Myriad interactions may have provided stimuli not only for the adoption of novel social practices but also for the perpetuation or enhancement of local traditions (e.g., Lightfoot et al. 1998).

Acknowledgments

My work at Garden Creek has been possible thanks to the careful excavations and record keeping of Bennie Keel, whose support and bottomless knowledge about Appalachian Summit history has proven invaluable. Vincas Steponaitis and Steve Davis provided much-appreciated assistance as I navigated the Garden Creek materials at the University of North Carolina. Thanks must also go to Cameron Gokee for guiding me through the ArcGIS help menus and to Tasha Benyshek for providing data from the Macon County Airport site. This chapter has benefited from comments from and conversation with Casey Barrier, Eddie Henry, Christina Perry, Ashley Schubert, Howard Tsai, and Rob Beck. Last, thank you to Edward Henry for the conversations and enthusiasm that motivated this volume.

8

Biltmore Mound and the Appalachian Summit Hopewell

LARRY R. KIMBALL, THOMAS R. WHYTE, AND GARY D. CRITES

Hopewellian ceremonies of the Appalachian Summit were undoubtedly varied and undertaken at a variety of locations across the landscape. However, it can be argued that only Garden Creek Mound No. 2 (31Hw2—Keel 1976; Wright, chapter 7, this volume) and Biltmore Mound (31Bn174—Kimball et al. 2010) are documented Hopewellian/Connestee phase mound sites in western North Carolina. Both have single mounds placed adjacent to secondary rivers and were encircled by relatively large habitation areas. The mounds are multistage earthen platforms that are oval to square and supported some sort of public architecture with fired floors. Each mound has at least one construction stage composed of two or more layers representing one ritual cycle. The mounds were constructed of variably colored and textured soils (from light/dark and water/dry-land sources) derived from a variety of locations. Biltmore Mound was primarily built out rather than up with several mantles, which, given the contemporaneity argued from the radiocarbon evidence (below), may have constituted a complete ritual cycle of mound construction. Ritual items, exotic ceramic and lithic artifacts, and organic materials were discarded on and adjacent to the mound.

Because of remarkable preservation, more specific insight into ritual use of Hopewellian platform mounds is manifest at the Biltmore Mound. This Connestee phase (AD 300–600) platform mound and associated 10 ha habitation area are on the south floodplain of the Swannanoa River just above its confluence with the French Broad River (figures 8.1 and 8.5). Situated in the center of the Asheville Basin, Biltmore Mound was surrounded by a huge climax chestnut forest with rich biodiversity and great relief ranging from rich valleys to very high mountain peaks. The site is also at the intersection of two major Native American trails—Rutherford's War Trace and the Catawba Trail (Myer 1971).

The mound comprises three fired structural floors. Around it is an approxi-

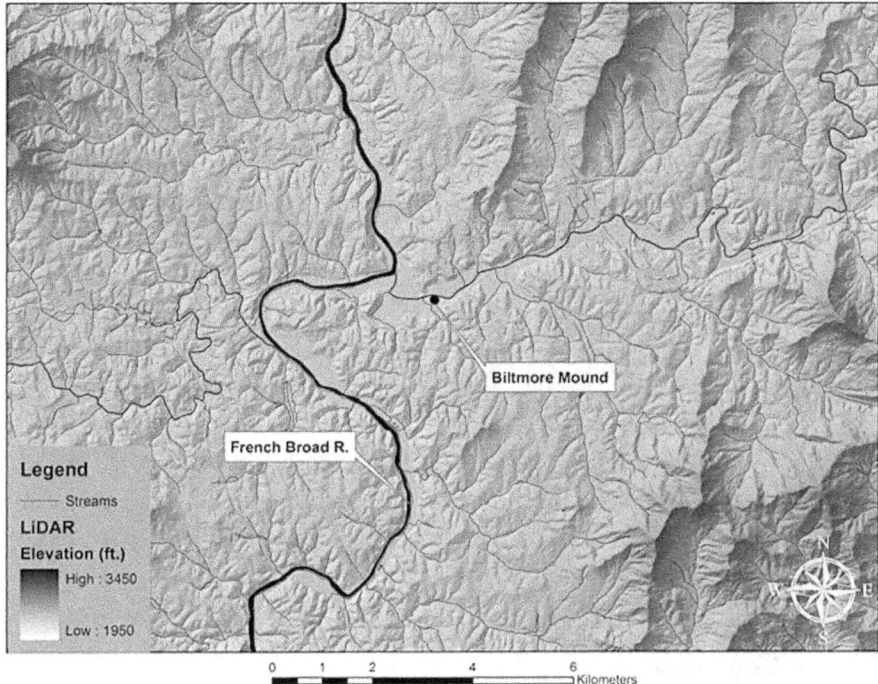

Figure 8.1. Location of Biltmore Mound in Buncombe County, North Carolina. Map prepared by Christopher R. Moore.

mately seven-meter-wide ditch excavated into subsoil. The in-filling of the ditch was initiated with sterile deposits of light-colored (tan and red) clays and a burned log. Next, ritual items (including "killed" carnivore jaws, copper, mica, bone awls, and so forth) and exceptional faunal and floral assemblages were deposited into it during the late spring through fall months. These could represent the remains from feasts and rituals undertaken on the mound. The ditch was in-filled with at least three episodes, and upon completion the wall of a very large (probably open arbor-like) structure was placed exactly down its centerline. At the center of the mound (and assumedly this structure), large posts were erected. Some of these posts and all of the posts centered on the ditch were pulled and then backfilled with light-colored sediment before the mound was abandoned.

The mechanisms of the involvement of South Appalachian Hopewell in the wider Hopewell phenomenon cannot be explained exclusively as reciprocal exchange of exotic goods between traders/shamans/elites at select villages in the region (Chapman and Keel 1979). This exchange model does not explain how or why ceremonies on mound structures at ceremonial centers occurred. It makes more sense to envision a variety of reasons that Hopewell peoples would travel afar and leave exotic items at Connestee mounds. Possibilities include scheduled communal feasts; construction of a multilayered earthen platform by diverse ethnic groups; creation of a ditch around the mound and centered on a very large ritual post, possibly symbolizing an "Axis Mundi" (Carr and Case 2005a: 194–96, 296; Case and Carr 2008: 295–303; Eliade 1972: 259–74; Hall 1997: 102–8); and observation of cosmogonic events such as summer solstice sunrises over Mt. Mitchell in alignment with the central ritual post.

The order of our discussion follows the evident (and arguably ritual) steps undertaken by the mound creators: mound construction; the erection of structures and ritual posts; the creation of a ritual space around the mound by a ditch (which was backfilled in a specific manner); what kinds of foods were consumed on the mound; and, finally, how the variously colored mound stages, the ditch, the mound structure, and the central ritual post together not only symbolize the "Axis Mundi" and three-world system but also were used to observe the summer solstice sunrise over Mt. Mitchell.

Mound Construction

Biltmore Mound comprises a low, wide multistage earthen platform on the north edge of a habitation area. Excavations over an area of 212 m², the southwestern quadrant of the mound, reveal a complex history of mound construction (figures 8.2–8.4; Kimball et al. 2010: figs. 3–5). Intrusive into this portion of the mound were 18 pits and 62 medium to large postholes, including those of pulled posts and one very large post with a post-insertion trench. All mound postholes are larger than those discerned in the habitation area (where only 100 m² have been explored).

The mound was built over premound middens overlying a yellowish-brown B-horizon (figure 8.2a). The lowest midden was dated to AD 390 ± 60 (Kimball et al. 2010: table 2). At some time between AD 400 and 600, two prepared floors separated from one another by about 10 cm of dark brown silty loam were sequentially laid upon these middens. Around AD 580–600, a third prepared floor (Floor 3 or Mound Stage L) was constructed over a 20 cm layer of dark brown silty loam. This distinctive fine silty subsoil sediment was derived from an off-mound source and then fired. It contains patches of pale brown ash and charcoal. Numerous pit features and postholes of later structures intrude Floor 3.

Floor 3 is overlain by Mound Stage K, an olive-gray clayey loam mixed with grayish-brown silty and red clayey loams. Abundant charcoal indicates that a combustion event contributed to its formation. At nearby Garden

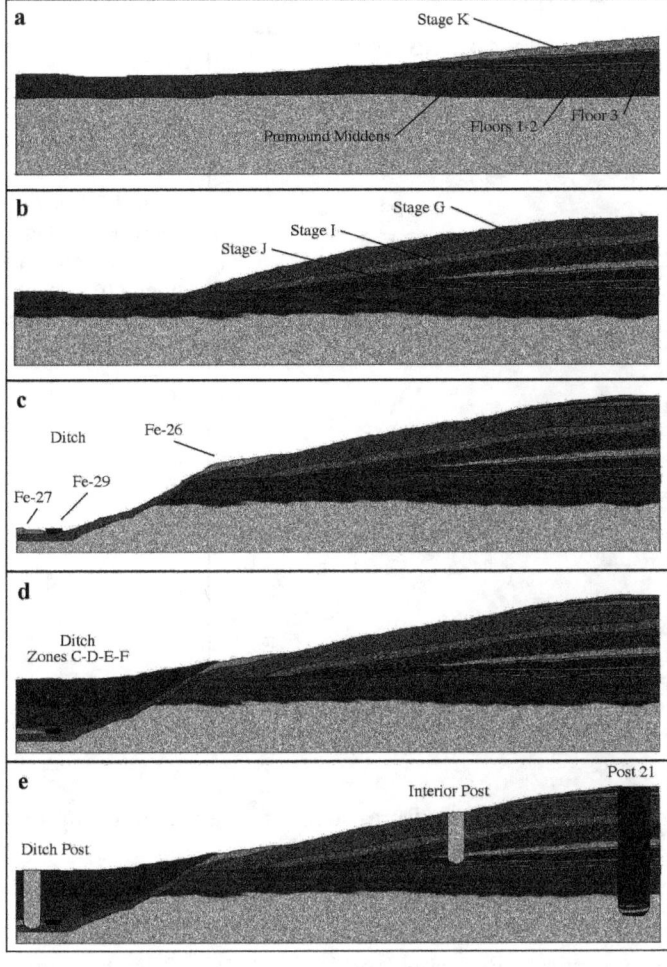

Figure 8.2. Construction stages of Biltmore Mound. Figure prepared by Larry Kimball and Thomas Whyte.

Creek Mound No. 2, Keel (1976: 78) noted a similar layer of ash above the prepared floor, which he considered to "have originated from the combustion of the roof" of the mound-top structure.

If Mound Stages L and K represent a prepared floor and overlying deposit that signaled the termination of the use of this surface (assumedly with a structure), then Mound Stage J (figure 8.2b) must represent the beginning of a new cycle of mound construction. This thick layer of dark grayish-brown silty loam represents a redeposited midden very rich in artifacts, faunal remains, fire-cracked rock, and carbonized plant remains.

Overlying this is a lighter and more homogeneous deposit (Mound Stage I) of dark grayish-brown silty loam (figure 8.2b). A charcoal layer at the top of Stage I is dated to AD 580 ± 50. Next is Mound Stage G, a thick, basket-loaded mixture of both A- and B-horizon soils. This mixing produced

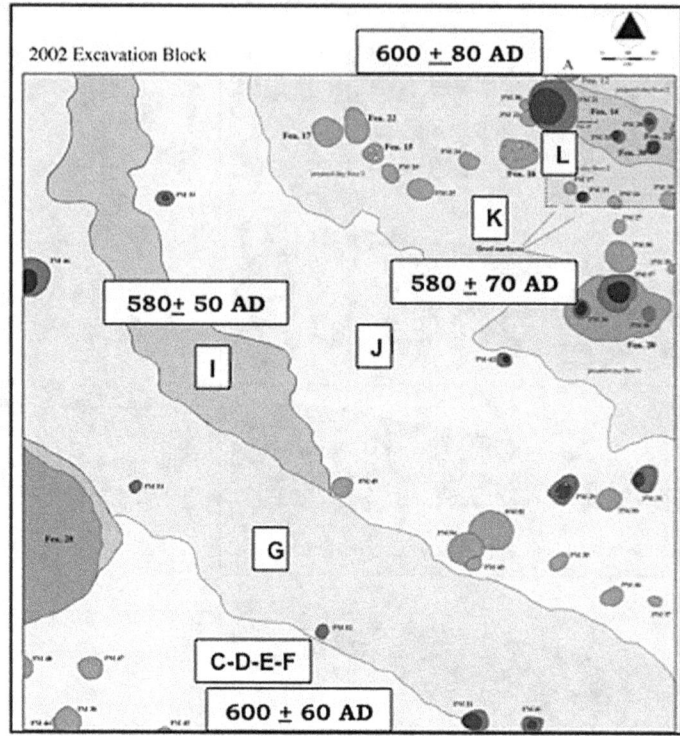

Figure 8.3. Plan view of construction stages of Biltmore Mound as seen from 2002 excavations, with relevant dates. Figure prepared by Larry Kimball.

a brownish-yellow silty loam mottled with brown silty loam containing few cultural remains.

Mound Stages J through G (figure 8.3) are concentric and represent the southwestern extent of the mound. Similar in shape to some Middle Woodland earthworks and structures (Benyshek and Webb 2009a, 2009b; Brown 1979: 214–15; Greber 1979: 30, 2009: 20; Jefferies et al., chapter 6, this volume; Keel 1976: 99; Keith 2010: 260–61, 264; Wright, chapter 7, this volume), the pattern of mound stages suggests a squared mound with rounded corners. The four overlapping radiocarbon assays that document all mound-building stages, the subsequent ditch (discussed below), and one of the internal posts of the mound structure indicate no significant time lapse between Mound Stage K (Prepared Floor 3) and the filling of the ditch.

Ditch

Flanking the mound and revealed in the southwestern corner of the excavation block is a midden-filled ditch (figures 8.2d and 8.4), approximately seven meters in width, that had been excavated into subsoil at the toe of Mound Stage G. Exhibiting a complex history, it was lined with a light brown silty

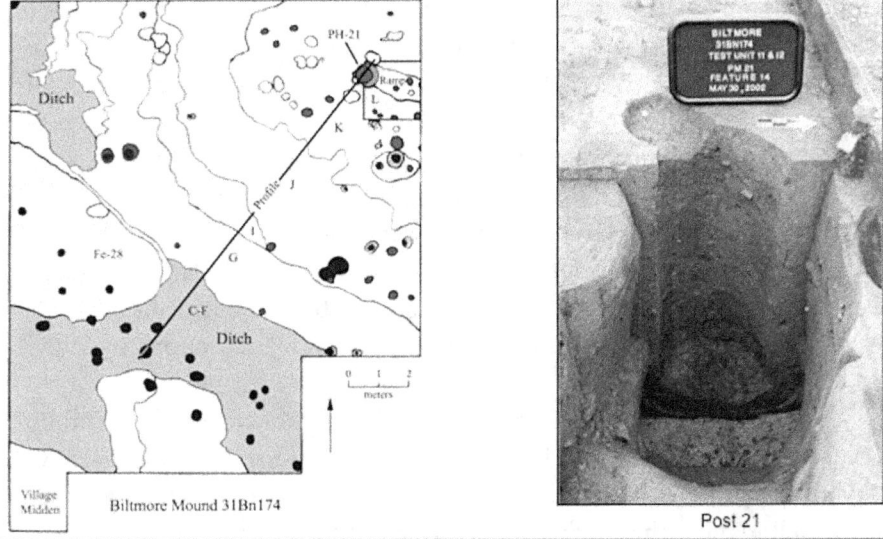

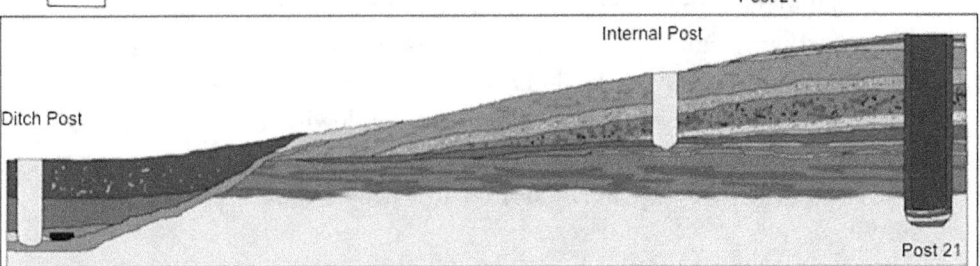

Figure 8.4. *Top left,* plan view of construction stages of Biltmore Mound as seen from 2008 excavations; *top right,* photo of large posthole (Post 21); *bottom,* profile showing construction stages with the posthole. Figure prepared by Larry Kimball and Thomas Whyte.

loam (Mound Stage F). Then a cap of coarse orange sand (Feature 26) was placed along the lip of the ditch and a small mound of tan clayey silt (Feature 27) was deposited in the bottom. Next to this was placed a burned log (Feature 29) that was dated to AD 600 ± 60.

The ditch, so prepared, was then filled with three subsequent midden-like deposits: Zones C, D, and E, each containing an abundance of artifacts, carbonized plant remains, and faunal remains. Artifacts include exotic and locally made pottery; items of marine shell, copper, and mica; fractured quartz crystals; and bladelets and projectile points of exotic flint. All of these items and the deposits that contain them likely had animistic meaning in a relational ontology (see Reynolds 2009; Zedeño 2009). In addition, items traditionally associated with ritual paraphernalia were found, including shaped carnivore jaws (black bear, red wolf, gray wolf, and dog) and a shaped black bear baculum. All items appear to have been ritually "killed" prior to deposition by fracture or burning.

Ditches are common features of sacred spaces in southeastern prehistory. A ditch was used at the Adena-age Biggs site to define sacred space around burial mounds (Clay 1986: 587). Comparable examples of ditches at Scioto Hopewell mounds include a "trench fence" outside the Big House beneath Edwin Harness Mound (Greber 1979: fig. 6.3), Hopeton Earthworks, and the Great Circle at Newark (Clay 1986: figure 23.3; Greber 2006: 89–91). At Edwin Harness Mound, trench features were observed to have a bottom yellowish stratum topped by a reddish layer, and finally with darker sediments forming the outside of the wall. No ditch had been recognized at Garden Creek Mound No. 2 until remote sensing and new excavations by Wright (2012).

Carr and Case (2005c: 44) believe that these kinds of features symbolize "water" as the encircling barrier, probably derived from the actual use of water barriers with Adena cultures. Possible examples from South Appalachian Hopewell include the ditch around two Swift Creek mounds at the Leake site in northern Georgia (Fairbanks et al. 1946; Keith 2007, 2010, chapter 9, this volume). A Late Woodland period example from North Carolina is the ditch enclosing a large rectangular grave at the Cullowhee School site (Moore 1992). A Mississippian example includes the ditch (Feature 7) associated with the early Mississippian site of Martin Farm in Tennessee (Schroedl et al. 1985).

We suggest that the combination of the very large post (Post 21; see below) at the center of the circle defined by the ditch may relate to the proposed Hopewellian variation of the Adena "Axis Mundi." This large central post in the center of the ditch would represent a "vertical conduit for traveling among layers of the cosmos," while the ditch would signify "a water barrier that horizontally separated the dead from the living on the earth-disk" (Case and Carr 2008: 295).

Mound Structures

After the filling of the ditch (and insertion of Feature 28), a series of posts was erected down the middle of the ditch (figure 8.4). All 20 postholes discovered to date were filled with yellow coarse sand, as were 11 other internal postholes, apparently after the posts had been pulled. If a single structure is represented by sand-filled postholes, its estimated width is 18 m with an area of approximately 324 m^2, well beyond the predicted upper limit of 85.5 m^2 for Hopewell domestic structures suggested by Smith (1992). However, these posts, which align with the mound periphery, could also represent an open structure or a "screen" for ritualized demarcation of the ceremonial space on the mound (but see Kimball and Johnson 2012 for an argument that this structure on Biltmore Mound was a roofed structure). Sand-filled postholes forming a structure centered beneath the earliest mound were also noted at Garden Creek by Keel (1976) and discussed further by Wright (chapter 7, this volume). Filling of postholes with yellow sand obtained from elsewhere appears to have been ritually prescribed.

A similar enclosure may have been present at McKeithen Mound A (Knight 2001: fig. 11.2, 321; Milanich et al. 1984). Here, a "screening wall" of charred pine posts was observed within a ditch ("screen trench") that was aligned with the southwestern periphery of the mound.

At the apparent center and summit of the Biltmore Mound (figure 8.4 upper right) is a large post (PH-21), with an associated post-insertion ramp. The feature is approximately 50 cm in diameter and nearly 1.2 m deep from the current ground surface. At least four thin lenses of alternating dark and light sediments were found beneath the base of the postmold. These clearly represent contemporaneous deposits intentionally placed just prior to seating the post.

The size of this post and its insertion ramp (or "post pit," following Kelly 2003) are comparable to four very large posts at Garden Creek Mound No. 2 (Keel 1976) and examples from Swift Creek mounds at Cold Springs (Jefferies 1994), Leake Mound A (Keith 2007, 2010), and the large post with post-insertion ramps at McKeithen Mound A and Walling Mound (Knight 2001). These large posts are sometimes referred to as "pageant poles" and are exemplified in the reconstruction of the Newark Earthworks (Lepper 2004: fig. 3). In size and construction, Posthole 21 compares favorably with "busk poles" identified at many Mississippian sites (e.g., Coe 1995: 93–95, among others).

The use of ritual posts at later Mississippian mound centers is well known (Fowler 1991; Kelly 1991, 1996, 2003). Their interpreted functions range from the structural (Knight 2001: 325; Milanich et al. 1984) to the symbolic (Kelly 2003: 124; Schroedl et al. 1985: 223; Williams 1927: 62). Multiple large postmolds are sometimes considered to be the result of serial enactments (Hall 1998).

In the case of Biltmore Mound, the large central post was positioned on a line connecting Mt. Mitchell, the highest peak east of the Rockies, with Mt. Pisgah, the second-highest peak of the Asheville Basin rim (figure 8.5). Preliminary study by Larry R. Kimball and Derek Johnson of the alignment of the southwestern corner of the mound structure from the ditch through the large ritual post (Post 21) strongly suggests an orientation with sunrise of the summer solstice in AD 590 directly over Mt. Mitchell (figure 8.6). This question has been examined more specifically by Kimball and Johnson (2012), and the overall orientation of the wall to the ritual post of the mound structure is shown to have alignments with summer and winter solstice sunrise and sunset events at this time.

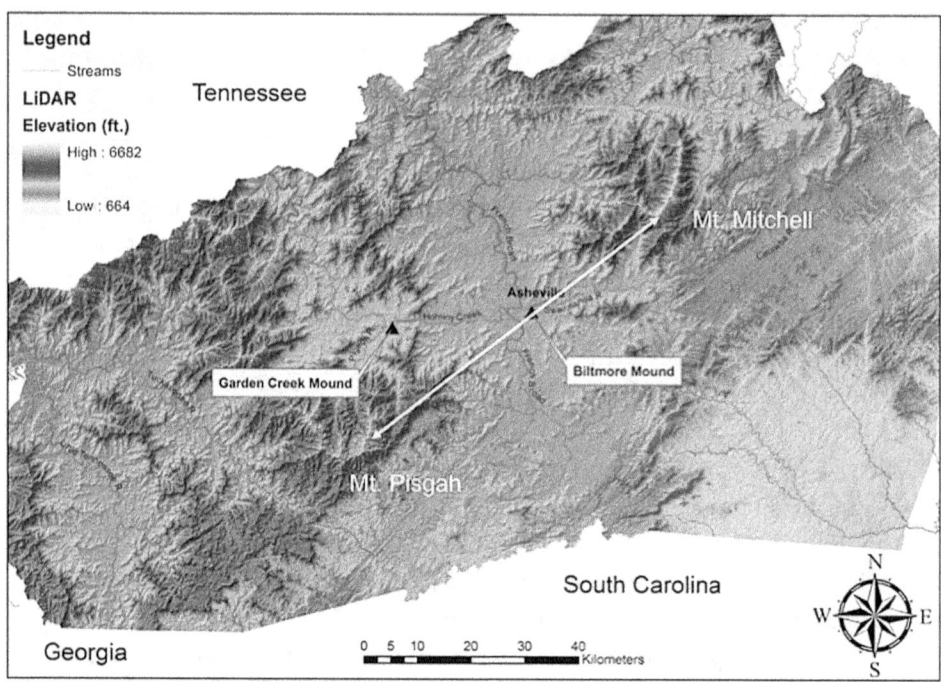

Figure 8.5. Location of Biltmore Mound between Mt. Mitchell (6,684 feet) and Mt. Pisgah (5,721 feet) in western North Carolina. Map prepared by Christopher R. Moore and Larry Kimball.

Figure 8.6. Summer solstice sunrise over Mt. Mitchell (AD 590), as viewed from Biltmore Mound, with Swannanoa River in the foreground. Figure prepared by Derek Johnson.

Color Symbolism

Sediment sources and colors (following numerous ethnographic sources and archaeological examples, such as Conley 2005: 9; Mooney 1900: 342; and Swanton 1979) played important roles in mound construction at Biltmore Mound and elsewhere (Buikstra et al. 1998; DeBoer 2005; Hall 1979, 1997; Van Nest 2006). Sediments were evidently selected because of their meaningful colors, textures, or origins and arranged in mound construction in a culturally prescribed sequence.

Examples from Biltmore contexts include the reddish-yellow-brown silts (light colored in fig. 8.2) of the prepared Floors 1–3 interspersed with dark brown silt loam strata (dark colored) underlying them, and the unusual olive-gray clayey loam of Mound Stage K (dark colored) that capped Floor 3. The next phase of mound construction was initiated by the covering of the mound with a dark grayish-brown midden (Stage J), followed by a lighter brown Stage I, and finally a mottled yellow-brown Stage G. This alternation of light and dark mound stages combined with redeposited midden and sterile subsoil mound stages appears purposively and meaningfully constituted. There could well have been color symbolism to mound fill (especially from allogenetic sources—following Van Nest 2006), as well as artifacts that may be manifest within structural (light/dark) and "three world" symbolic systems.

Material Contents of the Mound

Although a significant portion of the archaeofaunal and archaeobotanical remains, as well as a sample of 10,000 sherds (Kimball et al. 2010), has been studied thus far, our analyses of the material contents of the excavated portion of Biltmore Mound are ongoing. Here we focus on certain aspects of the faunal and botanical remains from the mound, as they contribute significantly to our understanding of the social and seasonal contexts of mound use.

Archaeofaunal remains (see Kimball et al. 2010: table 4) play a vital role in deciphering community function and the role of Biltmore Mound in the larger Hopewell culture. The exceptionally diverse faunal assemblage includes seldom-preserved fish scales, eggshell, terrestrial snail shells, ossified tendons of large birds, and costal cartilage of large mammals. The 34,532 specimens examined to date, all recovered from mound contexts, represent a minimum of 65 species, including those of crayfish, mollusks, fish, amphibians, snakes, turtles, birds, and mammals. Most astonishing is the sheer density of faunal debris on and within the mound versus off-mound contexts such as the immediately adjacent village area, where few animal bones were recovered. This disparity surely indicates deliberate deposition of animal remains in the construction of the mound and/or the conduct of activities on the mound that resulted in concentrated accumulation of animal remains. Immediate burial may have contributed to preservation; however, animal remains buried in village pit features did not enjoy the same degree of survival. The dense accumulation of osseous remains on the mound appears to have increased the soil pH to a level that reduced the rate of dissolution in the otherwise acidic matrix.

How and why, then, were so many animal remains deposited on the mound versus other parts of the site? The mere presence of animal remains on some Middle Woodland mounds has been interpreted as evidence of feasting. In other cases, such as McKeithen in northern Florida and Walling in northern Alabama (Knight 2001), the animal species and butchery units represented are viewed as evidence of feasting and of the sociopolitical structure of feasting. Feasting on or immediately near Biltmore Mound, and the primary or secondary deposition of feasting debris on the mound and in the circumferential ditch, provides the most parsimonious explanation for the abundance of animal remains in mound versus village contexts. The deposition of these remains, then, is interpreted as an action within a relational ontology that blurs the line between the profane and the sacred. Food remains, probably resulting from feasts, were a necessary component in sacred mound construction. Further evidence of this is the unusual frequency of burning and deliberate breakage, especially of bone implements and modified carnivore elements (Kimball et al. 2010).

In contrast to faunal assemblages from politically more complex Mississippian mound sites and certain Middle Woodland sites such as McKeithen and Walling, Biltmore's is taxonomically diverse, contains relatively few remains of exotic species, and is not in any way biased toward preferred butchery units. In taxonomy, anatomy, and seasonality, it resembles assemblages from egalitarian village contexts at other Woodland period sites in the Southeast (Clark et al. 2005; Egloff et al. 1994; Terrell 1998; Whyte 2003). If the assemblage resulted largely from feasting on the mound, then villagers provided for and participated in the feasting.

Archaeofaunal remains recovered by Keel's (1976) excavations at the nearby and contemporaneous Garden Creek Mound No. 2 were poorly preserved, perhaps because of more acidic soil chemistry. Consequently, beyond the matter of their association with the mound, they provide only weak evidence in support of ritual/ceremonial deposition (Whyte 2011).

Archaeobotanical remains from 16 mound flotation samples and two features (Features 32 and 36) from the 100 m² excavated village area are summarized in tables 8.1–8.3 (see Kimball et al. 2010: tables 5–7 for specific mound contexts). Represented nuts include hickory, walnut, acorn, American chestnut, and hazelnut. Fifteen identifiable plant genera are represented by seeds. Starchy-seeded plants such as lambs-quarters (*Chenopodium berlandieri*), erect knotweed (*Polygonum erectum*), maygrass (*Phalaris caroliniana*), and little barley (*Hordeum pusillum*) were clearly important (often cultivated) food resources during the Middle Woodland period in eastern North America (Gremillion 2006; Scarry 2003; Smith 2006). Oily-seeded plants represented in the samples include "squash" (*Cucurbita pepo* ssp. *ovifera*) and sumpweed (*Iva annua*). The sumpweed achene fragment from Feature 32

Table 8.1. Archaeobotanical remains from Biltmore Mound and village

		Village		
	Mound	Feature 32	Feature 36	Total
Volume (liters)	337	95	103	535
Nuts				
Carya sp.	2,254	1,433		3,687
(g)	48.91	46.64		95.55
Juglans nigra	38			38
(g)	0.91			0.91
Juglandaceae	51			51
(g)	0.26			0.26
Quercus sp.	878	6		6
(g)	6.52	0.01		0.01
Castanea dentata	52			52
(g)	0.27			0.27
Corylus sp.	4			4
(g)	0.07			0.07
Seeds	321	31		352
(g)	0.82	0.17		0.99
Cucurbita rind	58			58
(g)	0.09			0.09
Wood charcoal	19,002	5,633	10,175	34,810
(g)	160.62	84.98	574.22	819.82
Residue (g)	165.6	41	99.6	306.2
Total (g)	384.07	172.8	673.82	1,131.1

appears to be from a wild population. The sizes of the three achenes from mound contexts indicate a domesticated population of *Iva annua* var. *macrocarpa* (see Kimball et al. 2010: 51–52).

Seasonal availability of these seeds and mast include late spring through early summer, summer, and late summer through fall. The co-occurrence of many of these different seasonal indicators in features, postholes, and the ditch (as with the faunal remains) suggests that the overall pattern of mound use was from late spring through fall, rather than discrete seasonal usages.

The seasonality of maturation of the fruits from Feature 32 suggests spring through fall use of the village area as well as the mound. The plant remains suggest a human-plant interrelationship common during the Middle Woodland period in midlatitude eastern North America. Groups were harvesting

Table 8.2. Seeds from Biltmore Mound and village

Seed species	Mound	Feature 32 (village)	Total
Chenopodium berlandieri	48	2	50
Cyperaceae		1	1
Polygonum erectum	15	2	17
Polygonum sp.	4	2	6
Poaceae		2	2
Poaceae cf. *Elymus*		1	1
Galium sp.	122	3	125
Hordeum pusillum	32	8	40
Ipomoea sp.		1	1
Convolvulaceae		1	1
Ilex sp.		1	1
Phalaris caroliniana	2	3	5
Elymus sp.	77		77
Zizania aquatica	3		3
Carex sp.	2		2
Iva annua	3	1	4
Rubus sp.	2		2
Rhus sp.	4		4
Rhus cf. *glabra*		2	2
Vitis sp.	2	1	3
Gleditsia triacanthos	5		5
Total	321	31	352

Table 8.3. Identified wood charcoal from Biltmore Mound and village

Wood charcoal	Mound	Village Feature 32	Feature 36	Total
Quercus rubra	72	40	7	119
Quercus alba	16	0	0	16
Quercus sp.	22	1	0	23
Carya sp.	21	14	74	109
Castanea dentata	6	0	0	6
Gleditsia triacanthos	23	2	0	25
Robinia pseudoacacia	3	0	0	3
Acer sp.	5	5	1	11
Salix nigra	1	0	0	1
Pinus sp.	451	82	0	533
Fraxinus sp.	0	4	8	12
Ulmus sp.	0	2	0	2
Total	620	150	90	860

a variety of seasonally available resources and maintaining anthropogenic environments favored by weedy annual plants. Presence of domesticated sumpweed indicates segregation of selected populations of the plant from wild forms. Wood charcoals (table 8.3) indicate exploitation of several taxa occurring in the Southern Appalachian Section of the Oak-Chestnut Forest region (Braun 1950). The predominance of hickory (*Carya* sp.) in the Feature 36 sample probably is indicative of the feature's function as a hearth.

The botanical assemblage from prescribed ceremonial contexts at Biltmore Mound, in association with a remarkable faunal assemblage, suggests feasting. The difference in representation of plant remains from mound versus village contexts may also reflect feasting on the mound. Composition of paleoethnobotanical and faunal remains from other mounds helps strengthen such interpretation (e.g., Milanich et al. 1997; Pluckhahn et al. 2006; Scarry 1990). Earlier Middle Woodland expressions of ritual contexts and similar botanical assemblages are found at the early Middle Woodland/Adena Walker-Noe Mound (Pollack et al. 2005) and the Evans site, an off-mound Adena site where the dead may have been processed as part of a multistage mortuary program (Pollack and Schlarb, chapter 3, this volume). Brown (2006) has argued for the importance of tobacco in Hopewell ceremony. No tobacco seeds have been recovered from Biltmore. However, a chemical signature for nicotine was recently identified during gas chromatography/mass spectrometry analysis of residue removed from a pipe fragment recovered from Biltmore Mound (Carmody et al. 2011), thus strengthening Brown's claim.

Conclusion

The Biltmore Mound and its contents, context, and dating afford an opportunity to examine the functions of South Appalachian Hopewell mounds in a new light and from an alternative ontological vantage. This mound was constructed by a community within a brief interval of time (approximately 300 years) for communal ritual activities. The manner of its construction was evidently prescribed by an animistic relationship between humans, objects, sediments, and place.

It is obvious that the ways in which different Hopewellian peoples related to one another through the wider Hopewell phenomenon ought not be explained exclusively as reciprocal exchange of exotic goods between traders/shamans/elites at select villages in the region. This traditional exchange model does not explain how or why ceremonies on mound structures occurred. It makes more sense to envision a variety of reasons that Hopewell peoples would travel afar and leave exotic items at Connestee mounds. The Biltmore Mound evidence indicates that there was probably broad-scale participation by powerful religious practitioners, shamans (of various kinds), leaders, and possibly family groups from outside the Southern Appalachians, who came to this place to participate in the following:

1. Scheduled communal feasts and other activities, the by-products of which were incorporated into mound construction;
2. Construction of a multilayered earthen platform and peripheral ditch using sediments of varied color, texture, and from different sources;
3. Construction of a very large mound structure, whose wall was centered on the ditch;
4. Placement of a large (>50 cm) post having a ritual rather than structural function; and
5. The possible observation of summer solstice sunrises over Mt. Mitchell in alignment with the central ritual post, and probably other astronomical observations as well.

Scheduled ritual actions would have permitted and encouraged the exchange of goods, mates, information, ritual knowledge, medicinal plants, and so forth and cemented social ties and political alliances among distant and diverse social groups.

This model of Hopewell mound use in the Appalachian Summit, viewed from sample excavations and preliminary analyses of material remains and contexts at Biltmore Mound and through an alternative ontological lens (sensu Alberti and Bray 2009), is offered for consideration in light of forthcoming data from Biltmore and other sites and reexamination of old evidence derived and interpreted by other epistemologies.

Acknowledgments

The Biltmore Mound investigations have been supported by the Biltmore Estate (2000–2002 seasons), the National Geographic Society (grants 7321-02 and 7543-03 for 2002 fieldwork and 2003–2004 analyses) and the Appalachian State University archaeological field schools (2002, 2004, 2006, and 2008 seasons). We greatly appreciate the hard work of all the field school students and diverse volunteers. The fieldwork was supervised by Scott Shumate and John Preston with Larry R. Kimball as principal investigator. We thank Derek Johnson (ASU undergraduate) for his initial study and resultant animation of summer solstice sunrise over Mt. Mitchell at AD 590 as viewed from Biltmore Mound (figure 8.6). Stephen Carmody (Ph.D. candidate at the University of Tennessee–Knoxville) undertook the analysis by gas chromatography of residues from three pipes from Biltmore Mound. Dr. Christopher R. Moore (Savannah River Archaeological Research Program) created the LiDAR images used in figures 8.1 and 8.5. Our gratitude extends to any individuals at the Biltmore Estate who have supported these investigations in a number of ways, particularly Bill Cecil Jr., Ginger Cecil, Chuck Pickering, Dini Pickering, Bill Alexander, Ted Katsigianis, Hal Keiner, Rick King, and Ellen Rickman. We greatly appreciate the helpful comments of Jim Brown, Bennie Keel, Sharon Kimball, and Gerald Schroedl for this manuscript. We sincerely thank David Moore (1984) for discovering the Biltmore Mound. Finally, we appreciate the invitation of Alice Wright and Eddie Henry to participate in the symposium "The Ritual and Domestic Landscapes of Early and Middle Woodland Peoples in the Southeast" at SEAC in Lexington.

9

The Woodland Period Cultural Landscape of the Leake Site Complex

SCOT KEITH

Although it was occupied for approximately one millennium, from circa 300 BC to AD 650, the Leake site developed over a short period of time from a local domestic occupation early in its history into a large Hopewellian ceremonial and interaction center, which concomitantly served as a gateway community that geographically and culturally linked the Southeast and the Midwest during the Middle Woodland period. The Leake site complex (figure 9.1) comprises a local cultural landscape with residential areas, earthen mounds, a semicircular ditch enclosure, a large cave, a hilltop stone enclosure, and the stone-covered tomb of an important leader (Keith 2010). A broad spectrum of human activities accounts for these archaeological residues, including residential occupation, interaction, communalism, earthwork construction, feasting, and specialized item production. In an effort to examine the nature of domestic and ritual aspects of the local landscape at a large Middle Woodland center, I examine some of the archaeological contexts of the Leake site.

Leake Complex Overview

Several state-recorded sites (9Br2, 9Br663, 9Br664, 9Br665, 9Br666, 9Br667, and 9Br668) collectively make up the Leake site proper, which is situated in a large bend of the Etowah River approximately 3.5 miles downstream from the well-known Etowah Mounds (figure 9.2). The Leake site comprises the remains of three earthen mounds, a semicircular ditch enclosure, extensive midden deposits, and thousands of features such as postmolds, hearths, and cooking pits attributable to Cartersville and Swift Creek phase occupations of the site.

Rising 350 feet above the Etowah Valley one-half mile to the north and on the opposite side of the river, Ladd Mountain is a prominent feature of the Leake site viewshed. There were three archaeological sites on this ridge that I

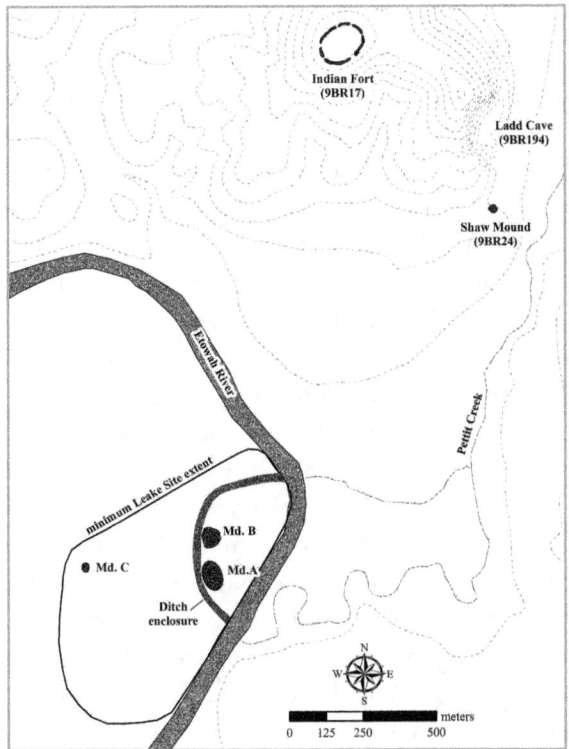

Figure 9.1. Map of the Leake site environs, including Shaw Mound, Ladd Cave, and Indian Fort in Bartow County, Georgia. Map prepared by Scot Keith.

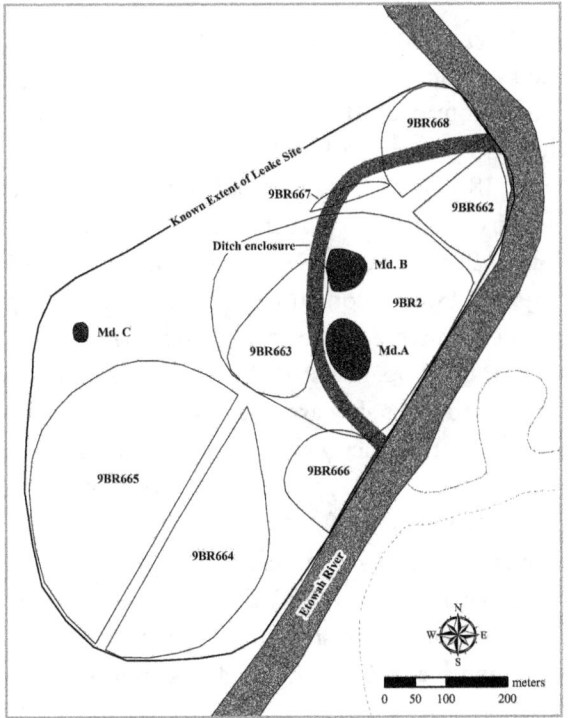

Figure 9.2. Map of the Leake site, including ditch and Mounds A, B, and C. Map prepared by Scot Keith.

contend were constructed and used by Middle Woodland peoples associated with the Leake site. Although all of these sites were largely destroyed as a result of mining and rock quarrying activities in the nineteenth and twentieth centuries, historic documentation provides significant clues as to their nature and association with the Leake site proper. All of these sites collectively make up the Leake Complex, encompassing an area of approximately 700 acres. These sites provide a view into the interconnected elements of a Middle Woodland Hopewellian ceremonial landscape situated at the geographic interface of the Southeast and the Midwest, a sacred place that was actively created and maintained by local and nonlocal peoples.

Indian Fort (9Br17) was a stone wall enclosure atop the summit of Ladd Mountain (P. E. Smith 1962; R. W. Smith 1936; Whittlesey 1883). With an approximate length of 400 m and a width of 3 m, the wall would have enclosed approximately 3.6 acres. Smithsonian researcher Charles Whittlesey (1883) documented six openings in the wall ranging in width from 3 m to 18 m, while a later description (Smith 1962: 18) stated that three "pits or circles" were built into the wall. Unfortunately the wall no longer exists, because its stone was quarried for road building material, and there are no known materials that might provide a construction date for the site. However, the wall's configuration and placement strongly suggest that it was built during the Leake occupation.

Ladd Cave (9Br194) was a large cavern with a vertical extent of 150 feet (Sneed 1998, 2007) located on the mountain's southern face, roughly between Indian Fort and Shaw Mound. In the 1880s, Smithsonian researchers documented and collected Pleistocene fossils and human bones from the cave (Anonymous 1885a, 1885b; Thomas 1894). Cave burials affiliated with the Middle Woodland period are known from other sites in the county, such as Pine Log Cave (Adams 2007; Harris 1950; Kelly 1950, 1951, 1952), prompting Arthur Kelly (1951, 1952) to conclude that such sites were part of the Copena tradition of the Tennessee River valley area. Because of the lack of diagnostic artifacts from the cave, its usage during the Leake occupation is speculative, yet one might reasonably assume that it figured into the Leake ceremonial landscape given the documented use of caves during the Woodland period (e.g., Crothers et al. 2002; Harris 1950; Kelly 1951, 1952; Walthall 1974; Walthall and DeJarnette 1974).

At the foot of Ladd Mountain on a ridge spur, the Shaw Mound (9Br24) was a stone burial facility. Also documented by Whittlesey (1883: 628), it was described as being a "regular cone, with small heaps attached around its base" approximately 49 m in length and 5.5 m in height. A later description states that the mound was 9 m in diameter and 3.6 m in height (Smith 1936).

Both descriptions mention a collapsed or sunken center. Shaw Mound was dismantled by the landowner in 1940, while local amateur archaeologist J. H. Wofford Jr. was present (Waring 1945). According to Antonio Waring Jr., who described the site in a 1945 *American Antiquity* article (1945: 119–20),

> At the base of the mound . . . directly in the center of the depression, were found the remains of an extended burial. . . . As Mr. Shaw, who knows nothing about archaeology, expressed it (without prompting), "The top of the pile was sunk in and looked as if the stone had been piled up on top of a log room that have [sic] caved in." . . . Covering its face and chest were several large sheets of mica. Lying on its chest was a plain, trapezoidal copper breastplate with double holes. . . . On each side of the head lay a tapered-based celt. Over the pelvis were several fragments of sheet copper which seem to have been parts of a large cut-design ornament. The expanded-bitted copper celt lay somewhere loose in the rock and hence went through the crusher and was slightly damaged.

Although we do not know precisely when the Shaw Mound personage lived, the nature of the burial facility and the grave goods are clearly Hopewellian. The burial treatment, including interment in what appears to have been a stone-covered log tomb, suggests that the individual was a ceremonial practitioner and communal religious leader of the Leake complex (sensu Carr and Case 2005a; Jefferies 1976; and Milanich et al. 1997). It may be that the person buried in the Shaw Mound was instrumental in the growth of Leake, perhaps acting as an intermediary between the Southeast and the Midwest.

Several archaeologists have previously touched on Leake's regional and interregional importance during the Middle Woodland period. Antonio Waring Jr. wrote a brief *American Antiquity* article in 1945 regarding the "Hopewellian" nature of the Shaw Mound. In his research on Tunacunnhee and the distribution of raw materials common at Hopewell sites, Jefferies (1976: 49) noted that Shaw Mound was located on top of a hematite and limonite deposit (specifically, Ladd Mountain). Pluckhahn (1998) directed testing excavations at Leake and recognized it as a population hub. Most recently, Anderson (1998: 279) suggested that Shaw Mound was likely a node within the Southeast-Midwest network of Middle Woodland centers. He points out that the distribution of major Swift Creek centers reflects in part a geographically strategic positioning designed to facilitate the movement of commodities. Further, Anderson (1998: 280) suggests that the Mann site— a contemporaneous Hopewellian center on the Ohio River in southwestern Indiana characterized by mounds and geometric earthworks and having a considerable quantity of Swift Creek complicated-stamped sherds—might have been a "gateway community or way station" linking the Midwest with the Southeast.

The prescience of Anderson's statement is underscored by the recent identification of a direct artifactual connection between Leake and Mann: a Swift Creek notched rim sherd found at Leake petrographically matches Swift Creek wares that were produced at the Mann site. Specifically, a Swift Creek sherd recovered at the Leake site (Keith 2010) is made of a grog-tempered paste that is petrographically similar to that used for the production of Swift Creek wares found at the Mann site (Ruby and Shriner 2005; Stoltman 2007). (Southeastern Swift Creek ceramics were typically made using sand or sand/grit temper.) Further, many of the fine-line simple-stamped wares found at Mann are petrographically and macroscopically similar to sand/grit-tempered Cartersville Simple Stamped wares common at Leake (Keith 2010; Stoltman 2007). My recent examination of the Mann Site collection held by the Indiana State Museum resulted in the identification of several sand-tempered Swift Creek sherds, providing additional evidence of direct interaction between these two sites. Taking Anderson's statement to its logical conclusion using this evidence, I posit that both Leake and Mann were geographical and cultural gateways into their respective regions and to each other, with a back and forth of people, materials, and ideas. Located at the edge of the Cartersville and Swift Creek cultural areas near the interface of the Tennessee River valley with several Gulf and Atlantic rivers systems, Leake became a large Middle Woodland ceremonial center and a gateway community at which both northward- and southward-bound travelers stayed and passed through. People came to sites such as Leake to interact with others and to participate in cooperative and public ceremonial and religious events, such as earthwork construction, feasting, purification, singing and dancing, and mortuary rituals.

Domestic and Ritual Contexts at the Leake Site

Earthworks

The earthworks at the Leake site are now for the most part found only below the modern ground surface, because of historic disturbances and river alluviation. The mounds—A, B, and C—were razed and used for road fill circa 1940 when the Dallas Rockmart Highway was relocated to its present position. Archaeologists working for the Smithsonian Division of Mound Exploration of the Bureau of Ethnology under the supervision of Cyrus Thomas provided the first known documentation of the Leake site in the late 1800s

(Middleton 1883; Rogan 1883; Thomas 1891, 1894). The site was later visited and described by Robert Wauchope (1966: 238) and Charles Fairbanks, Arthur Kelly, Gordon Willey, and Pat Wofford Jr. (Fairbanks et al. 1946) during the 1930s and 1940s. These early descriptions provide the only known descriptions of the mounds. These descriptions indicate that Mound A was flat-topped (i.e., a platform) and "loaf shaped" and approximately 7 feet in height; Mound B was conical and 5–18 feet in height; and Mound C was flat-topped and 8 feet in height (Fairbanks et al. 1946; Middleton 1883; Rogan 1883; Thomas 1894; Wauchope 1966).

The semicircular ditch enclosure at Leake was neither noted nor described by these early researchers, and there is very little surficial evidence for it. Portions of this feature were encountered by several excavations at the site (Hally, pers. comm. 2007, 2008; Pluckhahn 1998; Southerlin 2002; Southerlin et al. 2003) but were not recognized as an earthwork until a large-scale excavation of the site was conducted (Keith 2010). Portions of the ditch exposed and investigated during this investigation measured approximately 14 m wide and at least 1.7 m deep, although the bottom was not reached during excavations, because of safety issues (Keith 2010). Portions of the ditch enclosure are visible on 1938 aerial photographs, showing it beginning at the railroad and highway bridges that cross the river, arcing around the western sides of Mounds A and B, and ending at the southwestern edge of Mound A. A gap in the ditch is visible in the 1938 aerial photograph between Mounds A and B, yet excavations revealed that the ditch is now buried beneath historic fill, at least in the area excavated. Further, a recent ground-penetrating radar survey over a portion of the Swift Creek midden area and the area south and east of Mound A is providing additional evidence of this earthwork, including a possible embankment adjoining the interior of the ditch (Keith and Baughman 2011).

Geometric earthwork enclosures that form rectangles, squares, octagons, and circles have been documented at midwestern Hopewell area centers (Squier and Davis 1848) but are generally absent at southeastern centers (Anderson 1998: 286). While semicircular mounded embankment enclosures are present at a few major centers in the Southeast, including Pinson, Savannah, Marksville, and Kolomoki, semicircular ditch features are found at contemporaneous Fort Center in Florida (Pluckhahn and Thompson, chapter 12, this volume; Sears et al. 1982) and the nearby Mississippian period Etowah Mounds. Recently, ditch features have been identified at two Middle Woodland sites in the Appalachian Summit area, both with evidence of Hopewellian activities: Garden Creek (Wright 2012) and Biltmore Mound (Kimball et al., chapter 8, this volume). At Fort Center, Sears and colleagues

(1982) recorded a series of mounds and earthworks, including a semicircular ditch measuring 365 m in diameter and with each end connected to the river. At Etowah, Rogan (1883) felt that at least the western end of the ditch was originally open to the river but had been filled in by the landowner to prevent it from filling with water. Both Jones (1861) and Rogan (1883) argued that the Etowah ditch placed the mounds on an island. The shape and path of the ditch at Leake suggest that it may have extended continuously to join the river on both ends, a distance of 730 m. If this is the case, then the ditch would have enclosed Mounds A and B on a human-made "island."

If the ditch was a prominent earthwork at Leake, an immediate question that arises is why it was not noted or depicted by the early investigators of the site. The feature may have been filled in from centuries of floodplain alluviation. This possibility is supported by the mixed artifact stratigraphy that was documented during excavations within the ditch fill. Future geophysical work at the site will be designed to investigate this feature more fully.

Cartersville Early Middle Woodland Deposits

Evidence for domestic occupation at Leake comes from deposits found in the northeastern portion of the site, adjacent to the river, in the area of 9Br662 and 668. Dating circa 300–100 BC, these remains include pottery and stone tools of local slate and chert. Slate tool production and usage is evidenced by debitage and ground and worn bifaces. Several of the slate tools have use-wear patterns indicative of digging. While a few postholes and pits are present, no structural patterns are readily discernible. Local sand- and grit-tempered Cartersville check-stamped and Dunlap fabric-impressed wares dominate the ceramic assemblage. Limestone-tempered wares recovered from excavations may reflect interaction with peoples from the Tennessee River valley. Very low frequencies of artifacts and materials more commonly related to ceremonial contexts—a soapstone pipe bowl fragment, mica, ochre, hematite, limestone, mica schist, and siltstone—reveal that production of items from these materials was minimal in this area of the site during this time.

Communal Group Area

Other excavated areas of the site have yielded more equivocal evidence of domestic occupations. Specifically, artifacts traditionally considered domestic/utilitarian in nature are commonly found in association with items that are considered ceremonial. In the area immediately southwest of Mound B, numerous pit and post features are present (figure 9.3); radiocarbon dates (Beta-207560 and UGAMS# 02182) from features in this area place these remains between circa 100 BC and AD 125. While no structural patterns are readily discernible in the post features, nonpost features include shallow basin-shaped hearths, a deep circular cooking pit/earth oven, a mica cut-out storage pit, ceramic vessel busts, and pits of unknown function. While local Cartersville check- and simple-stamped wares predominate, nonlocal ceramics such as punctated/incised and red-filmed wares in the Weeden Island style, limestone-tempered types, and Cormorant Cord Impressed (variety Cormorant) point to interaction with peoples from the Gulf Coastal Plain, the Tennessee Valley, and the Tombigbee and Yazoo watersheds.

The low frequencies of typical domestic debris, such as chipped-stone tools and debitage, and the abundance of specialized items like gorgets, large chopping/digging tools, a small tubular piece of copper, and a mica sheet cut into a rectangular form indicate that this was not a domestic area. Rather, the remains suggest that this area was the scene of cooperative communal activi-

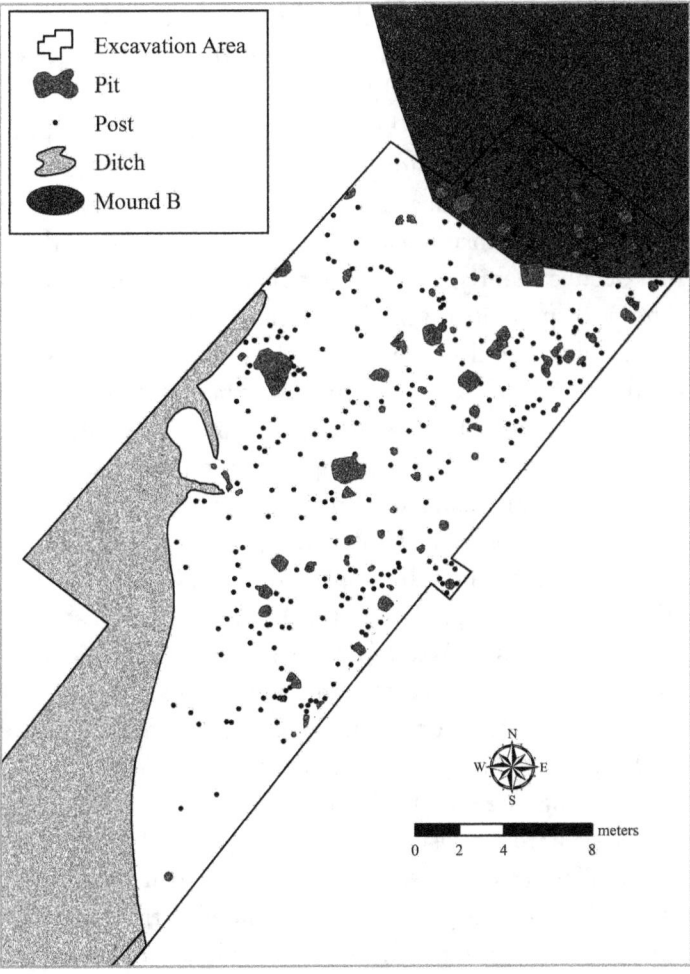

Figure 9.3. Pit and post features south of Mound B. Figure prepared by Scot Keith.

ties, possibly related to the construction of Mound B and the ditch enclosure. Interestingly, the dense concentration of features in this excavation area ends at the edge of the ditch enclosure. While the precise construction history of the ditch enclosure has not been worked out, the Cartersville period occupation inside the area of this enclosure appears to have ended as the intensive Swift Creek period occupation began in the area outside of it.

Swift Creek Midden

Outside of and adjacent to the ditch enclosure is a very dark and extensive midden with an extremely high artifact density. Referred to as the Swift Creek midden because of the predominance of this complicated-stamped pottery type, radiocarbon dates (Beta-109498, Beta-109499, Beta-207558, Beta-207556, UGAMS# 02181) situate this feature between circa AD 125 and 650. In addition to the dense features within and underneath it, the midden contains a mixture of utilitarian and ceremonial artifacts. Everyday items such as fire-cracked rock (FCR) and points and debitage made from local Ridge and Valley chert are found in association with ceremonial items and materials such as cut mica; sheet copper; ceramic human and animal figurines; prismatic blades of Ohio Flint Ridge chert, local chert, clear/crystal quartz, and possibly Wyandotte chert; modified quartz crystals and clear/crystal quartz debitage; graphite; hematite; greenstone; and phyllite. The majority of these ceremonial materials occur as debris, most likely remaining from the production of specialized items by participants in Hopewellian systems.

A high diversity of local and nonlocal ceramics was also present within this midden. The bulk of the identified ceramic assemblage comprises Swift Creek Complicated Stamped and plain pottery, while Cartersville Simple Stamped accounts for much of the remainder. Check-stamped, incised, punctated, red-filmed, rocker-stamped, cord-marked, fabric-marked, the rare diamond-dot Hopewellian type, and various other decorated ceramics are present at low frequencies, attesting to interaction with peoples from the Gulf and Atlantic coastal plains, the lower Mississippi Valley, the Tennessee Valley, and the Midwest. In addition, dozens of sherds of a previously unrecognized ceramic type are present. Named Ladds Stamped after the ridge across the river, this sand/grit-tempered ware was produced in the Swift Creek and Cartersville pottery tradition and appears to have been restricted to the Leake site.

The most obvious post alignment in the Swift Creek midden is a single linear arrangement of posts spanning a distance of 45 m (figure 9.4) (Southerlin 2002). The posts are similar in size and soil fill and are spaced at a regular interval of 1.7 m. If the azimuth of this post row was extended to the northeast, it would bisect Mound B (figure 9.4 inset). Coincidentally or not, this angle

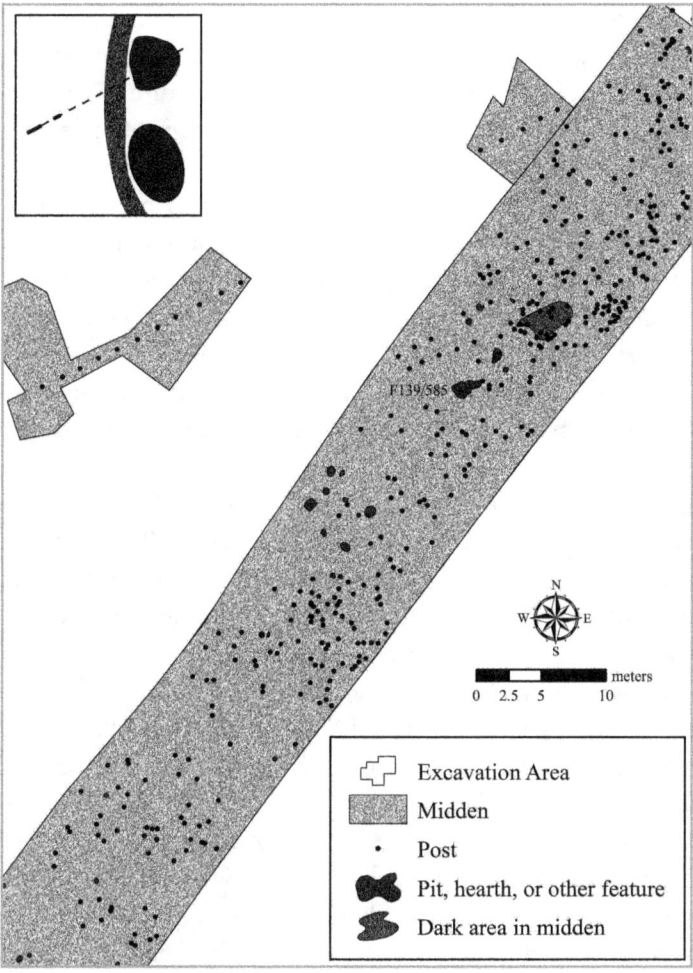

Figure 9.4. Post alignments in Leake site's Swift Creek midden. Figure prepared by Scot Keith.

set (63°/243°) is very close to those for the summer solstice sunrise (~61°) and the winter solstice sunset (~241°). Southerlin (2002) interpreted this row of posts as a possible palisade. However, this line of posts runs through the heart of the site, and palisade walls are not typically found at Middle Woodland mound centers. Rather than representing the remains of a palisade wall, this post row may represent evidence of a solar observatory associated with Mound B, which was historically described as conical (Fairbanks et al. 1946; Middleton 1883; Rogan 1883; Thomas 1894). Rigorous archaeo-astronomical analysis will be needed to test this hypothesis.

While there is a very dense concentration of posts within and under the midden, there are no clearly defined complete structural patterns, circular or oval, that are commonly interpreted as domestic houses in southeastern Woodland contexts. However, two parallel lines of posts mirroring the alignment just discussed are present, terminating at an area containing a dense array of posts and pits (figure 9.4). This configuration is reminiscent of one documented by Pluckhahn (2003: 148–57) at Kolomoki (Feature 57), which he argues represents a keyhole entrance to a pit-house structure. The density map of the Leake posts is suggestive of a circular structure grid north and east of this alignment. If so, it appears to have contained numerous interior posts. Alternatively, it may represent an unenclosed area where numerous activities occurred. Another alternative is that the posts are a keyhole entrance to a structure located to the west, predominantly outside of the excavation area. Several post features appear to run perpendicular to the south from the easternmost post of the southern parallel line, suggestive of a wall. The area west of this possible wall is relatively free of features; east of the wall is the dense post feature area.

Located along the west side of this possible wall, Feature 139/585 was a large dark stain with a large post in the southwestern corner. The post feature is quite wide and deep, measuring approximately 60 cm in diameter at the surface and extending 55 cm below the surface. Bordering this post was a concentration of FCR situated on a surface sloping down into the posthole, suggestive of a slide trench used for the post erection. Artifacts from this feature include Swift Creek Complicated Stamped, Cartersville Simple Stamped, Ladds Stamped, and a possible Marksville Incised sherd; mica; points, utilized flakes, cores, and debitage; a large crystal; and animal bone. A nearly whole ceramic spoonbill duck effigy was recovered from the feature area, as were another duck effigy head (with a straight rather than spatulate bill), a fragmented animal effigy that possibly represents a raptorial bird or a manatee, and several possible human effigy fragments. Identified bone from this feature includes white-tailed deer, large mammal, unidentified mammal, bird, drum, and fish (Matternes et al. 2007). In comparison to the other contexts that underwent faunal analysis, this feature contains a greater diversity of taxa, and the data indicate that a primary function of this feature was food processing. A radiocarbon date (Beta-207556) from Feature 139 returned a two-sigma calibrated date of AD 433–637, with a mean date of AD 545.

Within the dense concentration of post features a few meters away from Feature 139/585 was a relatively diffuse dark area of the midden. This area was visually prominent immediately upon stripping the plow zone prior to test unit excavation but became much less discernible from the surrounding midden as the soil moisture decreased. The artifact assemblage from this area is composed primarily of pottery, FCR, baked clay, and a few chipped-stone artifacts. There is very little in the way of effigies or other items commonly associated with ritual and Hopewellian activity. This assemblage is indicative of cooking and subsistence activities, perhaps directly related to food-processing remains located a few meters away.

Several nonlocal wares are present in this general area of the midden, including types resembling Marksville Incised, Alligator Bayou Punctated, Bayou la Batre, and Weeden Island Incised, as well as a simple-stamped and punctated sherd similar to Turner Simple Stamped B. Numerous Ladds Stamped sherds were present, and a Panola Diamond Check Stamped type was identified as well. In terms of local diagnostics, Swift Creek and Cartersville Simple Stamped wares account for approximately 80 percent of the assemblage by weight, with Ladds Stamped and Cartersville Check Stamped each contributing nearly 10 percent. Given that a food-processing feature (Feature 139/585) is situated just a few meters away, this may represent a communal feasting area, at which both local and nonlocal ceramic vessels were used to serve food and were subsequently deposited intentionally. Based on the context, I suspect that peoples intentionally deposited the items associated with feasting events at the feasting location.

Structures, Prepared Clay Area, and Ceremonial Feasting Pit

The most clearly discernible enclosed structural pattern at Leake was identified 175 m southwest of the Swift Creek midden in the 9Br665 excavation area (figure 9.5). Square in shape with rounded corners due to the lack of corner posts, the corners of Structure 1 are oriented to the cardinal directions. The posts are regularly spaced at 1.2 m intervals, forming walls approximately 11 m long and creating an interior area 110 m^2 in size. One of the posts yielded a mean radiocarbon date of AD 470 (UGAMS# 02186).

Designated Structure 2, a concentration of postmolds a few meters from Structure 1 displays a similar spatial arrangement, suggestive of a possible second structure comparable in size and shape (figure 9.5). A possible third structure, designated Structure Area 3, partially overlaps Structure 1 and is marked by an oval concentration of postmolds covering a 13 × 9 m area (figure 9.5). Among the dense array of postmolds within this block, there are many paired and overlapping posts, the latter indicative of rebuilding episodes.

A possible prepared clay surface is adjacent to Structure 1 and partially overlaps Structure 2 (figure 9.5). Markedly different in compaction and color from the surrounding red clay subsoil, the surface of this clay may have been stained by midden deposits that have since eroded. A thin lens of water-worn pebbles and cobbles was identified within one area of this clay feature. The function of this possible prepared clay feature is unknown. Waterworn cobble features reported in mound contexts at Hopewell sites in Ohio (Greber 1979:

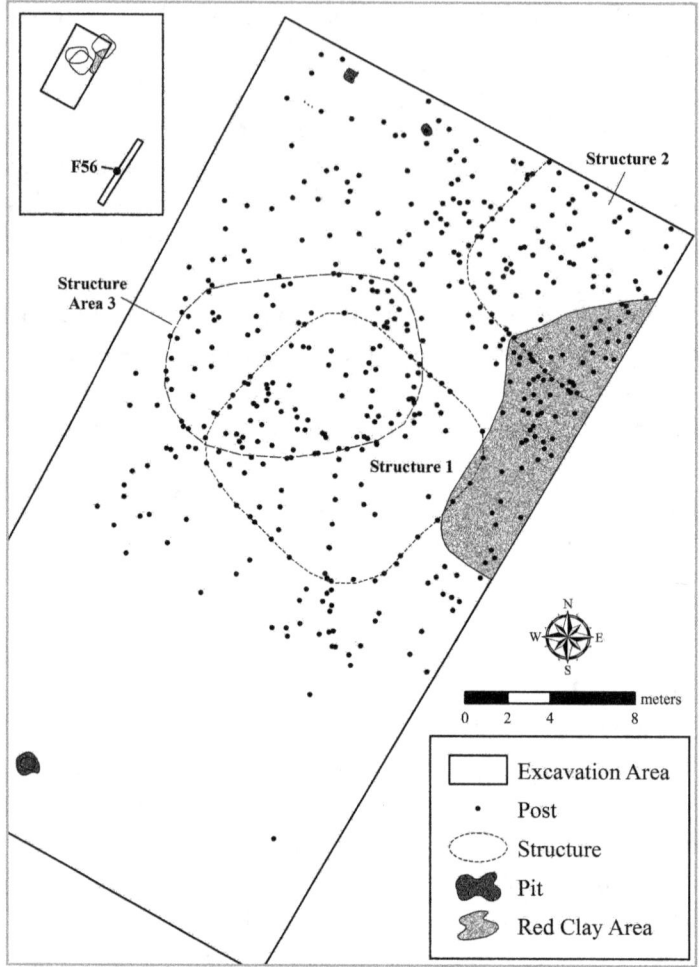

Figure 9.5. Structures in the 9Br665 excavation area at Leake. Figure prepared by Scot Keith.

fig. 1, 7; Greber 1983: fig. 1.1; Willoughby and Hooton 1922) have been interpreted as "water barriers," in that cobbles symbolically denote water in order to form a barrier between souls of the living and the dead (Carr and Case 2005c: 44; Hall 1976).

Approximately 50 m south of this red clay feature and Structure 1 was a large pit feature (Feature 56) that contained the remains of a ceremonial feasting event (figure 9.5 inset); two radiocarbon dates (UGAMS# 02185 and Beta-207555) situate the feature circa AD 600. This feature contained an incredibly dense assemblage of faunal remains (white-tailed deer, rabbit, turkey, turtle, and shark [Matternes et al. 2007]); crystal quartz debitage and utilized flakes; prismatic blades; mica; Swift Creek, simple-stamped, diamond check-stamped, and red-filmed Weeden Island pottery; local chert points and tools; and a human figurine head and other ceramic figurine fragments. The ceramic assemblage and a small nonfossilized shark's tooth evidence a strong Gulf Coast connection. Again, the context of this feature suggests that it was intentionally filled with symbolically charged materials directly associated with this feast.

Discussion and Conclusion

Sacred/secular, domestic/ritual—these dichotomous terms lend themselves to a dualistic interpretation, one that suggests a clear separation between activities, materials, and areas in these regards. Along the lines of Jon Gibson's (1998) inquiry into the nature of the sacred and the secular at Poverty Point, I have wrestled with the nature of the mixed deposits at Leake. While the earthworks are more obviously ceremonial, the Swift Creek midden and the area just southwest of Mound B contain a mixture of everyday and ceremonial items, begging the question, "What is sacred and what is secular?" As Gibson (1998: 21) puts it, "How secular can sacred be?" The association of artifacts traditionally thought of as domestic and ceremonial occurs at other large Middle Woodland centers, such as Tunacunnhee (Jefferies 2006) and Mann (Ruby 1997, 2006; Ruby and Shriner 2005; Ruby et al. 2005), as well as the Late Archaic Poverty Point site (Gibson 1998). Gibson argues that at Poverty Point, the two are inseparable, and I feel such is the case at Leake as well. In a discussion of interregional Hopewellian interaction, Carr (2005b: 590) argues that "pilgrims may manufacture utilitarian and ceremonial artifacts at sacred sites in their nonlocal styles out of local materials." Based on the presence of artifacts from throughout the Southeast and Midwest, it is evident that Leake was a relatively open and cooperative community (see Carr and Case 2005c: 42), at which nonlocals were welcome, perhaps even desired. Further, within the areas of the site where peoples from different areas interacted, there is no clear separation between materials traditionally considered "domestic" or "ritual."

Middens are often implicitly assumed to simply represent the buildup of debris and trash. However, the Swift Creek midden at Leake is certainly not just a refuse or dump area. The abundance of evidence for activities and structural facilities, including hearths, posts, ideologically charged items, feasting remains, the dense mixture of "utilitarian" and "ceremonial" items (for lack of better words), and the sheer amount and diversity of Swift Creek sherds within this midden cause me to wonder whether many of these materials were intentionally deposited and whether site participants actively *created* this Black Earth as they did the large earthen monuments. I suspect that many of the items within the midden may have been intentionally left as signifiers of the participants and memorials of religious and ceremonial events, in an active creation of this sacred cultural landscape.

Material debris found at Leake, particularly within the Swift Creek midden, suggests that some of the activities were likely related to mortuary ceremonies. Specifically, some of the debris of materials important within this system—mica, copper, graphite, hematite, and galena—may remain from the production of items to accompany those who were interred in local and regional caves. Discussions among Walthall, DeJarnette, and Kelly led them to posit a regional Hopewellian Copena-Cartersville mortuary tradition in the Tennessee River and Etowah/Coosa River drainages (Walthall 1980; Walthall and DeJarnette 1974). Downstream from Leake along the Coosa River in eastern Alabama, Walthall and DeJarnette (1974) argued that a village site (1Ta9) and a nearby burial cave (Kymulga Cave) represent a site complex in which the village occupants were buried in the cave. Such may have been the case with Leake and surrounding burial caves in northwestern Georgia (Harris 1950; Kelly 1950, 1951, 1952). To date, no Middle Woodland burials have been identified at the Leake site proper despite extensive excavations.

While this chapter is focused primarily on ceremonial contexts at the site, future investigation of the areas surrounding and outside the heart of the site—where the bulk of excavations have been conducted—may lead to insights regarding the nature of residential occupation and habitation at large centers. Are there deposits more similar to traditional "domestic" residential villages, remaining from peoples who lived at and near the site during the time it functioned as a large interregional center? Did groups establish housing that they abandoned and reoccupied according to scheduled ceremonial events at the site? Did nonlocal peoples from different areas live together at the site? Might there have been group housing? Hopefully, the rapidly expanding modern cultural landscape will not erase this prehistoric landscape before such questions can be addressed.

10

The Creation of Ritual Space at the Jackson Landing Site in Coastal Mississippi

EDMOND A. BOUDREAUX III

A defining trait of many Middle and Late Woodland societies across the Eastern Woodlands was the construction and use of various forms of monumental architecture (Anderson and Mainfort 2002a: 10–13; Carr and Case 2005c; Griffin 1967: 186; Knight 2001: 313; Mainfort and Sullivan 1998: 4; Steponaitis 1986: 379). In many locations, Woodland architects used culturally constructed features such as mounds and earthworks in combination with natural landforms and bodies of water to create large ceremonial centers and ritual landscapes. The scale of many of these sites with monumental architecture suggests that they were centers that integrated local populations at the regional and, perhaps, interregional levels (Mainfort 1988: 169; Mainfort and Sullivan 1998: 9, 15; Milner and O'Shea 1998: 200; Thunen 1988). Although local and regional traditions were important (Brose and Greber 1979; Carr and Case 2005c: 21; Ruby et al. 2005: 171–72; Thunen 1988), similarities in ritual activities—as indicated by shared artifact styles, the construction of similar forms of earthen monuments, and similarities in the arrangements of earthen monuments—suggest a sharing at some level of ideas about ritual among societies across the Eastern Woodlands during the Middle Woodland and early Late Woodland periods (Anderson and Mainfort 2002a: 9; Griffin 1967: 183; Kidder 2002: 79; Thunen 1988; Steponaitis 1986: 382; Toth 1988: 3–7). Important insights into ceremonialism, which include proposed functions for classes of sites with similar forms of monumental architecture (Cobb and Nassaney 2002; Knight 2001; Mainfort and Sullivan 1998), have been developed by considering these shared attributes from a regional perspective.

This chapter has two purposes. The first is to present information about the Jackson Landing site, an early Late Woodland period (AD 400–700) site on the Mississippi Gulf Coast with monumental architecture. The general absence of Jackson Landing from discussions about the Woodland period is ironic because the site's earthwork is one of the largest earthen constructions in the central Gulf Coast region (Blitz and Mann 2000: 39–40; Lewis 1988: 115) and because for some time archaeologists have known that this earthwork was built during the Woodland period (Williams 1987). Until recently (Boudreaux 2011a, 2011b), archaeological fieldwork at Jackson Landing has been relatively limited and little was known about the activities that occurred there during the early Late Woodland period. Consequently, the site has not been discussed in the archaeological literature beyond works that have focused exclusively on the Mississippi Gulf Coast (Blitz and Mann 2000: 39–40; Lewis 1988: 115; but see Phillips 1970: 899).

A second goal of this chapter is to use the limited information that does exist for Jackson Landing to develop some interpretations about how the site was used during the early Late Woodland period. Although the site's earthen monuments are known to have been built and used between AD 400 and 700 (Boudreaux 2011a, 2011b; Williams 1987), archaeological investigations have been too limited spatially to permit investigators to determine much about how Jackson Landing was used during that time. To facilitate a consideration of site function in the absence of site-wide investigations, the information that does exist from Jackson Landing—which consists mostly of basic observations about the size, shape, construction, and layout of the site's earthen monuments—will be compared with information from Woodland period sites with similar cultural attributes. In general, similarities among some Woodland sites regarding the form, spatial arrangements, and use of earthen monuments have been recognized across the Eastern Woodlands (Dancey 2005; DeBoer 1997; Knight 1990: 170, 2001: 313; Thunen 1988). More specifically, similarities among Jackson Landing and other sites in the Southeast have been noted for some time (Williams 1987: 61).

The use of analogies with other Woodland period sites generates some intriguing ideas about Jackson Landing's construction and use. Although any interpretations regarding site-wide activities and function will have to be evaluated against actual data from Jackson Landing as they become available, current information indicates that large-scale rituals involving large groups were the predominant, if not exclusive, activity undertaken there. Elements of the natural world, such as soil and water, were used to create a ritual landscape at Jackson Landing. The people who built the site's monuments used cultural activities to transform these natural materials into an earthwork and a platform mound; based on analogy with comparable sites in the Eastern Woodlands, these likely served, respectively, to delineate ritual space and as a stage for ritual performances (Knight 2001: 321; Mainfort and Sullivan 1998: 11–12). Also similar to a number of Woodland period sites, the monuments at Jackson Landing appear to have been used in combination with natural features of the landscape, such as existing water bodies and landforms, to create a large-scale ritual space that was physically and symbolically separated from the rest of the natural and cultural world (Cobb and Nassaney 2002: 532).

The Jackson Landing Site

Jackson Landing is located at the western end of Mississippi's Gulf Coast near the mouth of the Pearl River, which empties into Mississippi Sound about five kilometers to the south of the site (figure 10.1). Jackson Landing is located on a terrace surrounded by marsh. This natural landform is part of a relict shoreline that forms a low-relief bluff along the eastern side of the Pearl River near its

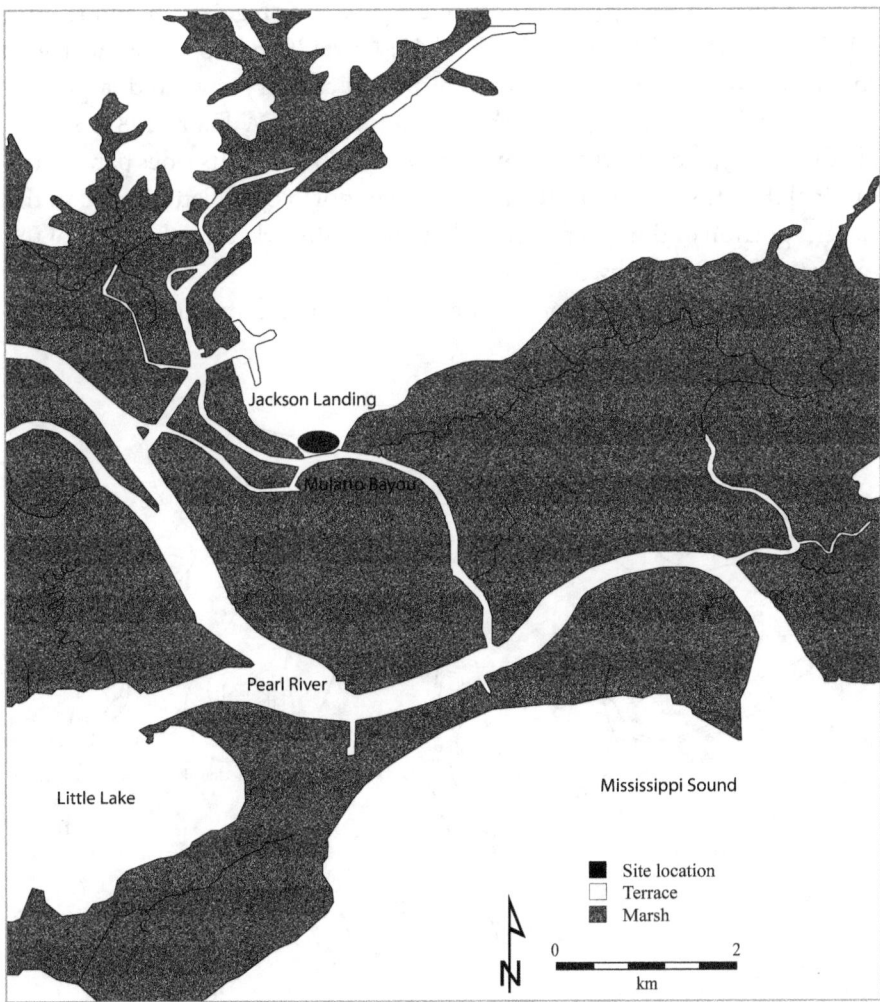

Figure 10.1. Map showing Jackson Landing's location near the mouth of the Pearl River on the Mississippi Gulf Coast. Map prepared by Edmond A. Boudreaux III, Amanda Keeney, and Joseph Roberts.

mouth (Gagliano et al. 1982: fig. 2.42; Otvos 1972: 241–48, 1975: 149). This terrace is the first substantial, elevated landform encountered when coming up the Pearl River from Mississippi Sound (Williams 1987: 5).

Jackson Landing consists of three major spatial elements that are visible on the site's surface: a large shell midden, a 460 m long earthwork, and a 1.5 m tall platform mound (figure 10.2). A shovel-test survey of much of the extensive area (approximately 60 acres) between the earthwork on the north and Mulatto Bayou on the south identified several widely separated areas that may have been used during the early Late Woodland, but much of this area does not appear to have been utilized (Boudreaux 2011a: 238–40).

Jackson Landing's earthwork, which is about 30 m wide and over 4 m tall in places, is one of the largest earthen monuments in the region (Blitz and Mann 2000: 39–40; Gagliano et al. 1982: 41–42; Lewis 1988: 115). The earthwork contains two gaps that have been interpreted as entryways, and large borrow pits are located along its northern, exterior edge (Williams 1987: 5). The platform mound measures approximately 50 × 70 m, and its sides parallel the cardinal directions. It is located about 200 m north of Mulatto Bayou in the eastern portion of the space enclosed by the earthwork, directly south of the eastern end of the earthwork.

Excavations in portions of the shell midden (Giardino and Jones 1996),

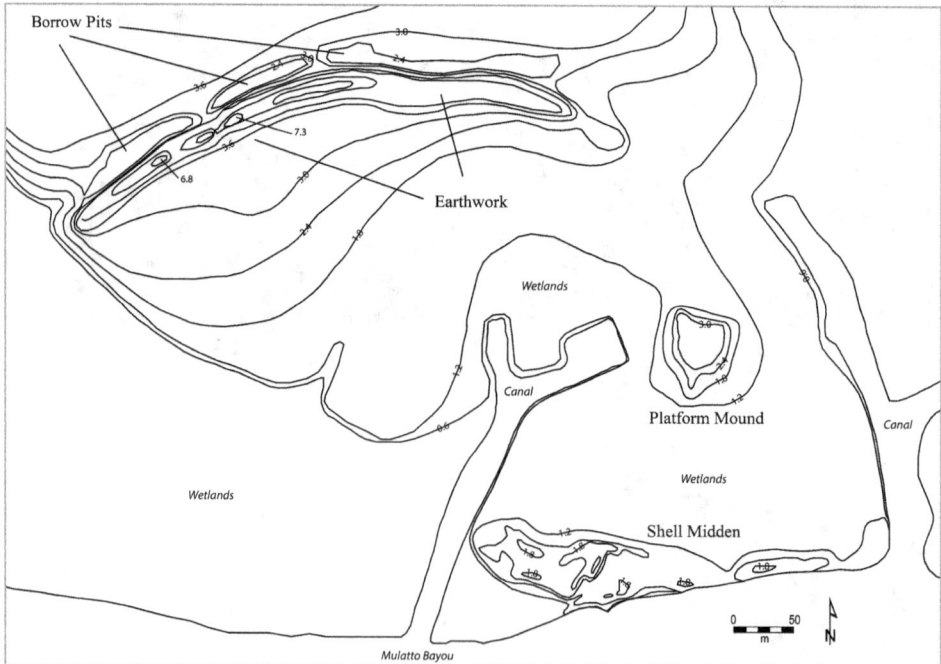

Figure 10.2. Jackson Landing site map (compiled from Gagliano et al. 1982: fig. 2.46 and Williams 1987: fig. 1). Map prepared by Edmond A. Boudreaux III, Amanda Keeney, and Joseph Roberts.

earthwork (Williams 1987), and mound (Boudreaux 2011a, 2011b) have demonstrated that the site was occupied as early as the Late Archaic period (circa 1900–1600 BC) and that Native American use of the site continued through the eighteenth century. The shell midden contains deposits from all of these periods, and it may have formed gradually over the course of thousands of years (Giardino and Jones 1996). In contrast, the mound and earthwork both were built during the early Late Woodland period between AD 400 and 700. Radiocarbon dates from the initial construction stage of the earthwork and a preconstruction context indicate that the earthwork was in place by cal AD 440–650 (Boudreaux 2011b: 358). A series of AMS dates from a premound midden, two mound summits, and an adjacent borrow pit indicate that the mound was built and used during a very brief interval around AD 655–60 (Boudreaux 2011a: 242–43).

Jackson Landing as a Ceremonial Site

The earthwork and platform mound at Jackson Landing were built and used within a context of local and regional social interaction. Given similarities observed among the construction techniques and spatial configurations of earthen monuments at Jackson Landing and several other Woodland sites, the plan for placing, building, and using the site's monuments likely was informed by ideas and practices that were broadly shared across the Southeast[1] and other parts of the Eastern Woodlands. Attributes that Jackson Landing shares with other sites include the use of an earthwork in combination with the local topography to define an interior space (Thunen 1998: 67 and fig. 4.1), the prominence of water features in the site's layout (Carr and Case 2005c: 44; Sears 1982: 165; Sunderhaus and Blosser 2006), the presence of a multiple-stage platform mound within the area enclosed by the earthwork (Knight 1990: 167, 2001; Thunen 1988: 112), and the use of distinctive soils for different stages of mound construction (Knight 1990: 158; Sears 1982: 162, 198; Thunen 1998: 64). In this section, these broadly shared attributes of site structure and earthen monument construction will be used as a basis for making analogies between Jackson Landing and selected Woodland period sites. As discussed previously, the purpose of making comparisons among sites where these broadly shared attributes are manifested is to develop ideas about the construction and use of the Jackson Landing site during the early Late Woodland period.

Defining and Gathering within Ritual Space

A number of Woodland sites with linear earthworks have been interpreted as spaces created for the performance of rituals that needed to be segregated from domestic areas (Cobb and Nassaney 2002: 532; Mainfort and Sullivan 1998: 12). In these cases, earthworks are seen as physical markers that delineate ritual space. The need to isolate ritual space may be expressed at Jackson Landing in the fact that the earthwork was placed so that it could be used in combination with the area's natural topography to enhance the site's separation and sense of isolation. The Jackson Landing site is located at the southern end of a terrace that is surrounded by an extensive system of marshes and waterways. The earthwork was built across most of the only dry-land access to the southern end of the terrace, but the earthwork does not extend across an approximately 200 m area directly north of the mound. Lewis (1988: 115) speculates that the earthwork did extend across this area at one time but this section has since been destroyed. I argue, however, that a section of the earthwork was never built across this area. An 1852 sketch shows the earthwork as it is now (Williams 1987: 65), indicating that it has been in its current configuration for some time. Also, the presence of intact eighteenth-century archaeological deposits on and around the eastern end of the earthwork suggests that this part of the site has not been significantly disturbed. I also argue that the earthwork was used in combination with an adjacent bayou-and-wetlands area to demarcate the southern end of the terrace. Aerial photographs from 1942 show that a modern canal currently located to the east of the earthwork closely follows the course of a former bayou (Boudreaux 2011b: 353). If this bayou and its adjacent wetlands were in the same location when the earthwork was built, then together they would have segregated the southern part of the terrace (i.e., the earthwork's interior space) through the combination of a cultural feature and natural waterway.

The placement of the site's earthwork on an elevated landform surrounded by lower ground is reminiscent of other Woodland period sites, and it is likely that the people who built these monuments used the local terrain in combination with culturally acknowledged barriers such as earthworks to isolate and delineate ritual space (Cobb and Nassaney 2002: 532; Thunen 1998: 67). The fact that Jackson Landing still would have been easily accessible from the south shows that the earthwork would have been effective only if acknowledged as a cultural barrier, because it did not actually prevent entry to the large space between it and Mulatto Bayou. Instead, multiple gaps in the earthwork may have served as prescribed points of access to the site from the north (Williams 1987: 5). The space between the eastern end of the earthwork and the bayou-and-wetlands area, which is directly north of the platform mound, was a likely point of entry as well.

In addition to sharing with several sites aspects of location and construction that enhanced its seclusion, Jackson Landing may be in the same class as many other Woodland period sites in the Southeast that appear to have been vacant ceremonial centers (Knight 2001: 313).[2] These sites do not appear to have been permanently occupied settlements but instead are interpreted as having been places for periodic gatherings (Cobb and Nassaney 2002: 535; Knight 2001: 313; Mainfort 1988: 169; Mainfort and Sullivan 1998: 9). In general, sites in the Eastern Woodlands with enclosures have been viewed as vacant centers because of their lack of dense midden deposits (Cobb and Nassaney 2002: 534–35; Knight 2001: 313; Mainfort and Sullivan 1998: 9). More specifically, it has been speculated that Jackson Landing represents a vacant ceremonial center based on the apparent lack of large, dense Woodland period midden deposits that would suggest the presence of a long-term habitation (Lewis 1988: 115). Although there clearly are areas south of the earthwork that were utilized during the early Late Woodland period, they are widely spaced, and large portions of the site were not used during this time (Boudreaux 2011a: 238–40).

Several aspects of Jackson Landing's location relative to the natural features and cultural landscape during the early Late Woodland period are consistent with the site's having been a place for social groups in the region, and perhaps beyond, to gather. The site's location on or near two of the region's most important waterways, the Pearl River and Mississippi Sound, would have facilitated the gathering of large groups at the site. A ritual center built at this spot would have been easily accessible because of its position on what was presumably a well-traveled waterway and highly visible because of its placement on a terrace that was prominent relative to the surrounding marshes. Furthermore, Jackson Landing was located at the margins of two archaeological regions: the Delta region near the mouth of the Mississippi River (Phillips 1970: 866) lies to the west of the site, and the Mississippi Sound region of coastal Mississippi lies to the east (Blitz and Mann 2000). This positioning suggests that activities at the site may have integrated populations at an interregional level (Boudreaux 2011b).

Water Bodies and Wetlands

Water bodies and wetlands constitute much of the space within and around the earthwork at Jackson Landing. The construction of the earthwork enclosed approximately 60 acres between it and Mulatto Bayou. However, about one-third of this space consists of water or wetlands. Two modern canals at the site mark the former locations of bayou-and-wetland areas east and west of the mound. Also, wetlands constitute much of the space south of the mound and in the central part of the site just south of the earthwork. This suggests that water features may have been integral parts of the site's layout and function. Although nothing is known directly about the use of water bodies or wetlands at Jackson Landing, these features appear to have been used for ritual purposes at several other Woodland sites. For example, the intensive use of an artificial pond at the Fort Center site in Florida led Sears (1982: 165) to the conclusion that the pond was a necessary part of the rituals that took place there during the Woodland period.

Comparatively, water features, both natural and cultural, appear to have been important for delineating space at other Woodland sites (Sunderhaus and Blosser 2006: 137–38). They may have been used to help demarcate boundaries at Jackson Landing as well. As discussed previously, a bayou-and-wetlands area appears to have been used in combination with the earthwork to define the northern edge of the site. Additionally, if large borrow pits located on the northern, exterior side of the earthwork held water during some seasons of the year, as they do now, it is possible that they served as culturally constructed water features (Sunderhaus and Blosser 2006: 137). If the two gaps in the earthwork and the space between it and the bayou-and-wetlands area served as prescribed points of access to the earthwork's interior, then one would not have been able to enter the site from the north without crossing between water bodies or wetlands. The clustering of water features around points of entry is a pattern seen at several Middle Woodland sites (Sunderhaus and Blosser 2006: 141). Water bodies and wetlands may have delineated space within the Jackson Landing site as well. Archaeological investigations of the site have identified three areas south of the earthwork that were utilized during the early Late Woodland period, and these widely spaced areas are separated from each other by either marshes or a bayou (Boudreaux 2011a: fig. 6.1). Speculations about the possible symbolism and meaning of water features integrated with Woodland period monuments include associations with ideas about supernatural barriers, origin stories, purity, or the underworld (Carr and Case 2005c: 44; Hall 1976; Sunderhaus and Blosser 2006: 141).

The Platform Mound

The contemporaneous construction and use of a platform mound within the space delineated by the earthwork at Jackson Landing indicates the importance of public ritual performance at the site, given that platform mounds at other Woodland sites appear to have served as highly visible stages on which publicly oriented rituals were performed (Knight 2001: 321). The placement of the mound in a prominent location, directly south of a possible entryway between the earthwork and the bayou-and-wetland area, suggests that the activities performed on its summit were a critical part of the overall activities that occurred within the space delineated by the earthwork. The Jackson

Landing mound was built in three stages (Boudreaux 2011a: 245–54, 2011b: 358), and the summit of each would have provided a raised area where a variety of activities could have taken place. Archaeological testing of the mound area has recovered evidence that the summits of the first two mound stages at Jackson Landing were associated with feasting and the erection of large posts (Boudreaux 2011a: 255–57), activities that have been associated with other Middle Woodland and early Late Woodland platform mounds across the Southeast (Knight 1990: 171–72, 2001: 319–23).

Not only does the presence of a platform mound indicate the prominence of ritual activity at Jackson Landing, but the choices made by its builders regarding the kinds of soils used for different mound-construction stages may indicate additional aspects of ritual. The first episode of mound construction at Jackson Landing created a low, approximately 60 cm tall platform of yellowish-brown clayey loam (fig. 10.3) (Boudreaux 2011a: 245). This ini-

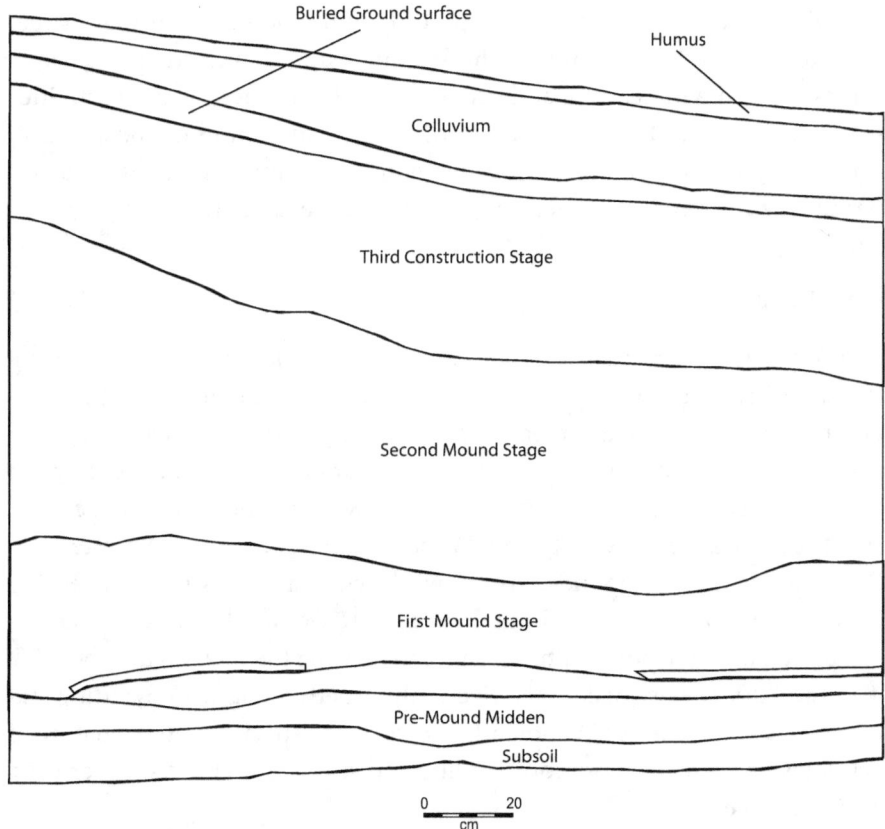

Figure 10.3. Drawing of mound excavation unit N183E19 north profile showing stages of mound construction. Figure prepared by Edmond A. Boudreaux III, Amanda Keeney, and Joseph Roberts.

tial layer, with its higher clay content, was very different from the mound's two subsequent construction episodes, which consisted of sandy loam. The distinctiveness of the initial mound stage suggests that it may have served a different purpose than subsequent layers did. Although very little of this first stage has been excavated, the presence of a low, clay platform as the initial stage of mound construction at the site is suggestive of another example of a regionally recognized pattern. Excavations at numerous Middle Woodland platform mounds across the Southeast have identified a similar construction sequence in which the mound's first stage consisted of a low, clay platform that was covered by subsequent layers of mound fill (Knight 1990: 158; Sears 1982: 162, 198; Thunen 1998: 64; Toth 1974: 18). The ubiquity of clay platforms as the initial stage of Middle Woodland platform mounds led Sears (1982: 198) to speculate that these distinctive clay features were a necessary part of mound rituals. Although these initial clay platforms have been identified at several Middle Woodland sites, the activities associated with them appear to have been quite variable. For example, while the clay platform at Fort Center was a place where one part of a multiple-stage mortuary ritual occurred (Sears 1982: 196–97), the Walling Mound in northern Alabama was associated with feasting and ritual exchange but not mortuary activities (Knight 1990: 161). At Jackson Landing, the initial mound-construction stage of more clayey soil was associated with a large midden deposit that appears to be the remains of a feasting event (Boudreaux 2011a: 245).

Conclusions

The construction of ritual space and monuments at Jackson Landing during the early Late Woodland period took place on a scale that rivals other ceremonial centers in the Southeast. The labor required to construct the site's platform mound and earthwork and the amount of space delineated by the latter serve as evidence that Jackson Landing was a major locus of large-scale ritual activity during the early Late Woodland period. The mere presence of this large site with its mound and earthwork begs many questions concerning how these monuments were built, how the site was used, and what role the site played in the region's cultural landscape during the interval between AD 400 and 700. The use of comparative analysis between Jackson Landing and other sites in the Eastern Woodlands allows one to speculate on the nature of activities performed at Jackson Landing and suggests that the site was used as ritual space.

Ironically, at present, very few overtly ritual objects have been recovered from Jackson Landing. Thousands of artifacts from surface collections and excavated contexts have included only one unusual object, a fragment of a possibly anthropomorphic figurine made of fired clay (Boudreaux 2011a: 192), and one possible nonlocal object, a ground-stone fragment that may be made from nonlocal stone (Boudreaux 2011a: 209). The near absence of ritual items and nonlocal materials at Jackson Landing is not surprising, however, because such items are rarely found at late Middle Woodland and early Late Woodland sites in the lower Mississippi Valley and adjacent Gulf Coast (Blitz and Mann 2000: 41; Kidder 2002: 74; McGimsey 2010: 128). Regardless, indications of Jackson Landing's use as ritual space lie in the scale of the landscape that was created rather than in the presence or absence of individual objects.

Woodland period enclosure sites in the Eastern Woodlands have been interpreted as places where people from multiple communities gathered to participate in large-scale, public rituals that integrated multiple communities (Byers 1998: 139; Cobb and Nassaney 2002: 532; Hall 1997; Knight 2001: 321; Mainfort and Sullivan 1998: 9–12). Current information available for Jackson Landing is consistent with its having been used in this way as well. The architects of Jackson Landing selected a prominent landform on the region's most important waterway and converted it into a ritual space. They did this by constructing monuments from various soil types and combining them with natural bodies of water and landforms to segregate and transform a portion of the natural landscape. This transformation created a ritual landscape within which large-scale, public ceremonies were the most prominent, if not exclusive, activities performed. The labor represented in the site's earthwork and mound implies a degree of intercommunity, and possibly interregional, group organization and cooperation. The scale of the earthwork, the size of the space it delineated, and the presence of a platform mound within this space all suggest that the rituals performed at the site were large-scale, publicly oriented events that involved large groups of people. The people who built and used the monuments at Jackson Landing almost certainly came from multiple communities, and the site's location at the edge of two archaeological regions suggests that activities performed at the site may have involved groups from multiple regions as well.

This chapter has served the purpose of presenting information about Jackson Landing to a broader audience. Additionally, archaeological information that is available from Jackson Landing has been considered in light of what is known from other sites with similar earthen monuments to develop some insights into the site's construction and use. The ideas presented here are speculative, and they undoubtedly will have to be modified or abandoned as more data from Jackson Landing become available. However, ideas about the site's construction and use as a large-scale, integrative, ritual space provide starting points both for situating Jackson Landing within the region's Woodland cultural landscape and for future investigations.

Acknowledgments

This chapter draws from several fieldwork projects that were conducted by the Mississippi Archaeological Association, the Louisiana Archaeological Society, Coastal Environments, Inc., and East Carolina University. Funding sources for these projects included the Mississippi Gulf Coast National Heritage Area and the Mississippi Department of Archives and History through a grant from the U.S. Department of Housing and Urban Development. SABIC Innovative Plastics, current owners of much of the site, have protected the site and supported recent investigations. Individuals who have contributed to the investigation of Jackson Landing include Jim Barnett, Aimee Bouzigard, Kay Erwin, Mike Fedoroff, Marco Giardino, Pam Lieb, Kelsey Lowe, and Rich Weinstein. This chapter has benefitted from discussions with John Blitz, Ian Brown, Ed Jackson, Mike Fedoroff, Jim Knight, Vin Steponaitis, and Rich Weinstein. Amanda Keeney and Joseph Roberts helped prepare the figures for this article. Finally, I want to thank the editors of this volume for improving this chapter and for inviting me to participate.

Notes

1. For example, the spatial arrangement of the platform mound and enclosure at Jackson Landing, with the former being located off-center within the interior space defined by the latter, is identical to the spatial arrangement of Middle Woodland platform mounds and enclosures at Little Spanish Fort (Jackson 1998: fig. 2), Leist (Phillips 1970: fig. 144), and Pinson (Mainfort 1988: fig. 3; Thunen 1998: 59) sites.

2. Middle Woodland sites that may have been vacant ceremonial centers include Fort Center in Florida (Sears 1982: 188), Marksville in Louisiana (Jones and Kuttruff 1998: 52; McGimsey 2010: 124), Little Spanish Fort (Jackson 1998: 217) and Ingomar in Mississippi (Rafferty 1990: 101), Pinson (Mainfort 1988: 162) and Old Stone Fort (Faulkner 1988: 85) in Tennessee, and the Florence Mound in Alabama (Boudreaux and Johnson 2000: 87).

PART THREE

Landscapes of Interaction

11

Late Middle Woodland Settlement and Ritual at the Armory Site

PAUL N. EUBANKS

The scale of interregional interaction in the Eastern Woodlands during the Middle Woodland period is generally thought to surpass that of any preceding prehistoric period. Characteristic of this interaction was the exchange of exotic materials and the sharing of ideas regarding the production of material culture, mound building, and mortuary ceremonialism (Chase 1998; Griffin 1967; Keel 1976; Kellar et al. 1962; Prufer 1964; Sears 1962; Wimberly and Tourtelot 1941). John Walthall (1985) argues that this period can be further characterized by the scheduled ritual gatherings of diverse ethnic groups at predetermined locations. Here, the term *pilgrimage center* is used to refer to such locations where individuals or groups of individuals assemble for the purposes of conducting ritual activities, while the term *ethnic group* is used somewhat loosely to refer to distinct potting traditions and their associated geographic boundaries. A pilgrimage, strictly speaking, does not necessarily entail the aggregation of multiple populations, yet it may be inferred that if ritual stimuli were the primary forces encouraging interregional aggregation, then the sites at which this aggregation occurred may be termed pilgrimage centers. This chapter focuses on one such potential pilgrimage center, the Armory site in central Alabama, with the goal of promoting a better understanding of Middle Woodland interaction across a subcontinental landscape.

Using data from the Ohio Hopewell and Southern Appalachians, Walthall (1985) argued that select Early Middle Woodland (AD 1–200) sites in the Southern Appalachians may have functioned as pilgrimage destinations for the Ohio Hopewell. Briefly cohabitating with their Southern Appalachian counterparts, these pilgrims may have conducted ritual activities such as mound and earthwork construction, ancestor veneration, the production of material culture, and "feasting with the dead," a ritual involving the preparation or the consumption of food by the living in the presence of the dead (Keith, chapter 9, this volume; Seeman 1979). Walthall's evidence for this argument rested largely upon two criteria: the presence of nonlocal artifacts and evidence for ritual activity. In this chapter, these criteria are discussed and augmented with a spatial distribution analysis of local and nonlocal pottery found at the Armory site, a late Middle Woodland (AD 300/400–500) mound center located in the middle Alabama River Valley (figure 11.1). Following this analysis, I argue that ritually motivated aggregations persisted into the late Middle Woodland subperiod and involved a greater number of ethnically diverse populations than has previously been recognized. While the results of the distributional analysis support the notion that Armory may have functioned as a pilgrimage center, this analysis is conducted using a relatively small sample ($n = 32$), since only a fraction of the pottery recovered from Armory was collected in a random or systemic fashion.

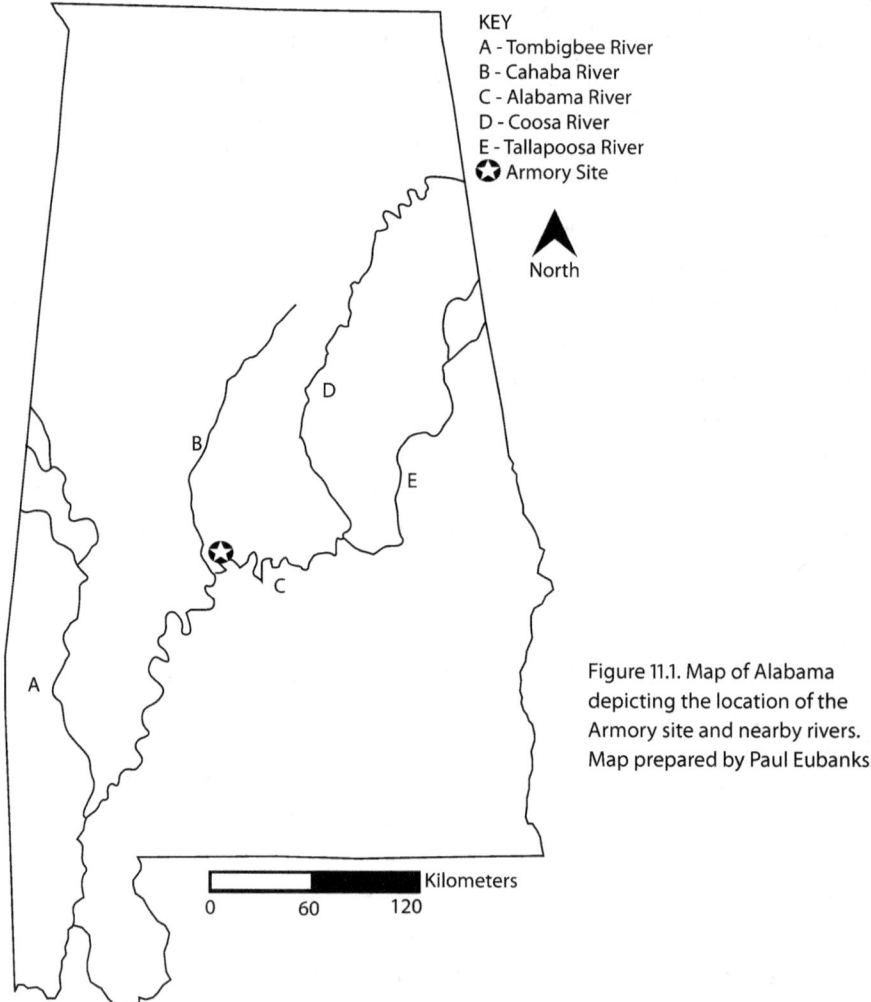

Figure 11.1. Map of Alabama depicting the location of the Armory site and nearby rivers. Map prepared by Paul Eubanks.

Settlement at the Armory Site

The Armory site is a U-shaped settlement flanked on its southeastern and northwestern sides by opposing mounds (figure 11.2). C. B. Moore may have documented the larger of these mounds, referred to here as Mound A, in 1899. This mound is currently 2 m high and measures 20 m north–south and 25 m east–west. Mound B, the smaller mound, was first observed during a survey conducted by the Alabama Historical Commission in 2007. This mound measures only 5 m north–south and 5 m east–west with a height of less than a meter and was not recorded earlier, because of its small size. Excavations conducted on or near these mounds suggest that they were used, and at least partially constructed, during the late Middle Woodland subperiod (AD 300/400–500) (Eubanks 2010).

While this site spans an area of at least two hectares, it is bordered to the north by a modern housing development, which envelops an unknown portion of the site. Given that large quantities of artifacts were recovered along the property line adjacent to the housing development, a considerable portion of the site could remain undocumented. The center of the settlement is relatively devoid of artifacts, suggesting that this area may have served as a cleared plaza. There are two artifact concentrations near each mound; these concentrations, however, are less dense than those encircling the plaza (figure 11.3).

A series of systematic shovel tests conducted in 2007 yielded two primary pottery classes: sand/grit tempered with check stamping and sand/grit tempered with rocker stamping. While the former pottery class is found in abundance throughout the middle Alabama River valley (Chase 1998; Cottier 1982; Dickens 1971; Nance 1976), the latter is typically associated with

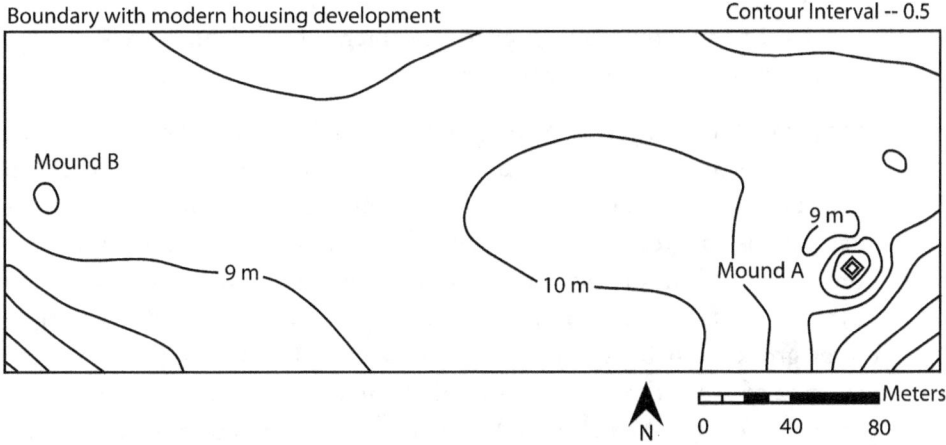

Figure 11.2. Contour map of and location of mounds at the Armory site. Map prepared by Paul Eubanks.

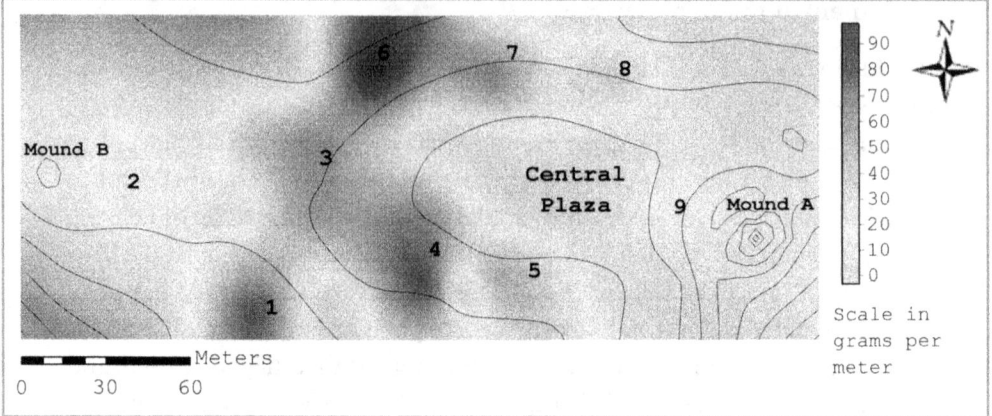

Figure 11.3. Distribution of the nine identified activity areas at the Armory site as defined by ceramic density. Figure prepared by Paul Eubanks.

the coastal regions of northwestern Florida, Alabama, Mississippi, and the Marksville Culture of the lower Mississippi Valley (Caldwell 1958; Phillips 1970: 125–27; Willey 1949; Wimberly 1960).

Aggregation

In his chapter discussing so-called Hopewellian encampments in the Southern Appalachians, John Walthall (1985) examined the function of five suspected aggregation centers using the following criteria:

1. If an abundance of nonlocal artifacts is found at a given site and such artifacts are absent from nearby contemporaneous sites, then this site is likely to have been occupied for some time by a nonlocal population.
2. If a site functioned as a pilgrimage center, then this site should contain evidence for ritual activities.

In this chapter, these criteria are used to assess the function of the Armory site. In addition, the results of a distributional analysis of local and nonlocal artifact classes are also presented in an attempt to better understand what effects, if any, aggregation and ritual had on the site's spatial organization. For instance, if cultural affiliations were made manifest on the landscape in the form of distinct ethnic enclaves, then the cohabitation of multiple ethnic groups may be inferred. It should be noted, however, that while the presence of such ethnic enclaves implies some form of aggregation, aggregation centers can be integrated socially without the presence of distinct ethnic boundaries.

Local and Nonlocal Artifact Classes

The Walling, Yearwood, Tunacunnhee, Garden Creek, and Icehouse Bottom sites discussed by Walthall (1985) all seem to fulfill the first criterion listed above, as each site contains a sizeable portion of nonlocal artifacts. Of particular interest to Walthall are prismatic blades, some of which are made of Flint Ridge (Ohio) chalcedony. The occurrence of these blades at these sites is striking given their general absence in the Southern Appalachian region. Despite their rarity in the Southern Appalachians, each of these sites contains multiple examples of these prismatic blades. Numerous other exotic artifacts were also found, including limestone-tempered sherds, rocker-stamped sherds, dentate rocker-stamped sherds, and cross-hatched rims. Given the presence and frequency of these artifact classes, their association with the Ohio Hopewell, and their general absence at other Southern Appalachian sites, Walthall concluded that Ohio Hopewell populations temporarily visited these locations.

The Armory site, located approximately 250 km south of the Walling site, Walthall's southernmost aggregation center (figure 11.4), also appears to fulfill the first criterion. The ratio of check-stamped sherds ($n = 39$) to rocker-

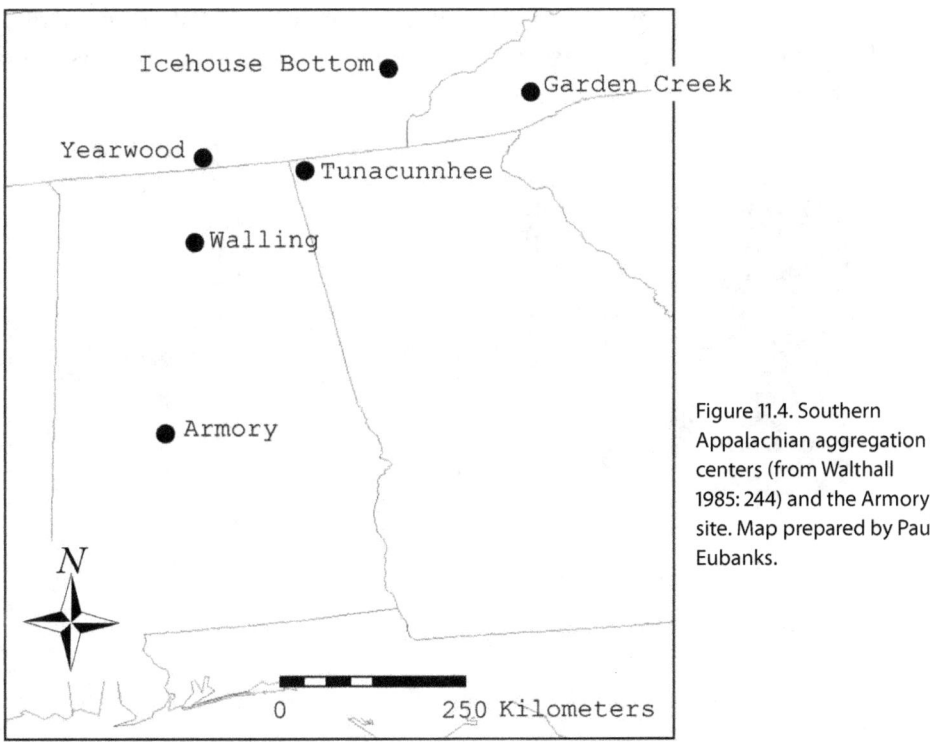

Figure 11.4. Southern Appalachian aggregation centers (from Walthall 1985: 244) and the Armory site. Map prepared by Paul Eubanks.

stamped sherds ($n = 37$) at this site is unusually high for central Alabama, where check stamping is generally the dominant mode of surface treatment during the Woodland period. The only other known Middle Woodland sites near Armory with rocker-stamped pottery are Site 1Mt209 and the Timberlands site, each of which were subject to much more thorough excavations than the Armory site and contained only a few rocker-stamped sherds (Chase 1998; Price 1999).

Assuming that the popularity of surface treatments gradually waxes and wanes through time, then local production is ill-suited to account for the large quantity of rocker-stamped sherds at the Armory site, as there are few sites in central Alabama with assemblages that could be indicative of this surface treatment's rising or declining popularity. This phenomenon can be displayed graphically using the most recent continuous cultural chronology for the middle Alabama River valley (figure 11.5). Notably absent from this seriation is a "battleship-shaped" curve for rocker-stamped pottery. Further, if nonlocal wares are assumed to tend to appear in much lower frequencies than comparable local wares, then the large amount of rocker-stamped sherds itself suggests that their presence at Armory is not a result of trade alone, as the ratio of check stamping to rocker stamping is nearly 1:1. Because the popularity of this surface treatment does not wax and wane through time and because it is found in substantial numbers in central Alabama only at the Armory site, its presence may be inferred to be the result of a migration from the nearby Gulf Coast region, where this surface treatment is more common.

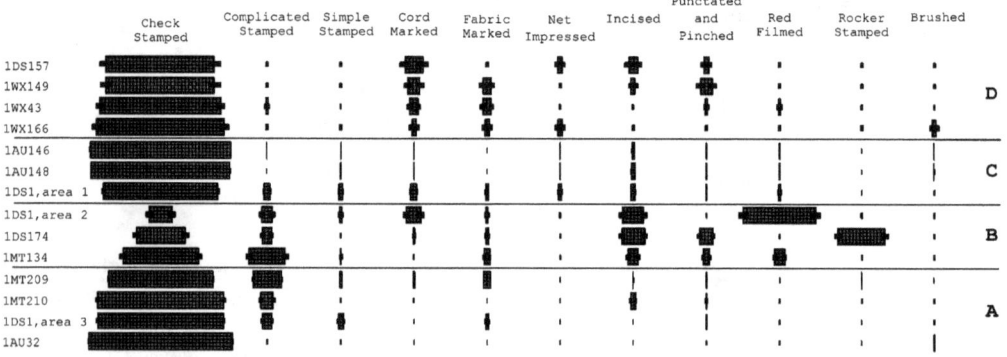

Key

A: Early Middle Woodland subperiod (A.D. 1-300/400)
B: Late Middle Woodland subperiod (A.D. 300/400-500)
C: Late Woodland period (A.D. 500-900)
D: Terminal Woodland period (A.D. 900-1200)

Figure 11.5. Augmented frequency seriation of ceramic assemblages from sites located near the Armory site. Figure prepared by Paul Eubanks.

Spatial Distribution Analysis at the Armory Site

Plotting the distributions of check- and rocker-stamped sherds from the 2007 shovel test pits makes it apparent that these sherds are concentrated in distinct, though partially overlapping, areas of the site. With the number of sherds per shovel test pit used as a weighting mechanism, the mean centers for both the check-stamped and the rocker-stamped sherds were calculated, and the distance between these two points was measured at approximately 50 m (figure 11.6). To test the statistical significance of this difference, the distributions of check- and rocker-stamped sherds along the north–south and east–west axes of the site were calculated and compared using a Wilcoxon rank sums test (tables 11.1 and 11.2). While the results of this test were not statistically significant at the .05 alpha level, there was some indication that the spatial distributions of these two pottery classes were reflective of a meaningful cultural pattern.

For the purposes of this analysis, it was assumed that if the check- and rocker-stamped distributions were statistically different along either axis, then they were representative of distinct activity areas where these sherds were deposited. At the .1 and .05 alpha levels, the distribution along the north–south axis was not significant ($p = .281$); however, the distribution of sherds along the east–west axis was significant ($p = .068$) at the .1 alpha level.

Though the difference between the depositions of these two pottery classes was statistically significant with a relaxed alpha level, their distributions were not mutually exclusive. Thus, if rocker- and check-stamped pottery was produced by distinct ethnic groups, then some areas of the site may have

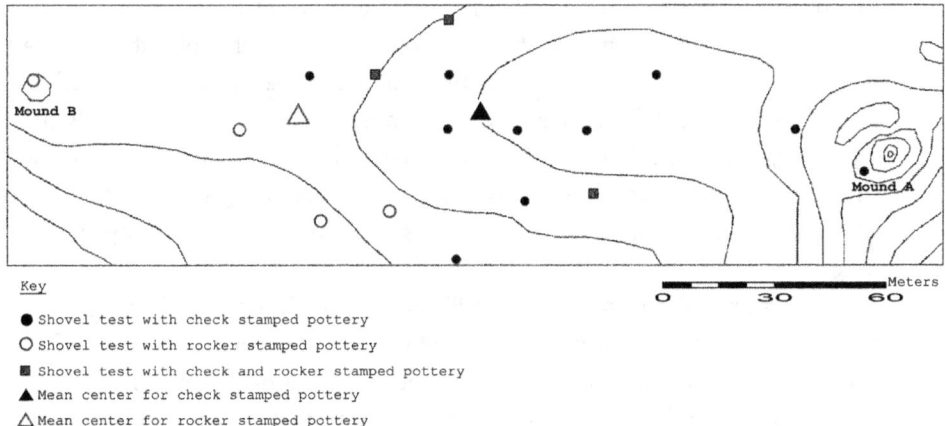

Figure 11.6. Distribution of check-stamped and rocker-stamped pottery at the Armory site. Figure prepared by Paul Eubanks.

Table 11.1. Significance of difference between the north–south distribution of check and rocker stamping

	Count	Mean rank	Sum of ranks
Rocker-stamped count < check-stamped count	6	5.25	31.5
Rocker-stamped count > check-stamped count	3	4.5	13.5
Rocker-stamped count = check-stamped count	4		
Wilcoxon rank sums test 2-tailed significance	0.281		

Table 11.2. Significance of difference between the east–west distribution of check and rocker stamping

	Count	Mean rank	Sum of ranks
Rocker-stamped count < check-stamped count	4	2.5	10
Rocker-stamped count > check-stamped count	0	0	0
Rocker-stamped count = check-stamped count	1		
Wilcoxon rank sums test 2-tailed significance	0.068		

been reserved for common usage. Additionally, the small sample size of the check- ($n = 22$) and rocker- ($n = 10$) stamped pottery used to conduct this statistical test must be highlighted. While more check- and rocker-stamped sherds have been recovered from the Armory site than were included in this analysis, they were not collected in a random or systematic fashion and thus could not be assessed statistically in the tests described above. In an attempt to redress this issue, Lauren Wiggins (2011) analyzed the check- and rocker-stamped pottery from three test excavation units and a shovel test pit located near the mean center for rocker-stamped sherds as part of an undergraduate research initiative at the University of Alabama in Tuscaloosa. From this analysis, Wiggins concluded that there were considerably more rocker-stamped sherds from these excavations than check-stamped sherds ($p = .068$), thus supporting the argument that the site was divided into two partially overlapping ethnic enclaves.

It is important to note that this differential distribution, even if highly significant, may be the result of several phenomena other than the cohabitation of distinct ethnic groups. First, an appreciable amount of time may have elapsed between the depositions of these two pottery classes. This does not seem to be the case, however, as Armory's dominant occupation appears to

Table 11.3. Significance of difference between the thicknesses of check- and rocker-stamped ceramics

	Count	Mean rank	Sum of ranks
Check stamped	33	36.89	1,217.5
Rocker stamped	35	32.24	1,128.5
Mann-Whitney U test 2-tailed significance	0.319		

have occurred within a relatively narrow span of time (Eubanks 2010). Further, because the thickness of pottery vessels is suggested to have increased during the late Middle Woodland and early Late Woodland subperiods in central Alabama (Nance and Mentzer 1980), the thicknesses of check- and rocker-stamped body sherds at the Armory site were compared using a Mann-Whitney U test (table 11.3). The difference between the thicknesses of these sherds was not significant at the .1 or .05 alpha levels ($p = .342$). There was also no stratigraphic evidence suggesting that a significant amount of time occurred between the deposition of these pottery classes. This evidence, however, must be tempered by the fact that much of the site's stratigraphy has been disturbed by modern cultivation.

Second, a single population living at the Armory site may have reserved certain areas of the site for the usage of specific pottery (Milanich 1994: 185). In such a scenario, one may expect either ceremonialism or social stratification to play a role in the differential distribution of these artifact classes. This explanation seems unlikely given the data at hand; there is little evidence supporting the existence of extensive social stratification during the Middle Woodland period in central Alabama. Further, there are no apparent ceremonial features or mounds located near the mean centers for check- and rocker-stamped sherds.

Third, the differential distribution of check- and rocker-stamped sherds may be the result of intracommunity preference. However, if such preferences are assumed to transcend the generational level beyond the occupation of a single site, then one would expect to find additional sites with a similar assemblage of ceramic material. Aside from the aforementioned Timberlands site and 1Mt209, such sites have yet to be documented in central Alabama. Therefore, given the weaknesses associated with these three possible scenarios, interregional aggregation is supported here; it accounts for the data at hand in the most parsimonious fashion.

Evidence for Ritual Activity

Following Walthall's second criterion, a pilgrimage center, as a milieu for ritual activities, should contain material remains associated with ritual activities. Walthall noted that the suspected aggregation centers in the Southern Appalachians yielded several material correlates suggesting that these sites served a unique ritual function. According to Walthall, the rituals conducted at these sites may have focused largely on mortuary activities, as four of these five sites were situated near burial mounds and the skeletal materials associated with these mounds or in other burial contexts exhibited elaborate mortuary treatment such as defleshing, cremation, and reburial. Evidence of food preparation and consumption was also found in the form of stone-filled hearths and globular fire pits. Among the Ohio Hopewell, the material correlates of food-related activities often occur in similar contexts as skeletal remains, suggesting that "feasting with the dead" was an important aspect of the rituals conducted at these sites (Seeman 1979; Walthall 1985).

Like the sites Walthall highlights in the Southern Appalachians, Armory yielded evidence indicative of possible mortuary and ritual activity. Mound A, which may have been excavated by C. B. Moore in 1899, contained at least

Figure 11.7. Copper ear spool possibly from Mound A at the Armory site. Reprinted with permission from the Smithsonian Institution's National Museum of the American Indian.

one burial (Moore 1899: 302–3). Unfortunately, Moore failed to note whether this burial received any mortuary treatment. Moore did, however, mention finding a bicymbal Hopewellian copper ear spool (figure 11.7) in a looter's debris pile. Though its exact context is unknown, this artifact, at the time of its deposition, may have been associated with a burial in Mound A.

In 2009, two two-by-two-meter excavation units were opened adjacent to Mound A's western flank. These units yielded three features related to food preparation and consumption. The largest of these features was an oval-shaped hearth filled with fire-cracked rock. Less than a meter to the north of this feature at the same depth was a smaller pit filled with lightly burned lumps of clay, some with a diameter larger than five centimeters. The final feature was a deposit of mussel shell located approximately five meters west of Mound A's base. The presence of these features and their association with Mound A lead to the inference that activities such as the preparation and consumption of mussels and possibly other foods occurred in close proximity to the site's possible burial mound. While the area surrounding Mound A has not been subject to thorough testing, if these features typify the areas surrounding Mound A, then a ritual akin to "feasting with the dead" may have been performed at Armory.

Other artifacts, such as large uniface choppers, scrapers, and projectile points, were also found in or near Mound A. Because these artifacts were located in or near a potential mortuary context in association with food-related features, they may have been involved in the procurement and processing of the food sources consumed during this ritual. Additionally, the relative abundance of decorated sand/grit-tempered pottery recovered from the Armory site, especially near Mound A, also suggests that the activities conducted at this site were not solely domestic in nature (Eubanks 2010: 147–48).

Interpretation

The evidence presented in this chapter suggests that the Armory site was an aggregation center where ritual activities were conducted. However, this does not necessarily imply that ritual or pilgrimage was the primary motivation for the coalescence of visitors at this site. A variety of other driving forces must first be considered before any one is given preference. Therefore, in this section, several potentially causal factors often associated with aggregation are briefly discussed as they relate to the Armory site and central Alabama.

Increases or decreases in a region's population may play some role in determining whether or not distinct ethnic communities will aggregate with one another. For instance, aggregation became common among many indigenous populations after the dramatic decrease in population following European contact (Merrell 1984, 1989; Perttula 1997; Snow and Lanphear 1988; Warrick 2003). Because thorough diachronic studies regarding population density have yet to be conducted in central Alabama, it remains unclear what effect, if any, fluctuations in population density had on aggregation in this region. There is, however, a notable increase in the number of sites and the median site size from the Middle Woodland period to the Late Woodland period in central Alabama, likely implying that the number of people living in this region was increasing during these periods (Eubanks 2010: 117–19; Jeter 1973: 235, 1977: 130). Though similar population data for the earlier Late Archaic and Early Woodland periods in central Alabama are not available, there is no immediate evidence suggesting that a dramatic decrease in population occurred following these periods. Thus, while it remains possible that population pressure had some effect on aggregation, it is doubtful that this force was a primary cause, because there is little evidence for such large-scale aggregation during the Late Woodland period, when population levels were presumably relatively high. Further, there is also no evidence for this phenomenon during the Early Woodland and Late Archaic periods, when population levels are believed to have been lower or roughly equivalent to those of the late Middle Woodland subperiod.

Warfare or raiding may also encourage populations to aggregate (LeBlanc 1999; Merrell 1989; Redmond 1998). An abundance of evidence for warfare and raiding during the Middle Woodland period, however, is generally lacking throughout the Southeast. Although this trend has not been the subject of rigorous testing in central Alabama, it appears to be generally applicable to this region. Thus, the threat or presence of warfare or raiding appears not to have been a primary motivation behind aggregation at the Armory site.

Changes in climatic conditions may also affect whether populations will be more inclined to aggregate. Favorable environmental conditions, for example, are usually assumed to encourage increased sedentism and higher population density among hunter-gatherers (Riede 2009). It is also possible, however, that communities with more readily intensified methods of production (i.e., plant cultivation or agriculture) may profit from having a larger workforce during periods of environmental stress. In either case, if the environment is a primary determinant for interregional aggregation, then large-scale fluctuations in the environment should correspond to periods of aggregation or dispersion.

Using tree-ring data, Karen Smith (2009: 150–60) argues that a below-average amount of rainfall between AD 388 and 420 significantly affected the social dynamics of populations living in the nearby Chattahoochee

River valley. Despite this decrease in rainfall, the majority of the late Middle Woodland subperiod is characterized by above-average rainfall (Smith 2009: 156–58). With a suspected occupation occurring sometime between AD 300 and 500, it is impossible to say with any confidence whether Armory's occupation correlates with one of these environmental trends. Although Smith's (2009: 156–58) data for the Late Woodland period (AD 500–900) reveal more dramatic fluctuations in the amount of annual rainfall compared to the late Middle Woodland subperiod (AD 300–500), sustained episodes of both above-average and below-average rainfall are present. Given that there is little evidence for interregional aggregation in central Alabama during the Late Woodland period, it is reasonable to assume that sustained or fluctuating rainfall was not the sole determinant for such population aggregations in the Late or Middle Woodland periods.

While none of these forces can be definitively eliminated as potentially causal, none appear to have been as influential a stimulus as ritual. Therefore, given the data at hand, I argue that ritual, perhaps in the form of pilgrimage, was a primary motivating factor for aggregation at the Armory site. This assertion does not imply that ritual was the only cause for aggregation at the Armory site, however, as other secondary forces may have played some determining role. These determinants, for instance, may have taken the form of preconditions where interregional aggregation was more likely when certain population densities were reached or when specific environmental conditions were met.

Conclusion

This chapter has attempted to elucidate a high-resolution understanding of a specific place on the landscape in order to facilitate a better understanding of the nature of subcontinental social interactions during the late Middle Woodland subperiod. At the Armory site, such interactions may have taken place in the form of interregional aggregation similar to the Southern Appalachian early Middle Woodland pilgrimage centers discussed by Walthall (1985). This interpretation relies on several lines of evidence. First, the high frequency of rocker-stamped pottery, a nonlocal artifact class typically associated with the Gulf Coast, suggested that nonlocal populations may have visited the Armory site for some period of time. Second, based on the presence of food-related artifacts and features found adjacent to the site's possible burial mound, I argue that ritual activities akin to "feasting with the dead" (Seeman 1979; Walthall 1985) may have been conducted at the Armory site. Third, the spatial organization of the site also seemed to reflect some possible ritual significance or separation, as the local check-stamped pottery tended to cluster on the eastern half of the site, while the nonlocal rocker-stamped pottery was found primarily on the western half of the site.

Given the evidence for interregional aggregation and ritual activity, several potentially causal forces often linked to population aggregation were considered in an attempt to ascertain the motivation for aggregation at the Armory site. Among these potentially casual forces, ritual seems to be the primary, though perhaps not the only, motivation for aggregation at Armory. Following the assumption that this interaction was motivated by ritual, I suggest that the Armory site may be termed a pilgrimage center (i.e., a place where people travel for the purposes of participating in ritual activity). However, the motivations of prehistoric populations are difficult to tease out from the archaeological record. Thus, while it can be said with some confidence that Armory functioned as an aggregation center where ritual activities were conducted, its proposed linkage with pilgrimage remains somewhat tenuous.

12

Constituting Similarity and Difference in the Deep South

The Ritual and Domestic Landscapes of Kolomoki, Crystal River, and Fort Center

THOMAS J. PLUCKHAHN AND VICTOR D. THOMPSON

Archaeological studies of the Woodland period societies of eastern North America have undergone a renaissance in recent years, with the appearance of a number of ambitious syntheses (Byers 2004; Carr and Case 2005a; Case and Carr 2008; Charles and Buikstra 2006; Romain 2009). The vast majority of this work, however, has focused on Middle Woodland societies in the Hopewell heartland of the Midwest. By comparison, the southeastern Woodland counterparts to these societies remain comparatively little studied and undertheorized, as Wright and Henry discuss in their introduction to this volume. While a number of new site-specific studies have been presented (e.g., Keith 2010; Kimball et al. 2010; Pluckhahn 2003; Pluckhahn and Thompson 2009; Pluckhahn et al. 2010; Thompson and Pluckhahn 2010; see also contributions to this volume by Boudreaux [chapter 10]; Dekle [chapter 13]; Eubanks [chapter 11]; Jefferies et al. [chapter 6]; Keith [chapter 9]; Kimball et al. [chapter 8]; and Wright [chapter 7]), there have been few attempts to draw comparisons and contrasts among sites in the region (but see contributors to Anderson and Mainfort 2002a; Knight 1990, 2001; see also contributions to this volume by Applegate [chapter 2]; Clay [chapter 4]; Henry [chapter 15]; Pollack and Schlarb [chapter 3]; and Wallis [chapter 14]). Indeed, we would suggest that for at least the past 30 years, the general tendency has been to view the Woodland sites of the Deep South in progressively more atomistic terms, with panregional commonalities in material culture attributed primarily to analogous evolutionary processes, rather than historical and social connections (e.g., Brose and Percy 1974; Milanich 2002: 371; Percy and Brose 1974).

We count ourselves fortunate to have now conducted research—individually and in collaboration—at three of the largest and most famous Woodland sites in the "Deep South" of the southeastern United States (figure 12.1): Kolomoki (9Er1) in the lower Chattahoochee Valley of southwestern Georgia (Pluckhahn 2003), Crystal River (8Ci1) on the west-central Gulf Coast of Florida (Pluckhahn et al. 2009; Pluckhahn and Thompson 2009; Pluckhahn et al. 2010; Thompson and Pluckhahn 2010), and Fort Center (8Gl13) near Lake Okeechobee in interior southern Florida (Thompson and Pluckhahn 2012; Thompson et al. 2013). While our work at these temporally overlapping sites is of varying intensity—and by no means complete—new field and laboratory research has allowed us to make relatively secure observations regarding the setting, scale, and form of these ritual and domestic landscapes. We review these, highlighting points of contrast and commonality, as a first, small step toward a broader synthesis of the archaeology of the region.

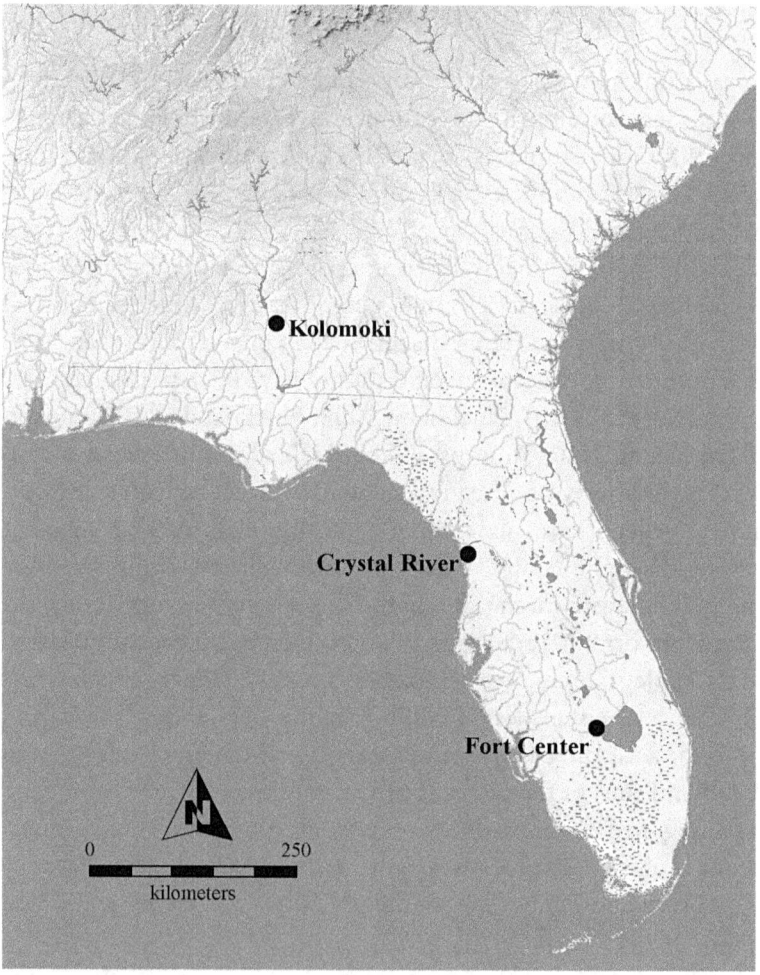

Figure 12.1. Location of Kolomoki, Crystal River, and Fort Center, Georgia and Florida. Map prepared by Thomas Pluckhahn.

Our review suggests to us that these landscapes were constructed in a manner that strategically emphasized both similarity and difference through variations on common themes, and thus exhibit a greater degree of historical and social connectedness than permitted by prevailing models. We suggest that the variety and similarity found in these mounded landscapes indicate a loose rather than highly structured monumental grammar, such as those found in later time frames (i.e., Mississippian period sites). The ability to construct similarities and differences in these landscapes provided the builders, as well as the larger population, with a way to build both a local and a larger regional identity (see Dillehay 2007 for an ethnohistoric example of this process from South America).

Setting

The first commonality we would note in regard to setting is that all three sites are located on or near the boundaries between distinct physiographic provinces or districts. These locations also generally correspond to boundaries between archaeological culture areas. Fort Center, for example, lies near the junction of the Eastern Flatlands, with its savannahs and pine flatwoods, and Big Cypress Swamp (Davis 1943: 43). Sears (1971, 1982) describes this as the Belle Glade culture area, a regional variant of the larger Glades culture defined by Goggin (1949) for southern Florida.

Milanich (1999, 2002: 368) has noted that Crystal River is located in one of the only areas of the Coastal Zone where hardwood hammocks extend to the coast proper, providing access to both upland and estuarine resources. Archaeologically, Crystal River is near the southern extent of the distribution of both Weeden Island and Swift Creek ceramics; assemblages from the site show a mix of these and the limestone-tempered Pasco and Perico Island types more common to the south (Weisman 1995).

Kolomoki is located near the boundary between two distinct divisions of the Coastal Plain: the Fall Line Hills, with hilly topography and an abundance of mast-bearing trees reminiscent of the Piedmont, and the Dougherty Plain, with pine flats more characteristic of the Coastal Plain (Pluckhahn 2003: 33–34; Steinen 1995, 1998; Veatch and Stephenson 1911: 28). The site marks the northernmost extent of the common occurrence of Weeden Island ceramics. Swift Creek ceramics, although not uncommon in areas to the south, are rarely found there in as large of quantities as at Kolomoki and other sites of southern Georgia.

Another commonality of setting worth noting is that all three of these sites are located in proximity to major bodies of water that likely held both cosmological and economic importance for their native inhabitants, an observation that has also been made for major Hopewell earthworks of the Scioto River valley (Romain 2000: 17–19). Crystal River's setting on the river of the same name is perhaps the most dramatic of the three; the site lies only a few kilometers upstream from the Gulf of Mexico and only a few kilometers downstream from the crystal-clear springs that give the river its name. The springs at Crystal River provide a haven for manatees during winter cold spells, drawing tourists today and probably hunters in the past—manatee remains have been recovered in quantity from portions of the middens at the site (Gary Ellis, pers. comm. 2010). In addition, Crystal River's location on the Gulf Coast at a point roughly midway on the Florida peninsula would have provided an obvious advantage in circumcoastal trade.

Fort Center is positioned only a few kilometers west of Lake Okeechobee, the second-largest freshwater lake in the contiguous United States (Florida Department of State 2010) and perhaps the only body of water in the interior Southeast where, while standing on one bank of the lake, one cannot see across to the opposite shore (an average distance of 48 km). Fisheating Creek, which lies adjacent to the site, is the major source of water for the lake from the west side. From Lake Okeechobee, water travel could continue north upstream along the Kissimmee River into central peninsular Florida, south downstream through the Everglades and the Miami River to the Atlantic Coast, or west along the Caloosahatchee to the Gulf Coast.

Kolomoki is located in relative proximity to the Chattahoochee River, widely assumed to have served as a major conduit for north–south Hopewellian trade (Anderson 1998). The cliffs adjacent to the river in this area reach heights of as much as 40 m, offering views of the river unparalleled elsewhere in the Coastal Plain. Less dramatic, but in closer proximity to the site, are numerous "steepheads" (Northwest Florida Environmental Conservancy 2006). These are active springs that cut back steep canyons to form microhabitats supporting plant and animal species unusual to the Coastal Plain.

Scale

Arbitrary definitions of archaeological site boundaries complicate efforts to compare the scale of these three centers. In addition, while we have conducted detailed topographic mapping at all three sites, the methods of mapping have varied: mapping at Kolomoki has been relatively comprehensive but limited in precision and detail by the use of an optical surveying transit; at Crystal River, the use of total stations provided much greater detail, albeit focused mainly on the core area of the site; at Fort Center, we have used selective total station survey to fill in gaps in publicly available LiDAR data, but the extent of the site has precluded us from filling all of those gaps. As a result, our maps are of varying resolution and precision. Nevertheless, in each case, they reflect a significant advance over previous efforts.

Fort Center (figure 12.2) is perhaps the largest of the three Woodland centers in terms of overall area, extending a minimum of 1.5 km east–west and 1 km north–south. As described by Sears (1982), the site includes a complex array of features: three circular ditches; five small mounds abutted by linear earthworks (Mounds 1, 2, 5, 8, and the UF Mound); one long oval mound (Mound 3); three small, round, flat-topped mounds (Mounds 10, 11, 12) (our mapping suggests that Mound 10 may also have an abutting linear earthwork); and finally, a mortuary complex comprising one large burial mound (Mound B) and one smaller platform mound (Mound A) separated by a charnel pond and partially surrounded by an earthen enclosure.[1] The Florida Master Site File lists two additional small mounds (Mounds X and W) in close enough proximity to the other earthworks to consider within the site boundaries. In addition, a sketch map of the site by Robert Carr (1975) shows several additional linear earthworks and small mounds; our map-

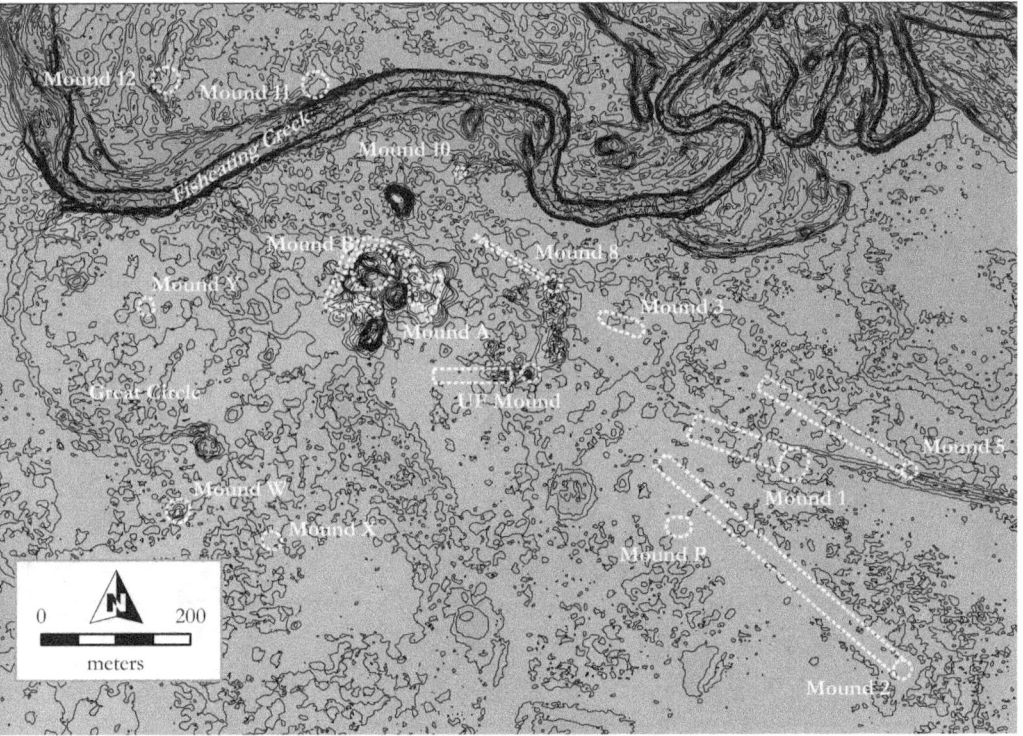

Figure 12.2. Map of the Fort Center site. Map prepared by Thomas Pluckhahn.

ping corroborates the existence of several of these features. While many of the mounds at Fort Center are spatially extensive, none are very tall; before Sears's excavation, Mound B was the tallest, at just 5.5 m.

Kolomoki (figure 12.3) is about the same size as Fort Center in terms of total area, stretching a little more than one kilometer east–west and an equal distance north–south. The site includes a minimum of eight mounds: two large burial mounds (Mounds D and E); one 16 m tall platform mound (Mound A); two smaller platform mounds (Mounds F and H); and one small linear mound (Mound L, not shown in figure 12.3) and four small dome-shaped mounds of uncertain function (Mounds B, C, G, and K, the latter not shown in figure 12.3). The area between Mounds D and E appears to have functioned as a plaza, as indicated by an absence of artifacts (Pluckhahn 2003). Historical accounts suggest the presence of a large but discontinuous earthen enclosure as well as two or three additional mounds (Palmer 1884; Pluckhahn 2003; Trowell 1998).

Compared to Fort Center and Kolomoki, Crystal River (figure 12.4) is relatively small and compact, extending about 500 m north–south and about 300 m east–west. However, there are historical accounts of several additional mounds in the area, and there is another large mound complex of apparent coeval occupation on the opposite side of the river only a short distance

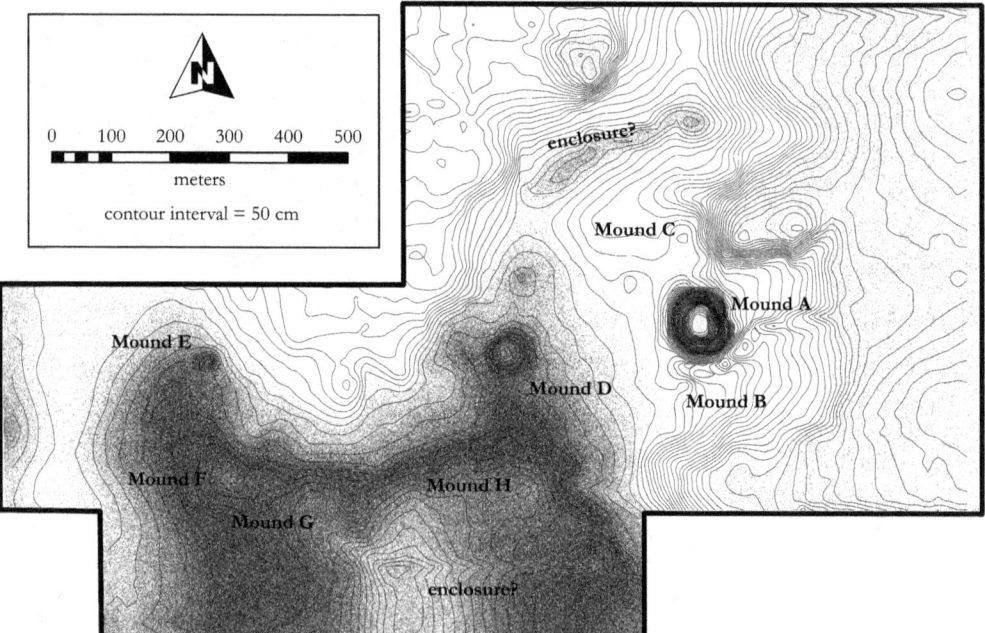

Figure 12.3. Map of the Kolomoki site. Map prepared by Thomas Pluckhahn.

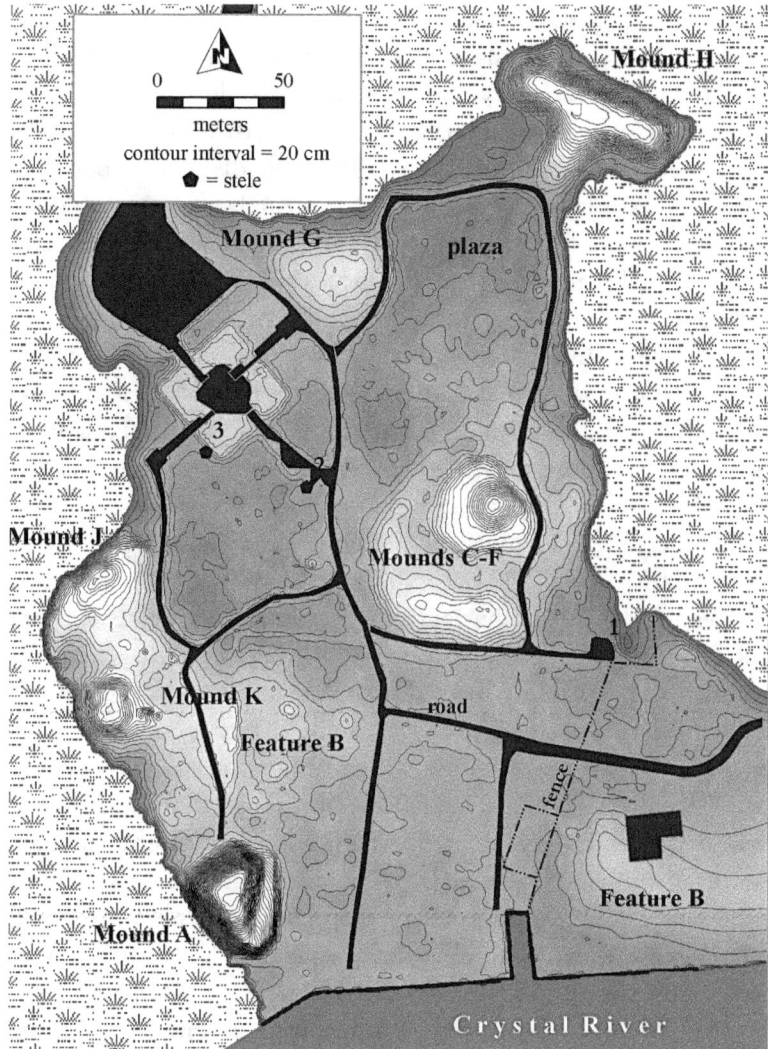

Figure 12.4. Map of the Crystal River site. Map prepared by Thomas Pluckhahn.

downstream (Weisman 1995). Documented earthworks at Crystal River include one low burial mound (Mound G); one 8 m tall platform mound (Mound A); two smaller platform mounds (Mounds H and K); one low, linear mound (Mound J); and a mortuary complex formed by a small mound (Mound F) on a low platform (Mound E) surrounded by a circular enclosure (Mound C), all of which contained burials.

Form

The caveats noted above in regard to scale apply equally to consideration of the form and layout of the three sites. In addition, we caution that although the approximate size, location, and extent of the domestic areas are well-known for Kolomoki and Crystal River, the same cannot be said of Fort Center.

Nevertheless, one commonality of form that we would stress is this: in contrast with their Hopewell counterparts to the north, all three of these sites clearly have extensive habitation areas. Thus, the distinction between ceremonial and domestic landscapes is blurred (see Applegate's contribution [chapter 2] in this volume for a contrast with Woodland sites in Kentucky). Pluckhahn (2003), following Sears (1956), suggests that Middle Woodland habitation at Kolomoki took the form of a roughly U-shaped village more than 500 m in diameter and possibly inhabited by as many as 400 people. At Crystal River, a comma-shaped midden (Feature B) of shell and bone, approximately 300 m long and 2 m deep, attests to a long period of relatively intensive and extensive domestic settlement. Finally, although the extent of the domestic habitation at Fort Center is poorly documented, we can say at a minimum that there are deep middens fronting Fisheating Creek for a distance of some 400 m.

All three sites include paired burial facilities. To varying degrees, these paired facilities were constructed in opposing locations across "empty" spaces, suggesting the possibility of dual social organization at each of the three sites. The opposition is perhaps most dramatic in the case of Crystal River, where Mound G and the Mound C–F burial complex face each other across a plaza. Carbon dates (described below) on burials confirm that interments in these two mounds were at least partially contemporaneous. At Fort Center, Mounds A and B are separated by an artificial pond that was used for mortuary purposes. Finally, Mounds D and E at Kolomoki are both located directly west of the plaza and Mound A but are separated by an area of unoccupied space, and thus are also suggestive of a dualistic opposition.

All three sites include circular earthworks. Historical accounts (McKinley 1873; Palmer 1884; Pickett 1851; see also Pluckhahn 2003; Trowell 1998) indicate that the enclosure at Kolomoki may have been the largest of these in terms of overall areal extent, with a diameter of approximately 675 m. If the discontinuous segments described in early accounts are counted, it probably had an overall perimeter of 950–1,200 m. The enclosure at Kolomoki was described as being about 6–9 m wide and 30–90 cm high. Mound D, a burial mound, was located near the center of the enclosure.

The Great Circle at Fort Center, comprising a more or less continuous ditch and adjacent spoil piles, is roughly the same length as the enclosure at Kolomoki, with a perimeter of around 1,130 m. It is approximately 365 m in diameter. There are hints of other, similar circular ditches, including one outside and two within the Great Circle. The arc of one preserved segment suggests that the outer circle may have been slightly larger than the Great Circle, with a diameter of about 380 m and a perimeter of approximately 1,200 m. Preserved sections of the interior circles suggest that they would have been smaller than the Great Circle, probably 200–220 m in diameter and 625–650 m in length. As at Kolomoki, there was apparently a small mound at the center of the Great Circle, although Sears (1982) provides little detail of his excavations there.

As noted briefly above, Fort Center and Crystal River each include smaller enclosures delineating burial complexes. Unfortunately, the enclosure at Fort Center was only minimally mapped by Sears (1982: fig. 9.5) and is difficult to discern today because of the many backfill piles Sears left behind. However, from his map we can suggest that it was an irregular circle or oval about 125 m in diameter, less than 1 m high, and perhaps 3 m wide. The circular enclosure at Crystal River was, at least as sketched by Moore (1903: 379), a nearly perfect circle about 90 m in diameter. It was reportedly about 2 m high and 20–25 m wide.

Both Crystal River and Kolomoki include plazas, defined by mounded architecture (including platform mounds at one end) and an absence of occupational debris. At Crystal River, one end of the plaza is further defined by a shell causeway. The plaza at Crystal River minimally measures about 90 m long (north–south) and 57 m wide (east–west). The plaza at Kolomoki, defined by the area between Mounds A and D, stretches over 200 m.

Timing

Although much remains to be done with regard to adequately dating the main features at these three Woodland sites, we have recently obtained a number of new radiocarbon dates that allow us to make some preliminary observations regarding the timing and tempo of settlement and earthwork construction. For consistency, we focus on the two-sigma calibrated ranges, determined using the OxCal 4.1 program and the Calib4.1 calibration data set.

Fifteen dates have been retrieved from the Crystal River site, including six from our own recent investigations (figure 12.5). These dates range from 800 cal BC to cal AD 966. Although sampling error is clearly a concern, the available dates suggest a possible brief hiatus in occupation and mound building at Crystal River during the Early or Middle Woodland; none of the dates with acceptable margins of error (<100 years) have two-sigma calibrated ranges covering the years between 417 and 166 cal BC.

Twenty-three carbon dates have been retrieved from Fort Center (figure 12.6), including 16 from our own investigations. Although additional dating

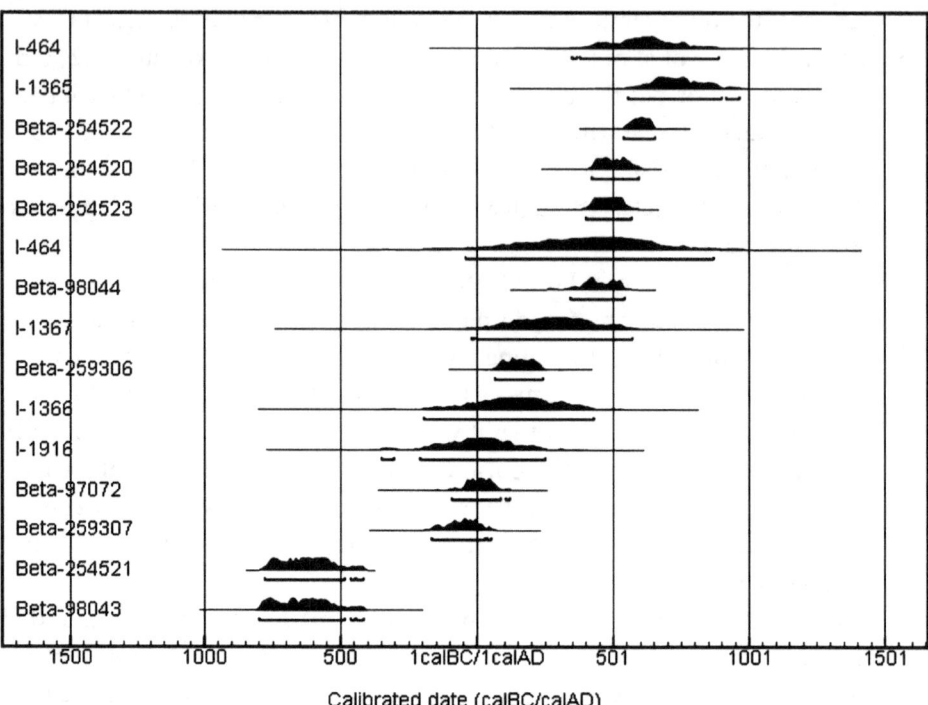

Figure 12.5. Calibrated radiocarbon dates from the Crystal River site. Date ranges and graph calculated using OxCal v4.1.7 (© Christopher Bronk Ramsey 2010) and the IntCal09 calibration curve (Reimer et al. 2009). Figure prepared by Thomas Pluckhahn.

could obviously change the picture, the dates from Fort Center are strikingly similar to those from Crystal River in several important respects. First, when several dates that presumably date to the later Mississippian or Seminole occupations are omitted, the two-sigma calibrated dates with acceptable errors from Fort Center exhibit a range almost precisely the same as those from Crystal River, extending from 799 cal BC to cal AD 950. Next, the Fort Center dates likewise point to a hiatus in the Early or Middle Woodland period; none of the two-sigma calibrated ranges on dates with acceptable errors fall between 386 and 20 cal BC.

For Kolomoki, we have obtained a total of 14 dates to supplement 2 with high errors retrieved by Sears (figure 12.7). These dates clearly indicate that Kolomoki has a more limited time range than Crystal River or Fort Center, dating exclusively to the Middle and Late Woodland periods. The two-sigma calibrated ranges for the 14 dates with acceptable errors begin at cal AD 253. The ending dates for Kolomoki more closely approximate those of Crystal River and Fort Center, extending to cal AD 1022.

Intriguingly, the earliest-dated features at all three sites are burial mounds,

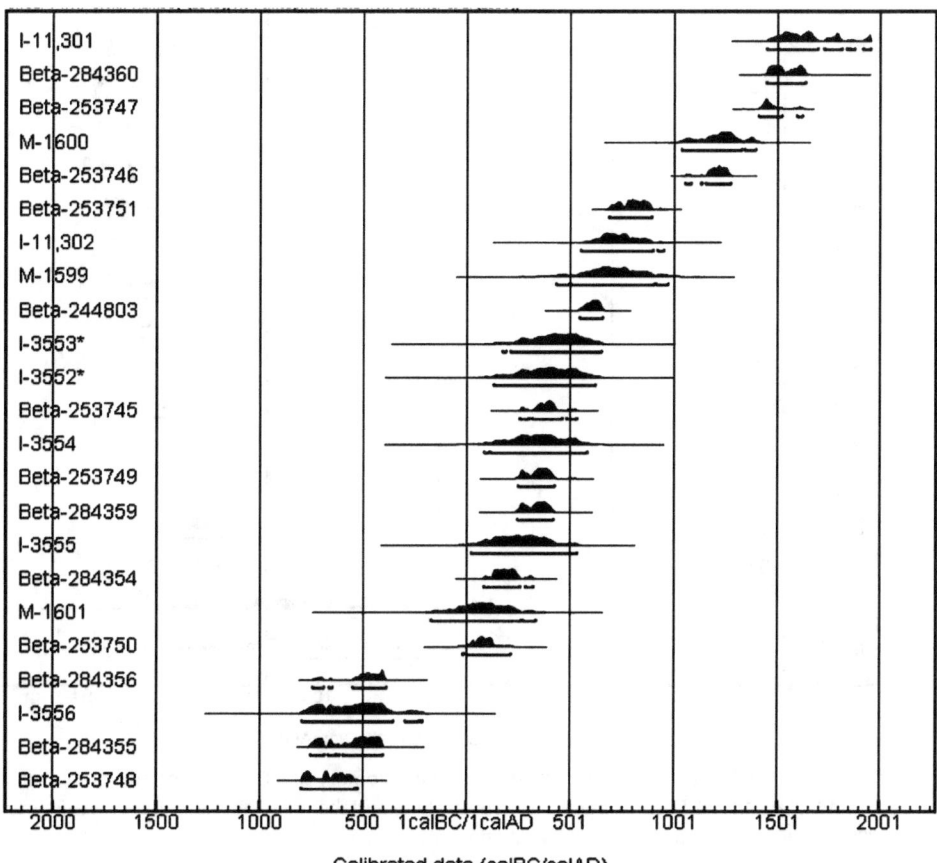

Figure 12.6. Calibrated radiocarbon dates from the Fort Center site. Date ranges and graph calculated using OxCal v4.1.7 (© Christopher Bronk Ramsey 2010) and the IntCal09 calibration curve (Reimer et al. 2009). Figure prepared by Thomas Pluckhahn.

or at least burial-mound-related features. Perhaps more intriguingly, at two of the three sites these mounds were initiated in the Early Woodland period, perhaps near the transition from the Late Archaic. In the case of Crystal River, carbon dates point to the initiation of a small burial mound (Mound G) between 800 and 416 cal BC and the circular enclosure (with burials) (Mound C) between 781 and 417 cal BC. One carbon date from Mound B at Fort Center closely matches these dates, with a two-sigma calibrated range of 799–524 cal BC (four other dates from Mound B are more recent, however). Mound construction apparently began much later at Kolomoki, with the earliest-dated context consisting of the midden below Mound D, which produced a date with a two-sigma calibrated range of AD 253–530.

At all three sites, the construction of small platform mounds apparently began during the Middle Woodland period. The single date from Mound A at

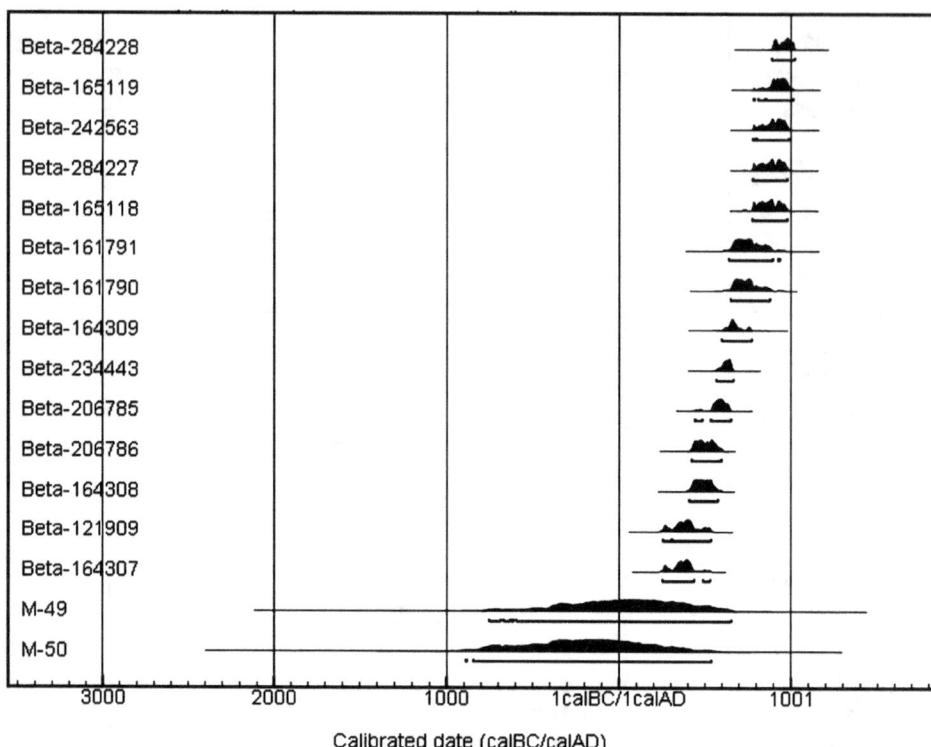

Figure 12.7. Calibrated radiocarbon dates from the Kolomoki site. Date ranges and graph calculated using OxCal v4.1.7 (© Christopher Bronk Ramsey 2010) and the IntCal09 calibration curve (Reimer et al. 2009). Figure prepared by Thomas Pluckhahn.

Fort Center has a two-sigma calibrated range of AD 132–621. A more precise date from a later construction stage in Mound H at Crystal River spans the interval from cal AD 422 to 596; geophysical evidence points to the existence of an earlier platform stage that would push this date back further (Pluckhahn et al. 2009). Mound H at Kolomoki has a two-sigma calibrated range of AD 597–773, and Mound F is assumed to date to around the same time, based on ceramic evidence (Pluckhahn 2003).

The much larger platform mounds at Crystal River and Kolomoki require additional dating but likewise appear to date to the terminal Middle Woodland or Late Woodland periods. Bullen's date for Mound A at Crystal River has a calibrated range of AD 556–966 (Weisman 1995). Mound A at Kolomoki has not been carbon dated, because modern excavations have never penetrated beyond the upper construction layers, but Pluckhahn (2003) suggests a date in the range of AD 450–650, based on ceramic evidence.

Discussion

Fort Center, Crystal River, and Kolomoki were temporally overlapping landscapes that shared a number of key features. At the same time, these features were expressed in varied settings, scales, and forms. We believe that this reflects the strategic constitution of similarity and difference by the inhabitants of these sites, rather than simply historical accident or convergent evolutionary process. In this final section of our chapter, we explore this idea by imagining how a resident of one of these landscapes might have experienced the other two if he or she encountered them as a visitor—an admittedly (but perhaps refreshingly) brief and superficial exercise in a phenomenology of landscape. Our exercise is entirely hypothetical but not outside the realm of possibility. Despite the distances between these sites, there are similarities in their artifact assemblages—from shell and stone plummets to Crystal River–like pottery—to suggest the possibility of direct, if only sporadic, contact through occasional pilgrimages or trading expeditions. The similarities in timing also make a case for direct connections between these sites; indeed, the strong correlation of radiocarbon dates suggests to us that the historical fortunes of Crystal River and Fort Center—and to a lesser extent Kolomoki—were intimately related.

Traveling from their home at one to another of these centers, visitors would no doubt have appreciated the exotic character of the setting, given the juxtaposition of different physiographic zones. They no doubt would have been awed by features of the natural landscape, from the size of Lake Okeechobee to the clarity of the springs at Crystal River to the height of the cliffs above the Chattahoochee River. But we probably do not climb too far out on the limb of phenomenological inference to suggest that the presence of these water features would have resonated with them at some deeper level as well. If much of Middle Woodland ceremony revolved around themes of rebirth and renewal, as has been claimed with increasing regularity in recent years (e.g., Buikstra and Charles 1999; Byers 2004; Carr 2005a; Hall 1979, 1997; Knight 1990, 2001; Romain 2000), then water would have been an appropriate metaphor, as many of these same authors have observed.

Standing on the plaza at Kolomoki, a visitor from Crystal River might be impressed by its size and by the height of the adjacent platform mound but would recognize the basic form and arrangement of these features. In contrast, a visitor from Fort Center might find the plaza and the size of platform mound unusual but would recognize the scale and form of the enclosure as similar to his or her own Great Circle. Indeed, several scholars point out common themes among Eastern Woodland native groups regarding such structures. For example, Hall (1976: 360; see also Gibson 1998, as well as Applegate's contribution to this volume [chapter 2]) suggests that circular earthworks served, in part, to "restrict the movement of spirits or to protect the enclosed area from unwanted supernatural influences." Other interpretations emphasize these architectural constructions in the context of myths. For example, Romain (2000: 182–97) has suggested that the circular enclosures with central burial mounds at Middle Woodland sites in Ohio materialized deep-seated beliefs about the cosmos, specifically, the earth-diver myths that were common to native peoples across much of North America. While we cannot say for sure exactly what these constructions represented, they were a common element to the built environment that, while taking slightly varied forms, would probably have evoked similar meaning for those who participated in their construction and use.

Observing a burial ceremony at Crystal River, visitors from Kolomoki and Fort Center might recognize the dualistic opposition in the placement of the two burial mounds, even if the scale and spacing of the mounds was dissimilar from their own experience. For a visitor from Fort Center, the arrangement of the Mound C–F burial complex would seem reminiscent of his or her own Mound B mortuary complex, particularly since there is evidence that Fort Center inhabitants also interred at least some burials in the earthen berm that surrounds the mound-pond complex (Milanich, pers. comm. 2011; Fort Center field notes, Florida Museum of Natural History).

For visitors to Fort Center, the linear earthworks and circular ditches might seem odd. But for the visitor from Kolomoki, the scale of the site and these features would not be unusual. And for the visitor from Crystal River, the approach to the site from Fisheating Creek, with the bluff of deep middens fronting the water, would recall home.

As we have argued elsewhere (Pluckhahn and Thompson 2009; Thompson and Pluckhahn 2010), and as our brief phenomenological exercise is meant to illustrate, the similarities among these sites would have served to facilitate participation in extralocal ceremonies and social networks. At the same time, the differences would have underscored the uniqueness of the community and the ceremonial practices that took place there. Thus, on the one hand, modification of the landscape by local groups provided a familiar setting for outsiders coming to the site for ceremonies, while on the other hand, it also served to distinguish Crystal River from other centers and provide a unique experience for visitors to the site (for parallels in Formative Peru, see Dillehay 1992, 2004).

The similarities and differences in setting, scale, and form of the three Woodland landscapes that we describe in this chapter thus do not merely reflect but were constitutive of connections among communities. We do not argue—as some have recently suggested for the Mississippian period (Blitz and Lorenz 2006; Pauketat 1994, 1997, 2004a, 2004b, 2007)—that these sites should be understood as part of a singular historical process. We do, however, suggest that there were much greater historical and social connections among these and other Woodland sites of the Deep South than many of our colleagues have been willing to grant. We hope this chapter has made a first small step toward identifying such connections and perhaps thus also stimulating a renaissance in the study of the Hopewellian societies of the Deep South.

Note

1. Sears (1982: 140–41) describes two additional small platform mounds, but these were located a kilometer or more away to the west and did not appear on his map. He also describes a possible mound at the center of the Great Circle but dismisses this as probable spoil from the excavation of one of the circular ditches (Sears 1982: 176).

13

Ritual Life and Landscape at Tunacunnhee

VICTORIA G. DEKLE

> If we are to understand fully the spatial, temporal, and symbolic dynamics of Middle Woodland sacred landscapes, we must look beyond the immediate boundaries of the burial site.
> Richard W. Jefferies, "Death Rituals at the Tunacunnhee Site"

As demonstrated by the chapters of this volume, Early and Middle Woodland ritual landscapes are variable and dynamic throughout Eastern North America. Our analyses of these phenomena, however, are uneven, because interpretations of landscapes result not only from local culture histories but also from our various academic backgrounds and theoretical persuasions. Landscape is a tricky and theoretically vague term, the definition of which tends to shift across disciplines or according to the available material data in question. In cultural geography, for instance, there is a disciplinary distinction between American geographical studies of the built environment (Sauer 1956) and the British concentration on landscapes as idealized expressions (Cosgrove 1983). As discussed in Wright and Henry's introduction, archaeological approaches to landscape also exhibit a transcontinental divide. American landscape approaches are often more aligned with regional studies (Buikstra and Charles 1999), while the British definition of landscape is often more sensual and experiential (Bender 1993; Ingold 1993, 2000; Tilley 1994).

A landscape analysis of the Tunacunnhee site in northwestern Georgia provides an opportunity to engage such different theoretical understandings of the landscape and, in the process, explore different individual and group identities at Tunacunnhee itself. Tunacunnhee is a rich Middle Woodland mortuary site that exhibits various interment styles and adornment materials, where people clearly referenced an ideological system shared across many subregions of eastern North America. Data sets from Tunacunnhee have been used to explore separate individual identities at the site, but they have never been considered at once, together. Landscape theory is one way to connect all these lines of data into a place-based study, and the landscape approach applied in this chapter explores the intersections of these different theoretical frameworks and various conceptions of Tunacunnhee through multiple scales of human interaction.

This landscape analysis of Tunacunnhee considers not simply the material concept of the built environment but also the experiences, motivations, and emotions connected to the built environment on multiple scales. As Adam Smith (2003: 72) states, "Landscape provides the conceptual apparatus for exploring the interconnections of the lived, conceived, and perceived." Thus, I do not consider landscape to be a mere reiteration of mound locations, river courses, or historically documented trade routes. Certainly these are integral elements within the landscape analysis—as I will illustrate with Tunacunnhee—but the landscape itself is also constituted of human interactions, perceptions, and imaginations of that space and within that place (Smith 2003). Tunacunnhee's landscape should not only be understood as an important location for influencing trade relations or as a regionally distinct set of human interments and mortuary practices but also as an arena for lived human experiences that created such a distinct landscape.

Scale is an ever-present issue in archaeological interpretations, and defining the particular scales of analysis is a methodological and conceptual necessity in landscape studies. Therefore, landscape approaches cannot simply be equated with bounded regional studies (Kowalewski 2008), because landscapes are multiscalar. While regional studies contribute much to our understanding of Middle Woodland life (e.g., Charles 1992; Tainter 1977), a detailed consideration of social possibilities and restrictions offered by a particular place adds further information to these geographic and temporal locations. Charles's (2010) chapter on Hopewellian landscapes in the Midwest is a good example of this experiential approach in action.

In this examination of the Tunacunnhee site, I incorporate multiple scales of archaeological data to explore ritual life in a particular place. Some of these interpretations consider identity information from mortuary adornments and body position, while other arguments question the broader social connection of Hopewellian exchange and mortuary ritual across Eastern North America. Obviously, certain aspects of Tunacunnhee's landscape have already been well documented and insightfully interpreted, such as the site's location along a major historical trade route in the east (Jefferies 1976, 1979). How did this connection, however, structure life in this particular location? What did the people at Tunacunnhee have to gain (or lose) from such a distant connection? How did ritual activity impact other social and political processes in daily life? My approach is a critical elaboration of Jefferies's original arguments. I emphasize his interpretations on interregional interaction and mortuary ritual, but I examine the nuances of ritual and interaction through a multiscalar landscape lens.

Site Description

Tunacunnhee (figure 13.1) is a well-known Middle Woodland site in Dade County, Georgia, that includes eight noncontemporary stone mounds across approximately an acre (Jefferies 1976: 3, 31). Tunacunnhee is most often cited in the Woodland literature for its regionally unique assemblage of Hopewellian funerary materials. In fact, much of the work at Tunacunnhee has focused on interpreting and sourcing these mortuary items (Goad 1976).

Joseph Caldwell directed the excavations of the mounds at Tunacunnhee in the summer of 1973 with students from the University of Georgia. Four of the eight mounds at the site were pre-Columbian constructions and contained human remains, while the other four were erected in modern times. The UGA crew also excavated a habitation area near the mounds. This area yielded many

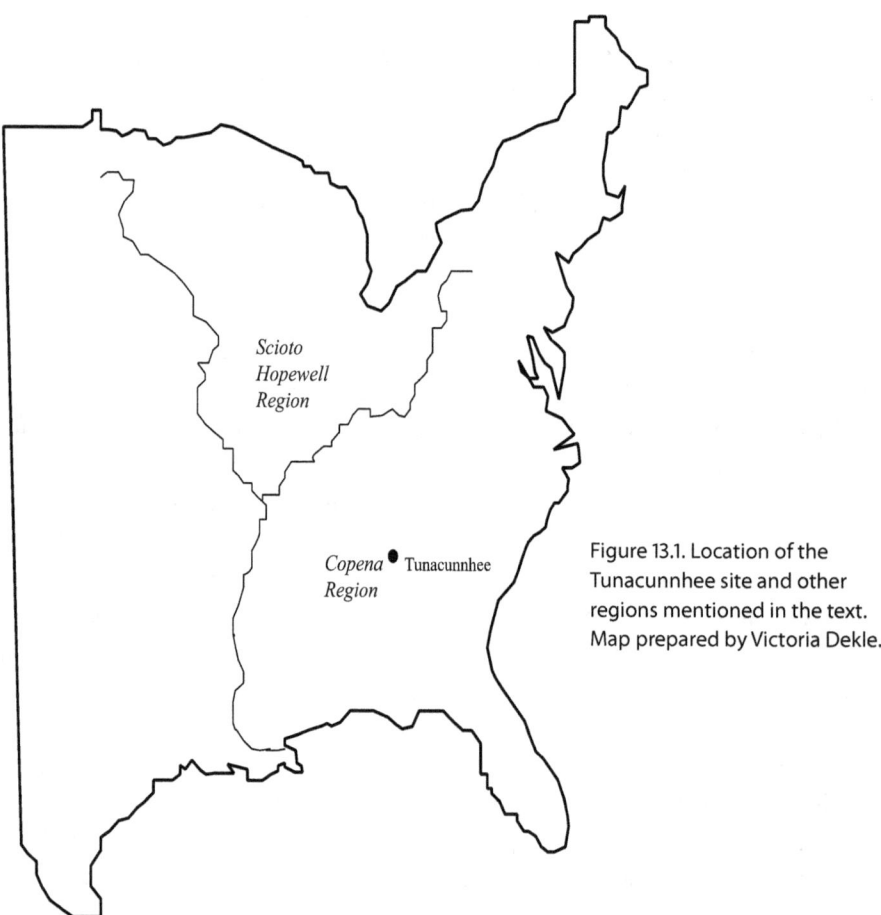

Figure 13.1. Location of the Tunacunnhee site and other regions mentioned in the text. Map prepared by Victoria Dekle.

specialized artifacts probably associated with the ritual manufacture of prismatic blades, crystal quartz, mica, and copper objects (Jefferies 2006). Data from the excavations of the mound and nonmound areas of the site supported interpretations about social hierarchy initially (Jefferies 1976) and later, scenarios concerning ritual specialists (Jefferies 2006; Turff and Carr 2005: 659).

Caldwell's crew excavated approximately 30 burials at the Tunacunnhee site, including some isolated human remains (such as mandibles) that were possible mortuary offerings (following Seeman 2007). As Jefferies (1976) illustrates in the original site report, there were many different burial styles, locations, and associated grave good materials throughout the Tunacunnhee site. He originally argued that the associated materials indicated social ranks (1976: 36–38), although his cluster analysis was limited by a small sample size ($n = 18$) (1976: 41); Jefferies (2006) deemphasized social ranking at Tunacunnhee in later publications. In sum, early interpretations of the data generated during the 1973 excavations underscore two important aspects of the identity of Tunacunnhee: it was not only a locus for the interment of the dead but also the site for the production of ritual objects. Follow-up analyses, in turn, highlighted the site's identity within a broader, regional landscape of social interaction.

Middle Woodland Interactions at the Interpersonal Scale

Tunacunnhee is located in Lookout Valley, a relatively isolated area between Lookout Mountain to the east and Sand Mountain to the west (Jefferies 1979: 162). Jefferies argued that this location was significant for interregional exchange, because it "would allow the inhabitants to have access to transportation and communication routes along the floor of Lookout Valley and over Lookout Mountain, which eventually leads to most of the Eastern United States" (Jefferies 1979: 170). As others have argued, most ethnographically documented exchange routes sat along major rivers and prehistoric overland trails (Chapman and Keel 1979; Goad 1979).

The sorts of interregional exchange postulated for Tunacunnhee have been a significant focus of Hopewellian research for decades. Previous work with the elaborate Middle Woodland contexts in the Southeast often focused on (1) the exchange of particular raw materials and (2) the Southeast's role in the generalized "Hopewell Interaction Sphere" (Caldwell and Hall 1964) or other such broad interaction networks (see Carr and Case 2005b for a recent summary of this extensive history). Significant advances in sourcing research in the Midwest and Southeast now demonstrate that many "exotic" Hopewell materials are not foreign at all but were instead locally produced (Carr 2005b: 592). Some of the materials at Tunacunnhee, such as copper ear spools (Ruhl 2005; Ruhl and Seeman 1998) and panpipes (Turff and Carr 2005), are from

South Appalachian sources (Carr 2005b: 592). In contrast, other materials at Tunacunnhee, such as marine shell, shark teeth, and a limited number of copper samples, are from more-distant regions. The movement of these materials and the stylistic traditions reflected in other artifacts (such as panpipes and ear spools) provide undeniable evidence for interregional exchange.

The interregional connections represented by these exchange goods and Tunacunnhee's location along a major trade route situate the site within a large-scale, regional landscape of interactions. What remain to be clarified are the implications of such connections for the lived experiences at Tunacunnhee. Were groups from distant locations traveling through Lookout Valley from Ohio to western North Carolina, where there is also evidence for Hopewellian interaction (Keel 1976; Kimball et al., chapter 8, this volume; Wright, chapter 7, this volume)? Alternatively, did people from northwestern Georgia make pilgrimages to the Midwest to learn or experience certain social traditions? What interpersonal experiences characterized such interactions? The questions about social interactions and motivations in the Tunacunnhee landscape are numerous and varied. Both economic and ritualistic mechanisms undoubtedly influenced interregional trade at Tunacunnhee, but the specifics of this interaction are elusive and require a multiscalar and contextual approach.

Panpipes offer one way to contextualize the experience of interregional interaction at Tunacunnhee, particularly at the scale of the individual interment. Panpipes are among the most unique constituents of the Tunacunnhee assemblage, and the Tunacunnhee panpipe assemblage is one of the largest concentrations of panpipes in any Hopewell site in eastern North America (Turff and Carr 2005: 650). The pipes are stylistically similar to panpipes across eastern North America (Richard Jefferies, pers. comm. 2011), although the Tunacunnhee panpipes occur with a more varied burial population than is commonly observed in the Midwest (Turff and Carr 2005: 661).

The way that panpipes were placed in the burials suggests that they were used to symbolize, at the scale of the individual, Hopewellian connections that linked groups across the eastern North American landscape. Instead of being beside the body or near the mouth, panpipes are most often located on individuals' chests as if they were adornments. Although this position is not ubiquitous across the site, the majority of panpipes appear to be "worn" by the deceased individuals in the mortuary context. Such position could communicate social affiliation (Wobst 1977) in addition to being a location for identity negotiation throughout one's life (Loren 2008). Dress in life and dress in death should never be uncritically equated, yet this class of mortuary adornment can still provide information about interaction and identity in life.

Following Mark Seeman's (1995) insights on foreigners and "otherness" in Hopewellian interactions, Turff and Carr (2005: 680–81) elaborate on how the panpipes might have served as a symbolic and functional indicator of interregional connections and power. They summarize (2005: 681):

> Distant peoples of Hopewellian traditions who considered each other outsiders could have used panpipes to communicate metaphorically some very basic concepts to each other when they met. Power and humanness are some reasonable possibilities with empirical support. Although persons from different Hopewellian traditions probably were not able to appreciate all the specific connotations that the copper, silver, and melodies of panpipes had in each other's cultures, they may have been able to grasp core aspects of each other's identities through the playing and presentation of panpipes. These messages would have encouraged mutual respect among Hopewellian peoples who were categorically outsiders and also provided motivation for interacting.

If Turff and Carr's impression of panpipe ownership is accurate, than Tunacunnhee's abundance of panpipes indicates possibly intensive social interactions with "foreign" individuals who would recognize the panpipe's significance. Whether the individuals interred at Tunacunnhee traveled to distant areas (such as the Hopewell core), were immigrants or visitors from the Midwest, or interacted with traders passing through the region, the people at Tunacunnhee understood the significance of panpipes and used them to engage visitors who were associated with a regional identity.

In this regard, panpipes can be productively interpreted as parts of a relational landscape, in which the interactions among the individual actors at Tunacunnhee proper effectively worked to create and perpetuate a landscape of interregional connections. As Tim Ingold has argued, "Landscape is the world as it is known to those who dwell therein, who inhabit its places and journey along the paths connecting them" (1993: 156). The Tunacunnhee landscape thus is more than the narrow passage by Lookout Mountain or the stone and earthen mounds; it also entails the experience of interregional connections among individuals and groups of people at this particular place.

Subregional-Scale Interactions: Contrast to Copena

Although Hopewell studies have traditionally emphasized archaeological phenomena in the Ohio Hopewell core (e.g., Brose and Greber 1979), recent analyses have reconsidered the large-scale unitary view of "Hopewell" (see Carr 2005b: 576–77) and urge more local approaches. The term *Copena* describes the localized Middle Woodland burial expressions in northwestern Georgia, northeastern Alabama, and southeastern Tennessee (Beck 1995; Goad 1980; Jeter 1984; Knight 1990; Walthall 1973). This term was created as a combination of *copper* and *galena,* referring to raw materials that are commonly observed in these funerary contexts (Walthall 1979: 200; Webb 1938). Copena sites are distributed in a linear fashion along the lower Tennessee River. Beck (1995) has documented a Copena social boundary extending along the Elk River, which is further supported by Ruhl's ear spool study (2005: 710).

The mortuary traditions exhibited at Tunacunnhee are materially distinct from those of its Copena neighbors to the west. The material culture at Tunacunnhee is more elaborate and more deliberately cites contemporary Hopewellian mortuary and adornment practices than does the material culture observed at Copena sites. Although Copena groups did participate in Hopewellian interregional exchange and cited certain styles and materials, they did so in a less direct way (Jefferies 1976: 43). In other words, although Tunacunnhee and the Copena groups both participated in interregional Hopewell exchange, they did so on different scales and with different social motivations. Although more research is needed to permit the specifics of this relationship to be discerned, the material differences between Tunacunnhee and Copena suggest that they were incorporated into relational landscapes of interregional interaction in different ways.

Although some of the material culture differences between Tunacunnhee and its western neighbors should be attributed to geographical and temporal factors, we should also recognize the social implications of this material distinction. As Goad (1979) and Jefferies (1979) both argue, Tunacunnhee is located in an important geographic location for access to trade items moving through eastern North America, such as materials from the Great Lakes and the Gulf and/or Atlantic Coasts. As a result, individuals at Tunacunnhee may have had the ability to influence some of the economic exchange through eastern North America or at least across the local subregion, which included Copena sites. For example, the symbolic weight of the Hopewellian materials (such as the canonical meanings of panpipes) would have provided the Tunacunnhee artifact possessors with a certain identity (and, possibly, with a resulting authority) to those who observed their material items.

The Hopewellian exchange advantage lent by Tunacunnhee's location may not have been available at Copena sites. As a result, we should expect that the material expressions of integration into a social landscape of interaction will differ between Tunacunnhee and Copena sites. In contrast to Copena sites, Tunacunnhee bears evidence of an ideological connection to the Midwest that was lived and experienced within Tunacunnhee society. Not only do the

Figure 13.2. Fabric-impressed ear spool from the Tunacunnhee site, Georgia. Photo by Richard Jefferies.

mortuary materials at the site create a larger Hopewell connection, but also the placement of these materials (such as the distinctive ear spool [figure 13.2] position in Burial 17 [Ruhl 2005]) indicates an intimate knowledge of Hopewellian mortuary rituals. These locally distinctive mortuary treatments indicate an understanding of and familiarity with the daily practices enacted through eastern North American Hopewellian culture.

Conclusion

While identifying the spatial and temporal distribution of Hopewell materials across the Woodland Southeast is very helpful for exposing trade connections and social patterns, more-fruitful questions ask how and why these materials were spread to individuals and communities across the broad region. Tunacunnhee's landscape was created and re-created every day through interpersonal interactions that drew on local and distant experience. Landscape analyses should be multiscalar, not simply considering where a place sits geographically but also exploring the actors within their spatial and temporal location. Landscapes are not simply composed of mountains, viewsheds, or trails. They are the places built by people, used by people, perceived by people, and imagined by people.

14

Swift Creek and Weeden Island Mortuary Landscapes of Interaction

NEILL J. WALLIS

Middle Woodland burial mounds in the lower Southeast were the ritualized locations for mortuary ceremonies and periodic population aggregation that probably included various other events. While there is some variation in the form and apparent function of these burial mounds, most mounds evidence a degree of social connection that extends beyond typical contemporaneous habitation sites. Indeed, burial mounds often contain exotic stone, mineral, and metal artifacts or raw materials, as well as pottery with distinctive formal or typological attributes that are not often found at nonmortuary sites in the region. The material culture of Swift Creek and Weeden Island burial mounds in the Gulf Coastal Plain, in particular, indicates a variety of connections between sites that have been explained in a number of ways, including interactions among close kin and proximate communities, interactions among distant communities, and long-distance exchange (e.g., Goad 1979; Milanich et al. 1997; Pluckhahn 2003: 193–94; Sears 1973; Smith and Stephenson 2010; Willey 1949: 540–41).

In western areas of Florida and Georgia, assorted copper artifacts, mica sheets or cutouts, worked animal jaws, ceramic human figurines, platform pipes, and bar gorgets, among other artifacts, at some Swift Creek mound sites have been interpreted as evidence of Hopewell exchange connections (Goad 1979; Keith, chapter 9, this volume), although Hopewell mostly predates Swift Creek. Swift Creek Complicated Stamped vessels also preserve evidence of social interaction among Swift Creek sites through paddle matches, that is, multiple vessels stamped with the same wooden paddle (Snow and Stephenson 1998; Stoltman and Snow 1998; Wallis 2011). Ceramics also provide evidence for interaction at Early Weeden Island (or Weeden Island I) mounds; these contain Late Swift Creek Complicated Stamped pottery in the Weeden Island "heartland" of northern Florida, southern Georgia, and eastern Alabama, as well as highly ornate vessels that are typically found in east-side caches (Milanich et al. 1997; Sears 1956; Willey 1949: 405). Finely crafted effigy vessels from various distant sites are so similar that they seem to have been made in the same location by a single artisan, and other Weeden Island series vessels may have been transported between sites as well (Cordell 1984; Milanich et al. 1997; Pluckhahn and Cordell 2010).

Clearly, then, Swift Creek and Weeden Island burial mounds were gathering centers of some kind. These landscape loci gathered not only people periodically from various places, perhaps from multiple kin groups, but also citations to other places in the form of nonlocal material culture that was deposited within them (Wallis 2008). Along these lines, William Sears (1973) once argued that the artifacts deposited in Deptford, Swift Creek, and Weeden Island burial mounds reflected changes in a ceremonial penchant for the "unique and the foreign," an interpretation that can now be thoroughly evaluated through materials analysis and careful considerations of object biographies (e.g., Wallis 2011).

Additionally, mound assemblages can be better understood by viewing the mounds themselves as locations for the assembly of disparate people and things, inscriptions that became salient points of reference for defining the social landscape. Situated among people who may have been seasonally mobile (e.g., Smith 2009), mounds can be usefully considered as "nodes in a matrix of movement" that were important mapping devices (Ingold 2000: 219). Following the approach taken by Tim Ingold (2000: 219–38), these mapping practices are quite unlike conventional "mapmaking," which simply provides representations of space. Rather, the mapping implicated in mounds constituted "ways of knowing" that were made up of stories and histories that could be inscribed in place. Places, or nodes, such as these are at once part of the past, present, and future, potentially uniting disparate histories and serving as platforms for asserting, affirming, and contesting histories, social connections, and social and cultural distinctions. Archaeological evidence indicates that many Swift Creek and Weeden Island burial mounds, much like other Woodland mounds across the southeastern United States, were indexical places that made reference to particular situated experiences and the paths between places through the deposition of artifacts within mounds (e.g., Wallis 2008, 2011). Simply put, burial mounds were not just repositories for the dead and their possessions (Charles 2005; Clay, chapter 4, this volume). Neither were mounds primarily territorial markers for particular groups of hunter-gatherers, as has been argued for some Hopewell mounds (e.g., Buikstra and Charles 1999; Charles and Buikstra 1983). While mounds may have served these purposes, in the Deep South they were most significantly places for the construction of histories and were constituted, in part, through the nuances of depositional practice that included the placement of nonlocal objects. These nuances can better inform our interpretations of Middle Woodland earthen mounds in the lower Southeast.

What sorts of histories or social relationships are indicated at Middle Woodland burial mounds? To address this question, this chapter considers variation in Swift Creek and Weeden Island burial mounds of the Gulf Coastal Plain (figure 14.1) in comparison to contemporaneous mounds on the Atlantic coast where materials analysis shows clear patterns of artifact distribution (Wallis 2011; Wallis et al. 2010). As evidence from this region demonstrates, practices at burial mounds were likely tied to definitions of lineage and kinship, but the objects that were deposited at mounds were probably not simply icons that were co-opted by resident kin groups. Instead, mound artifacts, particularly ceramic vessels (the focus of this analysis), are more likely to have been gifts in the sense that they came with obligations and indelible qualities of association; their burial in mounds was the end result of ongoing relationships between lineages or other social groupings. While Swift Creek Complicated

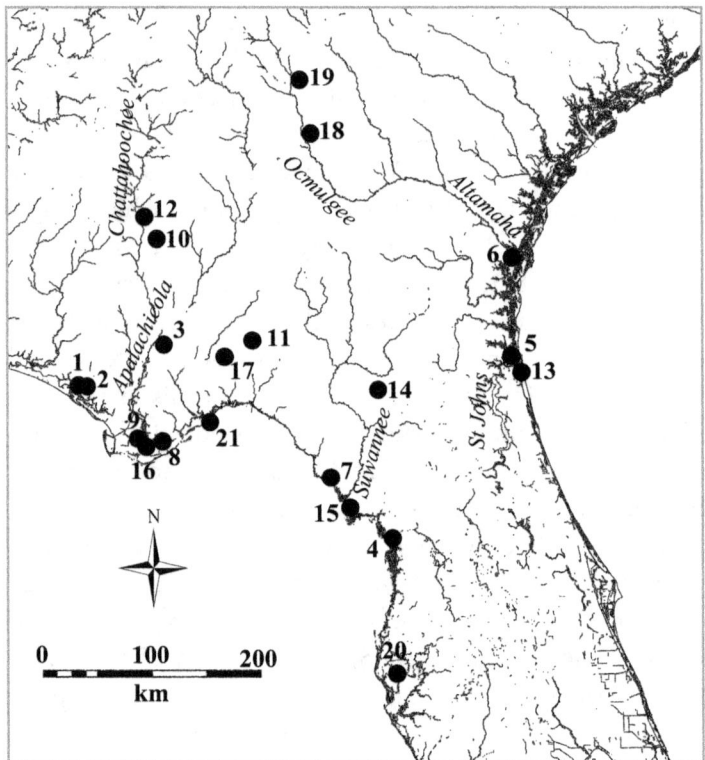

Figure 14.1. Sites mentioned in the text and other important Swift Creek and Weeden Island sites: (1) Alligator Bayou, (2) Anderson's Bayou, (3) Aspalaga, (4) Crystal River, (5) Dent, (6) Evelyn, (7) Garden Patch, (8) Green Point, (9) Huckleberry Landing, (10) Kolomoki, (11) Letchworth, (12) Mandeville, (13) Mayport, (14) McKeithen, (15) Palmetto Island, (16) Pierce, (17) Shelly Mound (Fla.), (18) Shelly Mound (Ga.), (19) Swift Creek, (20) Weeden Island, (21) Yent. Map prepared by Neill Wallis.

Stamped vessels seem likely to have been used to secure histories of alliance among lineages, east-side caches of vessels in general, and Weeden Island effigy vessels in particular, may require other explanations. Considering mounds as points of social reference, I outline some of the important differences that are apparent among Swift Creek and Weeden Island burial mounds and the types of social interaction that may be indicated with future materials analysis.

Swift Creek and Weeden Island Burial Mounds and Assemblages on the Gulf Coast

In the Gulf Coastal Plain, the Swift Creek (eastern northwest Florida) and Santa Rosa–Swift Creek (western northwest Florida) periods date from circa AD 100 to 300 and are followed by Weeden Island I from circa AD 300 to 750 (Milanich 2002). These temporal divisions have been defined primarily by ceramics: while both periods include Swift Creek Complicated Stamped vessels, the Weeden Island I period saw the advent of punctated, incised, and painted pottery types of the Weeden Island series, as well as elaborate vessel forms that include animal effigies (Milanich 2002: 354). Variability in calibrated radiocarbon dates for sites designated as Swift Creek or Weeden Island based on these criteria indicate regional disparities in the rates of adoption and the degree of Weeden Island ceremonialism (Milanich 2002; Milanich et al. 1997; Stephenson et al. 2002). Both of these archaeological cultures seem to represent panregional connections among distinctive societies and cultures. Indeed, differences in settlement patterns, subsistence, and material culture have long belied the equivalencies implied within the vast geographic and temporal expanses of these archaeological cultures (Ashley and Wallis 2006; Milanich 1980, 2002; Milanich et al. 1997; Sears 1973).

While the complexities of culture history that intersect and intertwine Swift Creek and Weeden Island archaeological cultures should be acknowledged, there are nonetheless important differences among burial mounds in the Gulf Coastal Plain. Some burial mounds were constructed by "continuous use," gaining width and height through time, sometimes over several centuries, as human remains, artifacts (sometimes in small caches), and new mantles of earth were periodically added (Sears 1962, 1973; Willey 1949). In addition, sometimes pits were periodically dug into mounds to deposit human remains and artifacts. In contrast, "patterned" mounds were constructed much more quickly (Sears 1962: 13). The stratigraphy and provenience of artifacts in these mounds indicate that the mound, or at least the final dramatic phase of mound construction, happened in a single event, on the order of days, weeks, or months, rather than centuries. Many of these essentially single-event mounds contain ceramic caches on their peripheries or east of the mound center, some with pathways "literally paved with potsherds" leading from the east side of the mound to the center (Willey 1949: 405). In some cases, nearly all of the mound contents, including burials, were concentrated in peripheral locations, especially on the eastern side (Moore 1902). Importantly, these patterned mounds became common only within the Weeden Island "heartland" in northwestern Florida, southeastern Alabama, and southwestern Georgia. Elsewhere, continuous-use type mounds continued to be customary among Weeden Island–affiliated cultures (Milanich 1980).

On the Gulf coast, these different types of mounds roughly correspond to the ceremonial complexes that Sears (1962, 1973) defined as a continuum of development. The late Deptford period Yent complex included continuous-use mounds at Crystal River, Pierce, and Yent (Sears 1962: 8). The Swift Creek period Green Point complex represented a shift from continuous-use mounds (such as at Green Point and Huckleberry Landing) to "patterned" mounds with east-side caches (such as at Anderson's Bayou and Alligator Bayou). Weeden Island mounds mark the end of continuous-use mounds and the predominance of east-side caches.

Alongside this trajectory in mound construction, Sears (1973) saw periods of waxing, waning, and then waxing again of a "sacred" and "secular" dichotomy, in which sacred contexts emphasized "the unique and the foreign." Yent complex mounds contained "one-of-a-kind" ceramic vessels, Hopewellian artifacts, and nonlocal vessels. Green Point mounds contained primarily local utilitarian wares, although some appeared to have been somewhat more carefully produced and a few were made with prefired kill holes. Finally, Weeden Island effigy vessels reinforced the sacred and secular dichotomy, though, according to Sears (1973), not as ostentatiously as within the Yent complex.

While the form of burials throughout both Swift Creek and Weeden Island periods is quite variable, including secondary, primary, extended, bundles, single skulls, and cremations, Willey (1949) and others (Brose and Percy 1974) note that there are more accoutrements with Swift Creek burials compared to later Weeden Island ones. In addition, central tombs and primary interments of a limited number of individuals are more common during the Swift Creek phase and dramatically decline through Weeden Island times (Brose and Percy 1974). In both Swift Creek and Weeden Island mounds, accoutrements with burials are most often nonceramic materials such as lithics, shells, copper, galena, and hematite; ceramic vessels were typically deposited peripherally in "communal" offerings. Again, however, vessels during Swift Creek times were more often placed singly or in small caches, while large east-side ceramic caches are more typical of Weeden Island.

In sum, the earlier Swift Creek burial mounds were mostly continuous use and sometimes had central tombs and a select number of burials with accoutrements, as well as variable burial treatments evident throughout mounds, and ceramics that seem largely utilitarian and equivalent to those deposited at local habitation sites. In contrast, Weeden Island burial mounds were "patterned" and had diverse burial treatments but fewer primary interments, few artifacts with burials, and caches of often exquisitely produced ceramics very different from domestic assemblages. The implication, for Sears (1973), at least, was that the people responsible for Swift Creek burial mounds did not value a sacred-secular dichotomy and were not particularly well connected interregionally. In contrast, Weeden Island ceremonialism indicates tremendous value placed on "the sacred" and burial ceremonies, and though Sears did not interpret them as such, many of the ceremonial vessels might be deemed "foreign" if they were made in only a few locations. Sears further argued that Weeden Island ceremonialism was marshaled to celebrate powerful individuals and that vessels were made by a specialized class of potters. However, the "communal" offerings could just as well be interpreted as an affirmation of egalitarianism.

More recent research might further blur the differences between Swift Creek and Weeden Island mortuary practices. For example, Smith and Stephenson's analysis (2010) of an assemblage from the Shelly Mound, a Weeden Island I mound near the Ocmulgee River in Georgia, revealed caches with different sizes of vessels compared to habitation sites: in particular, small vessels that might have been serving wares used during ceremonies. Similar assemblages of relatively small vessels have also been documented at contemporaneous Swift Creek sites in northeastern Florida (Wallis 2007, 2011), are generally common among earlier Swift Creek mounds on the Gulf coast, and are associated with *Busycon* shells that could represent early evidence of black drink ceremony (Milanich 1994: 149). There is, evidently, a "sacred and secular" dichotomy in ceramics associated with the Swift Creek phase, but mostly in terms of vessel form and function rather than typology.

This retreat from Sears's original sacred and secular distinction between Swift Creek and Weeden Island mortuary ritual is made even more necessary by the realization that many of the Swift Creek Complicated Stamped vessels that Sears considered to be local may have been nonlocal productions, as indicated on the Atlantic coast (Wallis 2011). Data from that region demonstrate the importance of originally domestic-use vessels as indexes, or referencing tools, in the salient contexts of mortuary ceremony. I believe that this realization is particularly significant in the interpretation of Swift Creek and Weeden Island ceremonialism and mortuary mounds, and their apparent diachronic transition, throughout the lower Southeast. In light of these and other new data, Sears's (1962, 1973) original formulation could be revised to acknowledge that Swift Creek burial mounds sometimes did include small ceramic caches, small bowls not found in habitation middens, and nonlocal village wares. The apparent shift between "continuous-use" mounds and mounds with east-side caches is probably not quite as dramatic as it was presented by Sears, nor is the shifting emphasis on the "unique and the foreign" so clear, but there nonetheless remain real changes through time in the contents and structure of Middle Woodland mounds that require explanation.

Swift Creek and Weeden Island Distinctions: Alternative Models

Burial mounds were obviously monuments concerned with death and religion, but they were also arenas for affirming and reworking social relationships (e.g., Battaglia 1983, 1990; Kan 1989; Weiner 1992). As such, the social implications of burial mounds have been interpreted by archaeologists in a number of ways, mostly by way of defining the diversity among social groups involved in mortuary ceremony and burial. These explanations are briefly outlined below and serve as alternative ways of understanding Swift Creek and Weeden Island mortuary landscapes and interactions, to be tested with materials analysis. While much of this empirical work is only just beginning, I offer a robust data set from contemporaneous contexts on the Atlantic coast as a useful comparison.

Many archaeologists have described both Swift Creek and Weeden Island burial mounds as repositories for the remains of local populations (e.g., Brose and Percy 1974; Milanich 1994: 169–70, 2002; Milanich et al. 1997: 41–42; Sigler-Lavelle 1980). More specifically, the mounds are supposed to have functioned as cemeteries for lineages, and interment might have included individuals from various surrounding residential communities within a single lineage (e.g., Milanich et al. 1997: 41–42; Willey 1949: 368). Accordingly, nonlocal artifacts would be the result of down-the-line exchange and, when associated with burials, are indicative of a limited degree of social rank, especially with Swift Creek (i.e., Green Point) burials.

In contrast to smaller mounds that served closely related kin groups, larger mounds and multimound complexes such as Weeden Island mound centers at Kolomoki, McKeithen, Aspalaga, or Garden Patch may have accommodated more numerous and diverse populations for ceremonial activities (Milanich et al. 1997: 187–95; Pluckhahn 2003: 193–94). If some of these larger mound centers were exchange "gateways" into the interior, as Anderson (1998) argues (see also Keith, chapter 9, this volume), then we might expect these places to be gathering locales for disparate populations. Taking this hypothesis a step further, Smith and Stephenson (2010) argue that all Weeden Island mounds and their contents are the result of ceremonies that were important as costly displays among multiple communities and kin groups.

I have argued that Middle Woodland mounds on the lower St. Johns River were inscriptions of relational identities that were constructed, in part, by the artifacts buried within them (Wallis 2008). In terms of the diversity of social groups involved, my assessment of these small, accretional Swift Creek mounds is quite similar to Smith and Stephenson's (2010) interpretation of single-event Weeden Island mounds. In fact, materials analysis for sites on the Atlantic coast, described below, demonstrates that these mounds were virtually filled with nonlocal ceramic vessels, many of which archaeologists have traditionally viewed as local.

According to these alternative interpretations, the construction and use of Middle Woodland burial mounds may have involved populations from local to extralocal and cosmopolitan. Stable isotope analyses are required to assess the diversity of the populations interred within burial mounds. But even if all the remains proved to be "local" to each site, the ubiquitous ceramic vessels interred in mounds might reflect the involvement, if not the direct participation, of diverse social groups in mortuary ceremony. Returning to the idea of mounds as devices for mapping the social landscape, the transformations between "Swift Creek" and "Weeden Island" burial mounds seem to indicate a shift in the structure of social relationships and their signification. The increasingly "costly display" (e.g., Smith and Stephenson 2010) represented by Weeden Island ceremonialism (quickly constructed mounds and finely crafted ceramic vessels and effigies) implicates increasingly heterogeneous groups in competition with one another. If labor is taken to represent degrees of concern with impressing "others," then the social distance of participants at mound ceremonies would be expected to increase from Swift Creek to Weeden Island times, from relatively local kin groups to more cosmopolitan gatherings. The distance of these social relationships can be effectively deciphered through provenance analysis, which may also serve to test the models described above. However, based on data from the Atlantic coast, I predict that the social distance of participants in mortuary ceremonies may not have changed significantly between Swift Creek and Weeden Island. Rather, the social relationships and forms of signification changed with the adoption of "single-event" mounds and east-side caches. The foundation for this idea comes from evidence of the "unique and foreign" that were imbued in Swift Creek vessels alongside Weeden Island series mortuary pottery.

Swift Creek and Weeden Island on the Atlantic Coast

Detailed syntheses of Swift Creek and associated Weeden Island on the Atlantic coast have been published elsewhere and will be only summarized here (e.g., Ashley et al. 2007; Ashley and Wallis 2006; Wallis 2011). On the Atlantic coast, Swift Creek pottery is found at sites from just south of the mouth of the St. Johns River to just north of the Altamaha River, a distance of about 120 km. Early Swift Creek sites (circa AD 200–500) are found only proximate to the lower St. Johns River, but between circa AD 500 and 800, and perhaps later, Late Swift Creek sites predominated throughout northeastern Florida and southeastern Georgia. Weeden Island series vessels, in minor proportions, are associated with Late Swift Creek sites, especially at burial mounds. At all "Swift Creek" sites in the region, both Early and Late, plain sherds tend to make up the majority of assemblages, followed by complicated-stamped sherds.

Swift Creek sites in this region consist of three basic types: small artifact scatters, large shell middens, and low sand burial mounds. These three site types may roughly correspond with special-use or procurement sites, villages, and ceremonial and mortuary centers, respectively. Many of the larger shell middens have circular or semicircular orientations that are presumed to represent the shape of villages and corresponding refuse disposal patterns (e.g., Stephenson et al. 2002; Wallis 2007). Contemporaneous sand mounds conform to Sears's (1962) continuous-use type, with many used throughout both Early and Late Swift Creek phases (Ashley 1992, 1998; Ashley and Wallis 2006; Wallis 2008). The distribution of these types of archaeological sites and their relationship to one another are noticeably variable across the region. Along the lower St. Johns River, a series of burial mounds are segregated from the villages represented by large shell middens (Wallis 2008). In contrast, there are few mounds recorded on the Georgia coast, possibly because of both site destruction and different burial practices (Ashley et al. 2007: 22). But where mounds are present in coastal Georgia, villages were placed nearby.

There are also differences in pottery assemblages between lower St. Johns sites and coastal Georgia sites. Early Swift Creek Complicated Stamped pottery generally occurs only at sites on the lower St. Johns, and much of this pottery is tempered with crushed wood charcoal, a conspicuous localized tradition (Wallis et al. 2011). Furthermore, Late Swift Creek vessels are, on average, tempered with different sizes of quartz sand in each region: coarse sand at sites along the Georgia coast and fine sand along the lower St. Johns River. Finally, vessel forms are slightly different between areas. While they are mostly all the same general shape, approximating a subconical pot with an open or slightly restricted orifice, vessels from lower St. Johns sites are, on average, significantly thinner than vessels from sites on the Georgia coast (Wallis 2011: 181–84).

Even in the context of these differences, there are direct connections between sites along the coast in the form of paddle matches among Late Swift Creek vessels (Wallis 2011: 77–86). Most significantly, several wooden paddles were used to impress vessels recovered from village sites on the Altamaha

River, Georgia, and at burial mounds on the St. Johns River, 100–115 km to the south (figure 14.2). Chemical and mineralogical data indicate that these paddle matches resulted from vessels being transported from the Altamaha River region to be deposited primarily within mounds on the St. Johns River (Wallis 2011; Wallis et al. 2010). Corroborating these identifications, the vessel thickness and size of quartz tempers among nonlocal vessels on the St. Johns River are also diagnostic of the Altamaha region.

The distribution of nonlocal vessels is significant. When demonstrably Early Swift Creek vessels are excluded from the tabulation of analyzed samples, nonlocal vessels make up 27 percent ($n = 9$) of burial mound assemblages but only 3 percent ($n = 2$) of habitation midden assemblages. This pattern is unlikely to be the result of traditional explanations offered for paddle matches: widespread residential mobility, exchange of goods transferred in ceramic containers, or the postmarital residence patterns of women curating their wooden paddles or ceramic vessels (cf. Stephenson et al. 2002; Stolt-

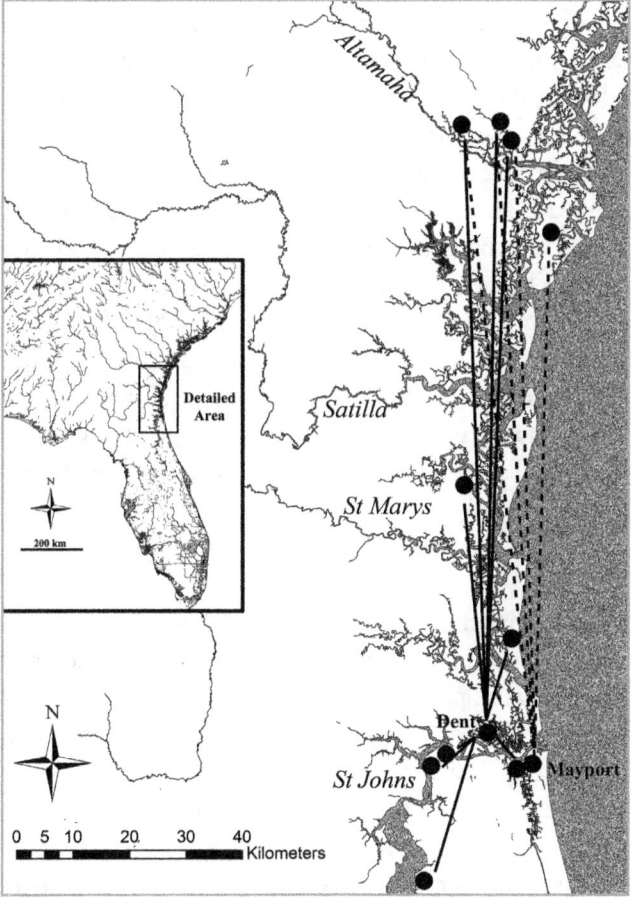

Figure 14.2. Select paddle match connections with the Dent (solid lines) and Mayport (dashed lines) mounds on the St. Johns River. Figure prepared by Neill Wallis.

man and Snow 1998). Each of these forms of interaction would likely result in many paddle matches and nonlocal vessels in middens, where pottery that was used and broken in domestic contexts was subsequently deposited. Paddle matches do occur between nearby midden sites that are presumed to have been villages on the Altamaha River. These same paddle designs, however, occur on the St. Johns River *only* in mounds, on vessels transported from the Altamaha River. More than 80 percent of nonlocal vessels on the St. Johns River are complicated stamped; the others are sand-tempered plain. Based on this evidence, I have argued that the foreign vessel assemblages found on the lower St. Johns River are composed of gifts intentionally placed at burial mounds (Wallis 2011).

These gifts were offered in mortuary contexts, perhaps given as recognition of social connections and repayment of debts. The nonlocal vessels exhibit considerable evidence of use in the form of soot, abrasions, and mend holes and seem to have been taken out of distant domestic contexts to be buried as symbols of connection. Elsewhere I have argued that Swift Creek Complicated Stamped vessels were powerful indexes that could make specific reference to other places where vessels were stamped with the same paddle, just as they do for archaeologists today (Wallis 2011: 192–204). On the Atlantic coast, the indexical power of complicated stamping was most significantly mobilized at burial mounds, which is where histories were continuously reworked and accumulated, particularly as they related to social alliances among lineages. In sum, vessels were deposited and commingled in mounds as a way to map out the social landscape, toward the retention of past alliances and extension of future ones (sensu Husserl 1962, 1964; Munn 1990). Buried among a definitively specialized mortuary assemblage that included Weeden Island series vessels in the form of multicompartment trays and small cups and bowls, complicated-stamped domestic cooking pots were gifts that brought some of the everyday substance of a lineage to be used as symbolic material in mortuary ceremony.

Discussion

Complicated-stamped vessels may have been transported and buried in similar ways at Swift Creek and Weeden Island burial mounds on the Gulf coast of Florida and throughout the coastal plain. While the evidence so far remains anecdotal, it is worth noting, for example, that Swift Creek Complicated Stamped pottery in assemblages from burial mounds in the north-peninsular Gulf Coast region tends to have a fine, hard, micaceous paste that is quite different from associated "local" pottery and more typical of the Florida panhandle, such as along the Apalachicola River. The "better than average craftsmanship" that Sears (1973) noted among some Swift Creek vessels in mounds on the Gulf coast might also have simply represented nonlocal manufacture, somewhere toward the north and west with different materials and according to a different tradition. As on the Atlantic coast, perhaps these vessels were made and used in domestic contexts and were disseminated as indexes of various distant social groups during mortuary ceremonies. If so, then continuous-use mounds and the repeated interment of complicated stamped pottery within them were oriented toward accumulations of social alliances, inscribed in place. The stamps on Swift Creek Complicated Stamped vessels were like calling cards of a lineage, place, or even a particular person, but the vessels also had qualities of heirlooms that accumulated through histories of use and preserved the evidence of physical contact with a wooden paddle (and a place and person) that was indelibly marked on each vessel. Vessels were notably drawn out of domestic contexts and transformed into ceremonial material with their use and deposition in burial mounds.

This tradition in the transport and deposition of domestic pottery may have continued even as Weeden Island single-event mounds became more common. Swift Creek Complicated Stamped pottery continued to be included in Weeden Island I mounds in the Weeden Island "heartland," and there is little reason to suspect that these vessels ceased to function as effective indexical tools. In fact, in some cases Late Swift Creek designs seem to have become more distinctive and more deliberately applied, perhaps signifying a heightened concern with creating clearly visible links among people and places (Wallis 2011; figure 14.3). But with the advent of single-event mounds, the importance of (vertical) accumulation, heirlooming, and deep time through repeated deposition in a single place gave way to an emphasis on (horizontal) extension and event-centered spectacles.

In comparison to the preceding mortuary traditions associated with Swift Creek, Weeden Island single-event mounds reflect a ramping up of religiosity that seems to have become more distinct and isolated from daily life at the same time that reminders of ceremony became more ubiquitous and unavoidable on the landscape. More work is needed to generate reliable absolute numbers, but site file data indicate that Weeden Island mounds significantly outnumber earlier Swift Creek mounds, at least in Florida. Even with some population growth, this trend should be expected, as Weeden Island I mounds represent construction events in new places, resulting in a mortuary landscape studded with numerous nodes. These mounds represent a transformation in ceremonial practice. Rather than mounds being reworked or added onto, as was the case among Swift Creek mounds, Weeden Island mounds were often constructed quickly and decisively sealed with sand, leav-

Figure 14.3. Late Swift Creek Complicated Stamped vessel with discrete paddle impressions in a zoned field. This stamp design is found at several sites throughout Georgia and northern Florida. Shelly Mound (8Le6), Collections of the Anthropology Division of the Florida Museum of Natural History, FLMNH Cat. No. 103710. Photo by Ellen Walker.

ing a more permanent inscription on the landscape that was not meant to be altered. Moreover, Weeden Island east-side caches reinforced this restricted temporal scale by offering a brief spectacle of many ornate objects brought together and quickly covered from view forever (or until they were unearthed by archaeologists). Caches are thus inherently more exclusive than the pottery buried in Swift Creek mounds, which might have been encountered near the surface with new additions to a mound and when pits were dug into them for new interments (e.g., Willey 1949: 370). Thus, compared to Swift Creek mounds, each Weeden Island mound marked an exclusive event, a reminder of the past that could not be reworked or reappropriated at a later time.

Accompanying this shift in the temporality and spatiality of burial mound construction and use was the introduction of new kinds of vessels that were rarely or never deposited in nonmound contexts, such as effigy vessels, multicompartment vessels, and "decorated" wares such as Weeden Island Zoned Red. Use wear suggests that mortuary-specific vessels were apparently not used very often or for very long, in stark contrast to some Swift Creek vessels. This apparently deepening "sacred" and "secular" dichotomy, though by no means absolute, marked a significant shift in the orientation of indexes. Swift Creek vessels, as village wares that were conscripted into mortuary rites, made tangible and probably intimate connections between villages (and villagers) and accumulating mortuary loci. In comparison, Weeden Island mortuary-specific vessels elided connection with villages in their divergence from village forms and formed indexical linkages only with other burial mounds that contained similar vessels.

In light of this transition, it is worth noting also the developmental trajectory of iconography that seems to have attended the shift from Swift Creek to Weeden Island ceramic vessel forms. The iconographic themes represented in many Swift Creek Complicated Stamped designs are arguably quite similar to Weeden Island effigy forms, including the fourfold rendering of the cosmos, various birds and other animals, and anthropomorphic and zoomorphic faces or heads (Wallis 2011). The basic difference between Swift Creek and Weeden Island representative forms is in their dimensionality—Weeden Island effigies were molded in three dimensions, whereas Swift Creek carved designs were rendered in two dimensions by split representation, a technique of representing a three-dimensional object in two dimensions by figuratively cutting it into parts to display every side at once (Wallis 2006, 2011). Cross-culturally, this technique tends to indicate an inextricability of image, object, and the signified, meaning that an image embodies and is part of the thing it "represents" (Gell 1998: 195; Lévi-Strauss 1963). Linked as it is to bodily presence, split representation implies a strict conformity of persons to their social roles (Lévi-Strauss 1963: 264). Furthermore, because motifs are critical to and inextricable from the constitution of social persons, the technique often corresponds with competitions among ranked lineages, in which ancestral identity is understood as embodied in living persons (Gell 1998; Lévi-Strauss 1963). The use of split representation makes sense in the context of cooking vessels that were taken out of villages and buried in far-off mounds. The vessels were literally embodied parts of kin groups that people used daily, and the images, by convention, were also embodiments of those groups.

I suspect that Weeden Island effigy vessels took this idea a step further by instantiating animal and human forms in three dimensions, increasing the visual effect and "presence" of the representations. These vessels may in fact demonstrate an even more heightened concern with ownership, in which various beings were made manifest in fired clay and were subsequently used or viewed only on select occasions, and probably only once. Indeed, Weeden Island effigy vessels were apparently designed only for mortuary contexts; contra Sears (1973), they appear not to have been heavily used. As many have surmised based on the quality of craftsmanship (e.g., Brose and Percy 1974; Pluckhahn and Cordell 2010; Sears 1973), effigy vessels, in particular, may have been made by specialists. Whatever the case, concerns with ownership may have been applied to the vessels themselves or to the knowledge to produce and use them properly, or both.

Conclusions

When all these trends are viewed together, Weeden Island burial mounds mark a fairly dramatic transformation of Swift Creek mortuary landscapes. Although Swift Creek mounds apparently contain more extended burials with grave goods than do Weeden Island mounds, a more holistic assessment shows an increase in the practices of exclusion with the advent of Weeden Island ceremonialism. Indeed, the most common Swift Creek burial mound artifact was domestic-use ceramic vessels, though these were not necessarily made locally. If mounds are viewed as the inscriptions of histories of social relationships, then the interment of these vessels marked acts of inclusion of temporally and spatially disparate villagers. Corroborating this idea is the continuous use of mounds over several centuries, which tended to mark the accumulation of more ancestors and more social alliances through time. In contrast, some Weeden Island mortuary vessels seem to have been made by a select group of individuals, perhaps a sodality of mortuary potters, and lacked the sort of organic connection to villages that was imbued in Swift Creek Complicated Stamped cooking vessels (which were also buried in Weeden Island mounds). What is more, mounds tended to be built quickly and with a finality that left no room for reworking the contents or configuration. Instead, each Weeden Island burial mound was a monument built anew that must have provided much more frequent encounters with a mortuary landscape that was segregated from village life.

This shift may have been associated with a change in the organization of leadership, as Sears (1973) thought, but more empirical research is needed to better outline the social relationships inscribed in mounded mortuary loci. A first step in the interpretation of Woodland burial mounds as inscriptions of social relationships will come through contextual investigations of the organization of vessel production, particularly the provenance of various Swift Creek and Weeden Island vessel forms.

15

Working Out Adena Political Organization and Variation from the Ritual Landscape in the Kentucky Bluegrass

EDWARD R. HENRY

This chapter examines the distribution of structural variation in Adena mortuary ritual and burial practices across three subregions of the Kentucky Bluegrass: the Northern Bluegrass, Central Bluegrass, and Eastern Bluegrass (Pollack 2008). This study is used as a foundation to conceptualize Adena leadership as situational and heterarchical in nature (Abrams and Le Rouge 2008; Byers 2011; Sahlins 1968). Such decentralized political organization could be a principal source of the variation documented across the Adena ritual landscape in the Kentucky Bluegrass. Intraregional patterns of premound mortuary rituals and mound interments reflect an observable degree of variation relating to the structure of specific ritual practices and/or events, even as common themes in the character of these premound and mounded practices are identifiable across the Bluegrass. This pattern may suggest that all subregions, each somewhat distinct from the others in its approach to mortuary ceremonies, relied upon a common ideological structure from which specific rituals could be drawn to fit a particular event or situation. The basic foundation of this ideological structure would have been understood across kin groups throughout the Bluegrass region.

In this regard, this chapter addresses a common issue with contemporary interpretations of Adena peoples. Recent archaeological discourse has cited variation in Adena material culture as one reason to move away from the taxonomic category of "Adena" and rewrite the concept altogether (Brown 2005; Clay 2005; Greber 2005). However, if variation in Adena assemblages represents typological problems attributable to how the "culture" was fabricated early on in our discipline's history, then how do we interpret gross similarities that continue to be observed across these assemblages? Perhaps the nature of variation within the Adena ritual structure is a result of a particular form of sociopolitical organization. I argue that the construction of the ritual landscape by highly mobile peoples, operating within a decentralized heterarchical sociopolitical atmosphere, led to the material variation we encounter today. From this perspective, variation becomes attributable to specific situations or events in which a ritual practice is selected from a common ideological theme.

Situating Adena in Time, Space, and Theory

Teasing out evidence of human social interactions from landscape-level analyses requires a thoughtful consideration of the peoples under examination. Furthermore, such analyses benefit from grounding the investigation within specific and explicit theoretical perspectives. For the purposes of this study, Adena social organization is regarded as consisting of multiple, dispersed autonomous tribal kin groups (Clay 1998; Railey 1991, 1996). These semimobile hunter-gatherer-gardeners periodically and temporarily coalesced into larger corporate groups in the middle Ohio Valley circa 500 BC to AD 250 (Clay 1998; Fenton 2001; Hays 2010; Railey 1991, 1996). Working with this definition of Adena allows for the classification of corporate Adena social units as tribes (Howey 2012; Parkinson 2002a; Sahlins 1961, 1968), rather than Big Man societies or chiefdoms (Clay 1992; Custer 1987; Mainfort 1989; Shryock 1987). Thus, Adena sociopolitical organization should be considered decentralized or noninstitutionalized rather than egalitarian (Howey 2012: 9; Parkinson 2002b: 8–9).

With this research placed in the broader context of tribal societies, a multiscalar landscape approach becomes especially well suited to studying the Adena ritual landscape. As Alice Wright and I (chapter 1, this volume) have emphasized, this approach allows for the inclusive assessment of the complex interactions between people, their natural environment, and overarching social structures. Utilizing landscape studies provides the ability to highlight the intimate relationships that peoples had with their built environment (Anschuetz et al. 2001: 177). Further, it places great importance on ritual events and places that helped organize and shape shared experiences (Anschuetz et al 2001: 178–79). Working on a landscape scale for this study stresses how Adena rituals were practiced at sites specifically, and organized across the Kentucky Bluegrass generally. It calls attention to the roles of situational leaders in coordinating the labor and selecting the mortuary rituals that constitute the ritual landscape in this region.

Acknowledging that some form of leadership would be required to coordinate the construction of the Adena ritual landscape reopens the debate of how decentralized (or noninstitutionalized) leadership is organized. In this situation, Crumley's (1979, 1987, 1995) ideas of heterarchy prove useful in conceptualizing Adena leadership roles. Crumley (1979: 144) describes heterarchy as a structure in which "each element possesses the potential of being ranked or unranked in a number of different ways." This definition suggests both spatial and temporal flexibility in authority (Crumley 1995: 4).

Perhaps most important to this discussion of decentralized leadership roles, as Crumley (1995: 4) noted, heterarchy can facilitate brief moments of hierarchical leadership even as it enables regression to noninfluential social positions when leadership is no longer needed. This characterization of leadership demonstrates the complexity required to maintain heterarchical structures. Howey (2012: 9) suggests that maintaining this type of sociopolitical organization may have required more investment—in the form of leveling mechanisms—than centralized or institutionalized hierarchies. From these perspectives, the concept of heterarchy can explain how Adena leaders obtained some level of influence over others, but only in very specific situations and for very brief amounts of time. When a given leadership role was no longer required, these temporary leaders would return to their typical social roles.

This highly situational and variable sociopolitical environment could result in variation in material practices. However, in order to explain how such subregional variation affected the overlying ideological structure of Adena ritual, the use of heterarchy benefits from a contextual grounding in Giddens's (1984) theory of structuration. Specifically, structuration is useful to help explain how subregional variation becomes maintained in this decentralized sociopolitical context. The basic premise of Giddens's theory is that change in society emerges from historical events that are a result of the ongoing reinterpretation and reorganization of an overlying social structure by human agents (Giddens 1984: 17). Structuration theory provides a framework to understand (1) how the structures of Adena mortuary ritual changed through the reinterpretation of mortuary practices by a variety of ritual leaders, and (2) how variation materialized at ritual locales. The pairing of these two theoretical approaches (heterarchy and structuration) is particularly relevant to this study because it helps contextualize how mobile peoples moving around and experiencing a ritually dynamic landscape could adopt a variety of particular practices derived from a common premise (i.e., so-called Adena ideology) without adopting an entire suite of uniform interrelated practices. When situational Adena leaders integrated and interpreted the particulars of a given ritual practice in new areas of the landscape, structuration could take place, in which the leaders' actions would stand to reorganize or reaffirm the social structure. By noticing where on the Bluegrass Landscape certain ritual themes and practices were (or were not) applied, we can begin to trace how they evolved through time, thus highlighting broader changes in the structure of Adena society.

Study Area and Methods

During the Early and Middle Woodland period, the inhabitants of Kentucky's Bluegrass Region participated in panregional exchange networks and the construction of monumental architecture, which included burial mounds. Mounds are commonly conical in shape and range in size from barely visible bumps on the landscape covering only one interment event to large multimeter-high earthen features containing a variety of interments and construction events (Clay 1998; Milner 2004: 57; Rafferty 2005; Webb 1943a; Webb and Elliot 1942). The Bluegrass Region can be divided into two separate physiographic zones: the Inner and Outer Bluegrass regions (figure 15.1). The Inner Bluegrass region is characterized by subtly rolling topography, while the Outer Bluegrass comprises deeply dissected uplands with prominent hills and ridges (McGrain and Currens 1978: 4–6, 12). Following the Kentucky Heritage Council's State Historic Preservation Plan, the Bluegrass was divided into three subregions for this analysis (Northern, Central, and Eastern Bluegrass) (Pollack 2008). The Northern Bluegrass subregion is situated in the Outer Bluegrass physiographic region, while the Central Bluegrass subregion falls within the Inner Bluegrass physiographic region (figure 15.2). The Eastern Bluegrass subregion straddles these two physiographic areas (figure 15.2).

Mounds attributed to the Early and Middle Woodland periods within each subregion were identified using data from the Kentucky State GIS site files. While numerous mounds are present in each of these subregions, my sample ($n = 17$) was limited to those that have been excavated in these areas

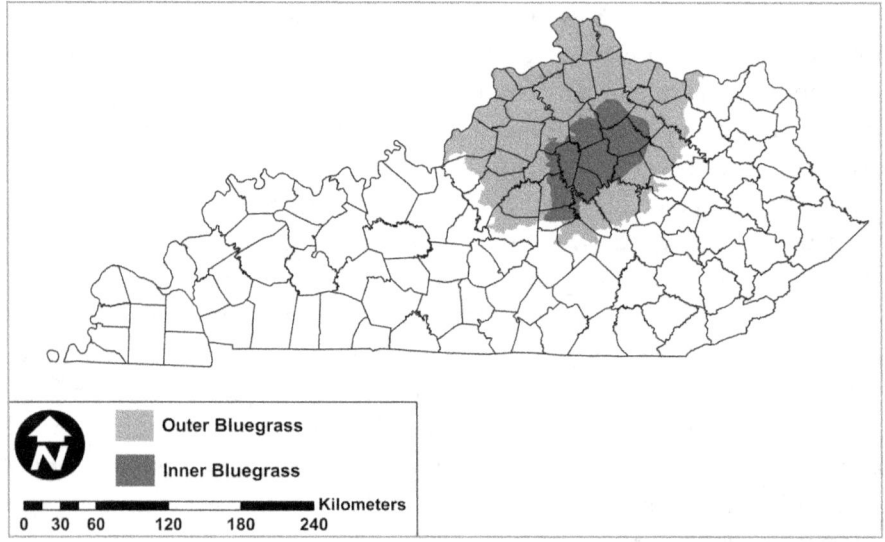

Figure 15.1. The Inner and Outer Bluegrass regions of Kentucky. Figure prepared by Edward Henry.

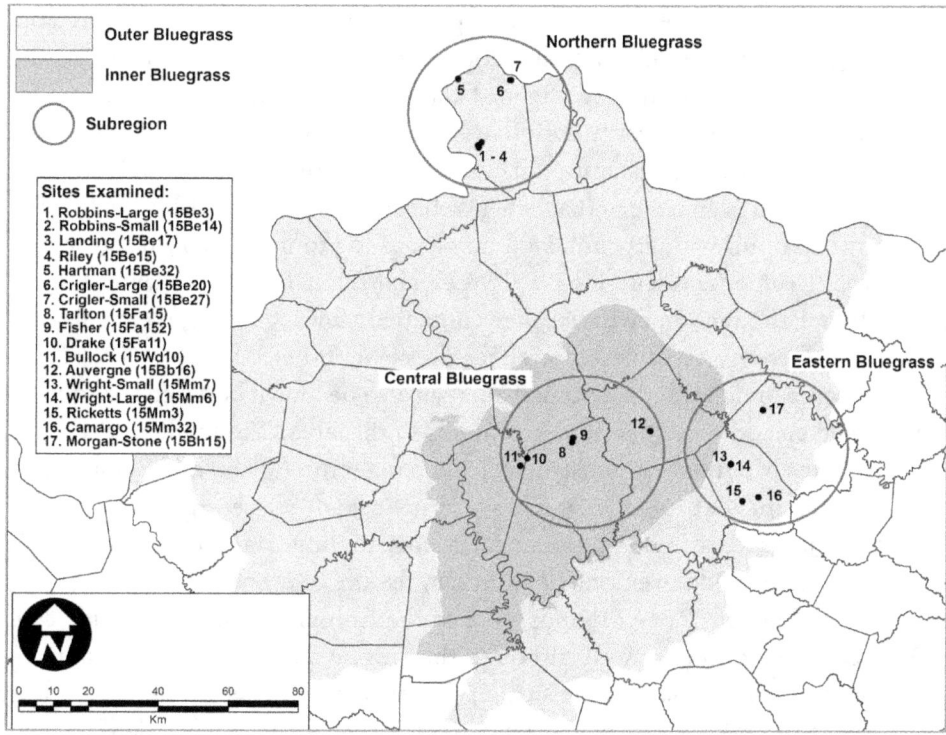

Figure 15.2. Subregions and sites examined in this analysis. Figure prepared by Edward Henry.

(Applegate 2008). To assess the structure of the ritual landscape in the Kentucky Bluegrass, I selected general but common mound attributes encountered and noted during excavations for this analysis. It was assumed that certain traits, such as evidence of specific premound rituals and the presence or absence of crypt-like interment strategies, would minimally indicate choices made by Adena leaders during mortuary ritual. Selected traits were added to maps of the Inner and Outer Bluegrass regions of Kentucky using ArcGIS 10 to aid in the recognition of subregional patterning among them. When radiocarbon dates were available, they were included in the analysis with the intention of delineating the changing structure of mortuary ritual through time. All dates discussed here are calibrated and reported at the two-sigma range. However, some problems emerge when chronometric dates are compared between these sites (these issues are discussed later).

Analyzing Adena Mortuary Ritual

Northern Bluegrass

Sites located in the Northern Bluegrass subregion include the Robbins Mounds (15Be3, 15Be14), Riley Mound (15Be15), Landing Mound (15Be17), Hartman Mound (15Be32), and the Crigler Mounds (15Be20, 15Be27) (table 15.1). This subregion's two large long-term-use mounds—the larger of the Robbins Mounds and the larger of the Crigler Mounds—revealed similar structures of mortuary ritual. Both were constructed in multiple episodes over paired-post circular structures that contained the remains of several individuals who had been cremated off-site (Webb and Elliot 1942; Webb 1943a). The large Robbins Mound contained numerous log tombs of varying structural types (Milner and Jefferies 1987; Webb and Elliot 1942). The larger Crigler Mound, though somewhat smaller, contained a few log tombs; their collapsed roofs were reused for newer tomb features (Webb 1943a).

Some organizational comparisons can also be drawn between the smaller, single-episode, short-term-use mounds in this area. The smaller of the two Robbins Mounds was constructed over a log tomb (Webb and Elliot 1942), and the smaller Crigler Mound was constructed over a central cremation. Although these are in no way identical events, it is important that both mounds were constructed over a single mortuary feature or event.

Landing and Riley Mounds, near to the Robbins Mounds, possibly covered single events as well, although they reveal a more complex history of mortuary ritual than do the smaller Robbins and Crigler Mounds. Landing covered a large pit that held extended interments and was encircled by other extended burials (Webb 1943b). Riley Mound covered two paired-post circular structures and one rectangular structure (Webb 1943b). The remains of many individuals—both cremated and extended inhumations—were identified on the premound surface (Webb 1943b).

Last, Hartman Mound was constructed over a pit that contained a partially cremated body (Webb 1943a). Around the edge of the pit, earth was piled up and covered with limestone slabs, forming an embankment around the mortuary pit.

In sum, the Northern Bluegrass subregion generally exhibits mounds placed over an important central ritual feature, such as a burial pit, a cremation, or a post structure that held cremated remains. When mounds were used over a long period of time, log tombs are the primary crypt-like interment feature.

Central Bluegrass

Mound sites examined in the Central Bluegrass subregion include Fisher (15Fa152), Tarlton (15Fa15), Drake (15Fa11), Bullock (15Wd10), and Auvergne (15Bb16) (table 15.1). Fisher and Tarlton Mounds were both small low-lying mounds. Fisher, the only multistage construction mound in this subregion, covered a central thermal pit, while Tarlton covered a single cremation (Webb and Haag 1947; Webb 1943b). The primary form of burial at

Table 15.1. Attributes observed from mounds across the Northern, Central, and Eastern Bluegrass subregions

Site name (no.)	Subregion	Construction episodes	Premound ritual activity	Crypt-like interments
Robbins Mound—Large (15Be3)	Northern Bluegrass	Multi	Circular paired-post structure w/ cremations	Log tomb
Robbins Mound—Small (15Be14)	Northern Bluegrass	Single	Log tomb	Log tomb
Riley Mound (15Be15)	Northern Bluegrass	Single	Paired-post structures w/ extended inhumations	N/A
Landing Mound (15Be17)	Northern Bluegrass	Single	Pit w/ extended inhumations	N/A
Hartman Mound (15Be32)	Northern Bluegrass	Single	Pit w/ cremations	N/A
Crigler Mound—Large (15Be20)	Northern Bluegrass	Multi	Circular paired-post structure w/ cremations	Log tomb
Crigler Mound—Small (15Be27)	Northern Bluegrass	Single	Cremation	N/A
Fisher Mound (15Fa152)	Central Bluegrass	Multi	Thermal pit	Puddled-clay basin w/ limestone cap
Tarlton Mound (15Fa15)	Central Bluegrass	Single	Cremation	N/A
Drake Mound (15Fa11)	Central Bluegrass	Single	Pit w/ cremations and inhumations	N/A
Bullock Mound (15Wd10)	Central Bluegrass	Unknown	Rectangular structure w/ cremation	N/A
Auvergne Mound (15Bb16)	Central Bluegrass	Single	Pit w/ inhumation	N/A
Wright Mound—Larger (15Mm6)	Eastern Bluegrass	Multi	Paired-post circular structure	Log tomb; puddled-clay basin
Wright Mound—Smaller (15Mm7)	Eastern Bluegrass	Unknown	Paired-post circular structure; cremation; inhumation	N/A
Morgan Stone Mound (15Bh15)	Eastern Bluegrass	Multi	Paired-post circular structure; inhumation	Log tomb
Ricketts Mound (15Mm3)	Eastern Bluegrass	Multi	N/A	Log tomb; puddled-clay basin
Camargo Mound (15Mm32)	Eastern Bluegrass	Unknown	Pit w/ cremation	N/A

Fisher consisted of the placement of extended individuals in puddled-clay basins covered by limestone slabs or surrounded by an embankment of limestone (Webb and Haag 1947).

The Drake Mound was constructed over a large multicolored prepared clay pit feature that was surrounded by an earthen embankment (Webb 1941a). The prepared clay pit contained the remains of cremated individuals and fragmented inhumations (Webb 1941b). Unlike Drake, the Bullock Mound covered a rectangular structure that confined multiple pit features and the remains of cremated individuals (Schlarb 2005). The Auvergne Mound covered the remains of one individual in a submound pit (Clay 1983).

Structural similarities between mounds in the Central Bluegrass subregion include the construction of a mound over a central pit that holds cremated remains and/or a skeletal inhumation. With the exception of Bullock Mound, submound ritual post structures are not present in this subregion. The construction and use of multicolored clay mortuary features is also prominent in mounds in this subregion and may be a substitute for log tombs. The Fisher Mound is the only accretional mortuary facility in this subregion. In the case of Fisher, extended burials were placed in puddled-clay basins. These interment features, leaving bodies accessible (under a limestone slab cover), may have served a crypt-like function similar to the log tombs in the Northern Bluegrass subregion. Mound construction over the other mortuary-centered sites in this subregion may symbolize the conclusion of each locale as a place where people were interred.

Eastern Bluegrass

Mounds examined in the Eastern Bluegrass subregion include the Wright Mounds (15Mm6 and 15Mm7), Ricketts Mound (15Mm3), Camargo Mound (15Mm32), and Morgan Stone Mound (15Bh15) (table 15.1). The larger of the two excavated Wright Mounds was constructed over a cluster of at least six overlapping paired-post circular structures and a possible rectangular structure (Webb 1940). Varying types of log tombs were by far the most common burial method within these mounds, but some puddled-clay basins were used (Webb 1940). Morgan Stone was built over a paired-post circular structure that was burned down over a central inhumation (Webb 1941b). Log tombs and a bark-lined pit were used to bury multiple persons in Morgan Stone.

Ricketts was constructed over bedrock limestone and primarily held puddled-clay basins and log tombs (Funkhouser and Webb 1935; Webb and Funkhouser 1940). The smaller of the two Wright mounds was constructed over a paired-post structure and covered a redeposited cremation and a poorly preserved extended inhumation placed in an oval pit (Webb 1940).

The Camargo Mound covered multiple dispersed postmolds and at least three crematory pits (Fenton and Jefferies 1991).

An interesting pattern in mortuary ritual noted for the Eastern Bluegrass subregion is an emphasis on long-term mound use—that is, mounds overlying evidence for a complex premound ritual history and showing multiple construction episodes. In this subregion, long-term-use mounds are typically constructed over a ritual post structure, and numerous log tombs and/or puddled-clay basins dominate the interment features. Camargo Mound is the only example in this region that might represent a mound used in the short term: it was constructed over cremations and exhibits possible evidence of underlying ritual architecture (scattered posts).

Comparing the Structure of Mortuary Ritual across Subregions

Shared patterns in the structure of mortuary ritual and the structure of burial mounds are present across each subregion of the Bluegrass. The practice of cremation and the presence of cremations inside submound ritual structures and/or submound mortuary pits are widely distributed across the study area (figure 15.3). The use of premound ritual architecture, defined here mainly as post structures but including the construction of elaborate submound mortuary pits, also is broadly distributed (figure 15.4). The existence of these mortuary rituals across the three subregions suggests that they were widely practiced in general but each event varied somewhat in the exact details of performance that were selected for it. In contrast, the use of log tombs is geographically more restricted (figure 15.5). A similar geographically restricted pattern in the use of puddled-clay basins, which could have served a similar crypt-like function as the log tomb, is recognized as well (figure 15.6).

Understanding the chronological relationships of these mound attributes is complicated. Only seven of these mounds have chronometric dates associated with them (table 15.2). Further, the majority of these mounds do not have reliably dated contexts. Instead, many of the dates presented here derived from samples in WPA-era collections or were subjected to very early radiocarbon dating methods, or both—leaving their reliability up for speculation. One of the more reliable dates comes from modern excavations at Auvergne Mound (Clay 1983). If nothing else, the date from this small, perhaps single-event mound proves that mounds with short use-histories were still used later in the Adena sequence (Clay 1991). The unreliability of these radiocarbon dates provides an avenue for future research, which should be aimed at better delineating the chronology of landscape use across the entire Bluegrass.

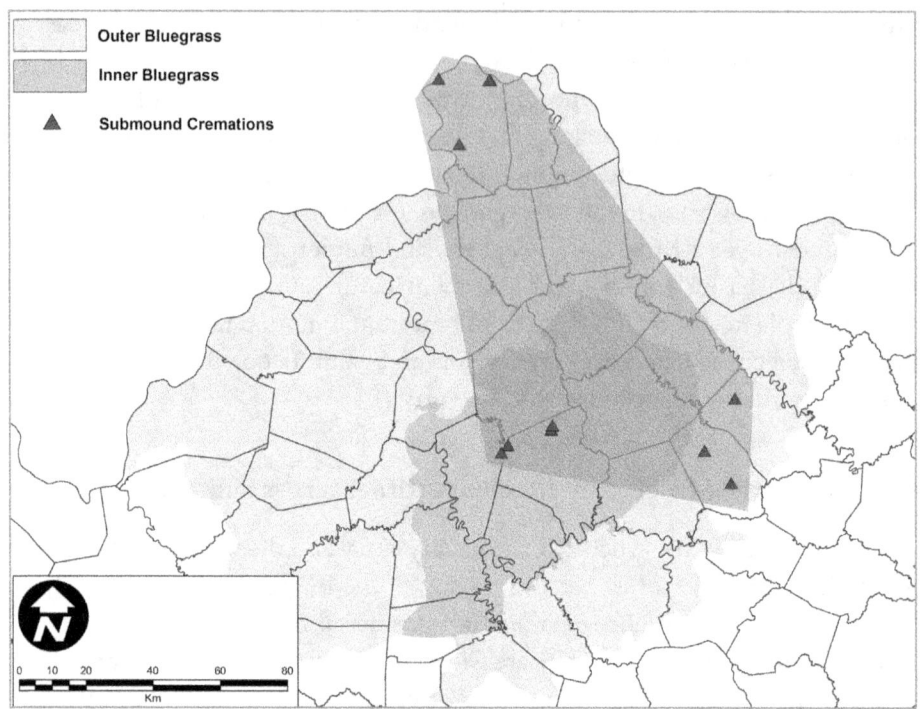

Figure 15.3. Distribution of submound cremations across subregions. Figure prepared by Edward Henry.

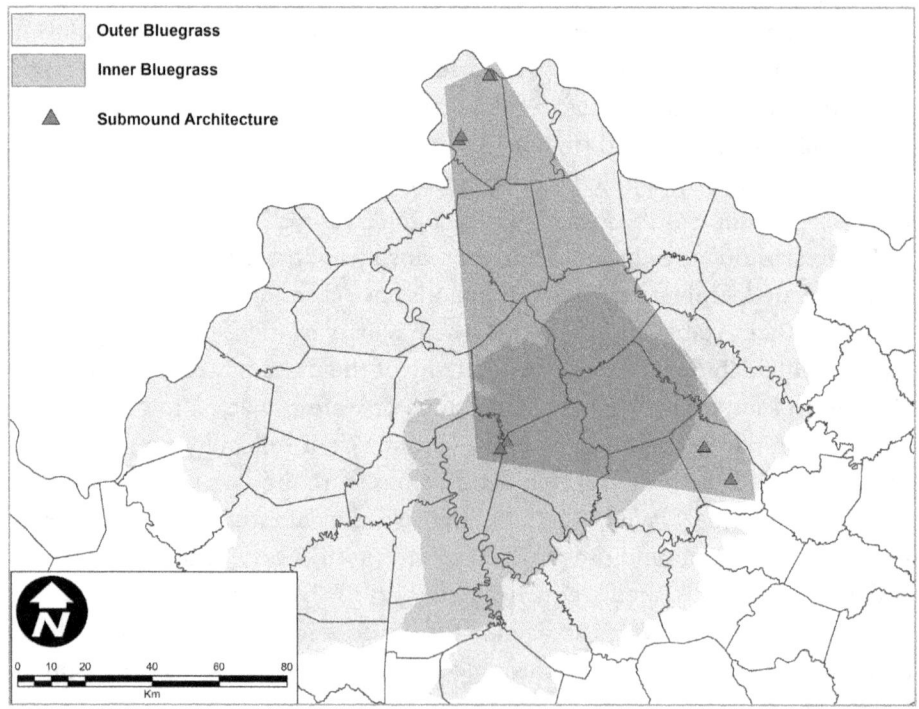

Figure 15.4. Distribution of submound architecture across subregions. Figure prepared by Edward Henry.

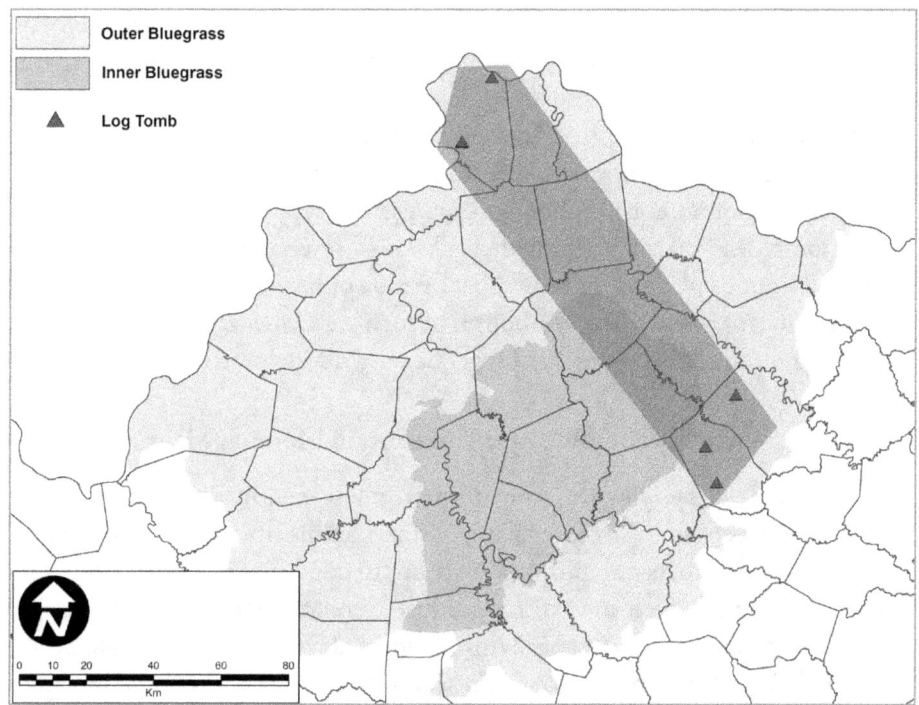

Figure 15.5. Distribution of log tombs across subregions. Figure prepared by Edward Henry.

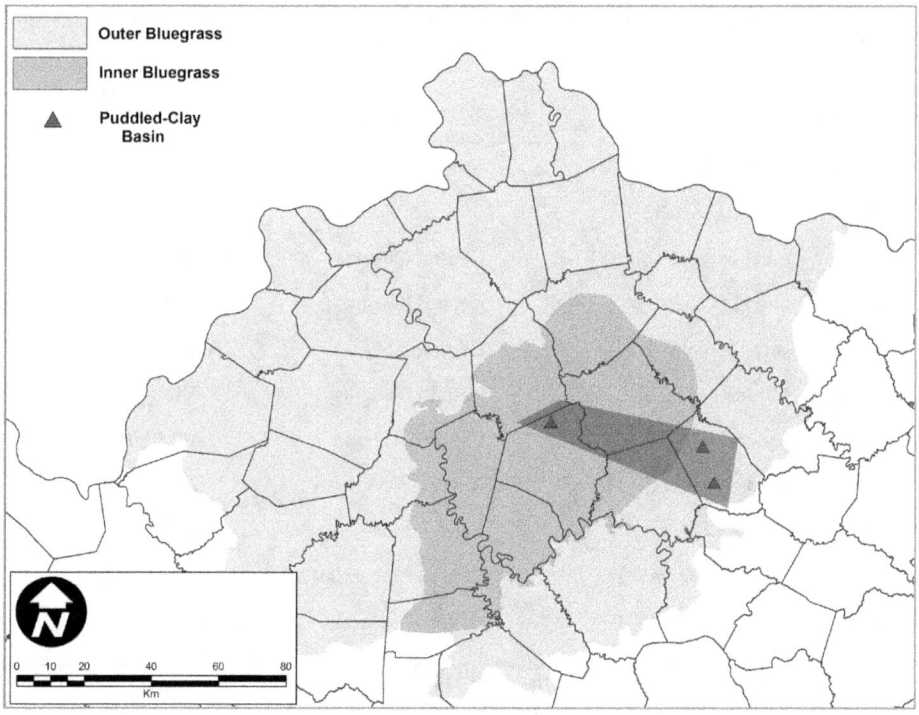

Figure 15.6. Distribution of puddled-clay basins across subregions. Figure prepared by Edward Henry.

Although the chronological relationships between these mounds cannot be appropriately assessed with extant dates, distinctions between mounds with short and long use-histories can still be made. Examination of mounds with long use-histories reveals that mortuary rituals evolved from the use of cremation, construction of mortuary pits, and construction of ritual post structures to include mound construction and the use of crypt-like interment features (log tombs and possibly puddled-clay basins). In comparison, the construction of mounds utilized for only short periods of time marks separate, but no less significant, events. The symbolism of such an exclusive event conveys that the premound surface would no longer be used during mortuary rituals.

A Discussion of Leadership and Variation in Mortuary Ritual

Though Adena peoples were not primarily engaged in a surplus-oriented subsistence economy, some level of political complexity was needed to organize the labor efforts of multiple kin groups to construct the ritual landscape examined here. Given the intimate nature of relationships between people and places on ritual landscapes (Anschuetz et al. 2001; Bradley 1998, 2000; Fennell 2010; Rodning 2010), this research assumes that the ritual practices

Table 15.2. Radiocarbon dates from examined mound sites in the Kentucky Bluegrass

Site name (no.)	Subregion	Calibrated 2-sigma radiocarbon date
Robbins Mound—Large (15Be3)	Northern Bluegrass	411 BC–AD 237
Hartman Mound (15Be32)	Northern Bluegrass	833 BC–113 BC
Drake Mound (15Fa11)	Central Bluegrass	827 BC–AD 340
Drake Mound (15Fa11)	Central Bluegrass	AD 603–1169
Bullock Mound (15Wd10)	Central Bluegrass	AD 1645–1953
Auvergne Mound (15Bb16)	Central Bluegrass	1735 BC–548 BC
Auvergne Mound (15Bb16)	Central Bluegrass	AD 87–602
Wright Mound—Larger (15Mm6)	Eastern Bluegrass	AD 3–235
Wright Mound—Larger (15Mm6)	Eastern Bluegrass	19 BC–AD 600
Camargo Mound (15Mm32)	Eastern Bluegrass	AD 88–397
Camargo Mound (15Mm32)	Eastern Bluegrass	AD 264–596

Note: Dates were calibrated using Calib (v. 5.0.2) (Stuiver and Reimer 1993) and the IntCal04 calibration data set (Reimer et al. 2004).

and participation that lead to the creation of these landscape features was not unplanned. Instead, I argue that the organization of singular ritual events and the selection of the particular practices that transpired at such events were systematically organized, selected for, planned, and carried out. However, this all would have been taking place within a decentralized sociopolitical environment where individuals managed specific circumstances, thus providing a means to introduce variation to ritual practices.

This form of Adena leadership would likely have been based on achieved status and would have been flexible enough to allow for the existence of multiple Adena leaders. With respect to mortuary rituals, temporary leadership could have been bestowed on those who, through their participation in earlier mortuary rituals, had the ability to organize, interpret, and undertake the rituals needed to process the dead and construct submound architecture or a mound.

As mentioned before, certain attributes that represent the organization and development of mortuary ritual across the Kentucky Bluegrass provide evidence that Adena mortuary ritual was structured around a common ideology. However, mounds in each subregion examined here exhibit variations on this theme. This variation may have resulted from the decisions made by leaders who chose and directed specific rituals during gatherings of the local corporate group. They would have selected these rituals based on their knowledge and experience of local mortuary traditions (Hays 2010). However, an additional contribution to the ritual decision-making process would have been the situation within which leaders were operating. The age, gender, and status of the deceased would likely have played a role in what rituals a leader selected. Thus, this heterarchical nature of Adena leadership, combined with the mobile nature of these peoples and the situations under which kin groups gathered, helps explain variation observed in subregional mortuary ritual, as well as changes that took place over time in the structure of mortuary ritual.

Interactions and shared experiences on the dynamic Adena ritual landscape would have exposed ritual leaders to new ideas that may have altered their interpretations of how the dead should be treated and how mortuary ritual should be conducted. Any change or variation in mound use, and therefore the structure of mortuary ritual, through time may simply have been a result of ritual leaders reinterpreting other mortuary events in which they were participants. However, those leaders who could have best influenced their kin groups would have had the most success in altering mortuary rituals. The agency of these individuals would then have led to the adoption of new ways of processing the dead and altering the mortuary rituals over time as they passed down their ideas to subsequent ritual leaders.

If remembering the dead is assumed to have been one of the purposes for these communal rituals (for an alternative perspective see Clay, chapter 4, this volume), then any mound constructed on the landscape would have served as a continual representation of ancestors placed there. As dispersed Adena kin groups assembled, ritual leaders organized and chose rituals from the overlying Adena ritual structure, as he or she understood it. In the context of premound rituals, these leaders may have chosen who was cremated and whether a mortuary pit or a post structure was appropriate for the situation. Any variation we see within the use of premound interment features may be the direct result of dynamic interactions that took place as many separate but allied groups came together to "work out" their losses (Clay 1998). Once the use of crypt-like interment features was widespread, leaders from one corporate group at one location may have interpreted the structure of ancestor veneration to include a log tomb, while the organizer of mortuary ritual for a different group may have relied more on a puddled-clay basin. If both served similar functions related to the Adena ideological structure, then their distribution may indicate different but important idiosyncratic symbols for the kin group using them.

Hays (2010) recently suggested similar intergroup ritual interactions as the cause of Adena mortuary variation in Ohio. He explained that stability and variation in the Adena mortuary paradigm derived from how social or isolated a kin group might have been (Hays 2010: 118). This could also be a result of their mobility. Hays (2010: 118) further mentioned that dramatic physiographic landscape features isolated groups from social interaction and thus prevented variation in mound structure by limiting the influx of outside ideas. The similarities in the theme of mortuary ritual across the three subregions examined here are present between drainages and across physiographic zones. However, specific variations in practices, such as the multicolored floor in the pit beneath Drake, remain confined at the subregional level. Additionally, there remains a Bluegrass-wide pattern that a long history of premound ritual gives way to mound construction. This distribution suggests that although individual practices may not have been comprehended among subregions, an overarching coherent Adena mortuary paradigm was present, possibly similar to what has been proposed by Striker (2008) and Clay (1998).

Conclusion

In this chapter, I have shown that there are general patterns in Adena mortuary ritual across the Bluegrass region that involved the use of cremations, the construction of premound post structures, and the presence of elaborate mortuary pits within short-term-use mounds. For those mounds that were used for more extended periods, there is a shift to the construction of complex crypt-like structures.

The source of change and variation in the structure of Adena mortuary rituals was grounded in the interactions between highly mobile kin groups moving around the landscape in space and time. As the leaders of Adena mortuary ritual continually reinterpreted how ancestors should be remembered, they were influenced by experiences and interactions that had previously taken place. When they successfully introduced new details on a common interpretation of how the dead should be treated, they changed (possibly inadvertently) the structure of mortuary ritual for future generations of participants in Adena ritual.

This heterarchical perspective of Adena leadership, coupled with structuration ensuing from the situational agency of particular leaders, suggests that the mobile nature and sociopolitical organization of Adena peoples led to a complex and varied Adena ritual landscape. This landscape was not static but constantly evolving for more than 700 years.

Acknowledgments

This chapter greatly benefited from discussions with A. Gwynn Henderson, David Pollack, and Jay K. Johnson. These three people not only talked through situational leadership with me but also provided very helpful comments on earlier drafts of this manuscript. My wife, Andrea Schuhmann, also proved an invaluable editing source. Finally, I thank Alice Wright, my coeditor for this volume and co-organizer for the 2010 Southeastern Archaeological Conference symposium that led to this volume, for her support, encouragement, and work ethic.

PART FOUR

Woodland Landscapes in Historical and Regional Perspective

16

On Ceremonial Landscapes

JAMES A. BROWN

This volume bears testimony to the growing evidence that landscape approaches in archaeology offer a very productive route to uncovering unexpected expressions of ritual practice found on sites of the Early and Middle Woodland periods. Ritual has been associated with the Middle Woodland period since the days of Squier and Davis (1848), when they identified "sacrificial altars" as a mark of the former presence of Mexican civilization in the forests of Ohio. To them, the very existence of mounds implicated ritual architecture, thereby making all of the earthworks blanketing the forests of eastern United States into a testimonial for bygone ritual practices. Moreover, mounds were believed to express in material terms the fact that in the past, more-complex cultures typified native peoples. By codifying this widely acknowledged Mound Builder myth, Squier and Davis set in motion perspectives that, even today, knowledgeable archaeologists have found hard to combat in their own work. This book takes an important step toward the eventual total dismantling of this myth.

Before I comment on the specific contributions to this volume, let me explain what I conceive of as the issue at stake. While the subject of landscape has been taken to be the framework around which these Early and Middle Woodland period studies are organized, in the Southeast and Midwest the long hand of Ohio Hopewell exercises a strong grip over the imagination. The central employment of landscape concepts helps to overcome some of the overhang of the Hopewell legacy—its splendid artwork and craftwork, and with its bewildering diversity of ritual practice that frequently involves the handling of human remains. It is not an overstatement to say that for southeastern archaeologists, Hopewell stands in the position of the "elephant in the living room" of the Woodland period. As an antidote, landscape helps place that romantically laden cultural phenomenon of Hopewell into a comparative context that allows it to be deconstructed.

Reactions to the proverbial elephant have ranged from denial to hearty embrace, and while the contributors here are definitely more comfortable with this elephant, I detect lingering doubts here and there. In large part one has difficulty squaring observations made in the fields of the Southeast with our often-distorted image of what Ohio Hopewell is or is not. It is not the place here to elaborate on this statement. But if one were to strip away some of the site specifics of artifactual forms and mortuary expressions, the similarities with the East as a whole would stand out far more obviously than they presently do.

The intellectual context that placed Ohio Hopewell in its key position within precontact history has been clearly articulated by Berle Clay (2005). It is part and parcel of the imperial Americanist vision. This perspective has left a legacy of diffusionism that clearly remains with us today (Brown and Kelly 2012). The "atomistic" label of Pluckhahn and Thompson (chapter 12) aptly fits archaeological perspectives that place the site at the center of the world and ignore alternative interpretations that visualize what takes place at the level of sites as part of a much larger social field (see Cobb and Nassaney 2002). Each site, no matter how large or small, is part of a larger entity. It is not a functional isolate. The position advanced here posits a cultural landscape on which human usage expands or contracts in accordance with the dynamics of a social process. As long as the conditions for this process are engaged, the features that mark it will either expand or increase until those conditions are no longer operative. The rituals of the Early Woodland and Middle Woodland are part of a single process involving an ever-increasing degree of periodic social aggregation under subsistence limitations preventing permanent aggregation. Landscape is a translation of the sacred. It is the material embodiment of cosmovision.

Exotics automatically become the result of some sort of exchange or logistical acquisition. It is therefore salubrious that Eubanks, Keith, Wallis, and other contributors have gone out on a limb to posit the presence of exotics in quantities as the material trace of visitation practices. I cannot agree more, although I would like to point out that the lowly bladelet has an unrecognized significance in this regard. The blade and core technology is a well-designed equipage for groups traversing territories with unfamiliar lithic source materials. Thus, it is no accident that the two periods well known for this technology are the Late Archaic of Poverty Point and Middle Woodland of the early centuries of the Common Era. Even the short presence of similar technology in Early Mississippian time can fit our expectations that visitors, or pilgrims if one chooses, repeatedly flocked to particular sites as centers of aggregation.

The distributions of the two core types are telling: one is centered in the Mississippi River valley, and the other lies across the flanks of the Southern Appalachians from Ohio to Georgia. These are two semiautonomous spheres. Add to this the fact that George Odell's (1994) comparative analysis of use wear on bladelets and flake tools revealed no differential functional usage, thereby undercutting the argument that the bladelet tool category has any performance advantage. Odell held out for a ritual advantage, but alternatively, bladelets could have been the expedient preference of mobile tool users—individuals who undertook long travels with minimal tool equipage. The weakness of the functional argument allows us to propose that the presence at a particular site of bladelets could be largely the consequence of special equipage being deposited that was designed for rapid transit. The long distances to the source deposits would then essentially index the travel distances undertaken by the visitors.

Both the neo-evolutionary and the diffusionist models have set up expectations that many have wrestled with but few have confronted satisfactorily (see Brose 1979: 149; Ford 1969; Jefferies 1979: 170; Smith 1979: 186). Should students of this time period expect a copy of the Ohio phenomenon, some selective replica, or some diagnostic trait? How does the chronological lead-up fit in, if at all? Or to sidestep the diffusionist positions, how does the increase in sedentism fit in and where does increase in plant use in the diet fit? These and other legitimate questions should be accepted as a challenge and not be dismissed with a shrug.

A robustly conceived conception of landscape as articulated in the introduction to this volume provides a working agenda that addresses these and other questions. That agenda works as an aid to conceptual integration as well as a format for explanation. While abstract conceptualization in that instance establishes a robust framework, I prefer to address landscape perspectives in terms of concrete conceptualizations current even today in native America.

The Immanent Universe

The specific details of movements of the sun, moon, and stars, the march of seasons, and details in plant movements and animal behavior have to be of fundamental importance. In an existence in which direct experience takes you only so far, the workings of natural phenomena provide logical connections for experience that otherwise would be imponderable. No student of natural history can avoid the immanent impact of the natural world on day-to-day existence, much less fail to privilege it in ritual practice and belief. As a consequence, much of what we observe (and even ignore) is an expression of this principle. To postulate a ceremonial world without a cosmic referent is as unthinkable in native belief today as it was in the past.

The continuities have been expressed by Richard Townsend (2004: 20), who stated, "It therefore seems possible to advance the idea of an analogous history of shared cultural themes, transmitted and adapted from Archaic times through the Woodland period and into the Mississippian centuries, continuing in modified form into the Colonial period and even lasting substantially in a few tribes down to the present time."

The forms these themes take, however, are diverse, and they often manifest themselves in ways that seem oblique or indirect to our Western senses. A useful study on this matter is the religious studies perspective of Lindsey Jones (2000) in analyzing pre-Hispanic Mexican architecture and ritual patterns. For these reasons I applaud the wholehearted commitment to the systematic exploration of this topic, not only in ceremonial earthworks that seem to demand this perspective but also in seemingly lowly practices easily confused with simple mechanical or economic activity. When it comes to explanation, we should not shrink from the subject of phenomenology raised in the book. One should distinguish between the unexamined or untested senses of potential, and a proposition that is couched in a form that is clearly confirmable or rejected. The mental source of any idea is irrelevant.

The investigation of spiritual landscapes is one of the many ways in which landscapes are useful in archaeology. It stands to become a particularly rich avenue of research for the Early to Middle Woodland periods, as the archaeological record in this block of time is particularly rich in evidence of ritual practice and the production of spiritually infused artifacts. This is not to downplay the utility of applications for later periods, but the increased visibility of an amazing variety of on-site evidence makes these periods ones in which the growth of ritual life can be monitored readily through material remains. Celebrating the spiritual was anything but routinely symbolized at that time. Later, during the period of cereal agricultural production in the Mississippian period, the material expression of spiritually activated belief and practice was clearly much more subject to routinization. In contrast to the sheer multitude of material expressions of, say, world renewal rites in Middle Woodland mortuary practices, the variety of corresponding practices in the Mississippian period is simultaneously narrowed and multiply replicated (Beck and Brown 2012). Clearly demarcated material practices can be identified repeatedly over a broad region. As Pluckhahn and Thompson observe (chapter 12, this volume), the grammar of monuments becomes more structured in the Mississippian period than it had been before.

Ritual Life in a Spiritual Landscape

The fingerprints of ritual are not only indicative of belief and practice but often provide links to larger patterns. The placement of sites and monuments can be puzzling without knowledge of the relevant natural phenomena. Built works readily supplement natural wonders in a spiritual landscape. Now that archaeologists have become comfortable with the reality that all people live within a spatial envelope occupied by numerous natural features, it is possible to project connections from one or more individual sites onto a larger sacred landscape. This includes those that have been modified and aligned to address spiritual needs as well as more-subtle configurations of human usage, whether modified or not. Good reasons exist for examining landscapes this way. Diverse and seemingly out-of-place features can be tied to a common landscape that makes sense as physical remnants of past spiritual observance. Radiocarbon dating makes feature tie-in across a vast area entirely feasible where previously it was simply a speculative gesture.

The scope of a sacred landscape often stretches to the skyline or other distant landmarks. In the Biltmore and Leake site cases, the landscape is structured by heights of land that bracket the principal earthwork locale. Kimball, Whyte, and Crites (chapter 8, this volume) cite the Biltmore Mound as aligned between two opposing peaks, Mt. Pisgah and Mt. Mitchell. The same conceptual anchor to heights has been detected in Ohio Hopewell (Seeman and Branch 2006). Seeman (2004: 66) observed that "the Seip-Overly complex in south-central Ohio . . . orients to Copperas Mountain, a unique 350-foot high (106 m) black shale cliff that is home to dozens of nesting vultures and that produces quartz crystals and other mineral[s]."

Pollack and Schlarb (chapter 3, this volume) address the evidence for Adena off-mound ritual. At the Evans site, they located basins among concentrations of yellow clay, cremated fragments, barite, mica, and diagnostic points and pottery. This off-mound ritual evidence was logically tied to the burials in the mounds. Although the occupation site was separated from the mound, it was located within a line-of-sight of the mound.

Linkages to pools of fresh water and other features of ideological significance can be identified. Seeman (2004: 66, citing Bacon 1980) said, "Old Stone Fort in central Tennessee where a rock and earthen enclosure occupies the tip of a promontory at the forks of the Duck River . . . is flanked by twin waterfalls." Keith (chapter 9, this volume) makes the plausible claim that the Leake site lies in the center of a sacred landscape that includes at least two other sites. The Leake site complex includes caves, wherein a connection with the cosmic "Beneath World" becomes plausible. So far caves and rockshelters have, regrettably, received little attention, although they are regarded in the Midwest as entryways to the Beneath World (see Franklin et al., chapter 5, this volume). The above comments affirm a kind of connection between parts of a cosmically ordained ritual system that stands in contrast to elements of a subsistence-settlement system.

In general the ceremonial site locations cited in this volume are not motivated by economic reasons, although a convergence of economic and ritual factors may well be in play in particular situations. I think a congruence can be seen in certain repeated uses of the same ritual place in later Middle Woodland occupations where occupation takes on a more permanent character. The Kolomoki center is a case in point. I think it is worthy of note that Kolomoki and other sites with similar evidence for permanent settlement occur late in the time frame adopted in this volume and are located in southern environments with a richer and more sustained resource productivity than is possible earlier and farther north.

Spiritual Centering in a Constructed Arena

Built constructions beg for an interpretation that is logically connected with their forms. An enclosure that is embraced by an embankment is a common combination that once gave rise to the fortification function, notwithstanding the awkward placement of gateways and the frequent placement of ditches on the interior. A much more promising way of interpreting these features is to situate them in commonplace Eastern Woodlands cosmovision. Enclosures become proxies for the "center-of-the-world" and stand as large versions of a multifaceted class that can be created in any medium and at any scale, for private and public benefit.

Circular enclosures are widely reported. All too often they have received rudimentary attention, although they were by far the most common earthwork form noticed by Squier and Davis (1848). The simplicity of the form has commonly not been given its due as a significant ceremonial landscape feature. But they are in fact very revealing. Wallis (chapter 14, this volume) argues that the post–AD 250 centers incorporated avenues for undertaking shared experiences of cosmic significance (e.g., world renewal). The gateways stood for entry into the interior. Other contributors (Wallis, Kimball et al., Wright, Pollack and Schlarb) argue that layers of deposits incorporate histories of ritual observance.

A good case can be made that the form itself replicates, in miniature, the surface of the earth on which humans live. The embankment becomes, in effect, a rim walling off the human world from the untamed cosmos beyond (see Hall 1997). I find intriguing the report that ditches are found interior to the embankments. Here there is a restatement of the same cosmic concept with the additional elaboration of a ditch setting off the elevated interior space (habitable earth) from the cosmic wall. The ditch then becomes a proxy for the waters on which the earth's surface rests. At the complicated Fort Ancient earthwork in southwestern Ohio, these interior ditches are modeled as filled with water. They complement spring-fed ponds outside of the embankment wall (Connolly and Lepper 2004). The numerous hilltop "forts" readily fall into the category of large-scale centering arena. The many entryways that these "forts" possess—in contrast to the simple circular earthworks—inform us as to systematic change in ritual format.

The contemporary realization of the centering arena is, of course, the Creek busk ground. Although an embankment is not an obligatory feature of the ground, its sacred precincts are duly sanctified prior to the ceremony. The surface is cleared of debris in preparation. Swanton (1928) offered a revealing description of the Old Tuckabachee ground in Oklahoma. In this case the act of sweeping clean the surface of the ground over several decades had resulted in an accidental earthwork, oval in shape with a one-meter-high embankment. Swanton was doubly impressed with the physical similarity to certain precontact earthworks in the mound that were created by the piling of ash and other debris after repeated cleaning the central fireplace. While this example in no way argues for the same process of earthwork creation in precontact time, it does pose the revealing connection between sacred performances and the earthworks that frame them, whether a part of the constructed landscape or not.

With these axiomatic associations in mind, it is possible to perceive relationships between small and simple earthworks and large and complicated ones. The multitude of forms these earthworks take can be visualized as expansions of these concepts along desired directions. In an important sense, enclosed and roofed space takes on parallel importance. In this regard I find it intriguing that Jefferies and colleagues (chapter 6, this volume) report that the interior space delimited by a ditch is sometimes square in form, not a replica of the circular embankment. Many structures reported for the Middle Woodland period are rectangular or rectangular with rounded corners. The shape of the habitable earth can be seen as homologous with the shape of the design of roofed buildings of ceremonial significance. The principle of homologous expansion is exemplified in the relationship of buried ritual buildings and the outline of the embankment of late Ohio Hopewell age at Mound City (Brown 2004).

Earthen constructions are tangible features in a ritual landscape. However, they have long occupied archaeological interest as having a practical purpose, for example, as religious centers (with sacrificial altars) or more commonly as having some social function (e.g., clan segregation). Edward Henry (chapter 15, this volume) has tied variability of Adena mortuary practices to the degree of mobility of those engaged in the funerals. Although his idea is couched in mobility patterns in the course of the subsistence cycle, I would think that long journeys to strange peoples at distant places is a kind of mobility that would have potentially great impact on experiences.

In this volume we have ancestor veneration inferred at Kolomoki (Pluckhahn and Thompson, chapter 12) but a denial for the Adena (Clay, chapter 4). This may be less of a contradiction than it seems, considering the great separation in time and space between the two cultural manifestations. Henry (chapter 15) has introduced another factor that I see as informing more generally on mortuary practices over the course of time within entire area. He noted that one effect of mobility would be the impact of new experiences on the creation of novel practices. The advantage of his perspective is that it addresses the submerged problem of diffusion as instrumental in the appearance of mound building practices in widely separated locations. Prior to the rise of processualism, diffusion was commonly invoked out of habit, and the appearance of "look-alike" practices in widely separated places inspired this explanation as much as any other. But if ceremonial sites of any reputation attracted a wide body of ceremonial participants, then the conditions favorable for borrowing and innovation would be in place.

Exchange among Cultural Isolates

Thirty years ago, Early and Middle Woodland scholars were brought together from wide-flung areas in the Eastern Woodlands to sum up what was then known about the subject (Brose and Greber 1979). A combination of evidence for long-distance movement of materials such as mica and marine shell made the Southeast relevant to a discussion that been dominated by a focus on the Midwest. Some participants expressed reservations about the applicability of the term *Hopewell* in the context of southeastern studies.

Discourse on the subject was still mired in taxonomic issues that focused on similarities and differences among these manifestations. The subjects of trade and exchange, mortuary practices, and technologies had yet to be freed from the culturally specific category in which these practices were found. One could not productively speak of exchange dynamics comparatively and separated from its cultural milieu. Without taxonomic certainty, not much could be claimed about the processes that took place in Hopewell, whether restricted to Ohio Hopewell or within a Hopewellian Interaction Sphere. The subject of ceremony was hardly discussed at all.

Little attention has been paid to the taxonomic affiliation of particular earthworks. Discussions of earthworks in the past have all too often focused on whether the earthworks are Hopewell, Adena, or some third taxon. The problem of pigeonholing used to be paramount to the point that the evidence of human use of a particular space was of little interest unless this use could be placed in a cultural context.

What Is Moving—Goods or People?

Nodes in networks are cited numerous times. The Leake site complex stands out in this respect. But are these networks actuated by exchange? Or are these nodes something else? I have in mind here the way exchange is customarily modeled as a reciprocal activity. The quite evident conjunction of large groups (at least periodically) and an abundance of raw material and finished artifacts of exotic origin make this a plausible conclusion. Where access to exotics is envisioned in this way, various distant locales contributed materials to a single locale from sources they had access to. Lost sight of here is the possibility that bearers from the source came to the locale in which the exotics were interred.

At one time the social and economic underpinnings of exchange would have been unquestioned. Struever and Houart (1972) explicitly made major mound centers located in logistically critical places as "transactional nodes" in a subcontinental network called the Hopewellian Interaction Sphere. While their interpretation of the Hopewellian Interaction Sphere had the advantage of being grounded in well-sourced material remains, it had the unfortunate effect of downplaying the morphological similarities present among far-flung mound building programs. The movement to ceremonial centers of small groups of peoples, sometimes from long distances, for the purposes of large-scale religious renewal, as well as a range of other activities, helps explain certain archaeological facts. It also brings in other motivations (e.g., marriage, alliance making, socializing, exchange of goods) and the all-important pooling of labor, even for very short periods of time (Beck 2003; Bernardini 2004). As long as the appearance of exotics is divorced from the scale of local aggregation, we will retain the atomistic focus that prevents a vision of connectivity associated with the Hopewellian Interaction Sphere. This connectivity, interestingly, is one that falls short of the degree of integration manifest in the Early Mississippian period (Beck 2003).

Where Are the Settlements?

The perceived differences that should obtain between ritual space and housing for common everyday purposes do not meet expectations. The distinction we impose may not have existed. Ritual could easily have involved ordinary cooking and serving vessels. Fabricating ritual regalia may have been undertaken near the location of its intended use (Spielmann 2002). The locus of some rituals may not have been segregated in the same fashion as in the later Mississippian period.

Many of the structures indicated as common dwellings located beneath mounds may have been key to ritual acts that are part of the ceremonial landscape. Size and simplicity of form is no guarantee of being the covered space of everyday life. As an example, several of the structures uncovered beneath individual mounds at the site of Mound City have walls composed of a single line of posts. The sizes are modest.

Many contributors to this volume (e.g., Applegate, chapter 2; Franklin et al., chapter 5) report the archaeology of small-scale settlements with few or modest indications of ritual artifacts or even layouts hinting of a network of connections on any appreciable scale. There are indications of unease with asserting larger connections in anything other than a temporal assignment in the Early or Middle Woodland periods. For this reason, the bold step toward stitching together specific locales within a landscape of connected places is all the more important. Such a step recognizes that small sites can be related in patterns that are diagnostic or near diagnostic of specific cultural phenomena. The expectation here and commonly expressed is "where's the excitement?" This is borne out of a reader's understanding of Ohio Hopewell, whereas the reality is not too different from experience in the Southeast. Domestic features are underwhelming to the point of making Griffin (1996) and other critics protest that villages should be present (see discussions in Dancey and Pacheco 1997): villages belong with a cultural expression as grand as Ohio Hopewell; settlements should be comparably grand as well. But we are dealing with cultural life before maize agriculture had an impact on settlement aggregation and duration in all but the most favorable foraging environments on the Coastal Plains and nearby freshwaters with year-round productivity. The lower Mississippi River and Indian River in Florida are well-documented locales that have sustained the likes of Poverty Point and Mount Taylor cultures (Beasley 2008).

Over 30 years have transpired since the 1978 Chillicothe Conference on Hopewell archaeology attempted to provide a unifying theme to the subject (Brose and Greber 1979). By that time already, it had become evident that the ceremonially laden concepts of Adena and Hopewell simply could not be stretched far enough beyond their respective homelands to encompass the variety of regionally specific manifestations uncovered throughout the Eastern Woodlands. Rather than stuff the Southeastern cases into those two taxa, this collection sidesteps the taxonomic debates by focusing on an important commonality that has all of the marks of being a manifestation of one or more processes (social and natural). What is most striking about the present set of contributions is the recognition of the importance of religion in discussing ritual centers in a region of the Southeast south of the Ohio and east of the Mississippi.

17

Social Landscapes of Early and Middle Woodland Peoples in the Southeast

DAVID G. ANDERSON

Exciting and important things were happening during the Early and Middle Woodland periods in the Southeast, the interval from roughly 3,200 to 1,500 calendar years ago, as made clearer by the chapters in this volume. In any region where a vast amount of fieldwork and data collection has been occurring, as has been the case for many decades in the Southeast, there is a continual need for papers and volumes directed toward synthesis and interpretation. Robert Mainfort and I argued for continued efforts along these lines some ten years ago, in an earlier volume that made an effort at synthesizing Woodland archaeology in the Southeast (Anderson and Mainfort 2002a: xvi). We noted then that while such volumes take a lot of work to produce, they are necessary and indeed essential guides to our region's prehistory, distilling and making sense of immense amounts and disparate kinds of information. We specifically encouraged our younger and presumably more energetic, and theoretically and intellectually more nimble, colleagues to produce such volumes. Happily, what Alice Wright and Edward Henry and their colleagues and contributors have produced fits the bill nicely. Rather than producing broad syntheses of specific geographic regions or topics such as plant and animal use, as the contributors to our earlier volume attempted, the authors in the present volume have directed their efforts toward delimiting the social landscape of Woodland peoples in different parts of the Southeast, from a number of theoretical and methodological perspectives and employing many kinds of archaeological data. While local area syntheses are an inevitable by-product, the larger landscape approach ties the chapters in the volume together, much as peoples in the Woodland period in the Southeast were connected in various ways, and should not be viewed in isolation.

A theme running through the chapters in the volume is that, to paraphrase Tim Pauketat (2001), "landscape history matters" in southeastern archaeology. That is, domestic and ceremonial features such as houses and work areas, or mounds, earthworks, and plazas, as well as intervening fields, forests, and waterways, should be thought of not as finished creations but as continually changing venues upon which communal activities are registered. Landscapes are thus processes in time, reflecting the history and traditions of the people who live in and shape them. Wright and Henry (chapter 1) argue that to understand past societies from a landscape perspective, a multiscalar analytical perspective must be employed, examining variation in the archaeological record over both space and time and at multiple scales. Landscapes subsume the social, biotic, and terrain features created, used, and experienced by humans, and ideally our research should strive to encompass both the totality and the changing nature of this landscape. Typically archaeologists have tended to focus at one level or scale of analysis, such as a site or group of roughly contemporaneous sites, sometimes also looking at changes within them over time. Now, however, while sites regarded as "centers" still receive appreciable research attention, they are increasingly seen as positioned within changing networks of settlement, land use, communication, and interaction.

A second theme running through many of the chapters is the demonstration that information recovered from sites excavated long ago, such as Crystal River, Kolomoki, and Tunacunnhee, can be reexamined and reinterpreted from contemporary perspectives, with new and important things learned in the process. Indeed, where new fieldwork is occurring, in many cases it has been inspired by a reanalysis of older materials. The examination of old collections reminds us that no site, whether it is surviving or not, is ever definitively reported and interpreted, highlighting the critical importance of responsibly curating the records and material remains of our research (e.g., Sullivan and Childs 2003). The materials we are collecting now, if properly conserved and curated, will almost certainly be examined by many researchers in the future.

A third theme is that variability and not uniformity characterizes Woodland occupations in the Southeast and that the archaeological record at many sites is more complex than our reporting traditions, which tend to encourage standardization and simplification in classification, might tend to indicate. That is, as Wright demonstrates in her chapter examining the myriad of features found at the Garden Creek Mound in North Carolina (chapter 7), we have to avoid assuming that there are standard patterns of structure size and shape, or burial practice, or that sites can be accurately described using taxa such as "vacant ceremonial center" and "special activity loci" or, in more functional terms, that they were used solely for aggregation or feasting or, alternatively, mundane day-to-day activities. Any such assessments must be demonstrated and not assumed, and the default inference should be that a wide range of behavior occurred at every site.

A fourth theme running through the volume is that a great deal of primary field research and data collection on Woodland period sites is ongoing in the Southeast. The classic sites have not all been excavated or destroyed; instead, it is clear that what will someday be regarded as classic sites such as Armory, Biltmore, Jackson Landing, and Leake are appearing all the time. The data being collected come from traditional excavation procedures as well as from newer remote sensing and geoarchaeological and paleosubsistence/paleoenvironmental sampling techniques, making our fieldwork ever more efficient and informative.

Approaches to Woodland Landscape Archaeology

Darlene Applegate's analysis of Early and Middle Woodland structures in Kentucky in the reconstruction of domestic landscapes (chapter 2) is a remarkably broad synthesis, showing what can be done with data from numerous sources, many of them cultural resource management (CRM) projects. Three spatial scales of analysis were employed: the microscale, with data from 70 structures examined; the intrasite level, encompassing structure and feature assemblages from several dozen sites where wide areas were exposed and excavated; and the intersite level, comparing settlement distributions in several major river drainages. A number of major conclusions were reached, illustrating that, while demanding in terms of time and effort, compiling data from multiple scales and sources is critically important to understanding landscape use in an area, during the Woodland or indeed during any time period. The widespread occurrence of lightly built structures intended for seasonal or one-time use, rather than extended year-round use, is a somewhat surprising outcome of her work. Permanent, well-built structures were present but were the exception rather than the rule. As in the Cumberland Plateau of Tennessee (see chapter 5), furthermore, many caves and rockshelters were used for domestic purposes. While two rough size classes of domestic structures were evident, perhaps corresponding to nuclear and multiple or extended family residences, reuse or rebuilding was far more characteristic of the larger buildings. Structure shape varied considerably, with circular and rounded structures common, although roughly a fifth of the structures were square to rectangular in shape, many with corners oriented to the cardinal directions. Daubing was rare, reinforcing the impression that many structures were used only for relatively brief periods, presumably in warmer weather.

True villages, or well-organized communities with multiple households and what Applegate calls "activity-specific space differentiation," do not appear until the Late Woodland locally, when a fundamental transformation of the domestic landscape appears to have happened. Land use differed over time, and while a wide array of settings were utilized, habitation was more common along tributaries during the Early Woodland and along larger drainages in the Middle Woodland. In both periods, ritual and domestic sites were spatially discrete. As Applegate concluded, who knew there was so much information out there and that, once it was compiled and patterns were recognized, it could guide research in parts of Kentucky lacking such coverage?

Pollack and Schlarb (chapter 3) examine ritual in Adena culture, demonstrating that it took place in varied settings and that it encompassed more than the well-known tomb and mound building behavior that has attracted archaeologists' attention for generations. At the nonmound Evans site in Kentucky, unusual yellow clay–filled pit features were found, where ritual activity, including the processing of the dead, appears to have occurred. The fieldwork was superbly documented, as made clear by the quality of the images used at the meeting session that resulted in this volume. I was particularly impressed with the authors' efforts to check below what they initially thought to be the bottom of a clay-filled pit feature, to be sure it was indeed the bottom. All too often our assumptions about site features and soil conditions can fool us; our excavations, like our arguments, need to be taken to unequivocal completion. The authors review evidence for the use of unusual clays at other Adena sites, notably, of durable water/weather-resistant colored clays in several mounds. Many Adena mounds and other nonmound features were apparently built with great care taken with both the engineering properties of the materials employed and ritual ceremonial considerations, specifically, what soil types, colors, and textures were used, and why; this is a research area seeing increasing attention at monuments of all periods in the region (e.g., Anderson 2012a; Anderson and Sassaman 2012: 168–71; Charles et al. 2004; DeBoer 2005; Pursell 2004; Sherwood and Kidder 2011; Van Nest et al. 2001). Similar care and consideration in the use of fills in construction was also apparent at the Biltmore Mound in western North Carolina, at Leake in northern Georgia, and at Jackson Landing in Mississippi, as documented in the chapters by Kimball, Whyte, and Crites (chapter 8), Keith (chapter 9), and Boudreaux (chapter 10). Mound building in many prehistoric societies in the Southeast was about far more than the unthinking piling up of dirt, and our labor estimates for this activity must consider the time and associated ceremony that went into the selection, processing, and placement of fills.

Berle Clay's chapter reminds us that there is much that can be learned through ethnographic research and that we need to be careful when imbuing behavior in past societies with value and meaning derived from our own (chapter 4). Clay's experience in New Guinea demonstrated to him, for example, that ceremonies associated with the treatment of the recently or long dead were of more value to their participants because of the concurrent feasting and ceremony that would occur than because of a desire to commemorate the deceased. There are parallels in our own society, where the reception and wake are as important and cathartic to the participants as are the more formal church and graveside services. We need to keep in our minds that while the human remains are clearly a necessary and important part of or prop in burial ceremonies, the ceremony itself may have been as important as or more important than the disposal of the body itself. Clay thus argues that it was the building of Adena mounds and the placement of the dead within them—creating locations and foci for present and future ritual—that was most important rather than the burials themselves or the completion of the mounds. That is, the mounds were important not solely as monuments memorializing ancestors or perhaps marking territories but as locations of and justifications for collective feasting and ceremony (see Milner 2004: 95; see also Wallis, herein). Coupled with this, Clay (attributing the idea to Hofman [1985]) suggests that variation in the processing of the recent dead may in some cases be situational, a means of facilitating "the execution of proscribed mortuary ritual" rather than or in addition to reflecting individual status. The kind of remains encountered may reflect how long it had been since death and how far the remains had to be transported; some processing of the dead may have been considered essential if ceremonies were infrequent. Clay's arguments about burial and feasting reminded me of Polly Wiessner's (2002) work with the New Guinea Enga, in her classic "Vines of Complexity" article, that showed how exchange networks and patterns of warfare could arise in tandem, reinforcing and structuring both behaviors, which grew over time in scale and complexity, leading to inequality and in some cases collapse. Things archaeologists commonly discuss separately, such as warfare and exchange, or burial and feasting, were in fact often closely bound together, and cannot and should not be completely disentangled. As Clay notes, we do not think about these things in combination as much as we should. As much an ethnographic commentary on our own culture as on Adena, Clay's chapter demonstrates that we must be careful to ensure that our archaeological interpretations are shaped by the evidence at hand, not by perceptions from our own historical tradition.

Jay Franklin, Meagan Dennison, and their colleagues examine Early and Middle Woodland use of the Upper Cumberland Plateau of middle Tennessee, showing through example the many seasons of fieldwork and the quantities of primary data that must be collected and analyzed to develop a local cultural sequence and to begin to understand patterns of landscape use (chapter 5). Their research, directed toward small site types—specifically, upland rock shelters—reminds us that while much prior Woodland research has been conducted at mounds and enclosures, these site types constitute only a small part of the cultural landscape. Mounds and earthworks, or even evidence for interaction with peoples at great distances, appear to be the rare exception rather than the rule in large parts of the east. While some caves and rock shelters clearly saw use in ritual (e.g., Faulkner 1997; Simek and Cressler 2004, 2008; Simek et al. 1998), most of the upland sites appear to be where day-to-day existence took place, and constitute what might be called a domestic landscape. Whether and why people in areas such as the Cumberland Plateau opted out of monumentality or exchange is something that must be documented and considered. The presence of seemingly ritually charged artwork at some upland sites, however, indicates that Woodland ceremonialism occurred in other parts of the landscape than at centers characterized by monumental architecture.

Jefferies, Milner, and Henry's chapter on the "sacred circle" at Winchester Farm (chapter 6) not only provides a detailed examination of this one site but also places it in regional context through an analysis of the sizes and shapes of 247 contemporary enclosures in the middle Ohio River valley. Like Applegate's compilation efforts with data from domestic sites noted earlier, we now have both the data and the recording and analytical tools to conduct such large-scale comparative analyses, which I expect will become increasingly commonplace, revealing important new things about the past. What is essential in all such studies, of course, is that the compiled primary data are both responsibly curated for the long term and made publicly available to other researchers, to avoid duplication of effort, allow for additional work with it, and permit the verification of results (e.g., Nature 2009; Schofield et al. 2009). The Winchester Farm earthwork, interestingly, was not on a high or even prominent point on the landscape, suggesting that we must be careful not to assume we know where such sites might occur; many have apparently been plowed down and hence lost or obscured, requiring discovery or relocation through nontraditional methods, such as remote sensing. The project's fine-grained topographic mapping and remote sensing work demonstrate how to do this; whenever possible, use of such procedures should be the first step in any field project, before any earth is moved. Multiple remote sensing procedures, this project also showed, provide a far better picture of what is present than any one technique can provide (see Hammerstedt et al. 2010; Lydick 2008; Maki and Fields 2010). Ground truthing of remote sensing results, of course, will always be important to their interpretation. Finally, the authors' tongue-in-cheek suggestion at the meeting that the terms *squircle* or *squarecle* be used to describe these earthwork shapes (circular embankments with circular to squared internal platforms) did not make it into the text, although I still think they have descriptive value and hope they won't be squelched. As the authors conclude their chapter, "Winchester Farm is not simply a circle or a square, but a combination of both."

Alice Wright's chapter on the feature record associated with the Garden Creek platform mound (chapter 7) shows that we have come a long way from the recognition more than 35 years ago that some southeastern platform mounds were pre-Mississippian in age, dating back to at least the Middle Woodland period (e.g., Dickens 1975; Knight 1990; Lindauer and Blitz 1997). Wright's research was directed in part to the submound deposits at Garden Creek, to determine what activities were occurring before the mound was constructed. Hearths, for example, were smaller on the average in the submound area than those on the mound summits, suggesting that fewer people were using them; given the unusual artifacts associated with some of the hearths, however, gift giving and feasting may have been occurring around them. Importantly, Wright's research presents methods for resolving structures from the myriad of posts documented below the mound. Confusing arrays of posts are a part of the archaeological record of many southeastern archaeological sites and are particularly common on landforms that have been occupied repeatedly by people building post-in-ground structures and where minimal deposition has occurred. In some cases, it is simply not possible to recognize structures in such arrays in the field, making the collection of as much information as possible from each apparent post critical. Wright provides explicit and iterative methods for recognizing structures that involve displaying subsets of features on site maps by ranges of size and depth values; the ranges for these values were determined, in part, by their occurrence in known structures, such as the one building conclusively identified under the mound. Significantly, she also made use of posthole data from approximately 49 Middle Woodland structures recently excavated by Tasha Benyshek at the nearby Macon County Airport site (Benyshek and Webb 2009a, 2009b) to develop expectations about what contemporaneous domestic structures at Garden Creek could be like. Using this approach, Wright was able to tentatively identify 5 additional unrecognized structures below the Garden Creek mound. Her innovative and comparative methods can be used widely, to make sense of similar, confusing archaeological records anywhere they may be found. Her research also shows how modern CRM data from large-scale excavations can help us better understand older site data sets. The variability in the Middle Woodland structures that were observed at Garden Creek and the Macon County Airport Site, in fact, shows that we have to be careful to avoid assuming that there are single ideal types of buildings at given mounds or during specific time periods. Wright's chapter demonstrates that analyses with structures should use large samples whenever possible, to make us aware of the variability that likely existed, and the reasons for it.

Kimball, Whyte, and Crites provide a detailed construction history for the Biltmore Mound in western North Carolina, providing in the process a good overview on the excavations as well as the analyses of the artifactual and paleosubsistence assemblage recovered (chapter 8). I had the pleasure of visiting the excavations while the fieldwork was under way, and found the mound and its elaborate fills and ditches, and the remarkable artifacts associated with it, to be every bit as exciting as the nearby Biltmore mansion, a popular tourist attraction and a symbol of nineteenth- as opposed to fifth- and sixth-century opulence. The Biltmore site has a truly remarkable artifact assemblage, with pottery decorations and microblades reminiscent of Ohio Hopewell. The dating of the premound and mound deposits, to between circa AD 390 and 600, however, is very late for Hopewell, and indeed postdates most sites so classified in Ohio. Instead of thinking of the site as "Hopewellian," we should probably be thinking about it as a part of the continuation of Middle Woodland ceremonialism and mound building that occurred across the lower Southeast for several centuries after classic Hopewell had ceased in the Midwest. As at the Evans site in Kentucky noted previously, considerable effort went into the selection of soils used in the Biltmore mound and ditch complex, indicating that great knowledge and ceremony were associated with the construction. The presence of vast quantities of paleosubsistence remains in the mound compared to the comparatively few found in the nearby village deposits indicates feasting behavior was also associated with the complex's construction and use. Unlike in many other parts of the lower Southeast (e.g., Gremillion 2002), an extensive assemblage of Eastern Agricultural Complex domesticates was recovered at Biltmore, indicating the importance of these crops to local populations. The people at Biltmore appear to have interacted with Hopewellian peoples to the north toward the very end of that culture in the Midwest, and may even have been visited or founded by them. The ditch at the site, reminiscent of Adena sacred circles, may represent another tradition derived from the north, although the association of mounds with surrounding water, or built over water, has a long history in the Southeast, dating well back into the Archaic in parts of the region (Anderson 2012a; Kidder 2011; Sassaman 2010).

Scot Keith's analysis of the Leake site complex in northern Georgia makes a good case for its being an integrated sacred landscape extending over hundreds of acres as well as a gateway community linking people in societies located far to the north and south during the Middle Woodland period. Leake's probable ties with the Mann site in southern Indiana are documented through petrographic analyses of sherds found at each site; Mann likely served as a comparable gateway community in the lower Midwest, making a comparisons of the two site complexes a potentially rewarding area for study. But the people at Leake also apparently had ties with other parts of the Eastern Woodlands, as evidenced by the presence of Marksville, Weeden Island, and other pottery types indicative of connections to the south and west. Determining how and where people moved across the region is a topic where research should prove useful, particularly at delimiting key nodes as well as intermediate sites in interaction networks. When least-cost pathway analyses of Hopewellian interaction are conducted (e.g., Anderson 2012b; Anderson et al. 2007), sites like Leake and Mann will need to be considered. Hopewellian interaction was not just north to south or vice versa, the assemblages from the Leake complex demonstrate, but included appreciable movement within the southeastern region. If possible pathways between major sites and areas can be determined, it may be feasible to locate intervening centers or at least suggest the routes by which peoples moved across the region during the Middle Woodland period.

The field research at Leake included remote sensing analysis, another demonstration, like that by Jefferies and his colleagues at Winchester Farm, that such procedures can locate and document surviving portions of monuments that may not be apparent on the surface. The work at Leake also shows how important new information or interpretations may be obtained from sites excavated or thought destroyed long ago. Both Leake and Biltmore, the chapters herein additionally demonstrate, offer examples of the kinds of activities that were occurring at major southeastern Middle Woodland centers. The commonalities between these two site complexes—evidence for feasting, artifacts from a wide range of source areas, and the presence of ditches, marker posts, and apparent alignments—indicate multiple areas where comparative analyses would be valuable. Perhaps what is most impressive about the work Keith and his colleagues have done is that a comprehensive and extremely detailed report on the fieldwork and subsequent analyses exists and is available in electronic form, making the primary data readily accessible to interested researchers (Keith 2010). This highlights an advantage of much of the work conducted in the modern era under the auspices of cultural resources management: the timely production of final reports as well as the curation of collections and records in perpetuity is mandated. Keith raises numerous questions for future research at Leake throughout his chapter; indeed, another important contribution of this and the other chapters in the volume is suggesting directions that future research should take.

Tony Boudreaux's work at the Jackson Landing site (chapter 10) brings renewed research attention to this extensive earthwork and platform mound complex, one of the largest yet least-known late Middle Woodland/early Late Woodland centers in the Southeast. The Jackson Landing site complex was carefully placed by its builders within natural landscape features (largely surrounded by water or marsh, a theme common in the region) to heighten its isolation and at the same time demarcate what was likely a ritual precinct. Boudreaux's thoughts on Jackson Landing's "catchment," the area over which and the numbers of people who regularly came together at the complex, is a subject that deserves more attention at centers across the region. His recognition that the site is located "at the margins of two archaeological regions" and may have integrated people from both is certainly testable, although to date no exotic or extralocal artifacts have been found at the site. Finally, Boudreaux's fieldwork, documented in his meeting presentation, shows how much can be learned about mound construction procedures using relatively small yet carefully excavated units. His work also highlights the importance of systematically examining areas around mounds and within earthworks and illustrates that vacancy (i.e., minimal long-term habitation) of centers must be demonstrated rather than assumed. Like many of the other chapters in this volume, the work at Jackson Landing shows the value of research directed in multiscalar fashion toward placing a site complex within a local and much larger regional perspective.

Paul Eubanks convincingly argues that what he calls "ritually motivated aggregations" continued into the late Middle Woodland at the Armory site in Alabama (chapter 11), a pattern of ceremonial behavior that, as the chapters in this volume demonstrate, appears to hold in many parts of the Southeast. As at Biltmore and Leake, pottery from other parts of the region was found at Armory, suggesting to Eubanks, building on the earlier work of Walthall (1985), that the site was a pilgrimage center where people came together to conduct ritual and no doubt other activities. Although the construction and use of such centers in the Southeast has been interpreted as the result of action and local reaction to visits by people from the Midwest, it has since become clear that no matter how some of them may have started, activities at many of these southeastern centers continued long after Hopewell had faded in the Midwest. The later Middle Woodland and early Late Woodland was a vibrant period in the lower Southeast, in fact, with interaction occurring over large areas. Eubanks examined the occurrence of ceramics at Armory to show that distinct concentrations of differing wares were present over the site area, suggesting the possibility that multigroup aggregation was occurring. Likewise, food debris found near a burial mound suggested feasting tied to mortuary behavior. Eubanks importantly argues that we need to be considering the reasons why aggregation at centers occurred, suggesting that it may be related to demographic trends over the region, perhaps to bring dispersed peoples together to maintain ceremonial, kinship, information, and mating networks. Neither warfare nor climate change appears to have been a motivating factor, as reflected in evidence for raiding and dendrochronologically derived rainfall records (see also Smith 2009). Ritual requiring large numbers of people, Eubanks argues, was the primary reason aggregation occurred.

Pluckhahn and Thompson's chapter examining the major Middle Woodland Crystal River, Fort Center, and Kolomoki centers (chapter 12) offers an excellent contemporary theoretical overview of how Woodland period archaeology has been approached in recent decades in the Southeast, and how research should be directed. They argue, as indeed many of the chapters in this volume suggest, that greater emphasis needs to be directed toward the social and historical connections between sites, something that may be missed when research focuses too closely on specific cases. Likewise, they argue that it is the process of monumentalization that we should be considering, rather than characteristics of finished monuments—the short- and long-term histories of building and using monuments and landscapes, the tempo and mode of their construction and use, and how this was a part of and helped define daily life and social identity. Pointing to the tremendous variation in the size and shape of southeastern Woodland monuments, they argue that there was no rigid architectural grammar in place dictating how sites were to be constructed, compared with during later Mississippian times, as some would have it (cf. Anderson 2012a and Lewis et al. 1998; contra Lewis et al., I suggest that the case for a rigid Mississippian architectural grammar is itself overstated, save at the most general level of mounds fronting on plazas). Pluckhahn and Thompson argue persuasively that the similarities between these centers would have facilitated visitation and a sense of commonality between their respective occupants, while at the same time the differences would have reinforced a sense of distinctiveness and local identity, creating what the authors elegantly describe as constructing a sense of "local and larger regional identity."

Like Jackson Landing, all three sites examined by Pluckhahn and Thompson are located on or near major ecotones—something Larson (1972: 388–89) noted for Mississippian centers such as Etowah, located a few miles from the Leake site—as well as near major watercourses or water bodies. The latter features, the authors suggest, may be tied to cosmological themes of death and renewal (i.e., a watery underworld) and may have provided reasons why each site was located where it was on the larger regional landscape. All three sites also were intensively occupied, with apparent paired burial facilities, indicating a probable dualistic/moiety organization; these were not "vacant" centers. All three also have large circular enclosures, earthworks on a scale commensurate with the largest centers in the region. Importantly, Thompson and Pluckhahn (2012) have also been collecting site data through remote sensing and demonstrating the effectiveness of LiDAR imagery, providing fine-grained mapping information over a much greater scale than can be obtained from hand-driven instruments. New dating by the authors indicates a possible hiatus in construction or use of each center in the first few centuries BC, with a transition from the burial mounds characteristic of the Early Woodland site use, before the hiatus, and platform mounds after, in the later Middle Woodland. If not an artifact of sampling or calibration, as is clearly a problem with dating events a few centuries earlier during the initial early Woodland (e.g., Anderson 2010; Thomas 2008), then this hiatus occurred just prior to and during the first centuries of initial Hopewellian emergence in the Midwest. Perhaps connections between these three sites, which would later become major centers in the Southeast, were not in place at this time, nor does it appear that connections were in place (yet) with areas farther afield, such as with the emerging Hopewellian world in the Midwest.

Victoria Dekle's excellent summary of the Tunacunnhee site (chapter 13) offers new interpretations about this classic Hopewellian center from a multiscalar approach to landscape. While rigorously grounded quantitative approaches such as viewshed and least-cost pathway analyses are becoming more common in North American landscape archaeology, Dekle's work shows how we must merge these with a consideration of possible meanings and relationships between the inhabitants of a location and the surrounding world. Her discussion of aspects of the Tunacunnhee artifact assemblage, for example, such as the suggestion that panpipes may have served as musical passports or ear spools as markers of identity, shows how classic Hopewellian artifacts are more than merely exotic extralocal items when found at a distance from their point of origin. In the proper social context they are active agents or drivers of personal and collective identity formation and maintenance, both locally and over large areas. Dekle argues effectively that identity construction is itself multiscalar in nature, depending on whether local or larger social environments and networks are being engaged. Hopewellian interaction, to Dekle, involved the creation and maintenance of relational landscapes between peoples, and these were structured by the accidental, fortuitous, or less commonly the intentional positioning of settlements.

Tunacunnhee's location along a major travel artery between the Gulf and the lower Midwest enabled its people to have a much wider involvement with the Hopewellian world than was available to those in societies at some remove from such pathways. I fully concur with her conclusion that landscapes are "built, perceived, and imagined by people" and have elsewhere argued that the ties between specific trading partners, ceremonial practitioners, or even entire peoples are critical, and when these relationships are lost, they are difficult to reconstitute (Anderson 2010: 284–87; see also Thompson 2010).

Neill Wallis's examination of Swift Creek and Weeden Island provides an excellent overview of mortuary behavior and vessel characteristics—including shape, design complexity, and iconography—within these major southeastern archaeological cultures (chapter 14). He makes the case that in both archaeological cultures, burial mounds were places where social identities, relationships, and group histories were constructed, in part through the gifting of ceramic vessels and perhaps their contents between the living as well as between the living and the dead. Wallis (2011, herein) convincingly documents a far greater number and diversity of extralocal versus local vessels in Swift Creek burial mounds and habitation areas, respectively, in the southern Atlantic Coast region. Swift Creek mortuary behavior in this region thus involved differing peoples, and the mound deposits, thanks to the uniqueness of Swift Creek paddle designs, served to document the social landscape, for Middle Woodland peoples and archaeologists alike. Indeed, Swift Creek vessel designs provide such wonderfully unique signatures that one can only wonder what behaviors would be observed if we had comparable artifacts in other parts of the region, at centers such as Marksville and Pinson, or in the Midwest, where effigy pipes like those found at Mound City and Tremper offer a contemporaneous example of possibly similar behavior yet are unfortunately a decidedly uncommon artifact type, unlike Swift Creek potsherds. In the Gulf Coast region, the continuation of vessel interments in Weeden Island is coupled with an increase in the complexity and care in application of Swift Creek designs, perhaps to better signal the identity of individual participants. This increased ceremony is reflected in the occurrence of more single-mound construction and vessel-caching events and increasingly elaborate vessel forms, perhaps made by specialists. Wallis suggests, following arguments advanced by Sears (1973), that these behaviors were both the result and the cause of increasing social complexity that may reflect competition between ranked lineages and possibly changes in leadership structures. The emergence of hereditary inequality in the region, although not unequivocal until some centuries later in Coles Creek and Mississippian cultures, may have derived from such competition and the social arenas it engendered.

The final chapter in part 3 of the volume, by Edward Henry, examines mortuary ritual in northern Kentucky Adena sites to suggest that leadership in the participating societies was short term and situational in nature, essentially occurring when the mortuary facilities were in use. His analysis of all known Adena mound sites in the Bluegrass region of northern Kentucky (chapter 15), comparable in geographic scale to the analyses Applegate and Jefferies and colleagues conducted in the same general area (chapters 2 and 6, herein), shows that appreciable variation in premound and mound use can be present within presumably uniform or closely related archaeological cultures. Indeed, the extent of this variation makes it difficult to consider Adena as anything but a broad, general category, perhaps a useful heuristic device, but lacking much specificity, much as concepts such as "Mississippian" or "Hopewell" and neo-evolutionary categories such as the "chiefdom" or the "state" have been similarly deconstructed (e.g., Marcoux and Wilson 2010; Pauketat 2007). Maintenance of a general tradition (i.e., "Adena") but with a diversification in specific practice in mortuary behavior was occurring over the landscape from site to site, as Henry's GIS-based analysis demonstrates. The contributions by Applegate, Henry, Jefferies and colleagues, and Wallis (chapters 2, 15, 6, and 14, respectively) show that comparative analyses employing large numbers of sites, artifacts, or features can be highly informative, although this also assumes that the individual cases in the sample have been well documented. One message that is clear from Henry's chapter is that while many Adena sites in his study area have been excavated, very few have been well dated with multiple determinations, and of those that have been dated at all, the use of conventional radiocarbon procedures has resulted in unacceptably large error ranges. With high-precision AMS dating now available, it should be possible to obtain much better information on the internal construction and use-history and external relationships (i.e., contemporaneity) of these sites in the future. In spite of these dating problems, however, Henry was able to demonstrate consistent changes in mortuary behavior over time at a number of mortuary mounds. At these sites, mound building and the use of crypts typically occurred after the area had first been used for a time to prepare the dead in mortuary structures and through cremation or the use of mortuary pits. Where this idealized pattern occurred, it probably meant that the societies present in the area enjoyed greater stability and continuity. Whether these mortuary complexes were used by local peoples or, as the Swift Creek case suggests (Wallis, chapter 14), by peoples coming from some distance, has yet to be determined.

Conclusion

The contributions to this volume offer a new means for considering Woodland occupations in the Southeast, based on the situating of people and sites within socially constructed and cognized landscapes. As such, the volume represents a welcome and important addition to the literature. It is needed, as the editors note in their introduction to the volume (chapter 1), referring to a paper entitled "Recent Developments in Southeastern Archaeology" that I delivered at the 2009 Southeastern Archaeological Conference, coauthored with Ken Sassaman (Anderson and Sassaman 2009). Wright and Henry correctly observed that we did not discuss research directed to the Early and Middle Woodland periods, and they took this to infer that either such research had not happened or, more likely, that it had not received much attention.[1] Wright and Henry took this as a challenge and an opportunity to rectify the situation by producing the present volume, showing that a great deal of important and indeed exciting work on sites and assemblages from these periods is actually taking place. I fully agree and am impressed with how quickly and thoroughly they were able to put this volume together.[2] It takes volume-length summaries like that provided here by Wright and Henry and their colleagues to document the richness of detail and diversity of approaches being brought to bear on individual time periods such as the Woodland. Such volumes are important in telling us not just what has been done and learned but how these findings were obtained, as well as what kinds of questions and research we should be considering in the future. I am grateful for their efforts and am confident that more such guides to exploring the region's rich and important archaeological record will be forthcoming.

Notes

1. In Ken's and my defense, however, I would note that our omission was more a matter of the time constraints of a 20-minute paper presentation and the way we organized the argument than any conscious intent to ignore specific periods. In our SEAC paper, we talked about recent developments primarily by topic or site type, discussing ten areas where we believed interesting things were happening. These included research directed toward delimiting occupations on the now-submerged continental shelf, into the complexity and diversity of later Archaic societies, on shell rings and middens, on site planning and monumental construction, and on the revolutions occurring in the areas of information management, remote sensing, and climate change. Admittedly, we did not use the word *Woodland* even once in our slides or text, but I would also note that neither did we use the word *Mississippian*, although we did illustrate several sites dating to the latter period. Our SEAC paper was a way to give notice and ask for help about a book-length

treatment we were writing on recent developments in southeastern archaeology. That volume, happily, has since been completed; in it we took a period-by-period approach to structure our discussion, and the Woodland received extended treatment (Anderson and Sassaman 2012).

2. One aspect of our recent book is a compilation by time period of the number of articles that appeared over the preceding 30 years in *American Antiquity* and in *Southeastern Archeology*. In both journals the Woodland period was not particularly well represented, constituting roughly 10 to 12 percent of the total number of papers. Only the Paleo-Indian and Historic periods received less attention (Anderson and Sassaman 2012: table 5-1). The data provide yet another reason why a book such as this one is needed and why the editors, Wright and Henry, and all the participants deserve our thanks.

References

Abrams, Elliot M.
1992a Woodland Settlement Patterns in the Southern Hocking River Valley, Southeastern Ohio. In *Cultural Variability in Context: Woodland Settlements of the Mid-Ohio Valley*, edited by Mark F. Seeman, 19–23. MCJA Special Paper no. 7. Kent State University Press, Kent, Ohio.
1992b Archaeological Investigation of the Armitage Mound (33-AT-434), the Plains, Ohio. *Midcontinental Journal of Archaeology* 41: 80–111.

Abrams, Eliot M., and Mary F. Le Rouge
2008 Political Complexity and Mound Construction among the Early and Late Adena of the Hocking Valley, Ohio. In *Transitions: Archaic and Early Woodland Research in the Ohio Country*, edited by Martha P. Otto and Brian G. Redmond, 214–31. Ohio University Press, Athens.

Adams, Andrea E.
2007 Revisiting Arthur Kelly's 1951 Field School and the Corra Harris Cave from Bartow County. *Early Georgia* 35: 71–98.

Adovasio, James M.
1982 *The Prehistory of the Paintsville Reservoir, Johnson and Morgan Counties, Kentucky*. Department of Anthropology, University of Pittsburgh, Pittsburgh.

Ahler, Stanley A.
1967 The Faust Shelter (40MO8). Manuscript on file, Frank H. McClung Museum, University of Tennessee, Knoxville.

Alberti, Benjamin, and Tamara L. Bray
2009 Animating Archaeology: Of Subjects, Objects and Alternative Ontologies. *Cambridge Archaeological Journal* 19: 337–43.

Allen, Kathleen M. S., Stanton W. Green, and Ezra B. W. Zubrow
1990 *Interpreting Space: GIS and Archaeology Applications of Geographic Information Systems*. Taylor and Francis, London.

Allen, Roger C.
1976 Archaeological Investigations at Two Sites in the U.S. Interstate Highway 24 Right-of-Way in Marshall County, Kentucky. Ms. on file, Office of State Archaeology, University of Kentucky, Lexington.

Anderson, David G.
1998 Swift Creek in Regional Perspective. In *A World Engraved: Archaeology of the Swift Creek Culture*, edited by Mark W. Williams and Daniel T. Elliott, 274–300. University of Alabama Press, Tuscaloosa.
2010 The End of the Southeastern Archaic: Regional Interaction and Archaeological Interpretation. In *Trend, Tradition, and Turmoil: What Happened to the Southeastern Archaic?* edited by David Hurst Thomas and Matthew C. Sanger, 273–302. Proceedings of the Third Caldwell Conference, St. Catherines Island, Ga., May 9–11, 2008. Anthropological Papers of the American Museum of Natural History 93. New York.

2012a Monumentality in Eastern North America during the Mississippian Period. In *Early New World Monumentality*, edited by Richard L. Burger and Robert M. Rosenswig, 78–108. University Press of Florida, Gainesville.

2012b Least Cost Pathway Analyses in Archaeological Research: Approaches and Utility. In *Least Cost Analysis of Social Landscapes: Archaeological Case Studies for Beginners and Experts Alike*, edited by Devin A. White and Sarah L. Surface-Evans, 239–57. University of Utah Press, Salt Lake City.

Anderson, David G., J. Christopher Gillam, Christopher Carr, Thomas E. Emerson, and Jon L. Gibson

2007 Resolving Interaction Networks in Eastern North America. Paper presented at the 72nd Annual Meeting of the Society for American Archaeology, Austin, Texas.

Anderson, David G., and Robert C. Mainfort Jr. (editors)

2002a *The Woodland Southeast*. University of Alabama Press, Tuscaloosa.

Anderson, David G., and Robert C. Mainfort Jr.

2002b An Introduction to Woodland Archaeology in the Southeast. In *The Woodland Southeast*, edited by David G. Anderson and Robert C. Mainfort Jr., 1–19. University of Alabama Press, Tuscaloosa.

2002c Epilogue: Future Directions for Woodland Archaeology in the Southeast. In *The Woodland Southeast*, edited by David G. Anderson and Robert C. Mainfort Jr., 540–42. University of Alabama Press, Tuscaloosa.

2002d Preface. In *The Woodland Southeast*, edited by David G. Anderson and Robert C. Mainfort Jr., xv–xvi. University of Alabama Press, Tuscaloosa.

Anderson, David G., D. Shane Miller, Stephen J. Yerka, J. C. Gillam, Erik N. Johansson, Derek T. Anderson, Albert C. Goodyear, and Ashley M. Smallwood

2010 PIDBA (Paleoindian Database of the Americas) 2010: Current Status and Findings. *Archaeology of Eastern North America* 38: 63–90.

Anderson, David G., and Kenneth E. Sassaman

2009 Recent Developments in Southeastern Archaeology. Paper presented at the 66th Annual Meeting for the Southeastern Archaeological Conference, Mobile, Ala.

2012 *Recent Developments in Southeastern Archeology: From Colonization to Complexity*. Society for American Archaeology Press, Washington, D.C.

Anderson, Jason M.

2003 *A National Register Evaluation of Site 15Mm140 in Montgomery County, Kentucky*. Cultural Resource Analysts, Lexington, Ky.

Anderson, Patricia K., William O. Autry, and Glyn D. DuVall

1992 *Archaeological Reconnaissance and Testing for the Proposed Kentucky Lock Addition, Tennessee River, Livingston County, Kentucky*. Duvall and Associates, Nashville, Tenn.

Anonymous

1885a Accession Card no. 16227. United States National Museum.

1885b Accession Card no. 16678. United States National Museum.

1915 Report on Ladd Quarries. Submitted to S. W. McCallie, state geologist, Atlanta, Ga.

Anschuetz, Kurt F., Richard H. Wilshusen, and Cherie L. Scheick

2001 An Archaeology of Landscapes: Perspectives and Directions. *Journal of Archaeological Research* 9: 157–211.

Applegate, Darlene

1997 Lithic Evidence of Prehistoric Rockshelter Use in Eastern Kentucky. Unpublished Ph.D. dissertation, Department of Anthropology, Ohio State University, Columbus.

2001   Archaeological Investigations at Alexander Shelter No. 1 and Hilda Martin Shelter, Edmonson County, Kentucky. Paper presented at the 18th Annual Kentucky Heritage Council Archaeological Conference, Highland Heights, Ky.
2007   *Archaeological Survey of the Western Kentucky University Upper Green River Biological Preserve, Hart County, Kentucky.* Vol. 1, *Literature Review and Phase I Survey.* Prepared for the Department of Biology, Western Kentucky University, Bowling Green.
2008   Woodland Period. In *The Archaeology of Kentucky: An Update,* vol. 1, edited by David Pollack, 339–604. State Historic Preservation Comprehensive Plan Report no. 3. Kentucky Heritage Council, Frankfort.
2011   Early–Middle Woodland Domestic Structures in Kentucky: An Initial Database. Manuscript in possession of the author.

Applegate, Darlene, and Jennifer Furlong
2001   Diachronic Patterns of Landscape Use in the Drakes Creek Drainage, Warren, Allen and Simpson Counties, Kentucky. Paper presented at the 18th Annual Kentucky Heritage Council Archaeological Conference, Highland Heights, Ky.

Applegate, Darlene, and Amy McCray
2006   The Plum Springs Site (15Wa981), a Woodland Habitation Site in Beech Bend of Barren River, Kentucky. Paper presented at the 23rd Annual Kentucky Heritage Council Archaeological Conference, Bowling Green, Ky.

Ashley, Keith H.
1992   Swift Creek Manifestations along the Lower St. Johns River. *Florida Anthropologist* 45: 127–38.
1998   Swift Creek Traits in Northeastern Florida: Ceramics, Mounds, and Middens. In *A World Engraved: Archaeology of the Swift Creek Culture,* edited by Mark Williams and Daniel T. Elliott, 197–221. University of Alabama Press, Tuscaloosa.

Ashley, Keith, Keith Stephenson, and Frankie Snow
2007   Teardrops, Ladders, and Bull's Eyes: Swift Creek on the Georgia Coast. *Early Georgia* 35: 3–28.

Ashley, Keith H., and Neill J. Wallis
2006   Northeastern Florida Swift Creek. *Florida Anthropologist* 59: 5–18.

Ashmore, Wendy
2002   "Decisions and Dispositions": Socializing Spatial Archaeology. *American Anthropologist* 104: 1172–83.

Ashmore, Wendy, and A. Bernard Knapp (editors)
1999   *Archaeologies of Landscape: Contemporary Perspectives.* Blackwell, Malden, Mass.

Aspinall, Arnold, Chris Gaffney, and Armin Schmidt
2008   *Magnetometry for Archaeologists.* AltaMira, Lanham, Md.

Aston, Michael, and Trevor Rowley
1974   Landscape Archaeology: An Introduction to Fieldwork Techniques on Post-Roman Landscapes. David and Charles, Newton Abbot, U.K.

Autry, William O., Jr., and Glyn D. DuVall
1985   Field Investigations at 15Bl52 and 15Bl59, U.S. Army Corps of Engineers Upper Cumberland River Flood Control Project, Pineville, Bell County, Kentucky. Interim report submitted to the United States Army Corps of Engineers, Nashville District, Nashville, Tenn.

Baby, Raymond S., and Suzanne M. Langlois
1979   Seip Mound State Memorial: Nonmortuary Aspects of Hopewell. In *Hopewell Archaeology: The Chillicothe Conference,* edited by David S. Brose and N'omi B. Greber, 16–18. Kent State University Press, Kent, Ohio.

Bacon, Willard S.
1980   Factors in Siting a Middle Woodland Enclosure in Middle Tennessee. *Midcontinental Journal of Archaeology* 18: 245–81.

Bader, Anne Tobe
1991   *Phase II Archaeological Investigation on the Beech Fork (15Bc168) and the Clover Creek Church (15Bc169) Sites in Breckinridge County, Kentucky.* Archaeological Resources Consultant Services, Louisville, K.
1996a Early Woodland Site Variation within the Constricted Ohio River Valley Bottomlands. In *Current Archaeological Research in Kentucky,* vol. 4, edited by Sara L. Sanders, Thomas N. Sanders, and Charles Stout, 89–114. Kentucky Heritage Council, Frankfort.
1996b *A Phase III Archaeological Data Recovery at the Rockmaker Site, 15Bc138, Breckinridge County, Kentucky.* MAAR Associates, Newark, Del.

Barrett, John C., and Ilhong Ko
2009   A Phenomenology of Landscape: A Crisis in British Landscape Archaeology. *Journal of Social Archaeology* 9: 275–94.

Bartram, Laurence E., Ellen M. Kroll, and Henry T. Bunn
1991   Variability in Camp Structure and Bone Food Refuse Patterning at Kua San Hunter-Gatherer Camps. In *The Interpretation of Archaeological Spatial Patterning,* edited by Ellen M. Kroll and T. Douglas Price, 77–148. Plenum Press, New York.

Battaglia, Debbora
1983   Projecting Personhood in Melanesia. *Man* 18: 289–304.
1990   *On the Bones of the Serpent: Person, Memory, and Mortality in Sabarl Island Society.* University of Chicago Press, Chicago.

Beasley, Virgil R.
2008   Monumentality during the Mid-Holocene in the Upper and Middle St. Johns River Basins, Florida. Ph.D. dissertation, Northwestern University, Evanston, Ill.

Beck, Lane A.
1995   Burial Cults and Ethnic Boundaries in "Southern Hopewell." In *Regional Approaches to Mortuary Analysis,* edited by Lane A. Beck, 167–87. Plenum Press, New York.

Beck, Robin A.
2003   Consolidation and Hierarchy: Chiefdom Variability in the Mississippian Southeast. *American Antiquity* 68: 641–61.

Beck, Robin A., Jr., and James A. Brown
2012   Political Economy and the Routinization of Religious Movements: A View from the Eastern Woodlands. In *Beyond Belief: Archaeology of Religion and Ritual,* edited by Yorke M. Rowan, 72–88. Archaeological Papers, American Anthropological Association, vol. 19. Washington, D.C.

Bender, Barbara (editor)
1993   *Landscape: Politics and Perspectives.* Berg, Oxford, U.K.
1998   *Stonehenge: Making Space.* Berg, Oxford, U.K.

Bense, Judith A.
1994   *Archaeology of the Southeastern United States: Paleoindian to World War II.* Academic Press, Orlando, Fla.

Benyshek, Tasha, and Paul Webb
2009a The Ravensford and Macon County Airport Sites. Paper presented at the North Carolina Appalachian Summit Archaeology Conference, Boone, N.C.
2009b Management Summary for the Archaeological Data Recovery Fieldwork for the Macon

County Airport Extension Project, Site 31MA77. Report submitted to the Macon County Airport Authority, Franklin, N.C.

Bernardini, Wesley
2004 Hopewell Geometric Earthworks: A Case Study in the Referential and Experiential Meaning of Monuments. *Journal of Anthropological Archaeology* 23: 331–56.

Bevan, Bruce W.
1998 *Geophysical Exploration for Archaeology*. Volume B, *Introduction to Geophysical Exploration*. Midwest Archeological Center Special Report no. 1. United States Department of the Interior, National Park Service, Midwest Archeological Center, Lincoln, Neb.

Binford, Lewis R.
1980 Willow Smoke and Dog's Tails: Hunter-Gatherer Settlement Systems and Archaeological Site Formation. *American Antiquity* 45: 1–17.
1983 *In Pursuit of the Past*. Thames and Hudson, London.

Bing
2010 Aerial Photograph of North Elkhorn Creek Area, Fayette County, Kentucky. Electronic media, http://www.bing.com/maps/default.aspx?q=&mkt=en-US&FORM=BYFD. October 15, 2010.

Black, Deborah B.
1979 Adena and Hopewell Relations in the Lower Hocking Valley. In *Hopewell Archaeology: The Chillicothe Conference*, edited by David S. Brose and N'omi B. Greber, 19–26. Kent State University Press, Kent, Ohio.

Blazier, Jeremy, AnnCorrine Freter, and Elliot M. Abrams
2005 Woodland Ceremonialism in the Hocking Valley. In *The Emergence of the Moundbuilders: The Archaeology of Tribal Societies in Southeastern Ohio*, edited by Elliot M. Abrams and AnnCorrine Freter, 98–114. Ohio University Press, Athens.

Blitz, John H., and Karl G. Lorenz
2006 *The Chattahoochee Chiefdoms*. University of Alabama Press, Tuscaloosa.

Blitz, John H., and C. Baxter Mann
2000 *Fisherfolk, Farmers, and Frenchmen: Archaeological Explorations on the Mississippi Gulf Coast*. Archaeological Report no. 30. Mississippi Department of Archives and History, Jackson.

Boedy, Randall D., and Charles M. Niquette
1987 *A Phase III Archaeological Examination of the Danville Tank Site (15Bo16), Boyle County, Kentucky*. Cultural Resource Analysts, Lexington, Ky.

Boisvert, Richard A.
1979 Excavations at the Spadie Site (15Jf14). In *Excavations at Four Archaic Sites in the Lower Ohio Valley, Jefferson County, Kentucky*, edited by Michael B. Collins, 804–82. Department of Anthropology, University of Kentucky, Lexington.

Boudreaux, Edmond A., III
2007 *The Archaeology of Town Creek*. University of Alabama Press, Tuscaloosa.
2011a *Archaeological Investigations at Jackson Landing (22Ha515): An Early Late Woodland Mound and Earthwork Site in Coastal Mississippi*. Department of Anthropology and Phelps Archaeology Labs, East Carolina University, Greenville. Submitted to Historic Preservation Division, Mississippi Department of Archives and History, Jackson.
2011b Dating the Construction of Early Late Woodland Earthen Monuments at the Jackson Landing Site in Coastal Mississippi. *Southeastern Archaeology* 30: 351–64.

Boudreaux, Edmond A., III, and Hunter B. Johnson
2000 Test Excavations at the Florence Mound: A Middle Woodland Platform Mound in Northwest Alabama. *Journal of Alabama Archaeology* 46: 87–130.

Bow, Sierra M., and Jay D. Franklin
2009   Luminescence Dating and the Pogue Creek Archaeological Survey. Paper presented at the 21st Annual Current Research in Tennessee Archaeology Meeting, Nashville.

Bradley, Richard
1998   *The Significance of Monuments*. Routledge, London.
2000   *An Archaeology of Natural Places*. Routledge, London.

Braun, E. Lucy
1950   *Deciduous Forests of Eastern North America*. Hafner Press, New York.

Breetzke, David
2001   *Phase II Archaeological Investigation of Site 15Be509 for Expansion of Facilities at the Cincinnati–Northern Kentucky International Airport in Boone County, Kentucky*. Environment and Archaeology, Florence, Ky.

Brenyo, Daniel, Jr.
1983   *Archaeological Investigations at the Harvey Tudor Site, Madison County, Kentucky*. William S. Webb Archaeological Society, Lexington, Ky.

Brose, David S.
1979   An Interpretation of the Hopewellian Traits in Florida. In *Hopewell Archaeology: The Chillicothe Conference*, edited by David S. Brose and N'omi B. Greber, 141–49. Kent State University Press, Kent, Ohio.

Brose, David S., and N'omi B. Greber (editors)
1979   *Hopewell Archaeology: The Chillicothe Conference*. Kent State University Press, Kent, Ohio.

Brose, David S., and George Percy
1974   Weeden Island Ceremonialism: A Reappraisal. Paper presented at the 39th Annual Meeting of the Society for American Archaeology, Washington, D.C.

Brown, James A.
1979   Charnel Houses and Mortuary Crypts: Disposal of the Dead in the Middle Woodland Period. In *Hopewell Archaeology: The Chillicothe Conference*, edited by David S. Brose and N'omi B. Greber, 211–19. Kent State University Press, Kent, Ohio.
2004   Mound City and Issues in the Developmental History of Hopewell Culture in the Ross County Area of Southern Ohio. In *Aboriginal Ritual and Economy in the Eastern Woodlands: Papers in Memory of Howard Dalton Winters*, edited by Anne-Marie Cantwell, Lawrence A. Conrad, and Jonathan E. Reyman, 147–68. Illinois State Museum Scientific Papers, vol. 30. Springfield.
2005   Reflections on Taxonomic Practice. In *Woodland Period Systematics in the Middle Ohio Valley: The Good Servant and Bad Master*, edited by Darlene Applegate and Robert C. Mainfort Jr., 111–19. University of Alabama Press, Tuscaloosa.
2006   The Shamanic Element in Hopewellian Period Ritual. In *Recreating Hopewell*, edited by Douglas K. Charles and Jane E. Buikstra, 475–88. University Press of Florida, Gainesville.

Brown, James A., and John E. Kelly
2012   The Importance of Being Specific: Theme and Trajectory in Mississippian Iconography. In *Enduring Motives: The Archaeology of Religion and Tradition in Native America*, edited by Linea Sundstrom and Warren DeBoer, 210–34. University of Alabama Press, Tuscaloosa.

Buikstra, Jane E., and Douglas K. Charles
1999   Centering the Ancestors: Cemeteries, Mounds, and Sacred Landscapes of the Ancient North American Midcontinent. In *Archaeologies of Landscape: Contemporary Perspectives*, edited by Wendy Ashmore and Alfred B. Knapp, 201–28. Blackwell Publishers, Malden, Mass.

Buikstra, Jane E., Douglas K. Charles, and Gordon F. M. Rakita
1998   *Staging Ritual: Hopewell Ceremonialism at the Mound House Site, Greene County, Illinois.* Center for American Archaeology, Kampsville, Ill.

Burks, Jarrod
2006   *Geophysical Survey at the Junction Group (33Ro28) Earthworks in Ross County, Ohio, 2005: A Progress Report.* Ohio Valley Archaeology, Columbus, Ohio.
2010   Rediscovering Prehistoric Earthworks in Ohio, USA: It All Starts in the Archives. In *Landscapes through the Lens: Aerial Photographs and Historic Environment,* edited by David C. Cowley, Robin A. Standring, and Matthew J. Abicht, 77–87. Oxbow Books, Oxford, U.K.

Burks, Jarrod, and Robert A. Cook
2011   Beyond Squier and Davis: Rediscovering Ohio's Earthworks Using Geophysical Remote Sensing. *American Antiquity* 76: 667–89.

Byers, A. Martin
1998   Is the Newark Circle-Octagon the Ohio Hopewell "Rosetta Stone"? A Question of Archaeological Interpretation. In *Ancient Earthen Enclosures of the Eastern Woodlands,* edited by Robert C. Mainfort Jr. and Lynne P. Sullivan, 135–53. University Press of Florida, Gainesville.
2004   *The Ohio Hopewell Episode: Paradigm Lost, Paradigm Gained.* University of Akron Press, Akron, Ohio.
2011   *Sacred Games, Death, and Renewal in the Ancient Eastern Woodlands: The Ohio Hopewell System of Cult Sodality Heterarchies.* AltaMira, Lanham, Md.

Byers, A. Martin, and DeeAnne Wymer (editors)
2010   *Hopewell Settlement Patterns, Subsistence, and Symbolic Landscapes.* University Press of Florida, Gainesville.

Caldwell, Joseph R.
1958   *Trend and Tradition in the Prehistory of the Eastern United States.* Memoir 88. American Anthropological Association, Springfield, Ill.

Caldwell, Joseph R., and Robert L. Hall (editors)
1964   *Hopewellian Studies.* Scientific Papers, vol. 12. Illinois State Museum, Springfield.

Carmody, Stephen B., Maria A. Caffrey, and Sally P. Horn
2011   Palynological and Chemical Analyses of Pipe Residues as Evidence of Tobacco Use in the Southeastern U.S. Paper presented at the Annual Meeting of the Association for American Geographers, Seattle, Wash.

Carr, Christopher
2005a   Scioto Hopewell Ritual Gatherings: A Review and Discussion of Previous Interpretations and Data. In *Gathering Hopewell: Society, Ritual, and Ritual Interaction,* edited by Christopher Carr and D. Troy Case, 463–79. Springer, New York.
2005b   Rethinking Interregional Hopewellian "Interaction." In *Gathering Hopewell: Society, Ritual, and Ritual Interaction,* edited by Christopher Carr and D. Troy Case, 575–623. Kluwer Academic, New York.

Carr, Christopher, and D. Troy Case (editors)
2005a   *Gathering Hopewell: Society, Ritual, and Ritual Interaction.* Kluwer Academic, New York.

Carr, Christopher, and D. Troy Case
2005b   The Nature of Leadership in Ohio Hopewellian Societies: Role Segregation and the Transformation from Shamanism. In *Gathering Hopewell: Society, Ritual, and Ritual Interaction,* edited by Christopher Carr and D. Troy Case, 177–237. Kluwer Academic, New York.
2005c   The Gathering of Hopewell. In *Gathering Hopewell: Society, Ritual, and Ritual Interaction,* edited by Christopher Carr and D. Troy Case, 19–50. Kluwer Academic, New York.

Carr, Robert S.
1975 An Archaeological and Historical Survey of Lake Okeechobee. Submitted to Central and South Florida Flood Control District. Miscellaneous Project Report Series no. 22. Bureau of Historic Sites and Properties, Florida Department of State, Tallahassee.

Carskadden, Jeff
2008 Observations on the Early Woodland Cultural Landscape in the Central Muskingum Valley of Eastern Ohio. In *Transitions: Archaic and Early Woodland Research in the Ohio Valley*, edited by Martha P. Otto and Brian G. Redmond, 232–70. Ohio University Press, Athens.

Case, D. Troy, and Christopher Carr (editors)
2008 *The Scioto Hopewell and Their Neighbors: Bioarchaeological Documentation and Cultural Understanding*. Springer, New York.

Chapman, Jefferson, and Bennie C. Keel
1979 Candy Creek–Connestee Components in Eastern Tennessee and Western North Carolina and Their Relationship with Adena-Hopewell. In *Hopewell Archaeology: The Chillicothe Conference*, edited by David S. Brose and N'omi Greber, 157–61. Kent State University Press, Kent, Ohio.

Chapman, Robert
2006 Middle Woodland/Hopewell: A View from Beyond the Periphery. In *Recreating Hopewell*, edited by Douglas K. Charles and Jane E. Buikstra, 510–28. University Press of Florida, Gainesville.

Charles, Douglas K.
1992 Woodland Demographic and Social Dynamics in the American Midwest: Analysis of Burial Mound Survey. *World Archaeology* 24: 175–93.
2005 The Archaeology of Death as Anthropology. In *Interacting with the Dead: Perspectives on Mortuary Archaeology for the New Millennium*, edited by George F. M. Rakita, Jane E. Buikstra, Lane E. Beck, and Sloan R. Williams, 15–24. University Press of Florida, Gainesville.
2010 Riverworld: Life and Meaning in the Illinois Valley. In *Hopewell Settlement Patterns, Subsistence, and Symbolic Landscapes*, edited by A. Martin Byers and DeeAnne Wymer, 19–35. University Press of Florida, Gainesville.

Charles, Douglas K., and Jane E. Buikstra
1983 Archaic Mortuary Sites in the Central Mississippi Drainage: Distribution, Structure, and Behavioral Implications. In *Archaic Hunters and Gatherers in the American Midwest*, edited by James Philips and James A Brown, 117–45. Academic Press, New York.

Charles, Douglas K., and Jane E. Buikstra (editors)
2006 *Recreating Hopewell*. University Press of Florida, Gainesville.

Charles, Douglas K., Julieann Van Nest, and Jane E. Buikstra
2004 From the Earth: Minerals and Meaning in the Hopewellian World. In *Soils, Stones and Symbols*, edited by Nicole Boivan and Mary A. Owoc, 43–70. University College of London Press, London.

Chase, David W.
1998 Prehistoric Pottery of Central Alabama. *Journal of Alabama Archaeology* 44: 52–98.

Cherry, John F.
1983 Frogs Round the Pond: Perspectives on Current Archaeological Survey Projects in the Mediterranean Region. In *Archaeological Survey in the Mediterranean Area*, edited by Donald R. Keller and David William Rupp, 394–97. International Series no. 155. British Archaeological Reports, London.

Childe, V. Gordon
1950 The Urban Revolution. *Town Planning Review* 21: 3–17.

Claassen, Cheryl
2010 *Feasting with Shellfish in the Southern Ohio Valley: Archaic Sacred Sites and Rituals.* University of Tennessee Press, Knoxville.

Clark, Anthony
1996 *Seeing Beneath the Soil: Prospecting Methods in Archaeology.* Rev. ed. Batsford, London.

Clark, Wayne E., J. T. Moldenhauer, Michael B. Barber, and Thomas R. Whyte
2005 *The Buzzard Rock Site (44RN2): A Late Woodland Dispersed Village.* Research Report Series no. 15. Virginia Department of Historic Resources, Richmond.

Clay, Brenda Johnson
1977 *Pinikindu: Maternal Nature, Paternal Substance.* University of Chicago Press, Chicago.

Clay, R. Berle
1972 The Persistence of Traditional Settlement Pattern: An Example from Central New Ireland. *Oceania* 43 (3): 40–53.
1976 Tactics, Strategy and Operations: The Mississippian System Responds to Its Environment. *Midcontinental Journal of Archaeology* 1: 137–62.
1983 Pottery and Graveside Ritual in Kentucky Adena. *Midcontinental Journal of Archaeology* 8: 109–26.
1985 Peter Village: 164 Years Later, A Summary of 1983 Excavations. In *Woodland Period Research in Kentucky,* edited by David Pollack Thomas Sanders and Charles Hockensmith, 1–41. Kentucky Heritage Council, Frankfort.
1986 Adena Ritual Spaces. In *Early Woodland Archaeology,* edited by Kenneth B. Farnsworth and Thomas E. Emerson, 581–95. Canter for American Archaeology, Kampsville, Ill.
1987 Circles and Ovals: Two Types of Adena Space. *Southeastern Archaeology* 6: 46–56.
1988 Peter Village: An Adena Enclosure. In *Middle Woodland Settlement and Ceremonialism in the Mid-South and Lower Mississippi Valley: Proceedings of the 1984 Mid-South Archaeological Conference,* edited by Robert C. Mainfort Jr., 19–30. Archaeological Report 22. Mississippi Department of Archives and History, Jackson.
1991 Adena Ritual Development: An Organizational Type in a Temporal Perspective. In *The Human Landscape in Kentucky's Past: Site Structure and Settlement Patterns,* edited by Charles Stout and Christine K. Hensley, 30–39. Kentucky Heritage Council, Frankfort.
1992 Chiefs, Big Men, or What?: Economy, Settlement Patterns, and Their Bearing on Adena Political Models. In *Cultural Variability in Context: Woodland Settlements of the Mid-Ohio Valley,* edited by Mark F. Seeman, 77–80. Kent State University Press, Kent, Ohio.
1998 The Essential Features of Adena Ritual and Their Implications. *Southeastern Archaeology* 17: 1–21.
2001 Complementary Geophysical Survey Techniques: Why Two Ways Are Better Than One. *Southeastern Archaeology* 20: 31–43.
2002 Deconstructing the Woodland Sequence from the Heartland: A Review of Recent Research Directions in the Upper Ohio Valley. In *The Woodland Southeast,* edited by David G. Anderson and Robert C. Mainfort Jr., 162–84. University of Alabama Press, Tuscaloosa.
2005 Adena: Rest in Peace? In *Woodland Period Systematics in the Middle Ohio Valley,* edited by Darlene Applegate and Robert C. Mainfort Jr., 94–110. University of Alabama Press, Tuscaloosa.
2006 Conductivity Survey. In *Remote Sensing in Archaeology: An Explicitly North American Perspective,* edited by Jay K. Johnson, 79–107. University of Alabama Press, Tuscaloosa.
2009 Where Have All the Houses Gone? Webb's Adena House in Historical Context. *Southeastern Archaeology* 28: 43–64.

Clay, R. Berle, and Charles M. Niquette
1992 Middle Woodland Mortuary Ritual in the Gallipolis Locks and Dam Vicinity, Mason County, West Virginia. *West Virginia Archaeologist* 44: 1–25.

Cobb, Charles R., and Adam King
2005 Re-inventing Mississippian Tradition at Etowah, Georgia. *Journal of Archaeological Method and Theory* 12: 167–93.

Cobb, Charles R., and Michael S. Nassaney
1995 Interaction and Integration in the Late Woodland Southeast. In *Native American Interactions: Multiscalar Analyses and Interpretations in the Eastern Woodlands*, edited by Michael S. Nassaney and Kenneth E. Sassaman, 205–26. University of Tennessee Press, Knoxville.
2002 Domesticating Self and Society in the Woodland Southeast. In *The Woodland Southeast*, edited by David G. Anderson and Robert C. Mainfort Jr., 525–39. University of Alabama Press, Tuscaloosa.

Coe, Joffrey L.
1995 *Town Creek Indian Mound: A Native American Legacy.* University of North Carolina Press, Chapel Hill.

Collins, Michael B.
1979 The Longworth-Gick Site (15Jf243). In *Excavations at Four Archaic Sites in the Lower Ohio Valley, Jefferson County, Kentucky,* edited by Michael B. Collins, 471–589. Department of Anthropology, University of Kentucky, Lexington.

Conley, Robert J.
2005 *Cherokee Medicine Man: The Life and Work of a Modern-Day Healer.* University of Oklahoma Press, Norman.

Connolly, James, and Mark Lake
2006 *Geographical Information Systems in Archaeology.* Cambridge University Press, Cambridge.

Connolly, Robert P., and Bradley T. Lepper
2004 *The Fort Ancient Earthworks; Prehistoric Lifeways of the Hopewell Culture in Southwestern Ohio.* Ohio Historical Society, Columbus.

Conyers, Lawrence B.
2010 Ground-Penetrating Radar for Anthropological Research. *Antiquity* 84: 175–84.

Conyers, Lawrence B., and Juerg Leckebusch
2010 Geophysical Archaeology Research Agendas for the Future: Some Ground-Penetrating Radar Examples. *Archaeological Prospection* 17: 117–23.

Cook, Sherburne
1972 Prehistoric Demography. *Addison-Wesley Modular Publications* 16: 1–42.

Cordell, Ann S.
1984 *Ceramic Technology at a Weeden Island Period Archaeological Site in North Florida.* Ceramic Notes no. 2. Occasional Publications of the Ceramic Technology Laboratory. Florida State Museum, Gainesville.

Cosgrove, Denis
1983 Landscapes and Myths, Gods and Humans. In *Landscape Politics and Perspectives*, edited by Barbara Bender, 281–305. Berg, Providence, R.I.
1984 *Social Formation and Symbolic Landscape.* University of Wisconsin Press, Madison.

Cottier, John W.
1982 The Archaeology of Ivy Creek. Report submitted to the United States Corps of Engineers, Mobile. Manuscript on file at Auburn University Department of Sociology and Anthropology, Auburn, Ala.

Cowan, Frank L.
2005   Stubbs Earthworks: An Ohio Hopewell "Woodhenge." In *Ohio Archaeology: An Illustrated Chronicle of Ohio's Ancient American Indian Cultures,* edited by Bradley T. Lepper, 148–51. Orange Frazer, Wilmington, Ohio.

Cowan, Wesley C.
1985   From Foraging to Incipient Food Production: Subsistence Change and Continuity on the Cumberland Plateau of Eastern Kentucky. Unpublished Ph.D. dissertation, Department of Anthropology, University of Michigan, Ann Arbor.

Cowan, Wesley C., H. Edwin Jackson, Katherine Moore, Andrew Nickelhoff, and Tristine L. Smart
1981   The Cloudsplitter Rockshelter, Menifee County, Kentucky: A Preliminary Report. *Southeastern Archaeological Conference Bulletin* 24: 60–76.

Crane, H. R.
1956   University of Michigan Radiocarbon Dates I. *Science* 124 (3224): 664–72.

Crane, H. R., and J. B. Griffin
1972   University of Michigan Radiocarbon Dates XIV. *Radiocarbon* 1: 155–94.

Creasman, Steven D.
1994   *Upper Cumberland Archaic and Woodland Period Archaeology at the Main Site (15Bl35), Bell County, Kentucky.* Cultural Resource Analysts, Lexington, Ky.
1995   *Archaeological Investigations at the Mills Site (15Bl80), Bell County, Kentucky.* Cultural Resource Analysts, Lexington, Ky.

Crothers, George M.
1987   An Archaeological Survey of Big Bone Cave, Tennessee and Diachronic Patterns of Cave Utilization in the Eastern Woodlands. Unpublished master's thesis, Department of Anthropology, University of Tennessee, Knoxville.

Crothers, George M., Charles H. Faulkner, Jan F. Simek, Patty Jo Watson, and P. Willey
2002   Woodland Cave Archaeology in Eastern North America. In *The Woodland Southeast,* edited by David G. Anderson and Robert C. Mainfort Jr., 502–24. University of Alabama Press, Tuscaloosa.

Crowell, David, Elliot M. Abrams, AnnCorrine Freter, and James Lein
2005   Woodland Communities in the Hocking Valley. In *The Emergence of the Moundbuilders: The Archaeology of Tribal Societies in Southeastern Ohio,* 82–98. Ohio University Press, Athens.

Crumley, Carole L.
1979   Three Locational Models: An Epistemological Assessment for Anthropology and Archaeology. In *Advances in Archaeological Method and Theory,* vol. 2, edited by Michael Schiffer, 141–73. Academic Press, New York.
1987   A Dialectical Critique of Hierarchy. In *Power Relations and State Formation,* edited by Thomas C. Patterson and Christine W. Gailey, 155–69. Archaeology Division, American Anthropological Association, Washington, D.C.
1995   Heterarchy and the Analysis of Complex Societies. In *Heterarchy and the Analysis of Complex Societies,* edited by Robert M. Ehrenreich, Carole L. Crumley, and Janet E. Levy, 1–5. Archaeological Papers of the American Anthropological Association no. 6. Washington, D.C.

Crumley, Carole, and William H. Marquardt
1990   Landscape: A Unifying Concept in Regional Analysis. In *Interpreting Space: GIS and Archaeology,* edited by Kathleen Allen Stanton Green and Ezra Zubrow, 73–79. Taylor and Francis, London.

Custer, Jay F.
1987   New Perspectives on the Delmarva Adena Complex. *Midcontinental Journal of Archaeology* 12: 33–54.

Dalan, Rinita A.
2006   Magnetic Susceptibility. In *Remote Sensing in Archaeology: An Explicitly North American Perspective,* edited by Jay K. Johnson, 161–203. University of Alabama Press, Tuscaloosa.

Dancey, William S.
2005   The Enigmatic Hopewell of the Eastern Woodlands. In *North American Archaeology,* edited by Timothy R. Pauketat and Diana DiPaulo Loren, 108–37. Blackwell, Malden, Mass.

Dancey, William S., and Paul J. Pacheco
1997   *Ohio Hopewell Community Organization.* Kent State University Press, Kent, Ohio.

David, Bruno, and Julian Thomas
2008   *Handbook of Landscape Archaeology.* Left Coast Press, Walnut Creek, Calif.

Davis, Daniel B., Leon Lane, Nancy O'Malley, and Jack Rossen
1997   *Phase II Testing and Phase III Mitigation of Three Sites in the Bardstown Industrial Park, Nelson County, Kentucky.* Archaeological Report no. 386. Program for Cultural Resource Assessment, University of Kentucky, Lexington.

Davis, John H., Jr.
1943   *The Natural Features of Southern Florida.* Bulletin 25. Florida Geological Survey, Tallahassee.

DeBoer, Warren R.
1997   Ceremonial Centres from the Cayapas (Esmeraldas, Ecuador) to Chillicothe (Ohio, USA). *Cambridge Archaeological Journal* 7: 225–53.
2005   Colors for a North American Past. *World Archaeology* 37: 66–91.

DeNeeve, Ian K.
2004   The Crab Orchard Ceramic Tradition Surrounding the Confluence of the Wabash and Ohio Rivers. Unpublished master's thesis, Department of Anthropology, University of Kentucky, Lexington.

Des Jean, Tom
1987   Looting Activity: A Folk Tradition of the Upper Cumberland. Paper presented at the 44th Annual Meeting of the Southeastern Archaeological Conference, Charleston, S.C.

Des Jean, Tom, and Joseph L. Benthall
1994   A Lithic Based Prehistoric Cultural Chronology of the Upper Cumberland Plateau. *Tennessee Anthropologist* 19: 115–47.

Dickens, Roy S., Jr.
1971   Archaeology in the Jones Bluff Reservoir on Central Alabama. *Journal of Alabama Archaeology* 17: 1–113.
1975   A Processual Approach to Mississippian Origins on the Georgia Piedmont. *Southeastern Archaeological Conference Bulletin* 18: 31–42.
1976   *Cherokee Prehistory: The Pisgah Phase in the Appalachian Summit Region.* University of Tennessee Press, Knoxville.

Dickens, Roy S., Jr., and Martin D. Fraser
1984   An Information-Theoretic Approach to the Analysis of Cultural Interaction in the Middle Woodland Period. *Southeastern Archaeology* 3: 144–52.

Dillehay, Thomas D.
1992   Keeping Outsiders Out: Public Ceremony, Resource Rights, and Hierarchy in Historic and Contemporary Mapuche Society. In *Wealth and Hierarchy in the Intermediate Area,* edited by F. Lange, 379–422. Dunbarton Oaks Research Laboratory, Washington, D.C.
2004   Social Identity and Ritual Pause: Uncertainty and Integration in Formative Peru. *Journal of Social Archaeology* 4: 239–68.
2007   *Monuments, Empires, and Resistance: The Araucanian Polity and Ritual Narratives.* Cambridge University Press, Cambridge.

Dowell, Michael Keith
n.d.   Original Field Notes, Maps, and Report Drafts for the Plum Springs Site (15Wa981). Original files in possession of the author, Bowling Green, Ky.
1979   A Study of the Middle Woodland Period of Kentucky, 200 B.C.–600 A.D. Ms. on file, Department of Folk Studies and Anthropology, Western Kentucky University, Bowling Green.
1981   The Plum Springs Site: An Early Woodland Component in Southern Kentucky. Ms. on file, Department of Folk Studies and Anthropology, Western Kentucky University, Bowling Green.

Dragoo, Don W.
1963   *Mounds for the Dead: An Analysis of the Adena Culture.* Carnegie Museum of Natural History, Pittsburgh, Penn.

Driskell, Boyce N.
1979   The Rosenberger Site (15Jf18). In *Excavations at Four Archaic Sites in the Lower Ohio Valley, Jefferson County, Kentucky,* edited by Michael B. Collins, 697–803. Department of Anthropology, University of Kentucky, Lexington.

Driskell, Boyce N., Cindy E. Jobe, Christopher A. Turnbow, and Mary Dunn
1984   *The Archaeology of Taylorsville Lake: Archaeological Data Recovery and Synthesis.* Archaeological Report no. 85. Department of Anthropology, University of Kentucky, Lexington.

Duerksen, Ken, John F. Doershuk, Christopher A. Bergman, Teresa W. Tune, and Donald A. Miller
1995   Fayette Thick Ceramic Chronology at the West Runway Site (15Be391), Boone County, Kentucky. In *Current Archaeological Research in Kentucky,* vol. 3, edited by John F. Doershuk, Christopher A. Bergman, and David Pollack, 70–88. Kentucky Heritage Council, Frankfort.

Duerksen, Ken, John F. Doershuk, Larry R. Kimball, and Christopher A. Bergman
1994   *Kramer Points and Fayette Thick Ceramics: Data Recovery at the West Runway Site (15Be391), an Upland Early Woodland Camp in Boone County, Kentucky.* 3D/Environmental Services, Cultural Resources Division, Cincinnati, Ohio.

Dunnell, Robert C.
1966a   *1965 Excavations in the Fishtrap Reservoir, Pike County, Kentucky.* National Park Service Southeastern Region, Richmond, Va.
1966b   *Archaeological Reconnaissances in Fishtrap Reservoir, Kentucky.* Department of Anthropology, Yale University, New Haven, Conn.
1972   *The Prehistory of Fishtrap, Kentucky.* Publications in Anthropology no. 75. Yale University, New Haven, Conn.
1992   The Notion Site. In *Space, Time, and Archaeological Landscapes,* edited by Jacqueline Rossignol and LuAnn Wandsnider, 21–41. Plenum, New York.

Dunnell, Robert C., and William S. Dancey
1983   The Siteless Survey: A Regional Scale Data Collection Strategy. In *Advances in Archaeological Method and Theory,* vol. 6, edited by Michael B. Schiffer, 267–87. Academic, New York.

Dunnell, Robert C., and James K. Feathers
1994   Thermoluminescence Dating of Surficial Archaeological Material. In *Dating in Exposed and Surface Contexts,* edited by Charlotte Beck, 115–37. University of New Mexico Press, Albuquerque.

Dye, Andrew D., Jeff Navel, Meagan E. Dennison, and Jay D. Franklin
2010   Archaeological Testing of Hemlock Falls Rock House (40Fn239), Pogue Creek State Natural Area. Paper presented at the 22nd Annual Current Research in Tennessee Archaeology Meeting, Nashville.

Ebert, James I.
1992 *Distributional Archaeology*. University of New Mexico Press, Albuquerque.
Egloff, Keith T., Michael B. Barber, Celia Reed, and Thomas R. Whyte
1994 Leggett Site (44HA23, Halifax County): A Dan River Agricultural/Riverine Community. *Archaeological Society of Virginia Quarterly Bulletin* 49: 89–120.
Eliade, Mircea
1972 *Shamanism: Archaic Techniques of Ecstasy*. Princeton University Press, Princeton, N.J.
Elmore, Chris, and Nancy Ross-Stallings
2006 *Phase II and Phase III Archaeological Investigations at the Miller Site (15Gd44), Located along the KY52 Realignment Project, Garrard County, Kentucky (Item no. 7-302.01)*. Cultural Horizons, Harrodsburg, Ky.
Ensor, H. Blaine, Steven Hunt, Marianne Marek, Anna Presley, Brian Shaffer, David Shanabrook, Donna Shepard, and Philip Waite
1996 *1993 Phase I Cultural Resource Survey and Archaeological Site Recordation Blue Grass Army Depot, Madison County, Kentucky*. Geo-Marine, Plano, Texas.
Espenshade, Christopher T.
2008 *Woodland Period Archaeology of Northern Georgia: Update 2008*. New South Associates Technical Report 1593. Stone Mountain, Ga.
Eubanks, Paul N.
2010 Interaction, Sedentism, and Aggregation in Woodland-Stage Central Alabama. Unpublished master's thesis, University of Alabama, Tuscaloosa.
Evans, Martin, Stephen Mocas, Roger Moeller, Renee Black, and Anthony O. Clark
1994 *Phase III Archaeological Investigation of the Yellowbank Site (15Bc164) in Breckinridge County, Kentucky*. Archaeology Resources Consultant Services, Louisville, Ky.
Evans, Susan, and Peter Gould
1982 Settlement Models in Archaeology. *Journal of Anthropological Archaeology* 1: 275–304.
Fairbanks, Charles H., Arthur R. Kelly, Gordon R. Willey, and Pat Wofford Jr.
1946 The Leake Mounds, Bartow County, Georgia. *American Antiquity* 12: 126–27.
Farnsworth, Kenneth B., and Donald L. Asch
1986 Early Woodland Chronology, Artifact Styles, and Settlement Distribution in the Lower Illinois Valley Region. In *Early Woodland Archaeology*, edited by Kenneth B. Farnsworth and Thomas E. Emerson, 326–457. Kampsville Seminar in Archeology, vol. 2. Center for American Archeology, Kampsville, Ill.
Faulkner, Charles H.
1968 A Review of Pottery Types in the Eastern Tennessee Valley. *Southeastern Archaeological Conference Bulletin* 8: 23–35.
1988 Middle Woodland Community and Settlement Patterns on the Eastern Highland Rim, Tennessee. In *Middle Woodland Settlement and Ceremonialism in the Mid-South and Lower Mississippi Valley*, edited by Robert C. Mainfort Jr., 76–98. Archaeological Report no. 22. Mississippi Department of Archives and History, Jackson.
1997 Four Thousand Years of Native American Cave Art in the Southern Appalachians. *Journal of Cave and Karst Studies* 59: 148–53.
2002 Woodland Cultures of the Elk and Duck River Valleys, Tennessee: Continuity and Change. In *The Woodland Southeast*, edited by David G. Anderson and Robert C. Mainfort Jr., 185–203. University of Alabama Press, Tuscaloosa.
Faulkner, Charles, and Charles R. McCollough
1974 *Excavations and Testing, Normandy Reservoir Salvage Project: 1972 Season*. Department of Anthropology, University of Tennessee, Knoxville.

Fennell, Christopher C.
2010   Carved, Inscribed, and Resurgent: Cultural and Natural Terrains as Analytic Challenges. In *Revealing Landscapes*, edited by Christopher C. Fennell, 1–11. Society for Historical Archaeology, Tucson, Ariz.

Fenneman, Nevin M.
1938   *Physiography of the Eastern United States.* McGraw-Hill, New York.

Fenton, James P.
2001   Early Woodland Burial Mounds of Kentucky: Symbolic Elements in the Cultural Landscape. In *Archaeology of the Appalachian Highlands*, edited by Lynne P. Sullivan and Susan C. Prezzano, 137–48. University of Tennessee Press, Knoxville.

Fenton, James P., and Richard W. Jefferies
1991   The Camargo Mound and Earthworks: Preliminary Findings. In *The Human Landscape in Kentucky's Past: Site Structure and Settlement Patterns*, edited by Christine Hensley and Charles Stout, 40–55. Kentucky Heritage Council, Frankfort.

Ferguson, Terry A.
1988   Lithic Analysis and the Discovery of Prehistoric Man-Land Relationships in the Uplands of the Big South Fork of the Tennessee Cumberland Plateau. Unpublished Ph.D. dissertation, Department of Anthropology, University of Tennessee, Knoxville.

Ferguson, Terry A., Robert A. Pace, Jeffrey W. Gardner, and Robert W. Hoffman
1986   An Archaeological Reconnaissance and Testing of Indirect Impact Areas within Selected Development Sites of the Big South Fork National River and Recreation Area. Final report of the University of Tennessee Big South Fork Archaeological Project. Submitted to U.S. Army Engineer District, Nashville.

Flannery, Kent V.
1972   The Origins of the Village as a Settlement Type in Mesoamerica and the Near East: A Comparative Study. In *Man, Settlement and Urbanism*, edited by Peter J. Ucko, Ruth Tringham, and G. W. Dimbleby, 23–53. Duckworth, London.
1976   *The Early Mesoamerican Village.* Academic Press, New York.

Fleming, Andrew
2006   Post-processual Landscape Archaeology: A Critique. *Cambridge Archaeological Journal* 16: 267–80.

Florida Department of State
2010   Lake Okeechobee Scenic Trail. Electronic document. http://www.dep.state.fl.us/gwt/guide/regions/south/trails/6_lake_okeechobee_scenictra.htm. Accessed September 22, 2010.

Foley, Robert
1981   Off-Site Archaeology: An Alternative Approach for the Short-Sited. In *Pattern of the Past: Studies in Honour of David Clarke*, edited by Ian Hodder, Glynn Isaac, and Normal Hammond, 157–83. Cambridge University Press, Cambridge.

Ford, James A.
1969   *A Comparison of Formative Cultures in the Americas: Diffusion or the Psychic Unity of Man?* Smithsonian Institution Contributions to Anthropology, vol. 11. Washington, D.C.

Fortier, Andrew C., Kathryn E. Parker, Thomas O. Maher, Joyce A. Williams, and Michael C. Meinkoth
1989   *The Holding Site: A Hopewell Community in the American Bottom.* American Bottom Archaeology FAI-270 Site Reports 19. University of Illinois, Urbana.

Foster, Gary S.
1972   Archaeological Survey of the Gasper River Drainage System. Ms. on file, Department of Folk Studies and Anthropology, Western Kentucky University, Bowling Green.

Fowke, Gerard
1902   *Archaeological History of Ohio: The Mound Builders and Later Indians.* Ohio State Archaeological and Historical Society, Columbus.

Fowler, Melvin
1991   Mound 72 and Early Mississippian at Cahokia. In *New Perspectives on Cahokia: Views from the Periphery,* edited by James B. Stoltman, 1–28. Prehistory Press, Madison, Wis.

Franklin, Jay D.
1999   The Rime of the Ancient Miners. Unpublished master's thesis, Department of Anthropology, University of Tennessee, Knoxville.
2001   Excavating and Analyzing Prehistoric Lithic Quarries: An Example from 3rd Unnamed Cave, Tennessee. *Midcontinental Journal of Archaeology* 26: 199–217.
2002   *The Prehistory of Fentress County, Tennessee: An Archaeological Survey.* Doctoral dissertation, Department of Anthropology, University of Tennessee, Knoxville. University Microfilms, University of Michigan, Ann Arbor.
2006a   An Archaeological Reconnaissance Survey of the Bluffs and Gorges of the South Sides of Fletcher Branch and North White Oak Creek to the Confluence of Mill Seat Creek, Fentress County, Tennessee. Report submitted to Holbrook and Peterson, PLLC, Knoxville, Tenn., and the Estate of Bruno Gernt, Inc., Allardt, Tenn.
2006b   Prehistoric Culture Chronology on the Upper Cumberland Plateau of Tennessee. Paper presented at the 63rd Annual Southeastern Archaeological Conference, Little Rock, Ark.
2007   Cave and Rock Shelter Excavations on the Tennessee River, Roane County, Tennessee. Paper presented at the 64th Annual Southeastern Archaeological Conference, Knoxville, Tenn.
2008a   Luminescence Dates and Woodland Ceramics from Rock Shelters on the Upper Cumberland Plateau of Tennessee. *Tennessee Archaeology* 3: 87–100.
2008b   Big Cave Archaeology in the East Fork Obey River Gorge. In *Cave Archaeology of the Eastern Woodlands: Essays in Honor of Patty Jo Watson,* edited by David H. Dye, 141–55. University of Tennessee Press, Knoxville.

Franklin, Jay D., and Sierra M. Bow
2008   The Upper Cumberland Plateau Archaeological Luminescence Dating Project. Paper presented at the 65th Annual Southeastern Archaeological Conference, Charlotte, N.C.
2009   Archaeological Exploration of Workshop Rock Shelter, Upper Cumberland Plateau, Tennessee. *Tennessee Archaeology* 4: 145–62.
2010   Archaeological Exploration of the Workshop Rock Shelter, Upper Cumberland Plateau, Tennessee. In *Pottery, Passages, Postholes, and Porcelain: Essays in Honor of Charles H. Faulkner,* edited by Timothy Baumann and Mark Groover, 53–69. Report of Investigations no. 53, Department of Anthropology, and Occasional Paper no. 22, Frank H. McClung Museum, University of Tennessee, Knoxville.

Franklin, Jay D., Michelle L. Hammett, and Renee B. Walker
2008   The Nelson Site: Late Middle Woodland Habitation on the Nolichucky River, Washington County, Tennessee. *Tennessee Archaeology* 3: 181–200.

Franklin, Jay D., Maureen A. Hays, Sarah C. Sherwood, and Lucinda M. Langston
2012   An Integrated Approach: Lithic Analyses and Site Function, Eagle Drink Bluff Shelter, Upper Cumberland Plateau, Tennessee. In *Lithic Analysis: Problems, Solutions, and Interpretation,* edited by Phillip J. Carr, Andrew P. Bradbury, and Sarah E. Price, 128–45. University of Alabama Press, Tuscaloosa.

Franklin, Jay D., Renee B. Walker, Maureen A. Hays, and Charlotte W. Beck
2010   Late Archaic Site Use at Sachsen Cave Shelter, Upper Cumberland Plateau, Tennessee. *North American Archaeology* 31: 447–49.

French, Michael W.
2004   *Phase I Archaeological Intensive Survey for the Proposed KY 61 Realignment Right-of-Way and Investigation Buffer in Cumberland County, Kentucky.* AMEC Earth and Environment, Louisville, Ky.

French, Michael W., and Anne Tobe Bader
2001   *A Phase I Archaeological Reconnaissance of 64 Acres of Proposed Borrow Area at Blue Grass Army Depot and Phase II Investigations at Site 15Ma218.* AMEC Earth and Environment, Louisville, Ky.

French, Michael W., Anne Tobe Bader, and David W. Schatz
2007   Terminal Late Archaic/Early Woodland Occupations at the Shippingport Site (15Jf702). Paper presented at the 24th Annual Kentucky Heritage Council Archaeological Conference, Natural Bridge, Ky.

Fritz, Gayle J.
1993   Early and Middle Woodland Period Paleoethnobotany. In *Foraging and Farming in the Eastern Woodlands*, edited by C. Margaret Scarry, 39–56. University Press of Florida, Gainesville.

Funkhouser, William D., and William S. Webb
1928   *Ancient Life in Kentucky.* Kentucky Geological Survey, Frankfort.
1929   The So-Called "Ash Caves" in Lee County, Kentucky. In *Reports in Archaeology and Anthropology* 1, 37–112. University of Kentucky, Lexington.
1935   The Ricketts Site in Montgomery County, Kentucky. In *Reports in Anthropology and Archaeology* 3, 70–100. University of Kentucky, Lexington.

Gagliano, Sherwood M., Charles E. Person, Richard A. Weinstein, Diane E. Wiseman, and Christopher M. McClendon
1982   Sedimentary Studies of Prehistoric Archaeological Sites: Criteria for the Identification of Submerged Archaeological Sites of the Northern Gulf of Mexico Continental Shelf. Coastal Environments, Inc., Baton Rouge. Submitted to U. S. Department of the Interior, National Park Service, Division of State Plans and Grants, contract no. C35003(79).

Gardner, Paul S.
1987   New Evidence Concerning the Chronology and Paleoethnobotany of Salts Cave, Kentucky. *American Antiquity* 52: 358–67.

Gell, Alfred
1998   *Art and Agency: An Anthropological Theory.* Clarendon Press, Oxford, U.K.

Giardino, Marco J., and Robert Jones III
1996   Archaeological Test Excavations at the Jackson Landing Site and Adjacent Ancient Earthwork, Hancock County, Mississippi. Manuscript on file, Historic Preservation Division, Mississippi Department of Archives and History, Jackson.

Gibson, Jon L.
1998   Broken Circles, Owl Monsters, and Black Earth Midden. In *Ancient Earthen Enclosures of the Eastern Woodlands*, edited by Robert C. Mainfort Jr. and Lynne Sullivan, 17–30. University Press of Florida, Gainesville.

Giddens, Anthony
1984   *The Constitution of Society: Outline of a Theory of Structuration.* University of California Press, Berkeley.

Gilman, Patricia A.
1987   Architecture as Artifact: Pit Structures and Pueblos in the American Southwest. *American Antiquity* 52: 538–64.

Goad, Sharon I.
1976   Copper and the Southeastern Indians. *Early Georgia* 4: 48–67.
1979   Middle Woodland Exchange in the Prehistoric Southeastern United States. In *Hopewell Archaeology: The Chillicothe Conference*, edited by David S. Brose and N'omi B. Greber, 239–46. Kent State University, Kent, Ohio.
1980   Copena Burial Practices and Social Organization. *Journal of Alabama Archaeology* 26: 67–86.

Goggin, John M.
1949   Cultural Traditions in Florida Prehistory. In *The Florida Indian and his Neighbors*, edited by John M. Goggin, 13–44. Inter-American Center, Rollins College, Winter Park, Fla.

Greber, N'omi B.
1979   A Comparative Study of Site Morphology and Burial Patterns at Edwin Harness and Seip Mounds 1 and 2. In *Hopewell Archaeology: The Chillicothe Conference*, edited by David S. Brose and N'omi B. Greber, 27–38. Kent State University Press, Kent, Ohio.
1983   *Recent Excavations at the Edwin Harness Mound, Liberty Works, Ross County, Ohio*. Mid-Continental Journal of Archaeology, Special Publication 5. Kent State University Press, Kent, Ohio.
1991   A Study of Continuity and Contrast between Central Scioto Adena and Hopewell Sites. *West Virginia Archaeologist* 43: 1–26.
2005   Adena and Hopewell in the Middle Ohio Valley: To Be or Not To Be? In *Woodland Period Systematics in the Middle Ohio Valley*, edited by Darlene Applegate and Robert C. Mainfort Jr., 19–39. University of Alabama Press, Tuscaloosa.
2006   Enclosures and Communities in Ohio Hopewell: An Essay. In *Recreating Hopewell*, edited by Douglas K. Charles and Jane E. Buikstra, 74–105. University Press of Florida, Gainesville.
2009   Stratigraphy and Chronology in the 1971–1977 Ohio Historical Society Field Data. *Midcontinental Journal of Archaeology* 3: 19–52.

Greenman, Emerson
1932   Excavation of the Coon Mound and an Analysis of the Adena Culture. *Ohio State Archaeological and Historical Quarterly* 41: 366–523.

Gremillion, Kristen J.
1994   Evidence of Plant Domestication from Kentucky Caves and Rockshelters. In *Agricultural Origins and Development in the Midcontinent*, edited by William Green, 87–104. Office of the State Archaeologist, University of Iowa, Iowa City.
1995   Botanical Contents of Paleofeces from Two Eastern Kentucky Rockshelters. In *Current Archaeological Research in Kentucky*, vol. 3, edited by John F. Doershuk, Christopher A. Bergman, and David Pollack, 52–69. Kentucky Heritage Council, Frankfort.
1996   The Paleoethnobotanical Record for the Southeastern United States. In *Archaeology of the Mid-Holocene Southeast*, edited by Kenneth E. Sassaman and David G. Anderson, 99–115. University Press of Florida, Gainesville.
1997   New Perspectives on the Paleoethnobotany of the Newt Kash Shelter. In *People, Plants, and Landscapes: Studies in Paleoethnobotany*, edited by Kristen J. Gremillion, 23–41. University of Alabama Press, Tuscaloosa.
1998   3,000 Years of Human Activity at the Cold Oak Shelter. In *Current Archaeological Research in Kentucky*, vol. 5, edited by Charles D. Hockensmith, Kenneth C. Carstens, Charles Stout, and Sara J. Rivers, 1–14. Kentucky Heritage Council, Frankfort.

2002   The Development and Dispersal of Agricultural Systems in the Woodland Period Southeast. In *The Woodland Southeast,* edited by David G. Anderson and Robert C. Mainfort Jr., 483–501. University of Alabama Press, Tuscaloosa.

2006   Southeast Plants. In *Environment, Origins, and Population.* Vol. 3 of *Handbook of North American Indians,* edited by Douglas Ubelaker, 388–295. Smithsonian Institution Press, Washington, D.C.

Gremillion, Kristen J., Katherine R. Mickelson, Andrew M. Mickelson, and Anne B. Lee

2000   Rockshelters at the Headwaters: Archaeological Survey in the Big Sinking Drainage of Eastern Kentucky. In *Current Archaeological Research in Kentucky,* vol. 6, edited by David Pollack and Kristen J. Gremillion, 76–93. Kentucky Heritage Council, Frankfort.

Gremillion, Kristen J., and Kristin D. Sobolik

1996   Dietary Variability among Prehistoric Forager-Farmers of Eastern North America. *Current Anthropology* 37: 529–38.

Griffin, James B.

1947   The Spruce Run Earthworks. *Ohio State Archaeological and Historical Society Quarterly* 56: 188–200.

1967   Eastern North American Archaeology: A Summary. *Science* 156: 175–91.

1996   The Hopewell Housing Shortage in Ohio, A.D. 1–350. In *View from the Core: A Synthesis of Ohio Hopewell Archaeology,* edited by Paul J. Pacheco, 4–15. Ohio Archaeological Council, Columbus.

Haag, William G.

1940   A Description of the Wright Site Pottery. In *The Wright Mounds, Sites 6 and 7, Montgomery County, Kentucky,* edited by William S. Webb, 75–82. Reports in Anthropology and Archaeology 5. University of Kentucky, Lexington.

Hall, Charles L., and Walter E. Klippel

1988   A Polythetic-Satisficer Approach to Prehistoric Natural Shelter Selection in Middle Tennessee. *Midcontinental Journal of Archaeology* 13: 159–86.

Hall, Christopher T.

2005   *Phase III Archaeological Investigations at the Hayes Site (15Cl67), Carroll County, Kentucky.* Cultural Resource Analysts, Lexington, Ky.

Hall, Robert L.

1976   Ghosts, Water Barriers, Corn, and Sacred Enclosures in the Eastern Woodlands. *American Antiquity* 41: 360–64.

1979   In Search of the Ideology of the Adena-Hopewell Climax. In *Hopewell Archaeology: The Chillicothe Conference,* edited by David S. Brose and N'omi B. Greber, 258–65. Kent State University Press, Kent, Ohio.

1997   *An Archaeology of the Soul: North American Indian Belief and Ritual.* University of Illinois Press, Urbana.

1998   A Comparison of Some North American and Mesoamerican Cosmologies and Their Ritual Expression. In *Explorations in American Archaeology: Essays in Honor of Paul Radin,* edited by Stanley Diamond, 19–52. Columbia University Press, New York.

Hally, David J.

2008   *King: The Social Archaeology of a Late Mississippian Town in Northwestern Georgia.* University of Alabama Press, Tuscaloosa.

Hammerstedt, Scott W., Amanda L. Regnier, and Patrick C. Livingood

2010   Geophysical and Archaeological Investigations at the Clement Site, A Caddo Mound Complex in Southeastern Oklahoma. *Southeastern Archaeology* 29: 279–91.

Hardesty, Donald L.
1965   The Biggs Site: A Hopewellian Complex in Greenup County, Kentucky. *Probes* 2: 14–21.
Hargrave, Michael L.
2011   Geophysical Survey of Complex Deposits at Ramey Field, Cahokia. *Southeastern Archaeology* 30: 1–19.
Harris, Corra
1950   A Sketch of the Pine Indian Cave. *Early Georgia* 1: 41–42.
Hayden, Brian
2001   Fabulous Feasts: A Prolegomenon to the Importance of Feasting. In *Feasts: Archaeological and Ethnographic Perspectives on Food, Politics, and Power*, edited by Michael Dietler and Brian Hayden, 23–64. Smithsonian Institution Press, Washington, D.C.
Hays, Christopher T.
2010   Adena Mortuary Patterns in Central Ohio. *Southeastern Archaeology* 29: 106–20.
Hays, Christopher T., and Richard A. Weinstein
2010   Tchefuncte and Early Woodland. In *Archaeology of Louisiana*, edited by Mark A. Rees, 97–119. Baton Rouge: Louisiana State University Press.
Hegmon, Michelle
2003   Setting Theoretical Egos Aside: Issues and Theory in North American Archaeology. *American Antiquity* 68: 213–43.
Heitman, Carrie C.
2007   Houses Great and Small: A Discussion of the House Model in Relation to Chaco Canyon, NM, AD 900 to 1150. In *The Durable House: House Society Models in Archaeology*, edited by Robin A. Beck, 248–72. Center for Archaeological Investigations, Southern Illinois University, Carbondale.
Henderson, A. Gwynn, and Eric J. Schlarb
2007   *Adena: Woodland Period Moundbuilders of the Bluegrass*. Educational Series no. 9. Kentucky Archaeological Survey, Lexington.
Henry, Edward R.
2009   *Geophysical Prospection and Excavation at an Early Woodland Ceremonial Circle in Bourbon County, KY*. Master's thesis, University of Mississippi, Oxford.
2011   A Multi-stage Geophysical Approach to Detecting and Interpreting Archaeological Features at the LeBus Circle, Bourbon County, KY. *Archaeological Prospection* 18: 231–44.
Henry, Edward R., and George M. Crothers
2010   Revisiting Webb's Old Friend Mount Horeb: New Research at an Early Woodland Circular Earthwork in Fayette County, Kentucky. Paper presented at the Kentucky Heritage Council Archaeological Conference, Cumberland Falls State Park, Ky.
Hensley, Christine K.
1991   The Green River Archaeological Study. In *Studies in Kentucky Archaeology*, edited by Charles D. Hockensmith, 11–26. Kentucky Heritage Council, Frankfort.
Herndon, Richard L.
2003   *Phase II National Register Evaluation of 15Lv222 (the Chestnut Lake Site) and 15Lv223 (the Crounse Site) in Livingston County, Kentucky*. Cultural Resource Analysts, Lexington, Ky.
Heye, George G.
1919   *Certain Mounds in Haywood County, North Carolina*. Museum of the American Indian Heye Foundation, New York.
Hofman, Jack L.
1985   Middle Archaic Ritual and Shell Midden Archaeology: Considering the Significance of Cremations. In *Exploring Tennessee Prehistory: A Dedication to Alfred K. Guthe*, edited by

Thomas R. Whyte, Clifford C. Boyd, and Bret H. Riggs, 1–22. Report of Investigations no. 42. University of Tennessee, Department of Anthropology, Knoxville.

Howey, Meghan C. L.
2012   *Moundbuilders and Monument Makers of the Northern Great Lakes, 1200–1600.* University of Oklahoma Press, Norman.

Husserl, Edmund
1962   *Ideas: General Introduction to Pure Phenomenology.* Collier Books, New York.
1964   *The Phenomenology of Internal Time and Consciousness.* Indiana University Press, Bloomington.

Ingold, Tim
1993   The Temporality of the Landscape. *World Archaeology* 25: 152–74.
1995   Building, Dwelling, Living: How Animals and People Make Themselves at Home in the World. In *Shifting Contexts: Transformations in Anthropological Knowledge*, edited by Marilyn Strathern, 57–80. Routledge, London.
2000   *The Perception of the Environment: Essays in Livelihood, Dwelling, and Skill.* Routledge, London.

Ison, Cecil R.
1988   The Cold Oak Shelter: Providing a Better Understanding of the Terminal Archaic. In *Paleoindian and Archaic Research in Kentucky*, edited by Charles D. Hockensmith, David Pollack, and Thomas N. Sanders, 205–20. Kentucky Heritage Council, Frankfort.

Jackson, H. Edwin
1998   Little Spanish Fort: An Early Middle Woodland Enclosure in the Lower Yazoo Basin, Mississippi. *Midcontinental Journal of Archaeology* 23: 199–220.

Jasanoff, Maya
2011   *Liberty's Exiles: American Loyalists in the Revolutionary World.* Alfred A. Knopf, New York.

Jefferies, Richard W.
1976   *The Tunacunnhee Site: Evidence of Hopewell Interaction in Northwest Georgia.* University of Georgia, Athens.
1978   Intersite Activity Variability in the Lookout Valley Area of Northwest Georgia. Unpublished Ph.D. dissertation, Department of Anthropology, University of Georgia, Athens.
1979   The Tunacunnhee Site: Hopewell in Northwest Georgia. In *Hopewell Archaeology: The Chillicothe Conference*, edited by David S. Brose and N'omi B. Greber, 162–70. Kent State University Press, Kent, Ohio.
1994   The Swift Creek Site and Woodland Platform Mounds in the Southeastern United States. In *Ocmulgee Archaeology, 1936–1986*, edited by David J. Hally, 71–83. University of Georgia Press, Athens.
2004   Regional-Scale Interaction Networks and the Emergence of Cultural Complexity along the Northern Margins of the Southeast. In *Signs of Power: The Rise of Cultural Complexity in the Southeast*, edited by Jon L. Gibson and Philip J. Carr, 71–85. University of Alabama Press, Tuscaloosa.
2006   Death Rituals at the Tunacunnhee Site. In *Recreating Hopewell*, edited by Douglas K. Charles and Jane E. Buikstra, 161–77. University Press of Florida, Gainesville.

Jeter, Marvin D.
1973   *An Archaeological Survey in the Area East of Selma, Alabama, 1971–1972.* Alabama Historical Commission, Montgomery.
1977   Late Woodland Chronology and Change in Central Alabama. *Journal of Alabama Archaeology* 23: 112–36.
1984   Materials, and Contingency Tables: Comments on Some Recent Analyses of Copena Burial Practices. *Midcontinental Journal of Archaeology* 9: 91–104.

Johnson, Jay K., Richard Stallings, Nancy Ross-Stallings, R. Berle Clay, and V. Stephen Jones
2000   *Remote Sensing and Ground Truth at the Hollywood Mounds Site in Tunica County, Mississippi.* Center for Archaeological Research, University of Mississippi, Oxford.

Johnson, Matthew
2007   *Ideas of Landscape.* Wiley and Sons, New York.

Jones, Charles Colcock, Jr.
1861   *Monumental Remains of Georgia,* part 1. John M. Cooper and Co., Savannah, Ga.

Jones, Dennis, and Carl Kuttruff
1998   Prehistoric Enclosures in Louisiana and the Marksville Site. In *Ancient Earthen Enclosures of the Eastern Woodlands,* edited by Robert C. Mainfort Jr. and Lynne P. Sullivan, 31–56. University Press of Florida, Gainesville.

Jones, Lindsey
2000   *The Hermeneutics of Sacred Architecture: Experience, Interpretation, Comparison.* 2 vols. Harvard Center for the Study of World Religions, Cambridge, Mass.

Joyce, Rosemary A., and Jeanne Lopiparo
2005   PostScript: Doing Agency in Archaeology. *Journal of Archaeological Method and Theory* 12: 365–74.

Justice, Noel D.
1987   *Stone Age Spear and Arrow Points of the Midcontinental and Eastern United States: A Modern Reference.* Indiana University Press, Bloomington.

Kan, Sergei
1989   *Symbolic Immortality: The Tlingit Potlatch of the Nineteenth Century.* Smithsonian Institution Press, Washington, D.C.

Kantner, John
2008   The Archaeology of Regions: From Discrete Analytical Toolkit to Ubiquitous Spatial Perspective. *Journal of Archaeological Research* 16: 37–81.

Keel, Bennie C.
1976   *Cherokee Archaeology: A Study of the Appalachian Summit.* University of Tennessee Press, Knoxville.

Keeley, Lawrence H.
1980   *Experimental Determination of Stone Tool Use: A Microwear Analysis.* University of Chicago Press, Chicago.

Keith, Scot
2007   Gateway to the Hopewell Heartland: The Cultural Trajectory of the Leake Site. Paper presented at the 64th Annual Meeting of the Southeastern Archaeological Conference, Knoxville, Tenn.
2010   *Archaeological Data Recovery at the Leake Site, Bartow County, Georgia.* Georgia Department of Transportation, Atlanta.

Keith, Scot J., and Pamela Baughman
2011   Ground Penetrating Radar at the Leake Site: Investigations, Results, and Interpretations. Presentation at the 68th Annual Meeting of the Southeastern Archaeological Conference, Jacksonville, Fla.

Kellar, James, A. R. Kelly, and Edward V. McMichael
1962   Final Report on Archaeological Explorations at the Manedeville Site, 9Cla1, Clay County, Georgia, Seasons 1959, 1960, and 1961. Manuscript on file at the Laboratory of Archaeology, University of Georgia, Athens.

Kelly, Arthur R.
1950   News and Notes. *Early Georgia* 1: 43–45.

1951 Limestone Caves in Bartow County, Georgia. Manuscript #284, on file at the Georgia Archaeological Site File, University of Georgia, Athens.
1952 North Georgia Burial Caves. Manuscript #32, on file at the Georgia Archaeological Site File, University of Georgia, Athens.

Kelly, John E.
1991 The Evidence for Prehistoric Exchange and Its Implications for the Development of Cahokia. In *New Perspectives on Cahokia: Views from the Periphery*, edited by James B. Stoltman, 65–92. Prehistory Press, Madison, Wis.
1996 Redefining Cahokia: Principles and Elements of Community Organization. *Wisconsin Archaeologist* 77: 97–119.
2003 The Context of the Post Pit and Meaning of the Sacred Pole at the East St. Louis Mound Group. *Wisconsin Archaeologist* 84: 107–25.

Kennedy, Mary C.
1992 Aboriginal Dates from Mammoth Cave. *CRF Newsletter* 20: 2–3.
1996 Radiocarbon Dates from Salts and Mammoth Caves. In *Of Caves and Shell Mounds*, edited by Kenneth C. Carstens and Patty Jo Watson, 48–81. University of Alabama Press, Tuscaloosa.

Kerr, Jonathan P., Andrew P. Bradbury, and Grant L. Day
2004 Excavations at 15Cu27: A Rockshelter in South-Central Kentucky. In *Current Archaeological Research in Kentucky*, vol. 7, edited by Charles D. Hockensmith and Kenneth C. Carstens, 35–54. Kentucky Heritage Council, Frankfort.

Kerr, Jonathan P., and Steven D. Creasman
1998 Middle Woodland Occupation at the Martin Justice Site (15Pi92), Pike County, Kentucky. In *Current Archaeological Research in Kentucky*, vol. 5, edited by Charles D. Hockensmith, Kenneth C. Carstens, Charles Stout, and Sara J. Rivers, 83–120. Kentucky Heritage Council, Frankfort.

Kerr, Jonathan P., Steven D. Creasman, Gary D. Crites, and Albert M. Pecora
1995 *Phase III Investigations at the Martin Justice Site (15Pi92) Pike County, Kentucky*. Cultural Resource Analysts, Lexington, Ky.

Kidder, Tristram R.
2002 Woodland Period Archaeology of the Lower Mississippi Valley. In *The Woodland Southeast*, edited by David G. Anderson and Robert C. Mainfort Jr., 66–90. University of Alabama Press, Tuscaloosa.
2006 Climate Change and the Archaic to Woodland Transition (3000–2500 cal B.P.) in the Mississippi River Basin. *American Antiquity* 71: 195–231.
2011 Transforming Hunter-Gatherer History at Poverty Point. In *Hunter-Gatherer Archaeology as Historical Process*, edited by Kenneth E. Sassaman and Donald H. Holly Jr., 95–119. University of Arizona Press, Tucson.

Kidder, Tristram R., Lori Roe, and Timothy M. Schilling
2010 Early Woodland Settlement and Mound Building in the Upper Tensas Basin, Northeast Louisiana. *Southeastern Archaeology* 29: 121–45.

Kimball, Larry R.
1988 Archaeological Investigations at Cumberland Ford I (15Bl59). Draft report prepared for DuVall and Associates, Franklin, Tenn.

Kimball, Larry R., and Derek Johnson
2012 The ritualized landscape at Biltmore Mound. Paper presented at the 77th Annual Meeting of the Society for American Archaeology, Memphis, Tennessee.

Kimball, Larry R., Thomas R. Whyte, and Gary D. Crites
2010   The Biltmore Mound and Hopewellian Mound Use in the Southern Appalachians. *Southeastern Archaeology* 29: 44–58.
King, Adam, Chester P. Walker, Robert V. Sharp, F. Kent Reilly, and Duncan P. McKinnon
2011   Remote Sensing Data from Etowah's Mound A: Architecture and the Re-Creation of the Mississippian Tradition. *American Antiquity* 76: 355–71.
Kline, Gerald W., Gary D. Crites, and Charles H. Faulkner
1982   *The McFarland Project: Early Middle Woodland Settlement and Subsistence in the Upper Duck River Valley in Tennessee.* Miscellaneous Paper no. 8. Tennessee Anthropological Association, Knoxville.
Knapp, A. Bernard, and Wendy Ashmore
1999   Archaeological Landscapes: Constructed, Conceptualized, Ideational. In *Archaeologies of Landscape: Contemporary Perspectives,* edited by Wendy Ashmore and A. Bernard Knapp, 1–32. Blackwell, Malden, Mass.
Kneberg, Madeline
1961   Four Southeastern Limestone-Tempered Pottery Complexes. *Newsletter of the Southeastern Archaeological Conference* 7: 3–15.
Knight, Vernon James, Jr.
1990   *Excavation of the Truncated Mound at the Walling Site: Middle Woodland Culture and Copena in the Tennessee Valley.* Office of Archaeological Research, Alabama State Museum of Natural History, Huntsville.
2001   Feasting and the Emergence of Platform Mound Ceremonialism in Eastern North America. In *Feasts: Archaeological and Ethnographic Perspectives on Food, Politics, and Power,* edited by Michael Dietler and Brian Hayden, 311–33. Smithsonian Institution Press, Washington, D.C.
2007   Conclusions: Taking Architecture Seriously. In *Architectural Variability in the Southeast,* edited by Cameron H. Lacquement, 186–92. University of Alabama Press, Tuscaloosa.
Knudsen, Gary D.
1985   Testing of Vandalized Sites, Is It Worth It? Two Woodland Examples. In *Woodland Period Research in Kentucky,* edited by David Pollack, 93–109. Kentucky Heritage Council, Frankfort.
Kolb, Michael J., Ross Cordy, Timothy Earle, Gary Feinman, Michael W. Graves, Christine A. Hastorf, Ian Hodder, John M. Micik, Barbara J. Price, Bruce G. Trigger, and Valerio Valeri
1994   Monumentality and the Rise of Religious Authority in Precontact Hawai'i [and Comments and Reply]. *Current Anthropology* 35: 521–47.
Kowalewski, Stephen A.
2008   Regional Settlement Pattern Studies. *Journal of Anthropological Research* 16: 225–85.
Kozarek, Sue Ellen
1997   Determining Sedentism in the Archaeological Record. In *Ohio Hopewell Community Organization,* edited by William S. Dancey and Paul J. Pacheco, 131–52. Kent State University Press, Kent, Ohio.
Kreisa, Paul P.
1987   Late Prehistoric Settlement Patterns in the Big Bottoms of Fulton County, Kentucky. In *Current Archaeological Research in Kentucky,* vol. 1, edited by David Pollack, 78–99. Kentucky Heritage Council, Frankfort.
1988   Second-Order Mississippian Communities in Western Kentucky. In *New Deal Era Archaeology and Current Research in Kentucky,* edited by David Pollack and Mary Lucas Powell, 162–71. Kentucky Heritage Council, Frankfort.

Kreisa, Paul P., and Charles Stout
1991   Trends and Trajectory in Western Kentucky Woodland Period Settlement Patterning. In *The Human Landscape in Kentucky's Past: Site Structure and Settlement Patterns*, edited by Charles Stout and Christine K. Hensley, 98–105. Kentucky Heritage Council, Frankfort.

Kvamme, Kenneth L.
1999   Recent Directions and Developments in Geographical Information Systems. *Journal of Archaeological Research* 7: 153–201.
2003   Geophysical Surveys as Landscape Archaeology. *American Antiquity* 68 (3): 435–58.

Kvamme, Kenneth, Jay K. Johnson, and Bryan S. Haley
2006   Multiple Methods Surveys: Case Studies. In *Remote Sensing in Archaeology: An Explicitly North American Perspective*, edited by Jay K. Johnson, 251–67. University of Alabama Press, Tuscaloosa.

KYTC
1952   Aerial Photograph of North Elkhorn Creek Area, Fayette County, Kentucky, March 1952. Photograph on file, Kentucky Transportation Cabinet, Frankfort.
1959   Aerial Photograph of North Elkhorn Creek Area, Fayette County, Kentucky, October 1959. Photograph on file, Kentucky Transportation Cabinet, Frankfort.

Lafferty, Robert H., III
1978   The Early Woodland Chronological and Cultural Affinities at Phipps Bend on the Holston River, Northeast Tennessee. *Journal of Alabama Archaeology* 24: 132–50.

Langston, Lucinda M., Meagan E. Dennison, and Jay D. Franklin
2010   Archaeological Testing at York Palace (40Fn220), Pogue Creek State Natural Area. Paper presented at the 22nd Annual Current Research in Tennessee Archaeology Meeting, Nashville.

Langston, Lucinda M., and Jay D. Franklin
2010   Archaeological Survey of Pogue Creek State Natural Area: A GIS Perspective. Paper presented at the 67th Annual Meeting of the Southeastern Archaeological Conference, Lexington, Ky.

Larson, Lewis H., Jr.
1972   Functional Considerations of Warfare in the Southeast during the Mississippi Period. *American Antiquity* 37: 383–93.

LeBlanc, Steven A.
1999   *Prehistoric Warfare in the American Southwest*. University of Utah Press, Salt Lake City.

Ledbetter, R. Jerald, and Lisa D. O'Steen
1992   The Grayson Site: Late Archaic and Late Woodland Occupations in the Little Sandy Drainage. In *Current Archaeological Research in Kentucky*,: vol. 2, edited by David Pollack and A. Gwynn Henderson, 13–42. Kentucky Heritage Council, Frankfort.

Ledbetter, R. Jerald, Andrea Shea, and Stan de Filippis
1991   *The Grayson Site: Phase III Investigations of 15Cr73, Carter County, Kentucky*. Southeastern Archaeological Services, Athens, Ga.

Lekson, Stephen H.
1996   Landscape with Ruins: Archaeological Approaches to Built and Unbuilt environments. *Current Anthropology* 37: 886–92.

Lepper, Bradley T.
2004   The Newark Earthworks. In *Hero, Hawk, and Open Hand: American Indian Art of the Ancient Midwest and South*, edited by Richard F. Townsend and Robert V. Sharp, 73–81. Yale University Press, New Haven, Conn.

Lévi-Strauss, Claude
1963   *Structural Anthropology.* Translated by C. Jacobson and B. C. Schoepf. Basic Books, New York.
Lewis, R. Barry
1988   Fires on the Bayou: Cultural Adaptations in the Mississippi Sound Region. *Southeastern Archaeology* 7: 109–23.
Lewis, R. Barry, Charles Stout, and Cameron Wesson
1998   The Design of Mississippian Towns. In *Mississippian Towns and Sacred Places: Searching for an Architectural Grammar,* edited by R. Barry Lewis and Charles Stout, 1–21. University of Alabama Press, Tuscaloosa.
Lewis, T. M. N., and Madeline Kneberg
1957   The Camp Creek Site. *Tennessee Anthropologist* 13: 1–48.
Lightfoot, Kent G., Antoinette Martinez, and Ann M. Schiff
1998   Daily Practice and Material Culture in Pluralistic Social Settings: An Archaeological Study of Culture Change and Persistence from Fort Ross, California. *American Antiquity* 63: 199–222.
Lindauer, Owen, and John H. Blitz
1997   Higher Ground: The Archaeology of North American Platform Mounds. *Journal of Archaeological Research* 5: 169–207.
Linden, Blanche
2007   *Silent City on a Hill.* University of Massachusetts Press, Amherst.
Littleton, Judith, and Harry Allen
2007   Hunter-Gatherer Burials and the Creation of Persistent Places in Southeastern Australia. *Journal of Anthropological Archaeology* 26: 283–98.
Livingood, Patrick C.
2009   Down the River and Through the Woods: Cost-Distance Calculations of Travel Time in the Mississippian. Paper presented at the 74th Annual Meeting of the Society for American Archaeology, Atlanta, Ga.
Lloyd, Timothy C.
1998   A Reconstruction of the Adena Site. *West Virginia Archaeologist* 50: 14–25.
Logan, Brad, and Matthew E. Hill Jr.
2000   Spatial Analysis of Small Scale Debris from a Late Prehistoric Site in the Lower Missouri Valley, Kansas. *Journal of Field Archaeology* 27: 241–56.
Loren, Diana DiPaolo
2008   *In Contact: Bodies and Spaces in the Sixteenth- and Seventeenth-Century Eastern Woodlands.* AltaMira Press, Lanham, Md.
Lydick, Christopher M.
2008   Sensor Fusion: Integrated Remote Sensing Surveys at Shiloh Mounds National Historic Landmark, Shiloh, Tennessee. M.A. thesis, Department of Anthropology, Florida State University, Tallahassee.
Mainfort, Robert C., Jr.
1988   Middle Woodland Ceremonialism at Pinson Mounds, Tennessee. *American Antiquity* 53: 158–73.
1989   Adena Chiefdoms? Evidence from the Wright Mound. *Midcontinental Journal of Archaeology* 14: 164–78.
Mainfort, Robert C., Jr., Mary L. Kwas, and Andrew M. Mickelson
2011   Mapping Never-Never Land: An Examination of Pinson Mounds Cartography. *Southeastern Archaeology* 30: 148–65.
Mainfort, Robert C., Jr., and Lynne P. Sullivan (editors)
1998   *Ancient Earthen Enclosures of the Eastern Woodlands.* University Press of Florida, Gainesville.

Maki, David, and Ross C. Fields
2010   Multisensor Geophysical Survey Results from the Pine Tree Mound Site: A Comparison of Geophysical and Excavation Data. *Southeastern Archaeology* 29: 292–309.

Mann, Rob
2005   Intruding on the Past: The Reuse of Ancient Earthen Mounds by Native Americans. *Southeastern Archaeology* 24: 1–11.

Marcoux, Jon Bernard, and Gregory D. Wilson
2010   Categories of Complexity and the Preclusion of Practice. In *Ancient Complexities: New Perspectives in Precolumbian North America*, edited by Susan M. Alt, 138–52. University of Utah Press, Salt Lake City.

Marquardt, William H.
1970   Archaeological Investigations in the Cave Run Reservoir, Kentucky: 1969 Season. Ms. on file, Department of Anthropology, University of Kentucky, Lexington.

Maslowski, Robert F., Charles M. Niquette, and Derek M. Wingfield
1995   The Kentucky, Ohio and West Virginia Radiocarbon Database. *West Virginia Archaeologist* 47(1–2).

Matternes, Hugh M., Linda Kennedy, R. Jeannine Windham, and Valerie Davis
2007   Zooarchaeology and Physical Anthropology from the Leake Sites. In *Archaeological Data Recovery at the Leake Site, Bartow County, Georgia*, vol. 2, *Appendices*, 6–111. Southern Research Historic Preservation Consultants, Ellerslie, Ga.

McAnany, Patricia A., and Ian Hodder
2009   Thinking about Stratigraphic Sequence in Social Terms. *Archaeological Dialogues* 16: 1–22.

McBride, Kim A. (editor)
1994   *Archaeological Investigations at the McKenzie Farmstead (15Jo67): A Multiple Component Occupation in Johnson County, Kentucky.* Archaeological Report no. 334. Program for Cultural Resource Assessment, University of Kentucky, Lexington.

McCollough, Major C. R., and Charles H. Faulkner
1973   *Excavation of the Higgs and Doughty Sites, I-75 Salvage Archaeology.* Tennessee Archaeological Society, Knoxville.

McGimsey, Charles R.
2010   Marksville and Middle Woodland. In *Archaeology of Louisiana*, edited by Mark A. Rees, 120–34. Louisiana State University Press, Baton Rouge.

McGrain, Preston, and James C. Currens
1978   *Topography of Kentucky.* Kentucky Geological Survey, University of Kentucky, Lexington.

McKinley, William
1873   Mounds in Georgia. Smithsonian Annual Report for 1872. Washington, D.C.

McKinnon, Duncan P.
2009   Exploring Settlement Patterning at a Premier Caddo Mound Site in the Red River Great Bend Region. *Southeastern Archaeology* 29: 248–58.
2010   Continuing the Research: Archaeogeophysical Investigations at the Battle Mound Site (3LA1) in Lafayette County, Arkansas. *Southeastern Archaeology* 29: 250–60.

Merrell, James H.
1984   The Indians' New World: The Catawba Experience. *William and Mary Quarterly* 41: 537–65.
1989   *The Indians' New World: The Catawba and Their Neighbors from European Contact through the Era of Removal.* University of North Carolina Press, Chapel Hill.

Mickelson, Andrew M.
2002   Changes in Prehistoric Settlement Patterns as a Result of Shifts in Subsistence Practices in

Eastern Kentucky. Unpublished Ph.D. dissertation, Department of Anthropology, Ohio State University, Columbus.

Middleton, James D.

1883 Material Concerning the Archaeology of Bartow County, Georgia. Manuscript 2400, Box 2, Georgia, Smithsonian Institution National Anthropological Archives, Smithsonian Museum Support Center, Suitland, Md.

Milanich, Jerald T.

1980 Weeden Island Studies—Past, Present, and Future. *Southeastern Archaeological Conference Bulletin* 22: 11–18.

1994 *The Archaeology of Precolumbian Florida*. University Press of Florida, Gainesville.

1999 Introduction. In *Famous Florida Sites: Crystal River and Mount Royal*, edited by Jerald T. Milanich, 1–27. University Press of Florida, Gainesville.

2002 Weeden Island Cultures. In *The Woodland Southeast*, edited by David G. Anderson and Robert C. Mainfort Jr., 353–72. University of Alabama Press, Tuscaloosa.

2004 Prehistory of Florida after 500 B.C. In *Smithsonian Handbook of North American Indians*, vol. 14, *The Southeast*, edited by Raymond D. Fogelson, 191–203. Smithsonian Institution, Washington, D.C.

Milanich, Jerald T., Ann S. Cordell, Vernon J. Knight Jr., Timothy A. Kohler, and Brenda J. Sigler-Lavelle

1984 *McKeithen Weeden Island, the Culture of Northern Florida, A.D. 200–900*. Academic Press, Orlando, Fla.

1997 *Archaeology of Northern Florida, A.D. 200–900: The McKeithen Weeden Island Culture*. University Press of Florida, Gainesville.

Mills, Barbara J.

2009 From the Ground Up: Depositional History, Memory and Materiality. *Archaeological Dialogues* 16: 38–40.

Mills, Barbara J., and William H. Walker (editors)

2008 *Memory Work: Archaeologies of Material Practices*. School for Advanced Research Press, Santa Fe, N.Mex.

Mills, W. C.

1922 Exploration of the Mound City Group. *Ohio Archaeological and Historical Society Quarterly* 18: 269–321.

Milner, Claire McHale, and John M. O'Shea

1998 The Socioeconomic Role of Late Woodland Enclosures in Northern Lower Michigan. In *Ancient Earthen Enclosures of the Eastern Woodlands*, edited by Robert C. Mainfort Jr. and Lynne P. Sullivan, 181–201. University Press of Florida, Gainesville.

Milner, George

2004 *The Moundbuilders: Ancient Peoples of Eastern North America*. Thames and Hudson, London.

Milner, George R., and Richard W. Jefferies

1987 A Re-examination of the W.P.A. Excavation of the Robbins Mound in Boone County, Kentucky. In *Current Archaeological Research in Kentucky*, vol. 1, edited by David Pollack, 33–42. Kentucky Heritage Council, Frankfort.

1991 A Reevaluation of the WPA Excavations of the Robbins Mound in Boone County, Kentucky. In *The Human Landscape in Kentucky's Past*, edited by Charles Stout and Charles Hensley, 33–43. Kentucky Heritage Council, Frankfort.

Milner, George R., and Virginia G. Smith

1986 *New Deal Archaeology in Kentucky: Excavations, Collections, and Research*. Occasional Papers in Anthropology 5. Program for Cultural Resource Assessment, University of Kentucky, Lexington.

Mocas, Stephen T.
n.d. Early Woodland and Middle Woodland Occupations at the Knob Creek Site (12Hr484). Ms. on file, Anthropology Laboratory, Indiana State University, Terre Haute.
1977 Excavations at the Lawrence Site (15Tr33), Trigg County, Kentucky. Ms. on file, University of Louisville Archaeological Survey, Louisville, Ky.
1991a Early Pottery in the Lower Tennessee-Cumberland Region: An Examination of the Ceramics from the Lawrence Site, Trigg County, Kentucky. In *Studies in Kentucky Archaeology*, 102–18. Kentucky Heritage Council, Frankfort.
1991b *Excavations at the Lawrence Site (15Tr33), Trigg County, Kentucky*. University of Louisville Archaeological Survey, Louisville, Ky.
2007 Early and Middle Woodland Structures in the Caesars Archaeological Project Area. Paper presented at the 24th Annual Kentucky Heritage Council Archaeological Conference, Natural Bridge, Kentucky.

Mocas, Stephen T., Michael W. French, and Duane B. Simpson
2010 *Intensive Archaeological Investigations at the McAlpine Locks and Dam, Louisville, Kentucky*, vol. 1, *Project Background and Investigations of the Late Archaic and Woodland Components at the Shippingport Site (15Jf702)*. CRM Report no. 2009-17. AMEC Earth and Environment, Louisville, Ky.

Mooney, James
1900 *Myths of the Cherokee*. Nineteenth Annual Report, Bureau of American Ethnology, Smithsonian Institution, Washington, D.C.

Moore, Clarence B.
1899 Certain Aboriginal Remains of the Alabama River. *Journal of the Academy of Natural Sciences of Philadelphia* 11: 289–348.
1902 Certain Aboriginal Remains of the Northwest Florida Coast, Part II. *Journal of the Academy of Natural Sciences of Philadelphia* 12: 127–358.
1903 Certain Aboriginal Mounds of the Central Florida West-Coast. *Journal of the Academy of Natural Sciences of Philadelphia* 12: 361–438.

Moore, David G.
1982 Test Excavations at Indian Fort Mountain, Berea, Kentucky. Paper presented at the 39th Annual Meeting of the Southeastern Archaeological Conference, Memphis, Tenn.
1984 Biltmore Estate Archaeological Survey Final Report. Technical report on file, North Carolina Department of Archives and History, Raleigh.
1992 Salvage Archaeology at the Cullowhee Valley School. *Newsletter of the North Carolina Archaeological Society* 2 (2): 1–2.

Moulton, Gary E. (editor)
1986 *The Definitive Journals of Lewis and Clark*. University of Nebraska Press, Lincoln.

Munn, Nancy D.
1990 Constructing Regional Worlds in Experience, Kula Exchange, Witchcraft, and Gawan Local Events. *Man* 25: 1–17.

Munson, Patrick J.
1986 Black Sand and Havana Tradition Ceramic Assemblages and Culture History in the Central Illinois River Valley. In *Early Woodland Archaeology*, edited by Kenneth B. Farnsworth and Thomas E. Emerson, 280–300. Kampsville Seminar in Archeology, vol. 2. Center for American Archeology, Kampsville, Ill.

Murphy, James L.

1989 *An Archaeological History of the Hocking Valley.* Ohio University Press, Athens.

Myer, W. E.

n.d. *Catalogue of Archaeological Remains in Tennessee.* Unpublished Manuscript on File at the Smithsonian Institution, Washington, D.C., and the Tennessee Division of Archaeology, Nashville.

1971 *Indian Trails of the Southeast.* Reproduction of *49th Annual Report,* Bureau of American Ethnology, Smithsonian Institution, Washington, D.C. Blue and Grey Press, Nashville, Tenn.

Nance, Jack D.

1974 *Ancient Men in the Land between the Lakes.* Tennessee Valley Authority, Nashville, Tenn.

Nance, Roger C.

1976 *The Archaeological Sequence at Durant Bend, Dallas County, Alabama.* Special Publications no. 22. Alabama Archaeological Society, Orange Beach.

Nance, Roger C., and E. Hollis Mentzer

1980 Changing Woodland Ceramic Functions and Technologies on the Northern Gulf Coastal Plain. *Southeastern Archaeological Conference Bulletin* 8: 51–55.

Nature

2009 Data's Shameful Neglect. *Nature* 461: 145.

Nelson, Nels C.

1917a Archaeology of Mammoth Cave and Vicinity: A Preliminary Report. *Scientific American* 83 (2157): 275.

1917b *Contributions to the Archaeology of Mammoth Cave and Vicinity, Kentucky.* Anthropological Papers no. 22 (1). American Museum of Natural History, New York.

Niquette, Charles M.

1989 *Phase III Investigations at the Graham Site, a Stratified Archaic/Woodland Site in the Proposed Yatesville Reservoir in Lawrence County, Kentucky.* Cultural Resource Analysts, Lexington, Ky.

1992 Woodland Settlement Patterns in the Kentucky/West Virginia Border Region. In *Cultural Continuity in Context: Woodland Settlements of the Mid-Ohio Valley,* edited by Mark F. Seeman, 15–18. Kent State University Press, Kent, Ohio.

Niquette, Charles M., and Randall D. Boedy

1986 *The Calloway Site (15Mt8): A Transitional Early to Middle Woodland Camp in Martin County, Kentucky.* Cultural Resource Analysts, Lexington, Ky.

Niquette, Charles M., Randall D. Boedy, Jonathan P. Kerr, Kristen J. Gremillion, and Paula Cross

1987 *National Register Evaluations of Thirteen Prehistoric Sites in the Proposed Yatesville Reservoir Area, Lawrence County, Kentucky.* Cultural Resource Analysts, Lexington, Ky.

Northwest Florida Environmental Conservancy

2006 Steepheads. Electronic document. http://www.nwflec.com/northwestfloridaenvironmental conservancypart2/id12.html. Accessed 2010.

O'Connell, James F.

1987 Alyawara Site Structure and Its Archaeological Implications. *American Antiquity* 52: 74–108.

O'Connell, James F., Kristen Hawkes, and Nicholas Blurton Jones

1991 Distribution of Refuse-Producing Activities at Hadza Residential Base Camps: Implications for Analysis of Archaeological Site Structure. In *The Interpretation of Archaeological Spatial Patterning,* edited by Ellen M. Kroll and T. Douglas Price, 61–76. Plenum Press, New York.

Odell, George H.
1994   The Role of Stone Bladelets in Middle Woodland Society. *American Antiquity* 59: 102–4.
O'Steen, Lisa D., Kristen J. Gremillion, and R. Jerald Ledbetter
1991   *Archaeological Testing of Five Sites in the Big Sinking Creek Oil Field, Lee County, Kentucky.* Southeastern Archaeological Services, Atlanta, Ga.
Ottesen, Ann I.
1985   Woodland Settlement Patterns in Northwestern Kentucky. In *Woodland Period Research in Kentucky,* edited by David Pollack, Thomas Sanders, and Charles Hockensmith, 166–86. Kentucky Heritage Council, Frankfort.
Otvos, E. G., Jr.
1972   Mississippi Gulf Coast Pleistocene Beach Barriers and the Age Problem of the Atlantic-Gulf Coast "Pamilco"—"Ingleside" Beach Ridge System. *Southeastern Geology* 14: 241–49.
1975   Late Pleistocene Transgressive Unit (Biloxi Formation), Northern Gulf Coast. *Bulletin of the American Association of Petroleum Geologists* 59: 148–54.
Pace, Robert A., and Christopher T. Hays
1991   Perspectives on Prehistoric Settlement in the Cumberland Plateau: The View from Station Camp. *Tennessee Anthropologist* 16: 115–49.
Palmer, Edward
1884   Mercier Mounds, Early County, Georgia. Report prepared for the Bureau of Ethnology Mound Survey, Smithsonian Institution. On file at the National Anthropological Archives, American Museum of Natural History, Smithsonian Institution, Washington, D.C.
Parkinson, William A. (editor)
2002a *The Archaeology of Tribal Societies.* International Monographs in Prehistory, Archaeological Series 15. Ann Arbor, Michigan.
Parkinson, William A.
2002b Introduction: Archaeology and Tribal Societies. In *The Archaeology of Tribal Societies,* edited by William A. Parkinson, 1–12. International Monographs in Prehistory, Archaeological Series 15. Ann Arbor, Michigan.
Parsons, Jeffrey R.
1972   Archaeological Settlement Patterns. *Annual Review of Anthropology* 1: 127–50.
Pauketat, Timothy R.
1994   *The Ascent of Chiefs: Cahokia and Mississippian Politics in Native North America.* University of Alabama Press, Tuscaloosa.
1997   Cahokian Political Economy. In *Cahokia: Domination and Ideology in the Mississippian World,* edited by Timothy R. Pauketat and Thomas E. Emerson, 30–51. University of Nebraska Press, Lincoln.
2001   Practice and History in Archaeology: An Emerging Paradigm. *Anthropological Theory* 1: 73–98.
2004a *Ancient Cahokia and the Mississippians.* Cambridge University Press, Cambridge.
2004b The Economy of the Moment: Cultural Practices and Mississippian Chiefdoms. In *Archaeological Perspectives on Political Economies,* edited by Gary M. Feinman and Linda M. Nicholas, 25–39. University of Utah Press, Salt Lake City.
2007   *Chiefdoms and Other Archaeological Delusions.* AltaMira Press, Lanham, Md.
Pauketat, Timothy R., and Susan M. Alt
2005   Agency in a Postmold: Physicality and the Archaeology of Culture-Making. *Journal of Archaeological Method and Theory* 12: 213–36.

Pearson, Mike, and Michael Shanks
2001   *Theatre/Archaeology*. Routledge, New York.
Percy, George, and David S. Brose
1974   Weeden Island Ecology: Subsistence and Village Life in Northwest Florida. Paper presented at the 39th Annual Meeting of the Society for American Archaeology, Washington, D.C.
Perttula, Timothy K.
1997   *The Caddo Nation: Archaeological and Ethnohistoric Perspectives*. University of Texas Press, Austin.
Perttula, Timothy K., Chester P. Walker, and T. Clay Schultz
2008   A Revolution in Caddo Archaeology: The Remote Sensing and Archaeological View from the Hill Farm Site (41BW169) in Bowie County, Texas. *Southeastern Archaeology* 27: 93–107.
Peter, Robert
1873a Ancient Mound, near Lexington, Kentucky. In *Annual Report for 1871*, 420–23. Smithsonian Institution, Washington, D.C.
1873b Ancient Mounds in Kentucky. In *Annual Report for 1872*, 420–21. Smithsonian Institution, Washington, D.C.
Phillips, Philip
1970   *Archaeological Survey of the Lower Yazoo Basin, Mississippi, 1949–1955*. Papers of the Peabody Museum of Archaeology and Ethnology, Harvard University, vol. 60. Cambridge, Mass.
Pickett, A. J.
1851   *History of Alabama and Incidentally of Georgia and Mississippi*. Birmingham Magazine Company, Birmingham, Ala.
Pluckhahn, Thomas J.
1998   Highway 61 Revisited: Archeological Evaluation of Eight Sites in Bartow County, Georgia. Submitted to Georgia Department of Transportation, Office of Environment/Location, Atlanta by Southeastern Archeological Services, Inc., Athens, Ga.
2003   *Kolomoki: Settlement, Ceremony, and Status in the Deep South, A.D. 350 to 750*. University of Alabama Press, Tuscaloosa.
Pluckhahn, Thomas J., J. Matthew Compton, and Mary Theresa Bonhage-Freund
2006   Evidence of Small-Scale Feasting from the Woodland Period Site of Kolomoki, Georgia. *Journal of Field Archaeology* 31: 263–84.
Pluckhahn, Thomas J., and Ann S. Cordell
2010   Paste Characterization of Weeden Island Pottery from the Kolomoki Site, Georgia. Paper presented at the 75th Annual Meeting of the Society for American Archaeology, St. Louis, Mo.
Pluckhahn, Thomas J., and Victor D. Thompson
2009   Mapping Crystal River: Past, Present, and Future. *Florida Anthropologist* 62: 3–22.
Pluckhahn, Thomas J., Victor D. Thompson, Nicolas Laracuente, Sarah Mitchell, Amanda Roberts, and Adrianne Sams
2009   Archaeological Investigations at the Famous Crystal River Site (8CI1) (2008 Field Season), Citrus County, Florida. Department of Anthropology, University of South Florida, Tampa. Submitted to Bureau of Natural and Cultural Resources, Division of Recreation and Parks, Florida Department of Environmental Protection, Tallahassee.
Pluckhahn, Thomas J., Victor D. Thompson, and Brent R. Weisman
2010   A New View of History and Process at Crystal River (8CI1). *Southeastern Archaeology* 29: 164–81.

Pollack, David
1993   Beta Analytic Report of Radiocarbon Dates for the Slack Farm Site (15Un28). Report in author's possession, Lexington, Ky.
Pollack, David (editor)
2008   *The Archaeology of Kentucky: An Update.* Kentucky Heritage Council State Historic Preservation Comprehensive Plan, Report no. 3. Frankfort.
Pollack, David, and A. Gwynn Henderson
2000   Late Woodland Cultures in Kentucky. In *Late Woodland Societies: Tradition and Transformation across the Midcontinent,* edited by Thomas E. Emerson, Dale L. McElrath, and Andrew C. Fortier, 613–42. University of Nebraska Press, Lincoln.
Pollack, David, Eric J. Schlarb, William E. Sharp, and Teresa W. Tune
2005   Walker-Noe: An Early Middle Woodland Mound in Central Kentucky. In *Woodland Period Systematics in the Middle Ohio Valley,* edited by Darlene Applegate and Robert C. Mainfort Jr., 64–75. University of Alabama Press, Tuscaloosa.
Prentice, Guy
1993   *Archeological Overview and Assessment of Mammoth Cave National Park.* National Park Service, Southeast Archeological Center, Tallahassee, Fla.
1996   Site Distribution Modeling for Mammoth Cave National Park. In *Of Caves and Shell Mounds,* edited by Kenneth C. Carstens and Patty Jo Watson, 12–32. University of Alabama Press, Tuscaloosa.
Prezzano, Susan C.
1988   Spatial Analysis of Post Mold Patterns at the Sackett Site, Ontario County, New York. *Man in the Northeast* 35: 27–45.
Price, George D.
1999   A Case for Increasing Sedentism in the Middle Woodland Prehistory of East Central Alabama. Unpublished master's thesis, University of Alabama at Birmingham.
Pritchard, Erin E.
2008   Deep Cave Mining: Archaeological and GIS Investigations of a Prehistoric Gypsum Mine at Hubbards Cave. In *Cave Archaeology of the Eastern Woodlands: Essays in Honor of Patty Jo Watson,* edited by David H. Dye, 97–116. University of Tennessee Press, Knoxville.
Prufer, Olaf H.
1964   The Hopewell Complex of Ohio. In *Hopewellian Studies,* edited by Joseph R. Caldwell and Robert L. Hall, 35–83. Scientific Papers, vol. 12. Illinois State Museum, Springfield.
Pursell, Corin
2004   Geographic Distribution and Symbolism of Colored Mound Architecture in the Mississippian Southeast. M.A. thesis, Department of Anthropology, Southern Illinois University, Carbondale.
Rafferty, Janet
1990   Test Excavations at Ingomar Mounds, Mississippi. *Southeastern Archaeology* 9: 93–102.
Rafferty, Sean M.
2005   The Many Messages of Death: Mortuary Practices in the Ohio Valley and Northeast. In *Woodland Period Systematics in the Middle Ohio Valley,* edited by Darlene Applegate and Robert C. Mainfort Jr., 150–67. University of Alabama Press, Tuscaloosa.
Rafinesque, Constantine S.
1820   Map of the Lower Alleghawee Monuments on North Elkhorn Creek. Manuscript on file, Special Collections, Margaret I. King Library, University of Kentucky, Lexington.
1821   Alleghawee Antiquities of Fayette County, Ky. *Western Minerva* 1: 53–57.

Railey, Jimmy A.
1991   Woodland Settlement Trends and Symbolic Architecture in the Kentucky Bluegrass. In *The Human Landscape in Kentucky's Past: Site Structure and Settlement Patterns*, edited by Charles Stout and Christine K. Hensley, 56–77. Kentucky Heritage Council, Frankfort.
1996   Woodland Cultivators. In *Kentucky Archaeology*, edited by R. Barry Lewis, 79–125. University of Kentucky Press, Lexington.

Redmond, Elsa M.
1998   The Dynamics of Chieftaincy and the Development of Chiefdoms. In *Chiefdoms and Chieftaincy in the Americas*, edited by Elsa M. Redmon, 1–17. University Press of Florida, Gainesville.

Reimer, P. J., M. G. L. Baillie, E. Bard, A. Bayliss, J. W. Beck, C. J. H. Bertrand, P. G. Blackwell, et al.
2004   IntCal04 Terrestrial Radiocarbon Age Calibration, 26–0 ka BP. *Radiocarbon* 46: 1029–58.

Reimer, P. J., M. G. L. Baillie, E. Bard, A. Bayliss, J. W. Beck, P. G. Blackwell, C. Bronk Ramsey, et al.
2009   IntCal09 and Marine09 Radiocarbon Age Calibration Curves, 0–50,000 years cal BP. *Radiocarbon* 51: 1111–50.

Renfrew, Colin
1973   Monuments, Mobilization and Social Organization in Neolithic Wessex. In *The Explanation of Culture Change: Models in Prehistory*, edited by Colin Renfrew, 539–59. University of Pittsburgh Press, Pittsburgh.

Reynolds, Fjion
2009   Regenerating Substances: Quartz as an Animistic Agent. *Time and Mind: The Journal of Archaeology, Consciousness and Culture* 2: 153–66.

Richmond, Michael D., and Jonathan P. Kerr
2005   Middle Woodland Ritualism in the Central Bluegrass. In *Woodland Period Systematics in the Middle Ohio Valley*, 76–93. University of Alabama Press, Tuscaloosa.

Richmond, Michael D., Jonathan P. Kerr, Renee Bonzani, R. Berle Clay, and Jessica Allgood
2002   *Phase II National Register Evaluation of the Cain Farmstead (15Mg33), the Short Fork Site (15Mg38), the Prime Farmland Site (15Fd78), and the Prater Site (15Fd81) in Magoffin and Floyd Counties, Kentucky*. Cultural Resource Analysts, Lexington, Ky.

Riede, Felix
2009   Climate and Demography in Early Prehistory: Using Calibrated 14C Dates as Population Proxies. *Human Biology* 81: 309–37.

Robinson, Kenneth W., and Steven D. Smith
1979   The Villier Site (15Jf110 Complex). In *Excavations at Four Archaic Sites in the Lower Ohio Valley, Jefferson County, Kentucky*, edited by Michael B. Collins, 590–696. Department of Anthropology, University of Kentucky, Lexington.

Rodning, Christopher
2010   Place, Landscape, and Environment: Anthropological Archaeology in 2009. *American Anthropologist* 112: 180–90.

Rogan, John P.
1883   Notes on Mounds in Georgia. Inventory of the George E. Stuart Collection of Archaeological and Other Materials, 1733–2006, Collection Number 5268, Wilson Library, University of North Carolina, Chapel Hill.

Rolingson, Martha A., and Michael J. Rodeffer
1968   The Zilpo Site, Bh 37: Preliminary Excavations in the Cave Run Reservoir, Kentucky, 1968. Report on file, Office of State Archaeology, University of Kentucky, Lexington.

Rolingson, Martha A., and Douglas W. Schwartz
1966   *Late PaleoIndian and Early Archaic Manifestations in Western Kentucky*. University of Kentucky Press, Lexington.

Romain, William F.
2000 *Mysteries of the Hopewell: Astronomers, Geometers, and Magicians of the Eastern Woodlands.* University of Akron Press, Akron, Ohio.
2009 *Shamans of the Lost World: A Cognitive Approach to the Prehistoric Religion of the Ohio Hopewell.* AltaMira Press, Lanham, Md.

Rossen, Jack
2007 Evans Site Archaeobotanical Remains. Ms. on file, Kentucky Archaeological Survey, Lexington.

Ross-Stallings, Nancy, and Richard Stallings
2007 Middle Woodland Settlement Patterning and Cultural Influences in Central Kentucky. Paper presented at the 24th Annual Kentucky Heritage Council Archaeological Conference, Natural Bridge, Ky.

Ruby, Bret J.
1997 The Mann Phase: Hopewellian Subsistence and Settlement Adaptations in the Wabash Lowlands of Southwestern Indiana. Unpublished doctoral dissertation, Indiana University, Bloomington.
2006 The Mann Phase: Hopewellian Subsistence and Settlement in the Wabash Lowland. In *Recreating Hopewell,* edited by Douglas K. Charles and Jane E. Buikstra, 190–205. University Press of Florida, Gainesville.

Ruby, Bret J., Christopher Carr, and Douglas K. Charles
2005 Community Organizations in the Scioto, Mann, and Havana Regions: A Comparative Perspective. In *Gathering Hopewell: Society, Ritual, and Ritual Interaction,* edited by Christopher Carr and D. Troy Case, 119–76. Kluwer Academic, New York.

Ruby, Bret J., and Christine M. Shriner
2005 Ceramic Vessel Compositions and Styles as Evidence of the Local and Nonlocal Social Affiliations of Ritual Participants at the Mann Site, Indiana. In *Gathering Hopewell: Society, Ritual, and Ritual Interaction,* edited by Christopher Carr and D. Troy Case, 553–72. Kluwer Academic, New York.

Ruhl, Katharine C.
2005 Hopewellian Copper Earspools from Eastern North America: Their Social, Ritual, and Symbolic Significance of Their Contexts and Distribution. In *Gathering Hopewell: Society, Ritual, and Ritual Interaction,* edited by Christopher Carr and D. Troy Case, 696–713. Springer, New York.

Ruhl, Katharine C., and Mark F. Seeman
1998 The Temporal and Social Implications of Ohio Hopewell Copper Ear Spool Design. *American Antiquity* 63: 651–62.

Sahlins, Marshall D.
1961 The Segmentary Lineage: An Organization of Predatory Expansion. *American Anthropologist* 63: 322–45.
1968 *Tribesman.* Prentice-Hall, Englewood Cliffs, N.J.

Sanders, Thomas N., and Lathel F. Duffield
1976 *Archeological Survey and Test Excavations in the Proposed Paintsville Lake Reservoir Project.* University of Kentucky, Museum of Anthropology, Lexington.

Sanders, William T., Jeffrey R. Parsons, and Robert S. Santley
1979 *The Basin of Mexico: Ecological Process in the Evolution of a Civilization.* Academic, New York.

Sasowsky, I. D.
1992 Evolution of Appalachian Highlands: Geochemistry, Hydrogeology, Cave Sediment Mag-

netostratigraphy, and Historical Geomorphology of the East Fork Obey River, Fentress County, Tennessee. Ph.D. thesis, Pennsylvania State University, State College, Pennsylvania.

Sassaman, Kenneth E.
2002 Woodland Ceramic Beginnings. In *The Woodland Southeast*, edited by David G. Anderson and Robert C. Mainfort Jr., 398–420. University of Alabama Press, Tuscaloosa.
2005 Poverty Point as Structure, Event, Process. *Journal of Archaeological Method and Theory* 12: 335–64.
2010 *The Eastern Archaic, Historicized.* AltaMira Press, New York.

Sauer, Carl
1956 The Education of a Geographer. *Annals of the Association of American Geographers* 46: 287–99.

Saunders, Joe W.
2010 Middle Archaic and Watson Brake. In *Archaeology of Louisiana*, edited by Mark A. Rees, 63–76. Louisiana State University Press, Baton Rouge.

Saunders, Joe W., Rolfe D. Mandel, C. Garth Sampson, Charles M. Allen, E. Thurman Allen, Daniel A. Bush, James K. Feathers, Kristen J. Gremillion, C. T. Hallmark, H. Edwin Jackson, Jay K. Johnson, Reca Jones, Roger T. Saucier, Gary L. Stringer, and Malcolm F. Vidrine
2005 Watson Brake, a Middle Archaic Mound Complex in Northeast Louisiana. *American Antiquity* 70: 631–68.

Scarry, C. Margaret
1990 Plant Remains from the Walling Truncated Mound: Evidence for Middle Woodland Horticultural Activities. In *Excavation of the Truncated Mound at the Walling Site: Middle Woodland Culture and Copena in the Tennessee Valley*, edited by Vernon James Knight Jr., 115–29. Alabama State Museum of Natural History, Division of Archaeology, Report of Investigations 56. University of Alabama, Tuscaloosa.
2003 Patterns of Wild Plant Utilization in the Prehistoric Eastern Woodlands. In *People and Plants in Ancient Eastern North America*, edited by Paul E. Minnis, 50–104. Smithsonian Books, Washington, D.C.

Schenian, Pamela A., and Stephen T. Mocas
1993 *The Combined Phase II/III Archaeological Investigation of Site 15Ml134 in the Hite Painting Barge Painting Facility at Tennessee River Mile 9.75, near Little Cypress, Marshall County, Kentucky.* Archaeology Service Center, Murray State University, Murray, Ky.

Schlanger, Sarah H.
1992 Recognizing Persistent Places in Anasazi. In *Space, Time, and Archaeological Landscapes*, edited by Jacqueline Rossignol and LuAnn Wandsnider, 91–113. Plenum Press, New York.

Schlarb, Eric J.
2005 The Bullock Site: A Forgotten Mound in Woodford County, Kentucky. In *Woodland Period Systematics in the Middle Ohio Valley*, edited by Darlene Applegate and Robert C. Mainfort Jr., 52–63. University of Alabama Press, Tuscaloosa.

Schock, Jack M.
1979 *An Archaeological Reconnaissance of Proposed Water and Sewer Improvements for the Bowling Green–Warren County Industrial Foundation at Bowling Green, Warren County, Kentucky.* Report submitted to G. Reynolds Watkins Consulting Engineers, Bowling Green, Ky.
1984 *An Archaeological Survey and Testing of the Proposed Gibson Greeting Card Plant Site in Kenton County, Kentucky.* Arrow Enterprises, Bowling Green, Ky.
1994 *Archaeological Testing of Sites 15Lv208–15Lv209 for the Proposed Ledbetter Community Treatment Plant Site at Ledbetter in Livingston County, Kentucky.* Arrow Enterprises, Bowling Green, Ky.

Schock, Jack M., Gary Foster, and Richard Alvey
1976   An Archaeological Survey of the Relocation of U.S. 119, between South Williamson and Pikeville, Pike County, Kentucky. Ms. on file, Department of Folk Studies and Anthropology, Western Kentucky University, Bowling Green.

Schock, Jack M., and Terry L. (Weis) Langford
1978   *An Archaeological Survey of the Proposed Carrs Site and Other Accessory Areas, Lewis County, Kentucky.* Arrow Enterprises, Bowling Green, Ky.
1979   An Archaeological Shoreline Reconnaissance of Barren River Lake, Allen, Barren and Monroe Counties, Kentucky. Report submitted to the Louisville District Corps of Engineers. Western Kentucky University, Bowling Green.
1980   *Archaeological Phase II Testing of the Proposed Carrs Site in Northern Lewis County, Kentucky.* Arrow Enterprises, Bowling Green, Ky.
1981   *Archaeological Phase II Testing of the Proposed Carrs Site in Northern Lewis County, Kentucky.* Arrow Enterprises, Bowling Green, Ky.

Schock, Jack M., Tacoma G. Sloan, and John Walker
1958a   Appraisal of the Archaeological Resources of the Rough River Basin, Kentucky. Ms. on file, Museum of Anthropology, University of Kentucky, Lexington.
1958b   Survey of the Archaeological Resources of the Rough River Basin. Ms. on file, Museum of Anthropology, University of Kentucky, Lexington.

Schock, Jack M., and Donna Stone
1985   Artifacts from 15He315B, a Middle Woodland Phase Site. Paper presented at the Second Annual Kentucky Heritage Council Archaeology Conference, Western Kentucky University, Bowling Green.

Schofield, P. N., T. Bubela, T. Weaver, L. Portilla, S. D. Brown, J. M. Hancock, D. Einhorn, G. Tocchini-Valentini, M. H. de Andelis, and N. Rosenthal
2009   Post-publication Sharing of Data and Tools. *Nature* 461: 171–73.

Schroedl, Gerald F., and Clifford C. Boyd Jr.
1991   Late Woodland Period Culture in East Tennessee. In *Stability, Transformation, and Variation: The Late Woodland Southeast,* edited by Michael S. Nassaney and Charles R. Cobb, 69–90. Springer, New York.

Schroedl, Gerald F., R. P. Stephen Davis Jr., and Clifford C. Boyd Jr.
1985   *Archaeological Contexts and Assemblages at Martin Farm.* Report of Investigations no. 39. University of Tennessee, Knoxville.

Schwartz, Douglas W.
1960   An Archaeological Survey of the Nolin River Reservoir. Ms. on file, Museum of Anthropology, University of Kentucky, Lexington.

Schwartz, Douglas W., Tacoma G. Sloan, and John Walker
1958a   Appraisal of the Archaeological Resources of the Rough River Basin, Kentucky. Ms. on file, Museum of Anthropology, University of Kentucky, Lexington.
1958b   Survey of the Archaeological Resources of the Rough River Basin. Ms. on file, Museum of Anthropology, University of Kentucky, Lexington.

Sears, William H.
1956   *Excavations at Kolomoki: Final Report.* University of Georgia Press, Athens.
1962   The Hopewellian Affiliations of Certain Sites on the Gulf Coast of Florida. *American Antiquity* 28: 5–18.
1971   Food Production and Village Life in the Prehistoric Southeastern United States. *Archaeology* 24: 323–29.

1973 The Sacred and the Secular in Prehistoric Ceramics. In *Variations in Anthropology: Essays in Honor of John McGregor,* edited by Donald W. Lathrap and Jody Douglas, 31–42. Illinois Archaeological Survey, Urbana.

1982 *Fort Center: An Archaeological Site in the Lake Okeechobee Basin.* University Press of Florida, Gainesville.

Sears, William H., Elsie O. Sears, and Karl T. Steinen
1982 *Fort Center: An Archaeological Site in the Lake Okeechobee Basin.* Florida Museum of Natural History, Ripley P. Bullen Series. University Press of Florida, Gainesville.

Seeman, Mark F.
1979 Feasting with the Dead: Ohio Hopewell Charnel House Ritual as a Context for Redistribution. In *Hopewell Archaeology: The Chillicothe Conference,* edited by David S. Brose and N'omi B. Greber, 39–46. Kent State University Press, Kent, Ohio.

1986 Adena "Houses" and Their Implications for Early Woodland Settlement Models in the Ohio Valley. In *Early Woodland Archaeology,* edited by Kenneth B. Farnsworth and Thomas E. Emerson, 564–80. Center for American Archaeology, Kampsville, Ill.

1995 When Words Are Not Enough: Hopewell Interregionalism and the Use of Material Symbols at the GE Mound. In *Native American Interactions: Multiscalar Analyses and Interpretations in the Eastern Woodlands,* edited by Michael S. Nassaney and Kenneth E. Sassaman, 122–43. University of Tennessee Press, Knoxville.

2004 Hopewell Art in Hopewell Places. In *The Hero, Hawk, and the Open Hand: American Indian Art of the Ancient Midwest and South,* edited by Richard Townsend, 57–71. Art Institute of Chicago, Chicago.

2007 Predatory War and Hopewell Trophies. In *The Taking and Displaying of Human Body Parts as Trophies by Amerindians,* edited by Richard J. Chacon and David H. Dye, 167–89. Springer, New York.

Seeman, Mark F., and James L. Branch
2006 The Mounded Landscapes of Ohio. In *Recreating Hopewell,* edited by Douglas K. Charles and Jane E. Buikstra, 106–21. University Press of Florida, Gainesville.

Sherwood, Sarah C., and Tristram R. Kidder
2011 The DaVincis of Dirt: Geoarchaeological Perspectives on Native American Mound Building in the Mississippi River Basin. *Journal of Anthropological Archaeology* 30: 69–87.

Shryock, Andrew J.
1987 The Wright Mound Reexamined: Generative Structures and the Political Economy of a Simple Chiefdom. *Midcontinental Journal of Archaeology* 12: 243–61.

Sigler-Lavelle, Brenda J.
1980 On the Non-random Distribution of Weeden Island Period Sites in North Florida. *Southeastern Archaeological Conference Bulletin* 22: 22–29.

Silliman, Stephen W.
2005 Culture Contact or Colonialism? Challenges in the Archaeology of Native North America. *American Antiquity* 70: 55–74.

Simek, Jan F., S. A. Blankenship, and Jay D. Franklin
2008 Prehistoric Rock Art in the Upper Cumberland Plateau. Paper presented at the 65th Annual Southeastern Archaeological Conference, Charlotte, N.C.

Simek, Jan F., and Alan Cressler
1998 Images in Darkness: Prehistoric Cave Art in Southeast North America. In *Discovering North American Rock Art,* edited by Lawrence L. Loendorf, Christopher Chippendale, and David S. Whitley, 93–113. University of Arizona Press, Tucson.

2004 Images in Darkness: Prehistoric Cave Art in Southeast North America. In *Discovering North American Rock Art*, edited by Lawrence L. Loendorf, Christopher Chippendale, and David S. Whitley, 93–113. University of Arizona Press, Tucson.

2008 On the Backs of Serpents: Prehistoric Cave Art in the Southeastern Woodlands. In *Cave Archaeology in the Eastern Woodlands: Essays in Honor of Patty Jo Watson*, edited by David H. Dye, 169–91. University of Tennessee Press, Knoxville.

Simek, Jan F., Jay D. Franklin, and Sarah C. Sherwood

1998 The Context of Early Southeastern Prehistoric Cave Art: A Report on the Archaeology of 3rd Unnamed Cave. *American Antiquity* 63: 663–77.

Skinner, Shaune M., and Rae Norris

1984 *Archaeological Investigations in the Adena Park Subdivision Including Excavations of the Connett Mounds 3 and 4, the Wolf Plains National Register District, The Plains, Ohio*. Ohio Historic Preservation Office, Columbus.

Smith, Adam

2003 *The Political Landscape: Constellations of Authority in Early Complex Societies*. University of California Press, Berkeley.

Smith, Betty A.

1979 The Hopewell Connection in Southwest Georgia. In *Hopewell Archaeology: The Chillicothe Conference*, edited by David S. Brose and N'omi B. Greber, 181–87. Kent State University Press, Kent, Ohio.

Smith, Bruce D.

1992 Hopewellian Farmers of Eastern North America. In *Rivers of Change: Essays on Early Agriculture in Eastern North America*, 201–48. Smithsonian Institution Press, Washington, D.C.

2006 Eastern North America as an Independent Center for Plant Domestication. *Proceedings of the National Academy of Sciences* 103: 12223–28.

Smith, Karen Y.

2009 Middle and Late Woodland Period Cultural Transmission, Residential Mobility, and Aggregation in the Deep South. Unpublished Ph.D. dissertation, University of Missouri, Columbia.

Smith, Karen, and Keith Stephenson

2010 Signaling Theory and Weeden Island Period Mortuary Ritual. Poster presented at the 75th Annual Meeting of the Society for American Archaeology, St. Louis, Mo.

Smith, Phillip E.

1962 *Aboriginal Stone Constructions in the Southern Piedmont*. University of Georgia Laboratory of Archaeology Series Report no. 4. Athens.

Smith, R. W.

1936 Unpublished Notes on the Archaeology of Quarry (Ladd) Mountain. Document in the Georgia Archives, Morrow, Ga.

Sneed, Joel M.

1998 Ladd's Cave: Story of a Destroyed Treasure. *National Speleological Society (NSS) News*, August.

2007 *Bartown County Caves: History Underground in North Georgia*. Joel Sneed, Flowery Branch, Ga.

Snow, Dean R., and Kim M. Lanphear

1988 European Contact and Indian Depopulation in the Northeast: The Timing of the First Epidemics. *Ethnohistory* 35: 15–33.

Snow, Frankie, and Keith Stephenson

1998 Swift Creek Designs: A Tool for Monitoring Interaction. In *A World Engraved: Archaeology of the Swift Creek Culture*, edited by J. Mark Williams and Daniel T. Elliott, 61–98. University of Alabama Press, Tuscaloosa.

Southerlin, Bobby G.
2002   Archaeological Evaluation of the 84 Lumber Tract, Cartersville, Georgia. Submitted to 84 Lumber Company, Eighty-Four, Pennsylvania, by Brockington and Associates, Inc., Atlanta, Ga.

Southerlin, Bobby G., Julie Wilburn Peeler, Dawn Reid, and Rachel Tibbetts
2003   Archaeological Evaluation of the Rockmart Highway Water System Improvement, Bartow County, Georgia. Report submitted to Bartow County Water Department, Cartersville, Georgia, by Brockington and Associates, Inc., Atlanta, Ga.

Spielmann, Katherine A.
2002   Feasting, Craft Specialization, and the Ritual Mode of Production. *American Anthropologist* 104: 195–207.

Squier, Ephraim G., and Edwin H. Davis
1848   *Ancient Monuments of the Mississippi Valley, Comprising the Results of Extensive Original Surveys and Explorations.* Contributions to Knowledge. Smithsonian Institution, Washington, D.C.

Stallings, Richard
2007   Phase III Mitigation of the Panther Rock Site (15Cl58): A Preliminary Report. Paper presented at the 24th Annual Kentucky Heritage Council Archaeological Conference, Natural Bridge, Ky.

Stallings, Richard, Nancy Ross-Stallings, Sarah Adams, Annette Ericksen, Flora Church, and Richard Bonnett
1995   *Phase III Mitigation at Sites 15Cr61 and 15Cr64, Located near Grayson, Carter County, Kentucky.* Cultural Horizons, Harrodsburg, Ky.

Steinen, Karl T.
1995   *Woodland Period Archaeology of the Georgia Coastal Plain.* Georgia Archaeological Research Design Paper no. 12, University of Georgia Laboratory of Archaeology Series Report no. 36. Athens.
1998   Kolomoki and the Development of Sociopolitical Organization on the Gulf Coast Plain. In *A World Engraved: Archaeology of the Swift Creek Culture,* edited by Mark William and Daniel T. Elliott, 181–96. University of Alabama Press, Tuscaloosa.

Stephenson, Keith, Judith A. Bense, and Frankie Snow
2002   Aspects of Deptford and Swift Creek on the South Atlantic and Gulf Coastal Plains. In *The Woodland Southeast,* edited by David G. Anderson and Robert C. Mainfort Jr., 318–51. University of Alabama Press, Tuscaloosa.

Stephenson, Keith, and Karen Smith
2008   Middle Swift Creek/Weeden Island I Ceremonialism in the Interior Coastal Plain of Georgia. Poster presented at the 65th Annual Meeting of the Southeastern Archaeological Conference Charlotte, North Carolina.

Steponaitis, Vincas P.
1986   Prehistoric Archaeology in the Southeastern United States, 1970–1985. *Annual Reviews in Anthropology* 15: 363–404.

Steward, Julian H.
1955   *Theory of Culture Change.* University of Illinois Press, Chicago.

Stokes, B. Jo, and Carl R. Shields
1999   *Woodland Occupations along Clear Creek in Southeastern Kentucky.* Kentucky Archaeological Survey. Research Report no. 2. Kentucky Heritage Council and the University of Kentucky Department of Anthropology, Lexington.

Stoltman, James B.
2007 Petrographic Observations on Middle Woodland Pottery from the Leake Site. In *Archaeological Data Recovery at the Leake Site, Bartow County, Georgia*. Vol. 2, *Appendices*. Southern Research Historic Preservation Consultants, Ellerslie, Ga.

Stoltman, James B., and Frankie Snow
1998 Cultural Interaction within Swift Creek Society: People, Pots, and Paddles. In *A World Engraved: Archaeology of the Swift Creek Culture*, edited by J. Mark Williams and Daniel T. Elliott, 130–53. University of Alabama Press, Tuscaloosa.

Striker, Michael
2008 Ancestor Veneration as a Component of House Identity Formation in the Early Woodland Period. Paper presented at the 6th World Archaeological Congress, Dublin, Ireland.

Struever, Stuart, and Gail L. Houart
1972 An Analysis of the Hopewell Interaction Sphere. In *Social Exchange and Interaction*, edited by Ed N. Wilmsen, 47–49. Anthropological Papers vol. 46. Museum of Anthropology, University of Michigan, Ann Arbor.

Stuiver, M., and P. J. Reimer
1993 Extended 14C Database and Revised CALIB Radiocarbon Calibration Program. *Radiocarbon* 35:215–230.
2005 Calib Radiocarbon Calibration Program Version 5.0.1. Copyright 1986–2005.

Stump, Nicole I., James Lein, Elliot M. Abrams, and AnnCorinne Freter
2005 A Preliminary GIS Analysis of Hocking Valley Archaic and Woodland Settlement Trends. In *The Emergence of the Moundbuilders: The Archaeology of Tribal Societies in Southeastern Ohio*, edited by Elliot M. Abrams and AnnCorinne Freter, 25–38. Ohio University Press, Athens.

Sullivan, Lynne P., and S. Terry Childs
2003 *Curating Archaeological Collections: From the Field to the Repository*. Alta Mira Press, Walnut Creek, Calif.

Sunderhaus, Ted S., and Jack K. Blosser
2006 Water and Mud and the Recreation of the World. In *Recreating Hopewell*, edited by Douglas K. Charles and Jane E. Buikstra, 134–45. University Press of Florida, Gainesville.

Sussenbach, Tom
1990 *Archaeological Site Distribution on the Cumberland Plateau of Eastern Kentucky*. Program for Cultural Resource Assessment, University of Kentucky, Lexington.

Swanton, John R.
1911 *Indian Tribes of the Lower Mississippi Valley and Adjacent Coast of the Gulf of Mexico*. Smithsonian Institution Bureau of American Ethnology Bulletin 43. Washington, D.C.
1928 The Interpretation of Aboriginal Mounds by Means of Creek Indian Customs. In *Annual Report of the Smithsonian Institution for 1927*, 495–506. Smithsonian Institution, Washington, D.C.
1979 *The Indians of the Southeastern United States*. Smithsonian Institution, Washington, D.C.

Tainter, Joseph A.
1977 Woodland Social Changes in West-Central Illinois. *Midcontinental Journal of Archaeology* 2: 67–98.

Terrell, William H.
1998 Zooarchaeology and Human Populations: A Case Study from the North Carolina Piedmont. Unpublished master's thesis, Wake Forest University, Winston-Salem, N.C.

Thomas, Cyrus
1891 *Catalogue of Prehistoric Works East of the Rocky Mountains*. Bureau of Ethnology, Smithsonian Institution, Washington, D.C.

1894 *Report on the Mound Explorations of the Bureau of Ethnology*. 12th Annual Report. Bureau of Ethnology, Washington, D.C.

Thomas, David H.
2008 Addressing Variability in the Pooled Radiocarbon Record of St. Catherines Island. In *Native American Landscapes of St. Catherines Island, Georgia*, edited by David H. Thomas, 435–74. Anthropological Papers of the American Museum of Natural History 88 (1–3). New York.

Thomas, Julian
1996 *Time, Culture, and Identity*. Routledge, London.

Thompson, Victor D.
2009 The Mississippian Production of Space through Earthen Pyramids and Public Buildings on the Georgia Coast, USA. *World Archaeology* 41: 445–70.
2010 The Rhythms of Space-Time and the Making of Monuments and Places during the Archaic. In *Trend, Tradition, and Turmoil: What Happened to the Southeastern Archaic?* edited by David Hurst Thomas and Matthew C. Sanger, 217–28. Anthropological Papers of the American Museum of Natural History no. 93. New York.

Thompson, Victor D., Philip J. Arnold III, Thomas J. Pluckhahn, and Amber M. Vanderwarker
2011 Situating Remote Sensing in Anthropological Archaeology. *Archaeological Prospection* 18: 195–213.

Thompson, Victor D., Kristen Gremillion, and Thomas J. Pluckhahn
2013 Challenging the Evidence for Prehistoric Wetland Maize Agriculture at Fort Center, Florida. *American Antiquity*, in press.

Thompson, Victor D., and Thomas J. Pluckhahn
2010 History, Complex Hunter-Gatherers, and the Mounds and Monuments of Crystal River, Florida, USA: A Geophysical Perspective. *Journal of Island and Coastal Archaeology* 5: 33–51.
2012 Monumentalization and Ritual Landscapes at Fort Center in the Lake Okeechobee Basin of South Florida. *Journal of Anthropological Archaeology* 31: 49–65.

Thompson, Victor D., and John A. Turck
2009 Adaptive Cycles of Coastal Hunter-Gatherers. *American Antiquity* 74: 255–78.

Thunen, Robert L.
1988 Geometric Enclosures in the Mid-South: An Archaeological Analysis of Enclosure Form. In *Middle Woodland Settlement and Ceremonialism in the Mid-South and Lower Mississippi Valley*, edited by Robert C. Mainfort Jr., 99–115. Archaeological Report no. 22. Mississippi Department of Archives and History, Jackson.
1998 Defining Space: An Overview of the Pinson Mounds Enclosure. In *Ancient Earthen Enclosures of the Eastern Woodlands*, edited by Robert C. Mainfort Jr. and Lynne P. Sullivan, 57–67. University Press of Florida, Gainesville.

Tilley, Christopher
1994 *A Phenomenology of Landscape: Places, Paths, and Monuments*. Berg, Oxford, U.K.
1999 *Metaphor and Material Culture*. Blackwell, Oxford, U.K.

Toth, Alan
1974 *Archaeology and Ceramics at the Marksville Site*. Anthropological Papers no. 56. University of Michigan, Ann Arbor.
1988 *Early Marksville Phases in the Lower Mississippi Valley: A Study of Culture Contact Dynamics*. Archaeological Report no. 21. Mississippi Department of Archives and History, Jackson.

Townsend, Richard F.
2004 American Landscapes, Seen and Unseen. In *The Hero, Hawk, and the Open Hand: American*

Indian Art of the Ancient Midwest and South, edited by Richard F. Townsend, 19–35. Art Institute of Chicago, Chicago.

Trigger, Bruce G.
1990   Monumental Architecture: A Thermodynamic Explanation of Symbolic Behavior. *World Archaeology* 22: 119–32.

Trowell, Christopher T.
1998   A Kolomoki Chronicle: The History of a Plantation, a State Park, and the Archaeological Search for Kolomoki's Prehistory. *Early Georgia* 26: 12–81.

Tuan, Yi-Fu
1977   *Space and Place: The Perspective of Experience*. University of Minnesota Press, Minneapolis.

Turff, Gina M., and Christopher Carr
2005   Hopewellian Panpipes from Eastern North America: Their Social, Ritual, and Symbolic Significance. In *Gathering Hopewell: Society, Ritual, and Ritual Interaction*, edited by Christopher Carr and D. Troy Case, 648–95. Springer, New York.

Turnbow, Christopher A., Cynthia E. Jobe, and Nancy O'Malley
1983   *Archaeological Excavations of the Goolman, DeVary, and Stone Sites in Clark County, Kentucky*. Archaeological Report no. 78. Department of Anthropology, University of Kentucky, Lexington.

Turnbow, Christopher A., Malinda Stafford, Richard Boisvert, and Julie Riesenweber
1980   *A Cultural Resource Assessment of Two Alternate Locations of the Hancock Power Plant, Hancock and Breckinridge Counties, Kentucky*. Archaeological Report no. 30. Department of Anthropology, University of Kentucky, Lexington.

Ucko, Peter J., and Robert Layton
1999   *The Archaeology and Anthropology of Landscape*. Routledge, London.

Vanderwarker, Amber M., C. Margaret Scarry, and Jane M. Eastman
2007   Menus for Families and Feasts: Household and Community Consumption of Plants at Upper Saratown, North Carolina. In *The Archaeology of Food and Identity*, 16–49. Occasional Paper no. 34. Center for Archaeological Investigations, Southern Illinois University, Carbondale.

Van Dyke, Ruth M.
2009   Chaco Reloaded: Discursive Social Memory on the Post-Chacoan Landscape. *Journal of Social Archaeology* 9: 220–48.

Van Dyke, Ruth M., and Susan E. Alcock
2003   Archaeologies of Memory: An Introduction. In *Archaeologies of Memory*, edited by Ruth M. Van Dyke and Susan E. Alcock, 1–13. Blackwell, Malden, Mass.

Van Nest, Julie
2006   Rediscovering This Earth: Some Ethnogeological Aspects of the Illinois Valley Hopewell Mounds. In *Recreating Hopewell*, edited by Douglas K. Charles and Jane E. Buikstra, 402–26. University Press of Florida, Gainesville.

Van Nest, Julie, Douglas K. Charles, Jane E. Buikstra, and David L. Asch
2001   Sod Blocks in Illinois Hopewell Mounds. *American Antiquity* 66: 633–50.

Veatch, O., and L. W. Stephenson
1911   *Geology of the Coastal Plain*. Bulletin 26. Geological Survey of Georgia, Atlanta.

Vento, F. J., James M. Adovasio, and J. Donahue
1980   *Excavations at Dameron Rockshelter (15Jo23A), Johnson County, Kentucky*. Department of Anthropology, University of Pittsburgh, Pittsburgh.

Versluis, Vincent
2004   Phase II Archaeological Testing of Sites 15He847, 15He848, 15He850, 15He852, 15He855, 15He863, and 15He873 for a Patriot Coal Mining Permit Area near Hebbardsville, Henderson County, Kentucky. Great Rivers Archaeological Services, Burlington, Ky.

Waldron, John, and Elliot M. Abrams
1999   Adena Burial Mounds and Inter-hamlet Visibility: A GIS Approach. *Midcontinental Journal of Archaeology* 24: 97–111.

Walley, Scott A., Rebecca A. Hawkins, and James C. Litfin
1997   Phase I Survey of the Proposed 350-Acre IDI Industrial Park, Phase II Evaluation of the Wackenstein Site, 15Be467, and Excavation of the Gaines-Graves Cemetery, 15Be474, Boone County, Kentucky. Algonquin Archaeological Consultants, Cincinnati, Ohio.

Wallis, Neill J.
2006   The Production of Meaning in Swift Creek Iconography. Paper presented at the 71st Annual Meeting of the Society for American Archaeology, San Juan, Puerto Rico.
2007   Defining Swift Creek Interaction: Earthenware Variability at Ring Middens and Burial Mounds. *Southeastern Archaeology* 26: 212–31.
2008   Networks of History and Memory: Creating a Nexus of Social Lives in Woodland Period Mounds on the Lower St John's River, Florida. *Journal of Social Archaeology* 8: 236–71.
2011   *The Swift Creek Gift: Vessel Exchange on the Atlantic Coast*. University of Alabama Press, Tuscaloosa.

Wallis, Neill J., Matthew Boulanger, Michael D. Glascock, and Jeffrey R. Ferguson
2010   Woodland Period Ceramic Provenance and the Exchange of Swift Creek Complicated Stamped Pottery in the Southeastern United States. *Journal of Archaeological Science* 37: 2598–2611.

Wallis, Neill J., Ann S. Cordell, and Lee A. Newsom
2011   Using Hearths for Temper: Petrographic Analysis of Middle Woodland Charcoal-Tempered Pottery in Northeast Florida. *Journal of Archaeological Science* 38: 2914–24.

Walthall, John A.
1973   Copena: A Tennessee Valley Middle Woodland Culture. Unpublished Ph.D. dissertation, Department of Anthropology, University of North Carolina, Chapel Hill.
1974   Appendix to Copena Burial Caves. *Journal of Alabama Archaeology* 20: 60–64.
1979   Hopewell and the Southern Heartland. In *Hopewell Archaeology: The Chillicothe Conference*, edited by David S. Brose and N'omi B. Greber, 200–210. Kent State University Press, Kent, Ohio.
1980   *Prehistoric Indians of the Southeast: Archaeology of Alabama and the Middle South*. University of Alabama Press, Tuscaloosa.
1985   Early Hopewellian Ceremonial Encampments in the South Appalachian Highlands. In *Structure and Process in Southeastern Archaeology*, edited by Roy S. Dickens Jr. and H. Trawick Ward, 243–62. University of Alabama Press, Tuscaloosa.

Walthall, John A., and David S. DeJarnette
1974   Copena Burial Caves. *Journal of Alabama Archaeology* 20: 1–59.

Wandsnider, LuAnn
1992   Regional Scale Processes and Archaeological Landscape Units. In *Unit Issues in Archaeology: Measuring Time, Space, and Material*, edited by Ann F. Ramenofsky and Anastasia Steffen, 87–102. University of Utah Press, Salt Lake City.

Ward, H. Trawick, and R. P. Stephen Davis, Jr.
1999   *Time Before History: The Archaeology of North Carolina.* University of North Carolina Press, Chapel Hill.

Waring, Antonio J., Jr.
1945   "Hopewellian" Elements in Northern Georgia. *American Antiquity* 11: 119–20.

Warrick, Gary
2003   European Infections Disease and Depopulation in the Wendat-Tionontate (Huron-Petun). *World Archaeology* 35: 258–75.

Watson, Patty Jo
1969   *The Prehistory of Salts Cave, Kentucky.* Illinois State Museum Report of Investigations no. 16. Springfield.
1974   *Archaeology of the Mammoth Cave Area.* Academic Press, New York.
1986   Prehistoric Cavers of the Eastern Woodlands. In *The Prehistoric Native American Art of Mud Glyph Cave,* edited by Charles H. Faulkner, 109–16. University of Tennessee Press, Knoxville.
2001   Ridges, Rises, and Rocks; Caves, Coves, Terraces, and Hollows: Appalachian Archaeology at the Millennium. In *Archaeology of the Appalachian Highlands,* edited by Lynne P. Sullivan and Susan C. Prezzano, 319–22. University of Tennessee Press, Knoxville.

Watson, Patty Jo (editor)
1997   *Archaeology of the Mammoth Cave Area.* Cave Books, St. Louis, Mo.

Watson, Patty Jo, Richard A. Yarnell, Harold Meloy, William Benninghoff, Eric Callen, Aidan Cockburn, Hugh Cutler, Paul Parmalee, Lionel Prescott, and William White
1969   *The Prehistory of Salts Cave, Kentucky.* Illinois State Museum, Springfield.

Wauchope, Robert
1966   *Archaeological Survey of Northern Georgia.* Memoirs of the Society for American Archaeology no. 21. Salt Lake City, Utah.

Weaver, Sarah A.
2009   A Middle Woodland House and Houselot: Evidence of Sedentism from the Patton Site (33AT990), the Hocking River Valley, Southeastern Ohio. Unpublished master's thesis, Ohio University, Athens.

Webb, William S.
1938   *An Archaeological Survey of the Norris Basin.* Bureau of American Ethnology Bulletin 118. Smithsonian Institution Press, Washington, D.C.
1940   *The Wright Mounds, Sites 6 and 7, Montgomery County, Kentucky.* Reports in Anthropology and Archaeology 5 (1). University of Kentucky, Lexington.
1941a *The Morgan Stone Mound, Site 15, Bath County, Kentucky.* Reports in Anthropology and Archaeology 5 (3). University of Kentucky, Lexington.
1941b *Mt. Horeb Earthworks, Site 1, and the Drake Mound, Site 11, Fayette County, Kentucky.* Reports in Anthropology and Archaeology 5 (2). University of Kentucky, Lexington.
1943a The Crigler Mounds, Sites Be20 and Be27 and the Hartman Mound Site Be32, Boone County, Kentucky. In *Reports in Anthropology and Archaeology 5 (6),* 505–79. University of Kentucky, Lexington.
1943b *The Riley Mound, Site Be15 and the Landing Mound, Site Be17, Boone County, Kentucky with Additional Notes on the Mt. Horeb Site, Fa1 and Sites Fa14 and Fa15, Fayette County, Kentucky.* Reports in Anthropology and Archaeology 5 (7). University of Kentucky, Lexington.

1943c A Note on the Mt. Horeb Earthworks, Site Fa 1, and Two New Adjacent Sites, Fa 14 and 15, Fayette County, Kentucky. In *The Riley Mound, Site Be 15, and the Landing Mound, Site Be 17, Boone County, Kentucky,* 640–66. Reports in Anthropology and Archaeology 5 (7). University of Kentucky, Lexington.

Webb, William S., and Raymond S. Baby
1957 *The Adena People No. 2.* Ohio Historical Society, Ohio State University Press, Lexington.

Webb, William S., and David L. DeJarnette
1942 *An Archaeological Survey of Pickwick Basin in the Adjacent Portions of the States of Alabama, Mississippi, and Tennessee.* Bureau of American Ethnology Bulletin 129. Smithsonian Institution, Washington, D.C.

Webb, William S., and John B. Elliott
1942 The Robbins Mounds, Site Be3 and Be14, Boone County, Kentucky. In *Reports in Anthropology and Archaeology 5 (5),* 377–499. University of Kentucky, Lexington.

Webb, William S., and William D. Funkhouser
1932 *Archaeological Survey of Kentucky.* Reports in Archaeology and Anthropology 2. University of Kentucky, Lexington.
1936a *The Ricketts Site Revisited, Site 3 Montgomery County, Kentucky.* Reports in Anthropology and Archaeology 3 (6). University of Kentucky, Lexington.
1936b Rock Shelters in Menifee County. In *Reports in Anthropology and Archaeology 3 (6),* 105–67. University of Kentucky, Lexington.
1940 Ricketts Site Revisited, Site 3, Montgomery County, Kentucky. In *Reports in Anthropology and Archaeology 3,* 211–69. University of Kentucky, Lexington.

Webb, William S., and William G. Haag
1947 *The Fisher Site, Fayette County, Kentucky.* Reports in Anthropology 7 (2). University of Kentucky, Lexington.

Webb, William S., William G. Haag, and Charles E. Snow
1942 The C. and O. Mounds at Paintsville, Sites Jo2 and Jo9, Johnson County, Kentucky. In *Reports in Anthropology and Archaeology 5 (4),* 297–372. University of Kentucky, Lexington.

Webb, William S., and Charles E. Snow
1945 *The Adena People.* Reports in Anthropology and Archaeology 6. University of Kentucky, Lexington.
1959 *The Dover Mound.* University Press of Kentucky, Lexington.

Weiner, Annette B.
1992 *Inalienable Possessions: The Paradox of Keeping-While-Giving.* University of California Press, Berkeley.

Weisman, Brent R.
1995 *Crystal River: A Ceremonial Mound Complex on the Florida Gulf Coast.* Florida Archaeology 8. Florida Department of State, Division of Historical Resources, Tallahassee.

Wheatley, David, and Mark Gillings
2002 *Spatial Technology and Archaeology: The Archaeological Applications of GIS.* Taylor and Francis, New York.

Whitley, Thomas G., and Lacey M. Hicks
2003 A Geographic Information Systems Approach to Understanding Potential Prehistoric and Historic Travel Corridors. *Southeastern Archaeology* 22: 77–91.

Whittlesey, Charles
1883 The Great Mound on the Etowah River, Georgia. In *Annual Report of the Board of Regents of the Smithsonian Institution for 1881,* 624–30. Smithsonian Institution, Washington, D.C.

Whyte, Thomas R.
2003 Archaeofaunal Remains from the Late Prehistoric Mount Joy Site in Botetourt County, Virginia. *Banisteria* 20: 45–52.
2011 Archaeofaunal Remains from Garden Creek Mound No. 2 (31HW2) in Haywood County, North Carolina. *North Carolina Archaeology* 60: 53–64.

Wiant, Michael D., and Charles R. McGimsey
1986 *Woodland Period Occupations of the Napoleon Hollow Site in the Lower Illinois Valley.* Research Series, vol. 6. Center for American Archeology, Kampsville, Ill.

Wiessner, Polly
2002 The Vines of Complexity: Egalitarian Structures and the Institutionalization of Inequality among the Enga. *Current Anthropology* 43: 233–69.

Wiggins, Lauren
2011 The Spatial Distribution of Check Stamped and Rocker Stamped Ceramics at the Armory Site in Dallas County, Alabama. Paper presented at the Undergraduate Research Conference at the University of Alabama, Tuscaloosa.

Willey, Gordon R.
1949 *Archaeology of the Florida Gulf Coast.* Smithsonian Institution, Washington, D.C.
1953 *Prehistoric Settlement Patterns in the Viru Valley, Peru.* Bulletin 155. Bureau of American Ethnology, Washington, D.C.

Williams, Mark J.
1987 *Archaeological Excavations at the Jackson Landing/Mulatto Bayou Earthwork.* Archaeological Report no. 19. Mississippi Department of Archives and History, Jackson.

Williams, S. C. (editor)
1927 *Lieut. Henry Timberlake's Memoirs, 1756–1765.* Watauga Press, Johnson City, Tenn.

Willoughby, Charles C., and Ernest A. Hooton
1922 *The Turner Group of Earthworks, Hamilton County, Ohio.* Papers of the Peabody Museum 8 (3). Harvard University, Cambridge, Mass.

Wimberly, Steve B.
1960 *Indian Pottery from Clarke County and Mobile County, Southern Alabama.* Geological Survey of Alabama, Museum Paper 36. University of Alabama, Tuscaloosa.

Wimberly, Steve B., and Harry A. Tourtelot
1941 *The McQuorquodale Mound: A Manifestation of the Hopewellian Phase in South Alabama.* Geological Survey of Alabama, Museum Paper 19. University of Alabama, Tuscaloosa.

Winters, Howard
1969 *The Riverton Culture: A Second Millennium Occupation in the Central Wabash Valley.* Report of Investigations no. 13. Illinois State Museum, Springfield.

Wobst, H. Martin
1977 Stylistic Behavior and Information Exchange. In *For the Director: Research Essays in Honor of James B. Griffin,* vol. 61, edited by Charles Cleland, 317–42. Museum of Anthropology, University of Michigan, Ann Arbor.

Wright, Alice P.
2010 Under the Mound: The Early Life History of the Garden Creek Mound No. 2 Site. Paper presented at the 67th Annual Meeting of the Southeastern Archaeological Conference Lexington, Kentucky.
2012 "Artifacts Writ Large": Ditch Enclosures and Middle Woodland Interaction in Southern Appalachia. Paper presented at the 77th Annual Meeting of the Society for American Archaeology, Memphis, Tenn.

Wyss, James D., and Sandra K. Wyss
1977   *An Archaeological Assessment of Portions of the Red River Gorge Geological Area, Menifee County, Kentucky.* Ohio Valley Archaeological Research Associates, Lexington, Ky.

Young, Bennett H.
1910   *The Prehistoric Men of Kentucky.* Filson Club Publications 25. John P. Morton, Louisville, Ky.

Zedeño, Maria N.
2009   Animating by Association: Index Object and Relational Taxonomies. *Cambridge Archaeological Journal* 19: 407–17.

Contributors

David G. Anderson is professor of anthropology at the University of Tennessee and the author of numerous books, monographs, and articles on Southeastern archaeology, including most recently *Recent Developments in Southeastern Archaeology: From Colonization to Complexity*, with Kenneth E. Sassaman.

Darlene Applegate is associate professor of anthropology at Western Kentucky University and the coeditor (with Robert C. Mainfort Jr.) of *Woodland Period Systematics in the Middle Ohio Valley*.

Edmond A. Boudreaux III is assistant professor of anthropology at East Carolina University and the author of *The Archaeology of Town Creek*.

James A. Brown is emeritus professor of anthropology at Northwestern University and the author of numerous publications on Southeastern archaeology and iconography. His major research projects have involved the Spiro Mounds (Oklahoma), Mound City (Ohio), Koster (Illinois), and Cahokia (Illinois).

R. Berle Clay is a principal investigator and geophysical specialist at Cultural Resources Analysts Inc., with a career spanning teaching, management, and CRM. He is the author of numerous articles on fieldwork in France, New Guinea, and the Mississippi Valley.

Gary D. Crites is the curator of paleoethnobotany at the Frank H. McClung Museum at the University of Tennessee and has published extensively on plant domestication and food production in the pre-Columbian Eastern Woodlands.

Victoria G. Dekle is a doctoral student at the University of Kentucky. Her dissertation research addresses Late Archaic (6000–3100 BP) hunter-gatherer settlement and subsistence strategies on the southern Atlantic Coast.

Meagan Dennison is a graduate student at the University of Tennessee. Her research focuses on prehistoric human-animal relationships on the Upper Cumberland Plateau.

Andrew D. Dye received his B.A. in anthropology from East Tennessee State University.

Paul N. Eubanks is a doctoral student at the University of Alabama. His dissertation research addresses specialization and the role of salt in the development of sociopolitical complexity in prehistoric Louisiana, Texas, and Arkansas.

Jay D. Franklin is associate professor of archaeology at East Tennessee State University. His research on the Upper Cumberland Plateau and Upper East Tennessee has been the subject of several articles and reports.

Maureen A. Hays is professor of anthropology at the College of Charleston and the coeditor (with Paul T. Thacker) of *Questioning the Answers: Resolving Fundamental Problems of the Early Upper Paleolithic*.

Edward R. Henry is assistant professor in the Department of Anthropology at Colorado State University. His PhD research at Washington University in St. Louis traced the construction timing and tempo of Middle Woodland earthen enclosures in the Bluegrass Region of Kentucky.

Richard W. Jefferies is professor of anthropology at the University of Kentucky. He has published numerous articles on prehistoric hunter-gatherers and Middle Woodland ritual life in the Eastern Woodlands. He has recently initiated research on Mission period interaction between Native Americans and Spanish in the coastal Southeast.

Scot Keith is a principal investigator and archaeologist at New South Associates. He has worked extensively across the Southeast and has recently focused his research on the Leake site in northwestern Georgia.

Larry R. Kimball is professor of anthropology and the director of the Laboratories of Archaeological Science at Appalachian State University. He has published research on the prehistoric Southern Appalachians and on Russia, including "Middle and Late Pleistocene Investigations of Myshtulgaty Lagat (Weasel Cave), North Ossetia, Russia" (with N. I. Hidjrati and T. Koetje).

George R. Milner is professor of anthropology at the Pennsylvania State University and the author of *The Moundbuilders* and *The Cahokia Chiefdom: The Archaeology of a Mississippian Society*.

Jeffrey Navel is an undergraduate student at East Tennessee State University.

Thomas J. Pluckhahn is associate professor of anthropology at the University of South Florida and the author of *Kolomoki: Settlement, Ceremony, and Status in the Deep South, A.D. 350–750*.

David Pollack is director of the Kentucky Archaeological Survey and the editor or coeditor of numerous professional publications on Kentucky prehistory. His book *Caborn-Welborn* assesses the reorganization of people on the landscape after the collapse of the Angel Chiefdom in southern Indiana.

Eric J. Schlarb is a staff archaeologist at the Kentucky Archaeological Survey and has served as president of the Kentucky Organization of Professional Archaeologists. He has conducted extensive research on Archaic and Woodland period sites in Kentucky and has published on his Adena research in central Kentucky.

Victor D. Thompson is assistant professor of anthropology at the University of Georgia and the coeditor (with James C. Waggoner Jr.) of *The Archaeology and Historical Ecology of Small Scale Economies*.

Neill J. Wallis is assistant curator of Florida archaeology at the Florida Museum of Natural History and the author of *The Swift Creek Gift: Vessel Exchange on the Atlantic Coast*.

Thomas R. Whyte is professor of anthropology at Appalachian State University and the author of several dozen professional papers on Southern Appalachian prehistory and zooarchaeology.

Alice P. Wright is assistant professor in the Department of Anthropology at Appalachian State University. Her PhD research at the University of Michigan examined the dynamics of Middle Woodland interaction networks in the Blue Ridge Mountains of North Carolina.

Index

Page numbers in *italics* refer to illustrations.

Activity areas, 35–37, 43, 48–50, 61, 173
Adena: in Bluegrass/core area, 40, 219–23; burial mounds, 14, 45, 51, 57, 63–67, 251; dating, 47, 61–63, 227; definition of, 9, 19; domestic landscape, 14, 19, 53; earthworks (general), 14, 92, 102–6, 254; leadership, 219–21, 231; mobility, 62–63, 220, 233; mortuary landscape, 45–47, 53, 243; off-mound sites, 45–49, 241, 250; ritual, 46–47, 54–61, 94, 128, 135, 220, 231–32; social organization, 219–20, 243–44, 260; taxonomy, 10, 70, 219, 244–45; use of clay, 47, 50–52
Agency, 231, 233
Aggregation: domestic, 43, 246; ritual, 13–15, 63, 167–70, 175–80, 204, 238, 245–48, 256–57. *See also* Assembly; Gathering
Alignments: astronomical, 124, 129, 136; cardinal directions, 118; geographic/natural landmarks, 124, 129, 136; of postholes, 118–19, 146–48, 255
Alliance building, 110, 136, 207, 214–18, 245
Alligator Bayou site, 208, 212
Altamaha River (Georgia), 212–14
American chestnut, 50, 54, 133
Ancestors, 45, 218, 232–33
Ancestor veneration, 167, 232, 244, 251
Anderson's Bayou site, 208
Animal jaws, 123, 127, 204
Apalachicola River (Florida), 214
Appalachian Summit, 109, 120–22, 137, 143. *See also* Southern Appalachians
Archaeoastronomy, 15, 36, 147
Archaeological prospection, 1, 7–8, 99–106, 144, 192. *See also* Geophysics; Remote sensing
Archaic Period: general, 1, 72, 80–84, 239, 254; Late, 8–10, 41, 63, 86–87, 157, 178, 191; Middle, 8, 63. *See also* Poverty Point

Architectural grammar, 257. *See also* Monumental grammar
Armory site, 169–75
Asheville Basin, 122, 129
Aspalaga site, 210
Assembly, 205. *See also* Aggregation; Gathering
Atlantic Coast (region), 184, 202, 206, 209–14, 259
Atomistic perspectives, 181, 238, 245
Auvergne Mound, 59–63, 69, 224–27
Axis Mundi, 124, 128

Base camp, 13, 39, 44, 86
Belle Glade culture area, 183
Big Man society, 220
Big Sandy River (Kentucky), 39, 41–42
Big South Fork (Tennessee), 79–80
Biltmore Mound site: alignments, 129–36, 143, 224, 254
Black Earth, 151
Blades (prismatic), 146, 150, 171, 199, 254
Bluegrass region (Kentucky): burial mounds (regional comparisons), 227–30; Central, 219, 224–26; Eastern, 219, 226–27; general location, 222; Northern, 219, 223–24; ritual landscape, 230–32
Borrow pits, 156, 160
Built environment, 4–9, 13–16, 194, 196–97, 220
Bullock Mound, 52, 226
Burial mounds: Adena (general), 9, 45, 49, 57, 222, 258; Adena (ritual), 14, 16, 45, 50–51, 59–67, 176, 227; single-event, 207, 211–12; Swift Creek and Weeden Island, 204–18, 259; symbolism, 128, 194. *See also* Adena; Kolomoki; Swift Creek; Weeden Island
Busycon shell, 209

Caldwell, Joseph, 198
Camargo Mound site, *107*, 226–27
Cartersville phase, 138, 144–46, 152
Caves: domestic occupation, 35–43, 249, 71–72; mining, 83–84; ritual, 35–43, 140–41, 241
Ceramics. *See* Pottery (major traditions)
Chalcedony, 78, 80, *81–82*, 171
Charnel house, 65
Chiefdom, 220, 260
Clay, ritual uses of: prepared clay pit or surface, 51–52, 226, 149–50; puddled clay basin, 51–52, 226–27, *229*; storage, 48
Climate change, 178–79
Cobble feature, 149–50
Coles Creek culture, 259
Color symbolism, 131
Communalism, 136. *See also* Feasting
Connestee phase, 111–12, 122
Coosa River, 152
Copena, 87, 140, 201–3
Copper: breastplate, 141; celt, 141; ear spool, *176*, 177, 199, *203*; exotic artifact, 127, 145–46, 199–201, 204, 208
Corporate groups, 220, 231–32
Cosmos/cosmology, 194, 217, 242
Costly display, 210–11
Crab Orchard, 39, 43
Craft production: craft specialists, 218; ritual objects, 54, 199
Creek busk ground, 243
Crigler Mound site, 51, 65, 224
Crystal quartz, 127, 146, 148, 150
Crystal River (Florida) (river), 183
Crystal River (site): chronology, 190–92; location, *182*, 183–84; site layout, 186–89, *187*, 194, 257
Cultural geography, 196
Cultural resource management (CRM), 9–10, 19, 44, 249

Debitage, 34, 59, *81–82*, 144–46, 148, 150
Deep South (geographic region), 181–82, 205
Delta (geographic region), 159
Domestic: activity areas, 35–39, 144–49, 188, 214–15; assemblages, 53, 119, 209; landscapes, 14, 44, 249; settlement patterns, 39–44; structures, 20, 28–31, 32–38, 115–16, 119–20, 249, 253. *See also* Base camp

Domestic/ritual dichotomy, 61, 151–52, 188, 246. *See also* Sacred/secular dichotomy
Drake Mound, 52, 224, 226, 232

Eagle Drink Bluff Shelter, 72–73, 77–79, 82–83, 86–87
Ear spool, *176*, 177, 199–201, *203*, 258. *See also* Copper
Earth-diver myths, 194. *See also* Water symbolism
Earth oven, 34, 36, 145
Earthworks: causeway, 189; ditches, 93–96, 100–106, 123–24, 126–28, 143–44, 185, 188, 242–43, 254–55; embankment, 93–96, 98–106, 143, 224–26, 242–43; enclosure, 91, 102–6, 129, 140, 143–46, 159, 185–18, 242; entryways/gaps, 94, 104–6, 156–58, 160, 241, 243; sacred/ceremonial circles, 91
Eastern Agricultural Complex, 13, 133–35, 254
East-side caches, 204, 207–8, 210–11, 216
Effigy vessels, 148, 205, 207–8, 211, 217–18
Egalitarianism, 132, 209, 220
Electromagnetic induction (EM), 99–100
Elk River (Tennessee), 202
Ethnic group, 124, 167, 170–75
Ethnographic analogy, 56–57, 131, 250–51
Etowah (site), 138, 143–44, 257
Etowah River (Georgia), 138, 152
Evans site, 47–55, 241, 250
Events: archeological correlates of, 113, 124, 219; communal, 142, 149, 163, 199; cosmogonic, 124, 130; extended, 59, 70; feasting, 152, 162; mortuary, 61–63, 67, 70, 204, 222–24, 231; in structuration theory, 221. *See also* Feasting; Single-event mounds
Exotic artifacts (general), 110–12, 171. *See also* Chalcedony; Copper; Galena; Mica
Experiential approach, 197. *See also* Phenomenology

Faunal remains, 61, 84, 111, 131–35, 150. *See also* Feasting
Feasting: communal, 110, 114, 120, 132, 149–51, 161–62, 248, 251; mortuary ritual, 46–50, 62, 64–65; with the dead, 167, 176–77
Figurines, 114, 120, 146, 150, 163, 204
Fire-cracked rock (FCR), 125, 146, 177
Fisher Mound site, 52, 226

Food processing, 36, 38, 148–49
Fort Ancient (culture/phase), 63

Galena, 152, 202, 208
Garden Creek site, 111–21
Garden Patch site, 210
Gateway communities, 138, 142, 210, 255
Gathering, 157–59, 167, 205, 210–11, 231. *See also* Aggregation; Assembly; Pilgrimage
Geographic information systems (GIS), 7, 115–16, 222–23
Geophysics, 7–8, 99–102, 104–6, 192. *See also* Archaeological prospection; Electromagnetic induction (EM); Ground penetrating radar (GPR)
Gorgets, 114, 119–20, 145, 204
Gradiometry/megnetometry, 99–102. *See also* Archaeological prospection; Geophysics
Great Circle (Fort Center), 188–89
Great Lakes (geographic region), 202. *See also* Copper
Green Point complex, 208, 210
Green Point site, 208
Green River (Kentucky), 40, 63
Ground penetrating radar (GPR), 99–100, 143
Gulf Coast (culture area), 151, 179
Gulf Coast (geographic region), 13, 153–55, 172, 182, 214, 259
Gulf Coastal Plain, 145, 204, 206–10
Gypsum mining, 84. *See also* Caves

Habitation areas, 122, 124, 188, 198, 259. *See also* Domestic
Hartman Mound site, 52, 224
Hearths, 34–37, 52–53, 110–19, 145, 176–77, 253
Heirlooms, 215
Hematite, 48, 141, 144, 146, 208
Heterarchy, 220–21
Historical connectedness, 183, 209 247, 257
Historical ecology, 5
Histories: culture, 196; of practice, 113; of mound use, 227–30, 257; of social relationships, 215, 218; ways of knowing, 205–7
Hopewell: definition of, 11–12; Interaction Sphere and influence, 87, 123, 151–52, 167, 170, 197, 200–201, 245; material culture, 141, 177, 199; monuments, 12, 66–67, 104, 122, 128, 143; mortuary ritual, 65, 202; in Ohio, 237–38, 243, 246, 254; religion, 12; in the Southeast, 122–24, 188, 244–45, 254
Huckleberry Landing site, 208

Icehouse Bottom site, 171, 259
Iconography, 217. *See also* Split representation
Identity, 47, 183, 197–202, 217, 257–59
Immanent universe, 239–40
Index (semiotics), 205, 209, 214–15, 217, 239
Indian Fort (Georgia), 140
Indian River (Florida), 246
Indian Rock House, 72, 78, 82–87
Inscription, 205, 211, 216, 218
Interregional interaction, 141, 151, 153, 159, 167, 175–80, 198–202, 199
Intra-site spatial patterning, 19, 35–39
Island (artificial), 144

Jackson Landing site, 157–62

Kentucky River (Kentucky), 40–41, 43
Kin group, 56, 205–6, 210–11, 217, 219–20, 230–32
Kolomoki, 242, 257, 143, 148, 182–84, 186–88, 190–92
Kolomoki pattern mounds, 13, 110, 114, 120
Kymulga Cave, 152

Labor, 211, 220, 230, 245, 250
Ladd Cave, *139*, 140
Ladd Mountain, 138–40
Lake Okeechobee, 184, 193
Landing Mound site, 223
Landscape archaeology: American approaches, 3–4; British approaches, 4; definition, 5–6. *See also* Cultural geography; Historical ecology; Phenomenology
Leadership, 219–21, 230–33
Leake site, 144–52, 245, 254–55
Lean-to, 20
Least-cost pathway analysis, 255
Leveling mechanisms, 221
Licking River (Kentucky), 40–41, 46
LiDAR, 185, 258
Lineage, 206–7, 210, 214–17, 259
Lithic use-wear analysis, 83–84
Lookout Valley (Georgia), 199–200

Mammoth Cave, 40
Mann site, 141–42, 255
Marksville culture, 170
Marksville site, 143, 259
McKeithen site, 110, 129, 132, 210
Memorialization, 56–59
Memory (collective/corporate), 45, 55
Mica, 48–50, 114, 120, 123, 141, 144–48, 199, 204, 241
Microsettlement, 21, 32–35
Midden, 35–38, 43, 110–14, 124–25, 146–49, 151, 159–62, 188, 194. *See also* Shell middens
Mississippian period, 129, 143, 183, 195, 238–40, 257
Mississippi River Valley (region), 238
Mississippi Sound, 155–56, 159
Monumental architecture, 12, 109, 153, 222, 252. *See also* Earthworks; Burial mounds; Platform mound
Monumental grammar, 183. *See also* Architectural grammar
Morgan Stone Mound site, 51, 226
Mortuary ritual and ceremonialism: adornment, 196–97, 200, 202; bundles, 208; cave burial, 140; cremation, 45, 49–54, 63, 65, 69, 176, 208, 224–30; grave goods, 141, 199, 218; inhumation, 45, 59, 63–65, 69, 224–26, 257; tomb architecture, 45, 51–53, 64–65, 141, 208–9, 224–32, 250
Mound Builder myth, 59, 67, 237
Mound City site, 114, 243, 246, 259
Mounds. *See* Burial mounds; Kolomoki pattern mounds; Platform mound
Mount Horeb site, 94–98
Mount Taylor culture, 246
Mt. Mitchell, 124, 129–30, 136, 241
Mt. Rogers, 49
Mulatto Bayou, 156, 158–59
Multiscalar research, 7, 19, 197–98, 200, 220, 248

Natural places, 3
Networks, 7, 121, 141, 194, 199, 222, 245–46, 251–58
New Deal archaeology, 96, 227
Nodes, 205, 215, 245, 255

Object biography, 205
Ochre, 52, 144

Off-mound activity, 61, 68
Off-mound ritual, 19, 46, 52, 135
Ohio River Valley (region), 29, 92–93, 97, 100, 252
Optically stimulated luminescence (OSL) dating, 74, 76–79

Paddle matches, 204, 212–14
Paired-post structures, 53, 63, 224–26
Paleo-environment, 10. *See also* Climate change
Panpipes, 199–202, 258
Papua New Guinea, 56–57, 250–51
Pearl River (Mississippi), 155–56, 159
Persistent place, 8, 108–9, 111, 120–21
Petrography (ceramics), 142, 255
Phenomenology, 4, 193–94, 240
Physiographic zones and boundaries, 72, 183, 193, 222, 232
Pierce site, 208
Pile Mound site, 87–88
Pilgrimage, 151, 167, 178–80, 193, 200, 238
Pilgrimage center, 167–70, 179–80, 256
Pine Log Cave, 140
Pinson Mounds site, 13, 143, 259
Pit features: borrow, 156–57, 160; cache, 34, 36; clay-filled, 46–49, 51–52, 250; feasting, 54, 150; mica-lined pit, 114–15, 120; mortuary, 38, 49, 64, 176, 207, 216, 224–33, 260; pit hearths, 34, 114; post pit, 129; refuse, 34, 36, 117; roasting, 36, 144–45; storage, 34, 36–38, 49–51
Pit-house structure, 148. *See also* Structures
Platform mound (general): construction, 124–26, 160–61, 190–91; Kolomoki pattern, 13, 109–10; ritual use, 157–58, 161–62, 193. *See also* Biltmore Mound site; Crystal River site; Great Circle (Fort Center) site; Garden Creek site; Jackson Landing site; Kolomoki
Plaza, 169, 186–89, 193, 248
Plummet, 193
Population increase/decrease, 177–78
Postholes: in structures, 33, 116–19, 128–29; large, 120, 127, 129, 148; scattered, 110–13, 115, 144, 253
Postmarital residence, 213
Pottery (major traditions): Adena, 47, 49, 53, 59; Cartersville, 142, 144–46, 148–49; Connestee, 79, 87, 118; Deptford, 205; Long Branch, 77; Marksville, 148–49, 169–70; Swift Creek, 146,

183, 204–5; Weeden Island, 145, 149–50, 183, 204–5, 207–8, 211–14
Poverty Point (culture), 238, 246
Poverty Point site, 151
Premound deposits: architectural, 116–21, 233; midden, 110–13, 124, 157; ritual, 219, 223–27, 232
Processualism, 3–4, 244
Proximate communities, 204

Refuse disposal, 38, 212
Relational landscape, 201–2, 258
Remembering, 62, 232–33. *See also* Ancestor veneration; Memorialization; Memory
Remote sensing, 91–101, 128, 249, 252, 255, 258. *See also* Archaeological prospection; Geophysics
Residential communities, 210
Ricketts Mounds site, 51, 226
Riley Mound site, 223–24
Ritual: architecture, 10, 32, 128–30, 227; landscape, 19, 32–33, 43; object, 12, 54, 162, 199. *See also* Exotic artifacts; Mortuary ritual and ceremonialism; Off-mound ritual; Structures (architectural)
Robbins Mounds site, 52, 63–65, 223–24
Rockshelters (site type), 37–38, 40–43, 71–74

Sacred/secular dichotomy, 151, 208–9, 217. *See also* Domestic/ritual dichotomy
Salts Cave site, 38
Seasonal mobility, 41, 86, 119, 205, 249
Seriation, 172
Settlement, 86–87, 169–70, 245–46. *See also* Village
Shark teeth, 150–51, 200
Shaw Mound, *139*, 140–41
Shell middens, 156–57
Shelly Mound site, *139*, 140–41
Shovel test, 156, 169, 173–74
Single-event mounds, 207, 211, 215, 227. *See also* Burial mounds
Soapstone, 144. *See also* Steatite
Social ranking, 199, 210, 217, 221, 259
Sociopolitical organization, 219–21, 231–33
Soil: drainage, 43; geophysical properties of, 99–101; in mound stratigraphy, 64, 96, 112, 124–26; symbolism of, 122, 131, 154, 161–63,

250, 254. *See also* Color symbolism; Water symbolism
Solstice, 129, *130*, 136, 147
Southeastern Archaeological Conference (organization), 1, 261
Southern Appalachians (region), 112, 135–36, 167, 170–71, 176, 238
Spiritual landscape, 240–44
Split representation, 217. *See also* Iconography
Squircle/squarecle, 252–53
St. Johns River (Florida) (river), 212
St. Johns River, lower (region), 211–14
Steatite, 73, 87, 115, 120. *See also* Soapstone
Structuralism, 131
Structuration, 221, 233
Structures (architectural): domestic, 20, 28–31, 32–38, 115–16, 119–20, 249, 253; paired-post, 53, 224, 225, 226; pit-house, 148; ritual (unspecified), 50, 112, 226–27, 233, 246; roofed, 110, 128–30, 249; single-post, 116–20, *117*, 149, *150*
Subsistence strategy, 39, 41, 43, 84–86, 238, 243, 254
Surface collection, 163
Swift Creek (ceramics), 12, 142, 148–50, 183, 207, *216*, 259
Swift Creek (mounds), 128–29, 205–18, 259
Swift Creek (phase), 138, 146–47, 207–9

Tarlton Mound, 224
Taxonomic approaches (material culture), 71, 244, 246
Tennessee River (Tennessee), 77, 140, 144, 152, 212
Territory, 66–67
Timberlands site, 72, 175
Topographic mapping, 97–99, *98*, 102, 106, 184, 252
Trade, 172, 184, 197, 202–3, 244
Trade routes, 197, 200
Tree-ring data, 178
Tribes/tribal societies, 220, 240
Tunacunnhee site, 141, 171, 196–203, 248, 258–59

Underworld, 160, 258. *See also* Water symbolism
Upper Cumberland Plateau (geographic region), 171–73, *173*, 251

Vacant ceremonial center, 159, 248
Viewshed, 68, 138, 258
Village, 39, 132–36, 152, 188, 210, 212–14, 217–18, 246, 249, 254. *See also* Settlement

Walling site, 110, 120, 129, 132, 162, 172
Warfare, 178, 251, 257
Water symbolism, 51, 122, 128, 149–50, 157–63, 183–84, 193–94, 241–43
Weeden Island (ceramics), 145–50, 183, 205–18
Weeden Island (mounds), 204–18

Weeden Island (phase), 204
Winchester Farm earthwork, 93–107
World renewal/renewal, 120, 193, 240, 242, 245, 258
WPA archaeology, 96, 227. *See also* New Deal archaeology
Wright Mounds site, 51, 226

Yearwood site, 171
Yent complex, 208
Yent site, 208

Ripley P. Bullen Series

FLORIDA MUSEUM OF NATURAL HISTORY

Tacachale: Essays on the Indians of Florida and Southeastern Georgia during the Historic Period, edited by Jerald T. Milanich and Samuel Proctor (1978)

Aboriginal Subsistence Technology on the Southeastern Coastal Plain during the Late Prehistoric Period, by Lewis H. Larson (1980)

Cemochechobee: Archaeology of a Mississippian Ceremonial Center on the Chattahoochee River, by Frank T. Schnell, Vernon J. Knight Jr., and Gail S. Schnell (1981)

Fort Center: An Archaeological Site in the Lake Okeechobee Basin, by William H. Sears, with contributions by Elsie O'R. Sears and Karl T. Steinen (1982)

Perspectives on Gulf Coast Prehistory, edited by Dave D. Davis (1984)

Archaeology of Aboriginal Culture Change in the Interior Southeast: Depopulation during the Early Historic Period, by Marvin T. Smith (1987)

Apalachee: The Land between the Rivers, by John H. Hann (1988)

Key Marco's Buried Treasure: Archaeology and Adventure in the Nineteenth Century, by Marion Spjut Gilliland (1989)

First Encounters: Spanish Explorations in the Caribbean and the United States, 1492–1570, edited by Jerald T. Milanich and Susan Milbrath (1989)

Missions to the Calusa, edited and translated by John H. Hann, with an introduction by William H. Marquardt (1991)

Excavations on the Franciscan Frontier: Archaeology at the Fig Springs Mission, by Brent Richards Weisman (1992)

The People Who Discovered Columbus: The Prehistory of the Bahamas, by William F. Keegan (1992)

Hernando de Soto and the Indians of Florida, by Jerald T. Milanich and Charles Hudson (1993)

Foraging and Farming in the Eastern Woodlands, edited by C. Margaret Scarry (1993)

Puerto Real: The Archaeology of a Sixteenth-Century Spanish Town in Hispaniola, edited by Kathleen Deagan (1995)

Political Structure and Change in the Prehistoric Southeastern United States, edited by John F. Scarry (1996)

Bioarchaeology of Native American Adaptation in the Spanish Borderlands, edited by Brenda J. Baker and Lisa Kealhofer (1996)

A History of the Timucua Indians and Missions, by John H. Hann (1996)

Archaeology of the Mid-Holocene Southeast, edited by Kenneth E. Sassaman and David G. Anderson (1996)

The Indigenous People of the Caribbean, edited by Samuel M. Wilson (1997; first paperback edition, 1999)

Hernando de Soto among the Apalachee: The Archaeology of the First Winter Encampment, by Charles R. Ewen and John H. Hann (1998)

The Timucuan Chiefdoms of Spanish Florida, by John E. Worth: vol. 1, *Assimilation;* vol. 2, *Resistance and Destruction* (1998)

Ancient Earthen Enclosures of the Eastern Woodlands, edited by Robert C. Mainfort Jr. and Lynne P. Sullivan (1998)

An Environmental History of Northeast Florida, by James J. Miller (1998)

Precolumbian Architecture in Eastern North America, by William N. Morgan (1999)

Archaeology of Colonial Pensacola, edited by Judith A. Bense (1999)

Grit-Tempered: Early Women Archaeologists in the Southeastern United States, edited by Nancy Marie White, Lynne P. Sullivan, and Rochelle A. Marrinan (1999; first paperback edition, 2000)

Coosa: The Rise and Fall of a Southeastern Mississippian Chiefdom, by Marvin T. Smith (2000)

Religion, Power, and Politics in Colonial St. Augustine, by Robert L. Kapitzke (2001)

Bioarchaeology of Spanish Florida: The Impact of Colonialism, edited by Clark Spencer Larsen (2001)

Archaeological Studies of Gender in the Southeastern United States, edited by Jane M. Eastman and Christopher B. Rodning (2001)

The Archaeology of Traditions: Agency and History Before and After Columbus, edited by Timothy R. Pauketat (2001)

Foraging, Farming, and Coastal Biocultural Adaptation in Late Prehistoric North Carolina, by Dale L. Hutchinson (2002)

Windover: Multidisciplinary Investigations of an Early Archaic Florida Cemetery, edited by Glen H. Doran (2002)

Archaeology of the Everglades, by John W. Griffin (2002; first paperback edition, 2017)

Pioneer in Space and Time: John Mann Goggin and the Development of Florida Archaeology, by Brent Richards Weisman (2002)

Indians of Central and South Florida, 1513–1763, by John H. Hann (2003)

Presidio Santa María de Galve: A Struggle for Survival in Colonial Spanish Pensacola, edited by Judith A. Bense (2003)

Bioarchaeology of the Florida Gulf Coast: Adaptation, Conflict, and Change, by Dale L. Hutchinson (2004; first paperback edition, 2020)

The Myth of Syphilis: The Natural History of Treponematosis in North America, edited by Mary Lucas Powell and Della Collins Cook (2005)

The Florida Journals of Frank Hamilton Cushing, edited by Phyllis E. Kolianos and Brent R. Weisman (2005)

The Lost Florida Manuscript of Frank Hamilton Cushing, edited by Phyllis E. Kolianos and Brent R. Weisman (2005)

The Native American World Beyond Apalachee: West Florida and the Chattahoochee Valley, by John H. Hann (2006)

Tatham Mound and the Bioarchaeology of European Contact: Disease and Depopulation in Central Gulf Coast Florida, by Dale L. Hutchinson (2006)

Taíno Indian Myth and Practice: The Arrival of the Stranger King, by William F. Keegan (2007)

An Archaeology of Black Markets: Local Ceramics and Economies in Eighteenth-Century Jamaica, by Mark W. Hauser (2008; first paperback edition, 2013)

Mississippian Mortuary Practices: Beyond Hierarchy and the Representationist Perspective, edited by Lynne P. Sullivan and Robert C. Mainfort Jr. (2010; first paperback edition, 2012)

Bioarchaeology of Ethnogenesis in the Colonial Southeast, by Christopher M. Stojanowski (2010; first paperback edition, 2013)

French Colonial Archaeology in the Southeast and Caribbean, edited by Kenneth G. Kelly and Meredith D. Hardy (2011; first paperback edition, 2015)

Late Prehistoric Florida: Archaeology at the Edge of the Mississippian World, edited by Keith Ashley and Nancy Marie White (2012; first paperback edition, 2015)

Early and Middle Woodland Landscapes of the Southeast, edited by Alice P. Wright and Edward R. Henry (2013; first paperback edition, 2019)

Trends and Traditions in Southeastern Zooarchaeology, edited by Tanya M. Peres (2014)
New Histories of Pre-Columbian Florida, edited by Neill J. Wallis and Asa R. Randall (2014; first paperback edition, 2016)
Discovering Florida: First-Contact Narratives from Spanish Expeditions along the Lower Gulf Coast, edited and translated by John E. Worth (2014; first paperback edition, 2016)
Constructing Histories: Archaic Freshwater Shell Mounds and Social Landscapes of the St. Johns River, Florida, by Asa R. Randall (2015)
Archaeology of Early Colonial Interaction at El Chorro de Maíta, Cuba, by Roberto Valcárcel Rojas (2016)
Fort San Juan and the Limits of Empire: Colonialism and Household Practice at the Berry Site, edited by Robin A. Beck, Christopher B. Rodning, and David G. Moore (2016)
Rethinking Moundville and Its Hinterland, edited by Vincas P. Steponaitis and C. Margaret Scarry (2016)
Handbook of Ceramic Animal Symbols in the Ancient Lesser Antilles, by Lawrence Waldron (2016)
Paleoindian Societies of the Coastal Southeast, by James S. Dunbar (2016; first paperback edition, 2019)
Gathering at Silver Glen: Community and History in Late Archaic Florida, by Zackary I. Gilmore (2016)
Cuban Archaeology in the Caribbean, edited by Ivan Roksandic (2016)
Archaeologies of Slavery and Freedom in the Caribbean: Exploring the Spaces in Between, edited by Lynsey A. Bates, John M. Chenoweth, and James A. Delle (2016; first paperback edition, 2018)
Setting the Table: Ceramics, Dining, and Cultural Exchange in Andalucía and La Florida, by Kathryn L. Ness (2017)
Simplicity, Equality, and Slavery: An Archaeology of Quakerism in the British Virgin Islands, 1740–1780, by John M. Chenoweth (2017)
Fit for War: Sustenance and Order in the Mid-Eighteenth-Century Catawba Nation, by Mary Elizabeth Fitts (2017)
Water from Stone: Archaeology and Conservation at Florida's Springs, by Jason O'Donoughue (2017)
Mississippian Beginnings, edited by Gregory D. Wilson (2017; first paperback edition, 2019)
Honoring Ancestors in Sacred Space: The Archaeology of an Eighteenth-Century African-Bahamian Cemetery, by Grace Turner (2017)
Investigating the Ordinary: Everyday Matters in Southeast Archaeology, edited by Sarah E. Price and Philip J. Carr (2018)
Harney Flats: A Florida Paleoindian Site, by I. Randolph Daniel Jr. and Michael Wisenbaker (2017)
Early Human Life on the Southeastern Coastal Plain, edited by Albert C. Goodyear and Christopher R. Moore (2018)
New Histories of Village Life at Crystal River, by Thomas J. Pluckhahn and Victor D. Thompson (2018)
The Archaeology of Villages in Eastern North America, edited by Jennifer Birch and Victor D. Thompson (2018)
The Cumberland River Archaic of Middle Tennessee, edited by Tanya Peres and Aaron Deter-Wolf (2019)
Pre-Columbian Art of the Caribbean, by Lawrence Waldron (2019)
Iconography and Wetsite Archaeology of Florida's Watery Realms, edited by Ryan Wheeler and Joanna Ostapkowicz (2019)

New Directions in the Search for the First Floridians, edited by David K. Thulman and Ervan G. Garrison (2019)

Cahokia in Context: Hegemony and Diaspora, edited by Charles H. McNutt and Ryan M. Parish (2019)

Archaeology of Domestic Landscapes of the Enslaved in the Caribbean, edited by James A. Delle and Elizabeth C. Clay (2019)

Contact, Colonialism, and Native Communities in the Southeastern United States, edited by Edmond A. Boudreaux III, Maureen Meyers, and Jay K. Johnson (2020)

Bears: Archaeological and Ethnohistorical Perspectives in Native Eastern North America, edited by Heather A. Lapham and Gregory A. Waselkov (2020)

An Archaeology and History of a Caribbean Sugar Plantation on Antigua, edited by Georgia L. Fox (2020)

www.ingramcontent.com/pod-product-compliance
Lightning Source LLC
Chambersburg PA
CBHW051048230426
43666CB00012B/2608